STUDIES IN SOVIET HISTORY AND SOCIETY

General Editors: R. W. Davies, Professor of Soviet Economic Studies, University of
Birmingham and E. A. Rees, Lecturer in Soviet History, University of Birmingham

Nicholas Lampert and Gábor T. Rittersporn (*editors*)
STALINISM: ITS NATURE AND AFTERMATH

Robert Lewis
SCIENCE AND INDUSTRIALIZATION IN THE USSR

Neil Malcolm
SOVIET POLITICAL SCIENTISTS AND AMERICAN POLITICS

Silvana Malle
EMPLOYMENT PLANNING IN THE SOVIET UNION: Continuity and Change

David Mandel
THE PETROGRAD WORKERS AND THE FALL OF THE OLD REGIME: From the
February Revolution to the July Days, 1917
THE PETROGRAD WORKERS AND THE SOVIET SEIZURE OF POWER: From the July
Days 1917 to July 1918

Catherine Merridale
MOSCOW POLITICS AND THE RISE OF STALIN: The Communist Party in the Capital,
1925–32

E. A. Rees
STATE CONTROL IN SOVIET RUSSIA: The Rise and Fall of the Workers' and Peasants'
Inspectorate, 1920–34

Christopher J. Rice
RUSSIAN WORKERS AND THE SOCIALIST-REVOLUTIONARY PARTY THROUGH
THE REVOLUTION OF 1905–07

Richard Sakwa
SOVIET COMMUNISTS IN POWER: A Study of Moscow during the Civil War, 1918–21

Jonathan R. Schiffer
SOVIET REGIONAL ECONOMIC POLICY: The East-West Debate over Pacific Siberian
Development

Nobuo Shimotomai
MOSCOW UNDER STALINIST RULE, 1931–34

Roger Skurski
SOVIET MARKETING AND ECONOMIC DEVELOPMENT

Daniel Thorniley
THE RISE AND FALL OF THE SOVIET RURAL COMMUNIST PARTY, 1927–39

J. N. Westwood
SOVIET LOCOMOTIVE TECHNOLOGY DURING INDUSTRIALIZATION, 1928–52

Professor Moshe Lewin

Stalinism: Its Nature and Aftermath

Essays in Honour of Moshe Lewin

Edited by

Nick Lampert

and

Gábor T. Rittersporn

 in association with the
Centre for Russian and East
European Studies
University of Birmingham

First published 1992 by
THE MACMILLAN PRESS LTD
Houndmills, Basingstoke, Hampshire RG21 2XS
and London
Companies and representatives
throughout the world

ISBN 0–333–54824–8 1001200338

A catalogue record for this book is available
from the British Library.

Printed and bound in Great Britain by
Antony Rowe Ltd, Chippenham, Wiltshire

11 10 9 8 7 6 5 4
04 03 02 01 00 99 98

Contents

List of Tables

Preface
Nick Lampert

In this volume a number of specialists in Russian and Soviet studies acknowledge their debts to a scholar who has been an inspiration in their field over the past twenty-five years, and who, approaching the start of his eighth decade, continues to work with undiminished vigour. The contributors – from the USA, Continental Europe and Britain – are not all well-known to each other, but they share one thing: a respect for the work of Moshe Lewin, who has greatly enriched our understanding of Soviet history and thus of the recent transformations in the USSR.

The title of our *Festschrift* relates to a central preoccupation in Lewin's work – the inter-war period of social and political upheaval which made a profound impact upon the character of the Soviet system. But the scope of Lewin's contribution is even broader than this suggests. It moves backwards and forwards in the attempt to grasp the overall dynamic of Soviet history, the relationship between Stalinism and the Tsarist past, and the ways in which, in its very formation, Stalinism prepared the ground for its demise.

There are several distinguishing features of Lewin's approach, which together make up a powerful synthesis. Starting with his first book, *Russian Peasants and Soviet Power*, published when the author was already in his forties and had a rich and varied life experience behind him, he brought to Soviet studies a new sense of the interplay of socio-economic, cultural and political forces. The cold-war climate of the post-war period had encouraged a singularly one-dimensional approach to the study of the Soviet Union in the West – an approach in which the 'total' claims of Soviet ideology and politics were all too often taken at face value. This perception, whether given a plus or a minus sign, was so strong that for many of us (the editors included) the first acquaintance with Lewin's work in the late 1960s had the quality of a revelation. For the first time we gained a sense of the complex relationship between political and social developments and the dynamic that they contained. Such a dynamic might be taken for granted in other contexts, but it had been successfully screened out of public consciousness by the cold war and by sheer ignorance about Soviet society that prevailed in the West.

Along with this multi-dimensionality there is another very attractive quality in Lewin's approach: a view of history from the bottom up as well as from the top down. He showed, with *Lenin's Last Struggle*, that he could tell a story about the political leadership as well as anybody. Yet it is the sense of becoming acquainted with ordinary people that is so refreshing in his work as a whole, a quality which is well conveyed in his collection of essays, *The Making of the Soviet System*. The 'grey masses' of Soviet society are not grey. All of them – whether peasants, workers, bureaucrats or intellectuals – are actors in the historical drama. All have been pushed about and harassed, their lives strongly affected – sometimes in murderous ways – by the grandiose schemes of the Soviet state, especially during the Stalin period to which this volume is primarily devoted. And yet these grey masses, including the bureaucratic servants of a highly centralised party and state machine, have constantly thwarted the efforts to control them and make them more predictable. People react to the world in their own way. By the same token, there has never been just one ideology in the Soviet Union, but a multiplicity of ideologies emerging from the variety of life experience of different groups and classes. Lewin's history is a 'popular' history in the best sense, imbued with a powerful humanism.

Much of this can be understood in the light of Lewin's own background. He was born in Wilno, then in Poland, in 1921, and lived there for his first twenty years. After fleeing eastwards from the Germans in June 1941, he ended up in provincial Russia. For two years he worked successively on a *kolkhoz*, in an iron-ore mine and in a metallurgical factory (as a blast-furnace operator), and in the summer of 1943 enrolled in the Soviet army. He was sent to officers' school and was promoted on the very last day of the war. During these five years he lived and worked close to the people, in his own words 'sharing their misery and hopes, learning about their uglier sides sometimes, but very often enchanted by their generosity and . . . their grandeur'.

In 1946 Lewin left the USSR for Poland and later for France, working in both countries among young people interested in life on kibbutz-farms in Palestine and Israel. During his teens he had been active in left-wing Zionist politics, which provided both an antidote to the virulent anti-semitism in Wilno under Polish rule, and a framework for a much broader socialist commitment. In 1951 he left for Israel where he spent ten years, working on a kibbutz and as a journalist, followed by studies in economics, history and philosophy.

Though he began studying late in life, Lewin felt from an early age that somehow it was his vocation to be a historian – a role that was only postponed by the turbulent fate of the countries in which he spent his youth and early adulthood. Furthermore, developments in Israel were increasingly out of tune with the inspiration that had led him there. In 1961 he received a research scholarship to study at the Sorbonne. Out of this came *Russian Peasants and Soviet Power*, and a distinguished academic career in Paris, New York, Birmingham and Philadelphia.

The scope of Lewin's explorations has been very wide, dealing with a panorama of social classes and groups, with the lower depths of society as well as the bosses, with informal social norms as well as formal law, with popular religion as well as established ideology. The range of his intellectual debts is also broad, owing as much to Weber as to Marx, emphasising as much the power of ideologies and myths in human behaviour as the weight of economic structure. The key thing is the perception of society as a socio-cultural whole, though Lewin always remains open to new pathways that might appear in the course of research, always eclectic in the best sense, always eschewing the pursuit of a grand theory for all history – a pursuit which only leads you away from the rich canvas of concrete human experience.

The range of Lewin's interests is reflected in this volume, though to represent them fully would have required a larger book. Methodological and historiographical questions are explored by Vladimir Andrle and Roland Lew, political developments by Gábor Rittersporn, Hans-Henning Schröder and Peter Kneen, social change by Alec Nove, Lewis Siegelbaum and Jean-Paul Depretto, and nationality issues by Ronald Suny. Bob Davies deals with the fate of the socialist idea in the light of the Soviet experience, and Peter Solomon with changing Soviet perceptions of law and legality. Maureen Perrie contributes an essay on historical parallels between the myths surrounding Stalin and earlier rulers.

The main focus is on the Stalin years, but the volume ranges backwards and forwards too. This befits a tribute to Lewin, who has throughout stressed the way in which current policies help to create social structures and ideologies which soon outgrow context in which they were formed. This theme is stated very clearly in his book on the Gorbachev reforms, *The Gorbachev Phenomenon*. *Perestroika*, far from being a bolt from the blue, was deeply prepared by the developments in the preceding decades, in particular by the rapid social changes of the 1960s and 1970s which the idea of 'stagnation' cannot convey. A new pluralism was already forming, although it could achieve only a very weak political expression.

The future of the Soviet Union, like its past, will be determined by the interaction of social, economic and political change. Its political structure has proved fragile and the civil society which Lewin was already identifying in the past two decades is now breaking the inherited patterns, though not necessarily the socialist idea as a whole. In the light of the approach to which this volume is a tribute, these riveting developments are not a sign of the 'end of history' but a further chapter in a continuing drama. They can be understood only with the benefit of historical perspective, and the style of investigation encouraged by Lewin is a very good place to start. Lewin has made a formidable contribution to our thinking about the Soviet Union, influencing a whole generation of younger scholars (and some of the older generation too, who are also represented in this book). In one way or another Russia and its neighbouring republics will continue to play a very big role on the world stage. The perspective developed by Lewin will greatly help to understand it.

Notes on the Contributors

Vladimir Andrle is lecturer in sociology at the University of York, England. He is the author of *Managerial Power in the Soviet Union* (1976) and *Workers in Stalin's Russia* (1988).

Robert W. Davies is Emeritus Professor of Soviet Economic Studies, University of Birmingham, England. He is the author of *The Development of the Soviet Budgetary System* (1958), co-author of vols 9 and 10 of E. H. Carr's *A History of Soviet Russia* (1969), and is now writing *The Industrialisation of Soviet Russia*, three volumes of which have already appeared. He is also the author of *Soviet History in the Gorbachev Revolution* (1989), and editor of *The Soviet Union* (1989).

Jean-Paul Depretto is associate professor in contemporary history at the University of Toulouse, France. He is the author (with Sylvie Schweitzer) of *Le Communisme à L'Usine* (1984) and of articles on Stakhanovism. His current field of research is the Soviet working class during the first five year plan.

Peter Kneen is lecturer in politics at the University of Durham, England. He was previously a research fellow at the Centre for Russian and East European Studies, University of Birmingham, England. He is the author of *Soviet Scientists and the State* (1980).

Nick Lampert is former senior lecturer at the Centre for Russian and East European Studies, University of Birmingham, England. He is the author of *The Technical Intelligentsia and the Soviet State* (1979) and *Whistleblowing in the Soviet Union* (1985).

Roland Lew is professor of political science at the Université Libre de Bruxelles. He is the author of *Mao Prend le Pouvoir* (1981), joint author of *La Société Chinoise Après Mao* (1986) and editor of *Une Dernière Chance à L'Est* (1989).

Alec Nove, FBA, FRSE, is Professor Emeritus, University of Glasgow. His books include *The Soviet Economic System* (1986), *An Economic History of the USSR* (1972), *The Economics of Feasible*

Socialism (1983), *Stalinism and After* (1989), and *Glasnost in Action* (1989).

Maureen Perrie teaches Russian history at the Centre for Russian and East European Studies, University of Birmingham, England. Her publications include *The Agrarian Policy of the Russian Socialist-Revolutionary Party* (1976), *The Image of Ivan the Terrible in Russian Folklore* (1987) and a number of articles on pre-revolutionary history. She is currently working on aspects of 'popular monarchism' from the sixteenth to the twentieth centuries, including pretenders and 'rebels in the name of the tsar'.

Gábor T. Rittersporn is senior research fellow at the Centre National de la Recherches Scientifique, Paris. He is the author of *Simplifications Staliniennes et Complications Soviétiques: Tensions Sociales et Conflits Politiques en URSS, 1933–1953* (1988) (shortly to appear in an English version), and of numerous articles on the political, legal and social life of the Stalin period.

Hans-Henning Schröder is senior research fellow at the Bundesinstitut für Ostwissenschaftliche und Internationale Studien, Cologne, and lectures in Russian and Soviet history at the Ruhr-Universität, Bochum. He has published on Soviet history of the twenties and thirties, on the history of the Khrushchev period and on Soviet military politics of the Gorbachev era.

Lewis H. Siegelbaum is professor of history at Michigan State University. He is the author of *Stakhanovism and the Politics of Productivity in the USSR, 1935–1941* (1988) and has written numerous articles and book chapters on Soviet labour history. He is currently working on a book, provisionally entitled *Between Revolutions: the Soviet State and Society, 1918–1929*.

Peter H. Solomon, Jr is professor of political science and a member of the Centre for Russian and East European Studies and the Centre for Criminology, University of Toronto. He is the author of *Soviet Criminologists and Criminal Policy: Specialists in Policy-Making* (1978) and *Criminal Justice Policy. From Research to Reform* (1983). He is currently completing a book on Soviet criminal justice under Stalin and is studying judicial reform under Gorbachev.

Ronald Grigor Suny is the Alex Manoogian Professor of Armenian History at the University of Michigan. He is the author of *The Baku Commune, 1917–1918: Class and Nationality in the Russian Revolution* (1972), *Armenia in the Twentieth Century* (1983) and *The Making of the Georgian Nation* (1988). He is the editor of *Transcaucasia, Nationalism and Social Change* (1983) and co-editor of *Party, State and Society in the Russian Civil War* (1989) and of *The Russian Revolution and Bolshevik Victory: Visions and Revisions* (1990). He is currently working on a study of the young Stalin and the formation of the Soviet Union.

1 Grappling with Soviet Realities: Moshe Lewin and the Making of Social History
Roland Lew

THE ANALYSIS OF SOVIET SOCIETY

For a long time, studying Soviet society seemed an impossible task. For many, in fact, understanding the Soviet Union was not simply a question of knowledge, since political and social issues, even civilisation itself, were at stake. Hence it was a topic far too important to be left to researchers. Would a sane person leave war to the military alone?

For decades one saw the triumphant reign of either apology or rejection. There was an ever more depressing contrast between the doctrinal promises of socialism and their outcome. For opponents of the USSR, the explanation was based on one massive idea, namely the preeminence of politics. In this one can recognise the central theme of the theories of totalitarianism. Although these theories were not the direct result of the study of the USSR – in fact they came initially from Mussolini and then from a very critical analysis of Italian fascism and German nazism – they nevertheless became increasingly focused on the Soviet system. Thanks to this concentration on the phenomenon of the 'homeland of socialism', the theories of totalitarianism acquired their maximum influence during the cold war period. They even became an instrument of this latent war. The USSR and the Socialist Bloc were thus presented as the embodiment of totalitarianism.

The central idea of the theory of totalitarianism was built on the search for the conditions that led to the emergence of an entirely new type of society, a system that completely crushes people and yet is deeply interiorized by them, that desires to smash individuals, to transform them into desocialised specks of dust. According to the theory, the success of totalitarian power led to an immobilization of

1

society and to making the system permanent and immutable. In this context one can recall George Orwell's impressive fictionalized description of such a society in his novel *1984* (published in 1949).

After the Second World War, the Soviet Union seemed the perfect candidate to exemplify this new and terrifying type of power. Politics was dominant, with an overwhelming presence of the state and a relentless and ostentatious ideological manipulation with constantly weakened and fragmented society. Why then was it necessary to look into the bowels of society to explain something that was so openly stated in the ideological discourse and in the state system of manipulation and repression? And why bother to study it when the most important thing was to fight it? Thus the theory soon degenerated into an anti-ideological ideology.[1]

On the other side, among the enthusiastic supporters of the USSR, one found the diametrical opposite, namely, a fervour for the Soviet system decked out with the most marvellous, the most magical, the most unreal, the most out-of-this-world attractions. Doing research in these conditions required special virtues – a certain intellectual courage, a highly developed critical faculty. And a great deal of sobriety.

How was it possible in this unusual situation to analyse and to understand rather than to make judgments about Soviet society? Research oscillated between the tendency to offer a normal study of an abnormal society, and an abnormal analysis of a normal society. Should one use the usual conceptual tools when faced with Soviet uniqueness? Or was it vital to devise an *ad hoc* theory, that would account for the pathology of a world full of familiar figures (cities, industry, decline or rural life . . .)?

The idea of the specificity of Russia, a recurrent theme that had become a stereotype of Russian intellectual life since the nineteenth century, was also widespread in the West. That idea was extended in a natural way to encompass the Soviet Union, amplifying all the traditional pre-1917 theories about Russian peculiarities and the immemorial continuity of these traits. It was a view that was unable to explain the complexity of an ever-changing situation. Something essential was missing: history and above all its vital social components.

The most recent period has seen the emergence of a more sober look at Soviet realities. It is clearly the result of the Gorbachev era and the discovery of a diversified and rapidly-evolving Soviet universe. In both the Eastern Bloc and in the West, people are increasingly open to the idea that all modern societies are subject to common problems, though there are undeniable Soviet peculiarities (backwardness, blockages, lack of coordination of the various levels . . .). It is thus that a multi-dimensional analysis becomes possible, leading to a study of the Soviet system and society in the framework of the long-term trends of Russian history and of the modernising process. It also becomes possible to see the stakes for which the revolutionaries were playing and their pre-1917 roots as well as the torment of the birth of a new society that claimed to be founded on these ideas, yet became radically separated from them.

This way of thinking about the Soviet Union has forerunners, one of whom is the social historian Moshe Lewin. As assessment of his work is long overdue.

THE ROAD TOWARDS A SOCIAL HISTORY OF THE USSR

Moshe Lewin is above all a historian of the Stalinist period which is at the heart of Soviet history. Yet Lewin's work is as much a defence and a demonstration of the value and necessity of a social history of the USSR, in line with Braudel's concept of *'la longue durée'*. It is a question of finding an alternative to the political theory and ideology of the totalitarian school. This project was initially implicit but has become explicit more recently.[2]

The conception of 'totalitarianism' had taken a firm hold in the field of Soviet studies. This term denotes the idea of a terroristic government seeking total control of the population by massive use of indoctrination, police and ideological brainwashing, monopoly of power as well as direct control over the economy:

> Though the term served quite well in its ideological function, it was useless as a conceptual category. It did not have much to say about where it was heading, what kind of changes it was undergoing, if any, and how to study it critically and seriously. In fact, the term was, in this context, itself 'totalitarian' in its empty self-sufficiency: it did not recognize any mechanism of change in the Soviet Union and had no use for even a shadow of some historical process.[3]

The change of perception in the 1960s led to the abandoning of the concept of totalitarianism and to the publication of serious studies. But Lewin adds:

On the whole, these analyses shared one important assumption with the "totalitarian school", the focus remained the study of the state-run economy, to the exclusion of most other aspects of Soviet experience . . . In sum, what had been missing was the idea of a Soviet "social system" and, in turn, the conceptualization of a dynamic process in which all the subsystems interact in time and space yielding ever more complex and intricate patterns.[4]

This rejection of the totalitarian school cannot be separated from Lewin's socialist and Marxist background, even if his research became increasingly separated from Marxism. Lewin's work is dominated by the desire to penetrate into the heart of a society, to grasp its inevitably complex structure and to measure its development. This requires a critical distance from one's own preconceived ideas, a lucid recognition of weaknesses in their explanatory power, a willingness to confront them with new historical facts.[5] Such a social history might be called materialist, though Lewin does not deny the exceptional nature of the events with which he is concerned. One should not forget that Lewin observed and lived enriching, dramatic and painful experiences in several countries, including the USSR during the Second World War. This helps to explain why his analysis has an ethical dimension. As in the case of the philosopher Simone Weil, this is one way to escape the madness of collective social pressures and to return to the lost paradise of the communion of the human spirit with the universe.[6]

A *leitmotiv* of Lewin's research is Spinoza's famous maxim: 'neither laugh nor cry, just understand'. It is this requirement that forces him to refrain from expressing his deep convictions as a passionate socialist intellectual, to the extent of holding in check his sensitive humanism in order to remain reserved and even cool in his scholarly writings. It is the same requirement that initially forced him to fulfill the meticulous 'ministry' of the historian (as Marc Bloch called it, or scholarship as vocation, in Max Weber's terms) with the indispensable carefulness that this task implies and the patient research which is the historian's daily lot. In addition, he also has the necessary qualities of imagination and intuition that guide his investigations and give his work such fertility.

These are the basic criteria of historical work. They are so evident that one should not have to mention them. Nevertheless, it is not as simple as that. Many historians have studied the USSR. Some remarkable works have been produced (we need only mention E. H.

Carr who is admired and often quoted by Lewin). Yet social history of the USSR was, and still is, a long and difficult conquest for which Lewin has been struggling, essentially as a pioneer. This is especially true for his exploration of the phenomenon of Stalinism. That Lewin could become a pioneer in this field in the 1960s, when the USSR as well as Lewin himself was approaching a fiftieth anniversary, gives an indication of his qualities as a historian, as well as highlighting the derisory state of research done by a large part of the academic establishment.

In his publications, as well as at his seminars, Lewin has insistently reminded us, even recently, of the enormous gaps in our knowledge of Soviet social history of the 1920s and 1930s. This state of affairs has broad implications. Soviet realities – society, regime and history – are a web of enigmas. They are not quite like Churchill's famous formula on the enigma surrounding a mystery, but rather a series of problems that have never really been systematically examined according to the strict rules of historical and social research. From this point of view Lewin's approach is a lesson and a vast 'work in progress' which calls for a great collective and critical research effort.

HISTORY AS THE HISTORY OF STAGES

In the approach of the totalitarism school the most important thing is to find a 'Principle' that is at work. It can be a new 'Principle' lodged at the core of a special type of modernity, or an old 'Principle' that is still unfolding (e.g. the 'Russian soul', irreducible slavic characteristics, etc . . .). One must understand this 'Principle', how it functions and what distinguishes it from all other 'Principles'. History has nothing to do here.[7] Familiar and ordinary ways of acting in or managing society are at best subordinate to the 'Principle'. There is no history and, therefore, no presenting of the stages and development of the system.

Lewin's approach is the exact opposite. Even if, for him, the 1930s and the Stalinist period are central to the formation of the USSR – the book which brings together his main studies of the topic, has the suggestive title of *The Making of the Soviet System* – it is only a stage preceded by several others and followed in turn by the formative moments of the present-day Soviet Union, a country that is experiencing profound changes which can no longer be ignored. This aim to define these stages is present in almost all of Lewin's works:

If we take the year 1914 or even 1917, we still have in place the main traits of the pre-revolutionary social system. But when we operate a leap to the not too far away 1921 – certainly a turning point – we discover immense changes. The peasantry of course was still there . . . but the ruling and privileged strata, aristocracy, gentry, the upper crust of the bureaucracy were all gone; capitalism and the capitalists were also wiped out, the old political system had gone. Towards the end of the NEP the main components of the post-Civil War social landscape remained the same, though somewhat complicated by the reappearance of the Nepmen and of some richer peasants. Important changes occurred in the party – but otherwise Soviet Russia was a case of a developing society. Let's now move up again by some 7 years to 1936. The old social structure didn't reappear . . . Skipping the war period next we observe after Stalin's death, his crisis-ridden system ushering in a long period of rather peaceful and mostly gradual developments . . . The transition to a stage of different tonality and intensity of social development was remarkable and new.[8]

The determination to situate the 1930s in their broad but delimitated framework is well illustrated in an important book whose publication in 1974 was a kind of turning-point: *Political Undercurrents in Soviet Economic Debates*. This is an analysis of the critical views of Soviet economists in the 1960s on the growing problems of Soviet society and its economy. It was not only a matter of showing that the suggested solutions were a return to the great debates of the 1920s and above all to Bukharin's proposals – even if this was the main theme of the book. It was equally a question of setting out the stages of Soviet history.

Lewin distinguished at least two main stages for the period prior to the Stalinist years – War Communism and NEP. There is perhaps a third period, if one adds the brief stage of the first months of the Soviet regime. They are very distinct stages and they offer often decisive elements for understanding the subsequent period.

The First Months

The Bolsheviks immediately found themselves confronted with realities that were very different from those predicted in revolutionary programmes and textbooks. Lenin insistently proposed state capitalism in this completely unexpected context. In his view there was only one task – to gain time and catch up with more advanced countries. One thus observes the rapid transition from the revolutionary period to the management of a revolutionary society that was immediately in a crisis. In any case, this eight months interlude 'is too short to allow any extensive conclusions about the theory and practice involved in the policies of Lenin's government at that stage'.[9] And if Lenin was so much in favour of state capitalism, to the surprise, or rather the indignation of his close colleagues, it was because he felt that a full transition to socialism was a matter of at least a generation if not longer'.[10]

War Communism (1918–1921)

War Communism was initially an expedient simply aimed at winning the terrible Civil War at any price. But it was also an outburst of enthusiasm – the utopia of achieving communism immediately. 'This new formula had no specific theoretical antecedent in the Bolshevik program that could be quoted to buttress it.'[11] In fact it was a state, and even a military communism, or at least a militarised form of 'communism' that came about by the deployment of a hypercentral-ised state system, a way 'of identifying the spread of Socialism with statism'.[12] The Bolsheviks did not hesitate to substitute the party for the working class in the absence of movements by the masses, who were exhausted, starving and discouraged (apart from some groups of workers that made up the solid supports of the new regime). Urban society broke down. And Bolshevism became militarised. It was, as well, the end of many revolutionary illusions about potential peasant 'allies'.

A new world emerged that was astonishing and unexpected, and constituted a profound break with the past. One was confronted with 'a dictatorship in the void'.[13] In this context, 'the party now exercised absolute power and was outside the control of any social force whatsoever'.[14] The most decisive factor but probably the least clearly seen by contemporaries was the irreducible gulf between the regime and the social sphere. It was the peasantry which gained most from the revolutionary events, yet the time-honoured rural way of life stood in the way of a statist Bolshevik party that wanted to rapidly transform and modernise the country. A void remained between the two, a void that resulted from the elimination during the Civil War of the intermediate groups between the proletariat and the peasantry.[15]

This three-year period for Lewin does not elicit a description of a colourful drama, of exalting heroism and human weaknesses and failures. This period was that of the formation, or more exactly deformation of the new society.[16] It showed the weight of what Lewin called 'the rural nexus', the stronger-than-ever presence of the imme- morial rural vastness at the centre of a project whose objective was nevertheless a radical break with the past and an attempt to leap into the twentieth century.[17] In addition, 'the spread of socialism was identified with the spread of state power, statism became a synonym for socialism, and any autonomous factor came to be considered antisocialist anarchism'. People were thus prepared for the idea of a 'full-fledged command economy'.[18] War Communism 'served as a sedative that anaesthetized the revolutionary Bolsheviks and made them build a Leviathan when they thought they were entering the free world of their dreams'.[19]

The NEP (1921–1928/29)

As we know, this was a period of forced retreat. The Bolsheviks realised their isolation. Only one force – the party – was still active. It was clear that it must now become a government and undertake the management of society. In brief, Bolshevism went through a meta- morphosis into a party-state. Authoritarianism was present every- where and stemmed from the pitiless period of the civil war and the militarisation of the Communist Party. Debate, where it still existed, took place only within the party. The only way for a non-Bolshevik to exercise any influence was to intervene in the debate within or on the periphery of the Communist Party, often through the role of special- ist adviser.

But one must take into account a gradual change in the vision of the NEP. It came to be seen more and more as a long-term solution to the problems of modernisation – a transition towards a rather distant socialism. Lenin admitted that War Communism had been a grave error and that one now had to bring about changes very prudently and by small stages. He viewed the modernisation of the country – dragging it out of its backwardness – as an elitist and statist project (but this would be a less pervasive statism than during the civil war). Modernisation would shape and educate society, especially the peasantry. Therefore, one had first to create the preconditions of modernisation. The Bolshevik leader was so aware of the gravity of the Russian situation that he proposed all this with some hesitation.

Tensions and even discord appeared among the Bolsheviks about which direction to follow.

Lenin's role was important and the consequences of his illness were perhaps decisive. That, at least, is Lewin's opinion and it is expressed in his attempts at reconstructing 'if history'.[20] He also stresses the weaknesses of Lenin's possible heirs (Bukharin and Trotsky) who were certainly remarkable figures, men of strong convictions, but who were not capable of being politicians, in the powerful and positive sense of the term, which might require the imposition of untested and risky policies. They lacked the determination, skills and cunning that this required.

The 1930s: The Stalinist Period

This period is characterised by the failure on the part of those in authority to appreciate the stakes and the true consequences of an often improvised policy. One solution carried the day, a solution that had its roots in the crisis-ridden atmosphere of the age, and was tied to what Bolshevism came to be: a structure for the efficient wielding of power, but extremely authoritarian and crude; a bureaucratic statism separated from the masses, and rather hostile to the peasantry.

> A new 20th century technology and an emerging 20th century social structure were suffused with repressive treatment of labour, in industry and especially in the countryside, and coexisted with a big sector of serf-labour (or slave labour, if one prefers) in the labour camps. In consequence, before the system managed to develop terms more congruent with modernity, both society and culture experienced deep setbacks and the state system too underwent an "archaization" or a "primitivization" of its own . . . After Stalin's death many of those particularly archaic, primitive or incongrous traits, especially mass oppression of labour, were quickly dismantled – and with them were the essence of the phenomenon called Stalinism . . .[21]

We are at the heart of Lewin's research, starting with his doctoral thesis, *Russian Peasants and Soviet Power* – a remarkable monograph and to some extent a manifesto for social history, and which was followed by studies that were in part collected in *The Making of the Soviet System*. In attempting to understand the complexities of the

Stalinist period, Lewin has widened our angle of vision. He has drawn from various disciplines, including economics and sociology, anthropology, folklore, demography and statistics. His aim has been to reconstruct the complex reality of life, the sense of dynamism and commitment, as well as the resistance within the regime and in society at that time.

Lewin has constantly multiplied the angles of vision and the analytic perspectives. These were the formative years of the USSR. But they were only a stage of development, certainly decisive and unbelievably cruel and dramatic, but which could not last for long. By the end of the 1930s, the dynamism and to a certain extent, the might of Stalinism began to wane. This is the area of research in which Lewin has contributed his most original thinking, by following two lines of analysis in order to shed light on the reasons for the strength of Stalinism and its relatively short duration.

> The instability inherent in the social structure could permit only a temporary stalemate that finally broke down during the leap undertaken under Stalin's leadership . . . But a "society in turmoil" . . . was also producing its own defensive measures, quite legitimate in the given situation, and finally some of its own strategies to stabilise and normalise the system . . . By now the political order seemed to have lost the capacity to discern between signals from the social base that expressed anarchy and those that expressed the need and the means for restoring an equilibrium.[22]

Lewin provides a fine description of the crisis that was brought about at the end of the NEP, and the strengthening of increasingly authoritarian currents. He traces in detail the transition from an authoritarianism which tended to exacerbate the crisis to a state close to chaos, which favoured the autonomy and the increasingly unfettered despotism of Stalin.

This was the triumph of extremism as policy-making.[23] Lewin shows in an original way, in what was perhaps only an outline for future research, that Stalinist despotism deliberately rooted itself in Russian tradition, and to a certain extent consciously relied on a deep-seated popular, peasant demonology, all the while being contaminated by it. This was a demonstration of the vitality of a peasant civilisation that was nevertheless about to be broken by Stalinist policies that were determined to destroy the traditional pattern of the Soviet landscape.[24] In fact, the entire society was in flux. Urban expansion led to deruralisation in the countryside and a ruralisation of the cities. Industrialisation was as all-embracing as the presence of the peasantry.

The despot alternately breathed life into and weighed down upon the party and state machine, a machine which in turn held society at arm's length and eventually drove it to labour camps – a society that was mobilised, disoriented, brutalised and broken. This was a very powerful movement which provided the foundations of the modern Soviet experience, and which generated lasting difficulties that are still being felt to this day.

However – this is one of Lewin's central ideas – if the inner logic of the system was to prevail, then the chaotic and completely despotic nature of the regime could not endure. The main reason was not the threat of popular revolt, since the regime inherited a fairly passive society, and once the revolutionary fervour of 1917 had been exhausted it encouraged that passivity and reinforced the atomisation of society. It was due rather more to the new logic of social domination buit up – partly deliberately and partly despite itself – by the politics of Stalinism. This entailed the growth of the party-state and through the extension of bureaucracy the establishment of a dominant elite which would seek to broaden its power base and legitimacy, so as to acquire the physionomy, ethos and ideology appropriate to a coherent and functional social category.

This bureaucracy learnt to cope with its job and became less crude and more sophisticated. It gradually realised its own strength and, bit by bit, found the means to go against the dictator's orders.[25] Step by step, this bureaucracy turned the despotic disorder into authoritarian bureaucratic order, into a controlled and regular bureaucratic routine. At the end of the 1930s this process was well under way, a process that was at the same time both fragile and irresistible.[26] The highly specific period of the Second World War served as a cruel test but also as a paradoxical respite for Stalinism. It was a test of the solidity of the regime. This period, which Lewin experienced on the spot and which played a great role in motivating his research and nourished his evident love for the peoples of the USSR,[27] is not analysed as such in his writings.

The Exit from Stalinism and the Road to Perestroika

The Stalinist period was a profoundly formative one for Soviet society. However, it was just as much a deforming period and a source of permanent dysfunctioning. The post-Stalin era was marked by a painful search for solutions to the problems bequeathed by Stalinism. The presence of new realities and new stages became more pronounced. Lewin was very perspicacious in this respect. He stressed the emergence of new social forces, increasingly urban, more educated and, despite appearances, more active. In addition, the party-state became more sophisticated and acquired a more nuanced image of Soviet society. This did not happen without some resistance from the authoritarianism that was encrusted in its habits and privileges. In his *Political Undercurrents*, Lewin showed the relevance of the debates of the 1920s, especially Bukharin's ideas, and thus the existence prior to Stalinism of an alternative to the Stalinist model that was still relevant at the beginning of the 1970s. He pointed out the regressive features of the Brezhnev period which was a negation for Khrushchev's reformism. And yet within this bitter bureaucratic relapse, this golden age for rigid bureaucratic apparatuses, this period which, in addition, brought out once more the worst of wooden language, Lewin spotted the 'civil society recovery'.[28] In the same way, he brought to light important cleavages in the apparatus, a frustration in the lower ranks of the cadres who were kept in strict subordination, suffering an ever more intolerable straitjacket. All this summed up a regime that was on the brink of splitting up. Reading Lewin's analysis of Soviet society at the start of the 1970s, rather desperate years of widespread repression and bureaucratic paralysis, one can sense the Gorbachev experiment seeking the means to break through.

A main characteristic of the new period is the disappearance of the peasantry, 'an important feature that characterised Russia for centuries and dominated its social landscape',[29] while the cities emerged as the centre of Soviet society. Previously, they dominated politically. Now they dominate sociologically as well.[30]

> The popular masses and the different groups of intelligentsia, mostly urban dwellers by now, do have a better grasp of their interests in the rather stable environment . . . of today and there is no doubt that they find ways to express those interests and fight for what they want. They all, unavoidably, especially the intelligentsia, produce their own vistas, moods and ideologies.[31]

It is therefore important to explore the theme of 'civil society'. This concept 'helps us to realise that *à la longue* Soviet statism . . . could not and cannot fully control, shape at will or supress the social body and its development. Classes, cultures, publics, develop, exist and persist'.[32] In any case, 'after Stalin died, the political system, heavily corrupted and incapacited by his rule, was badly in need of repair. The economy was a shambles. The standard of living of the masses was lamentable and agricultural production was at or below the per capita standard of tsarist Russia. The party was in disarray . . .'[33]

Lewin understood the changes in Soviet society and the effects of these changes on the regime. These include irresistible modernisation and the tensions that result from confrontation between the benefits and costs of this modernisation. We have here a dynamic contradiction out of which Gorbachevism emerged, not as the invention of a leader coming from nowhere, but as a somewhat belated result of the in-depth evolution of society. What is more, this is a reformist leader who was not anticipated by observers either without or within Soviet society. Gorbachevism is the consequence of pressures that were expressed more and more loudly and finally screamed out by powerful yet heterogeneous social forces. This is what Lewin comments on in his recent study of *The Gorbachev Phenomenon*; a small book that is also the summary and reaffirmation of his ideas: the result, and even the updating, of many years of research.

It is again the attentive examination of social transformation and its interaction with the regime that enables Lewin to gain a clear view of Soviet realities. This way of looking at things is no doubt the most striking aspect of Lewin's work. It is the art of combining an immense mass of research with a sharp sense of what life is all about. It is also the talent of making his sources talk, of understanding, for example, that behind a stereotyped speech by Molotov at the end of the 1920s lies the regime's real view of the peasantry.[34]

Sources are the raw material of knowledge, the possibility of escaping from ignorance. But they are also a safety-net: the means of testing one's initial intuitions and ideas. Hence the rare sense of the concrete that is so characteristic of Lewin, his talent for bringing individuals to life, with their projects, their cunning, their pettiness and their grandeur.[35] The reader of his publications meets a humanist intellectual who is sensitive about and attracted to the people, to a people of workers and peasants and peasant-workers who are at the centre of Lewin's analysis of Soviet society. Social history brings back the people to the front of the stage, with its strengths and weaknesses, even if the most important event for Lewin is still the modernising process and the end of backwardness. And with the end of this backwardness we find the emergence of a political society that is still feeling its way, and that is perhaps the most salient aspect of the Gorbachev period.

SOCIAL HISTORY OF THE USSR: RESEARCH IN SEARCH OF ITSELF

A good deal of Lewin's work is the fruit of endeavours that might be considered normal for a historian: a rigour, a tireless quest for information, an inventiveness and sensitivity. It is only in the light of the overheated ideological debates of the academic establishment that this achievement can appear surprising. Indeed, it was not accepted by a substantial part of the scholarly community.

The social history of the USSR is still a discipline in search of its identity. Its results are so far only partial, its methodology is not yet very certain. Its obvious links with Marxism, together with a certain critical distance from it, are not clearly articulated. This Marxist influence is especially present in the attempt to show the Soviet social system as a whole, as the integration of a great number of different elements, and as the effect of an uneven development of its constituent parts. Of course, Lewin could have found the motivation for his research elsewhere, but in his case it really does seem that Marxism played a role. The categories of social history are not specified and what distinguishes them from Marxist categories is not obvious. These uncertainties stem from the fact that in the Russian case one had first to respond to the elementary task of recognising the existence of a society. This is not as obvious as it might seem.[36] The historiography shows, for the prerevolutionary period as well as in the case of the theory of totalitarianism, a tendency to look for a central factor that explains Russian specificity. This type of research does not bother with investigating the 'social system' as 'a complex network of interrelations, or communications, visible or invisible'.[37]

Besides, social history is difficult to define as a discipline or subdiscipline. This has much to do with the fact that its practitioners are far from agreeing among themselves about its object, scope, methods, sources and (ab)uses. It is almost impossible to reach an agreement on how to define the categories of social history in an unambiguous way: economy, society, civilisation, social groups and mentalities are terms that are subject to different and conflicting definitions. Another uncertainty is that a supposedly unimpassioned and professionalised historiography is fortunately still charged with passion, with second thoughts and with convictions. One must recognise that there is a good deal of indetermination, or more precisely a creative choice for those who want to deliminate the field of social history. As one author put it: 'Whereas the social historian must define a class or other group having no formal boundaries, and pull together bits and pieces of information from sources as dispersed as its individual members, the biographer has a life and (in the best possible case) a neat collection of papers and works to go with it'.[38]

This uncertainty appears in Lewin's work as prudence, as a wish to leave questions open and explains the somewhat vague categories he uses. Thus, when defining the central characteristics of historical periods, Lewin often uses, though sometimes with reservation, the term Stalinism to speak about the 1930s, even if, for him, Stalinism was above all extreme repression. Once the scope and arbitrariness of this repression were reduced (the passage from despotism to authoritarianism) Stalinism, as he says, ended. In other words, the term Stalinism has a more restricted sense for him both in terms of time and its proper significance, than it is given in many analyses of Soviet society.

In the same way, Lewin uses the terms party-state and bureaucracy to speak about the dominant group, without defining them or exactly stating their nature (class, sub-group, new social category . . .). Thus, writing about the Gorbachev period, he talks of 'a new authoritarianism of quite different type'[39] without any further precision. This vagueness is also present in the oft-discussed question of the relationship between the Soviet system and capitalism. One can sense a desire not to settle the question, a rejection of self-confident and reductionist explanations that lack a solid factual basis. In other words, Lewin wants to avoid, as Marx would have said, creating science before science could exist. He has adopted this approach because the gaps are still considerable, and he repeats this tirelessly from one article and one book to the next. The preface to the 1985 collection of articles (*The Making . . .*) on the 1930s puts forward a catalogue of questions and the embryos of answers. They open a number of routes, and exhort the scientific community to go further and elsewhere by exploring new directions and new sources.

In his eyes, the weaknesses of the trade are largely in empirical research, and this at every level. One could even say that for Lewin, as soon as one scratches the surface and goes beyond mere appearances – the actions of the authorities, the battles between the leaders

– and when one gets rid of the certitudes of militant anti-Stalinism, such as the omnipresence of repression, lower down and all around we find ignorance. While historians as well as political activists have been quarrelling over the significance of major ideological debates, about the places to be accorded to Bukharin and Trotsky, about the real historical role of Stalin, the true nature of the party in all its depth, with its lower and middle cadres, is often shrouded in mystery. Worse still, these areas have provoked hardly any interest among researchers.

Such unknowns are everywhere, though there are many promising trails to follow. This is confirmed by works that clear the ground, by preliminary inquiries and even by the simple sketches Lewin draws of peasant religiosity, of the relationship between popular demonology and the demonology of the Stalinist period, or of the paradoxes of the 'cultural revolution' of the 1930s. Here he shows the combination of the cultural betterment of the masses with the loss of traditional urban culture as cities become subject to industrial growth, and to a massive inflow of peasants who had great difficulty in adapting to an industrial and modern way of life.[40]

In other words, much remains to be explored in all the nooks and crannies of Soviet society before conceptual analysis can function in a useful and fertile way. This is not to say that Lewin does not have a more or less firm view of many aspects of these questions. Although Stalinism is a phenomenon that has strict chronological limits, he does not deny its central importance and the extreme violence that it brought to Soviet society. In this respect he differs from a recent trend in historiography which, though partly inspired by his own work, tends to remove the Stalinist dimension from this period, to remove the man and the personal power that he embodied, and to locate the source of the extreme violence elsewhere.[41]

In Lewin's case there is a certain reserve and hesitation when it comes to conceptualisation. It is, no doubt, a question of temperament. First one must reconstruct life with its suffering, measure the weight of historical phenomena. This approach recalls in some ways the work of E. P. Thompson, the historian of the making of the English working class, and his uneasy relationship with the young Marxists of the *New Left Review*. Perhaps Lewin could also be imagined writing about the inability of theoreticians to reconstruct the fabric of history, as Thompson did in relation to Althusser. Like Thompson, having the rare ability to reconstruct life experience, he is reluctant to enter the conceptual dimension. From this vantage point the historian's job is to add something new, however great or small, which the theoretician can by no means be certain of doing. Very often too this also involves demystifying the magnificent dreams and grandiose intellectual visions.

Lewin gives an excellent illustration of this in his analysis of the divergence between Left and Right currents in the 1920s – apparently a controversy about questions of life and death – where what was at stake was nothing less for participants than the future for socialism and mankind. Yet, Lewin observes soberly that the importance of the confrontation is limited in the light of its impact. Similarly, when he studied Lenin's last struggle, Lewin quite rightly described not a battle for socialism in general, given the dramatic conditions of the period, but a desperate and almost tragic attempt to introduce a form of modernisation, or better still, to escape from backwardness or even from a certain barbarism – an attempt to lay the foundations of the foundations! The rest was largely hot air in Lenin's eyes. Carrying Lewin's thoughts a stage further, one could say that it was a modernisation project that was rather reminiscent of other similar attempts of the twentieth century. In short, Lenin presented an increasingly realistic evaluation of the incredible weight of Russia's backwardness at the end of the Civil War, of the burden of the 'Asian heritage' – '*Aziatshchina*' – violently rejected by the revolutionary intellectual as well as by the head of state.

Lewin's work gives us the impression of a busy construction site. He makes a considerable effort to exploit a vast range of knowledge, not only about the Soviet Union (economics, sociology, demography and anthropology) but also about general issues in the social sciences, for example in relation to bureaucracy. He contributes especially to an understanding of the social context of politics. The difficulties of reaching a synthesis of scattered findings are vast, and explain the occasionally groping and uncertain way in which he makes use of these disciplines. However, the openness of his research strategy, the desire to achieve a high degree of intellectual flexibility, the attempt to dig deep into the topic, to seize it (in an almost military sense) rather than taking a stand on its precise significance – all this does not prevent the expression of firm convictions.

What are the reference points of Lewin's work beyond socialist and Marxist influences? What is the specific methodology of the social history of the USSR? No doubt they are diverse, but there is none that stands out in particular. One can talk of eclecticism. Priority is always given to whatever enables one to dive more deeply into a phenomenon. The essential thing is the capacity to render the vitality of each moment and of each epoch – and also of each individual. If one had to characterise the specific tonality of Lewin, one might say that he often does the work of a perspicacious psychologist, though not as it is understood today, but as Nietzsche would have defined it, as a demystifier of the real motives that lie behind false appearances.

In fact Lewin is at the height of his talents when he situates prominent figures in their epoch, and interprets epochs in their prominent figures. He does this remarkably well for Lenin, Trotsky, Bukharin and Stalin, showing each time how the period weighed on the individual, but also showing how the ethos of the individual reacted to unexpected events of the period. The weaknesses as well as the intensity of the intellectual and emotional reactions of Trotsky and Bukharin are remarkably dissected and minutely weighed on an ultra-sensitive balance. How well Stalin, the rational politician and the uncontrolled pathological despot, is understood![42] However, it is above all Lenin's confrontation with a completely unique situation in the post-revolutionary period that is admirably depicted. One finds here an almost physical sense of the ingredients that make up the lives of individuals and periods. That is what makes Lewin such an engaging researcher – he applies himself to the task of reconstituting the atmosphere – one could almost say the face, the smell of historical events.

If one wants to be exhaustive, one should also add to this list of influences the French *Annales* School and the Frankfurt School – the latter rather a limited influence, even though Lewin has a sharp sense of contemporary alienation and of the tension between the private and public domains. One could also mention the link with the work of Max Weber, who is commented on in highly favourable terms for his analyses of bureaucracy. Nevertheless, these influences remain limited, in spite of an effort to take a distance from a past that was perhaps too exclusively rooted in socialist doctrines and to look elsewhere for conceptual tools.[43]

THE HISTORIAN AND THE SOCIALIST TRADITION

For even the superficial reader, Lewin is a historian inspired by socialist conviction. While his objectivity can hardly be questioned, no one can be in any doubt that he belongs to the socialist tradition and has a certain Marxist heritage.[44] His task has not been helped by this, given that he has worked for the last twenty years in the Anglo-Saxon world which is often hostile to this tradition (or, more exactly, to its Marxist element). Are we therefore dealing with a socialist history of Soviet Russia? And is it a Marxist history (if this term means anything) that does not dare to say what it really is? Or should we conclude that his realisation of the complexity and unique-ness of the subject, and even the fundamental needs of the historian's trade, forced Lewin to distance himself from the basic categories of socialist thought, to be more prudent, more eclectic, to follow the rules of the historian's craft, which are valid whatever one's beliefs?

Confronted with an area of research like the USSR, which needs an ability to demystify, a departure from one's preconceived ideas is an elementary requirement of intellectual hygiene – a requirement that is, nevertheless, rarely exercised. Is it not the only way of having a sober and lucid look at what is fundamentally an object of passion? One can certainly achieve an excellent quality of work as an historian with openly avowed socialist and Marxist convictions, as the very different examples of Isaac Deutscher, Franz Mehring and E. P. Thompson attest. One can even quote Trotsky, who was above all a Marxist militant. But in the Soviet case, there is such a hiatus between that which was hoped for and promised, and what actually occurred after the Revolution, that a work of analysis and historical reconstruction demands a cold lucidity – if that is ever possible – about the subject and about one's own convictions.

Has Lewin solved all the problems in this respect? Probably less than he thinks. What does 'real Bolshevism' mean for him? He emphasises a deliberately elitist view in the Leninist project. Facing the trials of the post-revolutionary period, socialism meant above all cultural, economic and social progress – a form of non-capitalist modernisation. The emancipatory dimension, the self-emancipation of the oppressed, does not seem relevant in the case of Russia. From 1918 onwards, we are far from the declarations – that only dated from 1917! – in Lenin's famous *State and Revolution* with its perspective of a quick withering-away of the state. The vision of the Leninism of Lenin confronted with his own works seems to bring Lewin close to ultra-left views. However, he never professed these himself, and no doubt he would distance himself from their self-confident and peremptory characterisations, which are often founded on limited knowledge of historical realities. After all, Lewin seems to approve of modernisation by an elite, whereas the ultra-left wants to be its implacable critic.

For Lewin, Marxism is a complex and contradictory social theory. In many respects it is still valid for him as an analysis of societies, even if a certain number of problems require new and more nuanced approaches and a radical renewal of perspectives. Marx provided

> a study of a social system, an effort to offer a method for defining the character of an epoch a society is living in, or entering into, or leaving. Anyone who feels he needs answers to this kind of questions will turn to Marx for inspiration . . . Marx, when he talks about economies, naturally raises the problem of social classes . . . Of course, Marx's choice of 'the carrier' of progress, the proletariat . . . [was] partly mythical and produced important miscalculations, such as his theory on the growing pauperization of the proletariat, or his reliance on a basically two-class model as the main force.[45]

In any case, Lewin needs a flexible theory that is able to account for the complex, multi-faceted and changing realities of the Soviet Union.

But the professional historian that Lewin became at a quite mature age was too deeply marked by socialism for this profound influence not to leave its trace in his works. Its presence does however sometimes lead to a certain narrowing of Lewin's perspective that leads him, for instance, to identify Bolshevism with socialism. He is not always as far from Bolshevism as he thinks. One sometimes has the impression that for him Bolshevism is unavoidable, not only because its victory made it the historian's subject matter, but also because of its intrinsic merits. In fact, one senses without difficulty a sympathy for Lenin, for whom Lewin has such a feeling, both for his talent and his limitations.

He shows in a convincing way the existence of a conception that is specific to Lenin – the Lenin of the last texts, 1922–3 – a vision of the NEP that contained the seeds of an alternative, and not an unrealistic one, to the Stalinist project of the future.[46] In the same way, for Lewin, Bukharin elaborated a credible project that followed the line of Lenin's last texts, at least from 1926 onwards and, above all, in 1928–9. It is as if the only remedy to the dangers on the horizon was to be found within Bolshevism. He shows little interest for anything non-Bolshevik. Is it only a question of realism? Is it the simple observation that only Bolshevism is still on the stage, as the unique actor? Can one, as many readers have felt, detect a trace of his allegiances there? Or, in a more favourable hypothesis: can one see in this a courageous refusal to take part in the anti-Soviet hysteria that has for so long dominated the historiography of the USSR?

Lewin is perhaps somewhat reluctant to show the intrinsic limits of Bolshevism, whatever the divergences among its different currents. Neither Bolsheviks, nor the overwhelming majority of people who wrote about them, saw a clear alternative to the system after the late 1920s – including people like Bukharin or the *émigré* Mensheviks. Authoritarianism was the sole possible method in the eyes of all Bolshevik currents. Lewin notes on several occasions that Lenin was haunted by the central Menshevik objection – the classical Marxism of the Second International that had for a long time been taken for granted and defended by Lenin – of the impossibility for backward Russia to bypass the capitalist stage. One can see that clearly in a 'testamentary' text of January 1923, *On our Revolution*. Lenin answers this objection through expressing revolutionary faith and saying that the Bolsheviks had to seize an extraordinary occasion. One engages the battle and then one sees what it is all about, said Lenin quoting Napoleon's famous dictum.[47] And as this was a bit thin as a response to a fundamental problem, and quite insufficient to meet the gigantic challenge of the period, Lenin turned the Mensheviks' argument against them by stating that it was up to the new revolutionary power to create the solid bases of modernity and civilisation – the precondition for socialism. It was easy to say but very complicated to implement. But it was too late to step backwards. What followed would inevitably be full of drama, even if the Stalinist calvary could no doubt have been avoided. The reduced space within which the Bolshevik government manoeuvred in the 1920s partly determined what was to follow and thus conditioned the analysts' outlook on the USSR.

It did so until the problems of the contemporary world confronted Sovietologists with evidence similar to Menshevik 'maledictions' that Lenin was close to acknowledging. Today the USSR has to replay part of the drama, or at least repair the colossal errors of the past. It is hard to see adepts of the emancipatory project in the present turmoil. And one can say that, like many liberal intellectuals, Lewin has been moving away from a schematic vision of the inevitable path and stages of progress, toward a rather simple desire for an emancipatory dimension of social existence whose forms, content, or even vague contours became increasingly difficult to see in contemporary realities – be they Soviet ones or ours. In such conditions, a sober and lucid attitude of study, and a non-complacent one, offers the best way of understanding the changing Soviet realities. And to that, the social history of the USSR, as it is practised by Lewin, still has a good deal to offer us and much to make us think.

NOTES

1. R. Lew and V. Thanassekos, 'Les enjeux du débat actuel sur le totalitarisme', *Contradictions* (1987) No. 51, p. 47 sqq.
2. Cf. the preface to the French edition of *The Gorbachev Phenomenon: A Historical Interpretation* (Berkeley, 1988); *La grande mutation soviétique* (Paris, 1989).
3. *The Gorbachev Phenomenon*, pp. 2–3.
4. Ibid., pp. 4–5.
5. Cf. the 1982 interview on his life and scholarly evolution in *Visions of History* (New York, 1984).
6. S. Weil, *Oppression et liberté* (Paris, 1967) p. 162.
7. For ahistorical aspects in the research of H. Arendt's *Origins of Totalitarianism* (1951) see Raymond Aron's 'L'essence du totalitarisme', *Critique*, January 1954.
8. 'Do the Russians have a Society?', unpublished manuscript, 1985, pp. 13, 14, 15.
9. *Political Undercurrents in Soviet Economic Debates: From Bukharin to the Modern Reformers* (Princeton, 1974) p. 74.
10. Ibid., p. 75.
11. Ibid., p. 77.
12. Ibid., p. 82.
13. This is the title of the first chapter of *Lenin's Last Struggle* (London, 1968).
14. Ibid., pp. 8, 10.
15. Ibid., first and second chapters.
16. *The Making of the Soviet System* (New York, 1985) pp. 16 sqq.
17. Ibid., pp. 12 sqq.
18. *Political Undercurrents*, p. 83.
19. Ibid., p. 82.
20. *Lenin's Last Struggle*, pp. 128 sqq.
21. 'Do Russians . . .', p. 19.
22. Ibid., pp. 16–17; see also *The Making . . .*, pp. 24 sqq.
23. *The Making . . .*, pp. 26 sqq.
24. Ibid., pp. 16–17; 57 sqq.
25. Cf. J. A. Getty, *Origins of the Great Purges: The Soviet Communist Party Reconsidered, 1933–1938* (Cambridge, 1985) and G. T. Rittersporn, *Simplifications staliniennes et complications soviétiques: Tensions sociales et conflits politiques en U.S.S.R., 1933–1953* (Paris, 1988).
26. *The Making . . .*, pp. 231 sqq.
27. Cf. *Visions of History*, pp. 284 sqq.

28. *Political Undercurrents* . . ., pp. 249 sqq.
29. 'Do the Russians . . .', p. 26.
30. Ibid., p. 27.
31. Ibid., pp. 28, 30.
32. Ibid., p. 3.
33. *The Gorbachev Phenomenon*, p. 101.
34. Cf. *La paysannerie et le pouvoir soviétique, 1928–1930* (Paris, 1966) pp. 67 sqq.; a book which relies on sometimes fragile sources that are nevertheless remarkably carefully and well exploited by Lewin.
35. This term is used about the Russian people in the autobiographical interview in *Visions of History*, p. 285.
36. Cf. the discussion about Stalinism by those who have been described as a new school of Soviet research in *The Russian Review*, vol. 45 (1986) pp. 355–413, vol. 46 (1987) pp. 375–431). Without always admitting it, this school continues the pioneering work of Lewin, even though it questions some of its aspects.
37. 'Do the Russians . . .', pp. 1 sqq.
38. H. Liebersohn, 'Weber and Women,' *Telos* (Winter 1988–9) No. 78, p. 123.
39. *The Gorbachev Phenomenon*, p. 152.
40. *The Making* . . ., pp. 38 sqq.
41. *The Russian Review*, loc. cit.
42. Cf. the highly critical review of Ulam's book *Stalin* (New York, 1973) by Lewin, 'Stalin and the Fall of Bolshevism', *Journal of Interdisciplinary History* (1976) No. 7, pp. 105–17.
43. For Lewin's views concerning the limits of socialist discourse and Max Weber cf. *Visions of History*, pp. 290–93. For a critical appraisal of M. Weber and his vision of the bureaucratisation of the world see P. Piccone, 'Rethinking Protestantism, Capitalism and a Few Other Things', *Telos* (Winter 1988–9) No. 78, pp. 95–108.
44. Cf. *Visions of History*, pp. 282–3, 290.
45. Ibid., p. 291.
46. *Lenin's Last Struggle*, pp. 129 sqq.
47. Ibid., pp. 109–10.

2 Demons and Devil's Advocates: Problems in Historical Writing on the Stalin Era

Vladimir Andrle

If it is true to say that English-language scholarship on the USSR on the whole prefers facts to theories, it is something of an event when one of its journals publishes, in a single issue, five articles on the merits of a 'new trend' in the historiography of Stalin's Russia in the 1930s, which are couched in such general terms as to render any particular points of factual evidence almost irrelevant. Although well-mannered, the debate betrays signs of a keenly-felt division between American specialists on Soviet history. It contests issues which arise from the pre-factual and post-factual phases of historical writing, i.e., the *a priori* ideas that shape research topics and weave findings into readable versions of reality. The purpose of this paper is to summarise the debate and reflect further on the following three problem areas: the ascription of normal phenomena to the Stalin period; the attribution of responsibility for Stalinist crimes; and the presence of dogmatic thought in the historiography of the period.

A SUMMARY OF THE *RUSSIAN REVIEW* DEBATE[1]

In her opening article, Sheila Fitzpatrick announces the arrival of a 'new cohort' of students of the 1930s who are distinctive for two reasons: firstly, they approach their subject as *historians* rather than political scientists, by which she means that they explore the available documentary evidence in freedom from the preconceptions that tend to be encoded in the 'totalitarian state' model; and secondly, they are *social* historians, which means that they seek to understand the historical process in terms of social divisions, conflicts and alliances, rather than in terms of regime actions imposed upon an undifferentiated and essentially passive 'people'. In so doing the 'new cohort' are offering a new understanding of the regime as well. They are discovering repressive actions that were a response to problems of social order rather than a gratuitous expression of absolutist power; policies that were pursued by means of persuasive appeals to the differentiated self-interest of particular social groups as well as by means of coercive threats; and policies that were modified or indeed compromised in a complex process of implementation by 'informal social negotiation'. The Young Turks in the ranks of the 'new cohort' even see state policies that were 'initiated from below', although this vision is considered by Fitzpatrick to be based more on a desire to challenge orthodoxy than on a careful sifting of the evidence. Overall, however, Fitzpatrick considers the 'from below' perspectives of the new historians to be breaking down the limitations on thought that have been visited upon the Sovietological field by Cold War ideologies. Shared as they are with the wider field of social history, the 'from below' perspectives deliver the new historians of Stalinist Russia out of the intellectual isolation suffered by orthodox Sovietologists and make the subject open to fresh approaches and ideas.

On this point Fitzpatrick's 'sympathetic description' of the 'new trend' turns to prescription. The new historians, she complains, are still preoccupied with the totalitarian model, and still asking the old Sovietological questions about the political system, as if the only significant social relations were those in which society related to government. They should instead concentrate their talents on formulating new questions and developing 'a real social-history perspective on the Stalin period' such as might enable them to make their proper contribution to the field: to find 'that Stalinism had some *social* as well as political dynamics'. At the centre of their focus should be not the actions of the state, but the dynamic of relationships between different social strata and classes; the prevalent social distinctions and their significance in the lives of individuals; the ways in which individuals could improve their status and protect themselves; the various aspects and repercussions of social mobility; and the ways in which some features of the social hierarchy could persist or emerge in spite of, rather than because of, the actions of the regime. In addition to coming to grips with all these topics, the social historians will also have to decide what kind of elite there was at the top of the social hierarchy, whether it amounted to a Marxist sense of the 'ruling class' or 'simply [to] the group with highest status and economic advantages in society'.

All the four other contributors express the view that Fitzpatrick mis-characterises the field of scholarship on Stalin's Russia in order to exaggerate the originality and importance of the contribution made by her 'new cohort'. The field is a lot more varied in its topics and a lot less dominated by the totalitarian orthodoxy than Fitzpatrick implies, and always has been. The topics already included social stratification at the time of the Harvard Project studies almost forty years ago. The discovery of 'chaos on the ground' that afforded the regime only a partial and illusiory control over the behaviour of its subjects likewise goes a long way back, as do indeed frontal attacks by scholarly 'revisionists' on the totalitarian model. And, since Fitzpatrick's 'new cohort' are demonstrably not the first students of Stalin's Russia to define their subject as 'social history', her reasons for heralding their arrival on the scene as a landmark event seem rather obscure.

Three contributors – Stephen Cohen, Peter Kenez and Geoff Eley – also make the point that Fitzpatrick and the 'new cohort' assume a 'from below' perspective which leads to a serious distortion of historical reality in as much as it happens to obscure the full scale and significance of the state terror that took place during the 1930s. While Cohen argues that the terror clearly had direct implications for the social phenomena of the period that Fitzpatrick and her 'new cohort' for some reason seem determined to ignore, Kenez observes that much of the 'new cohort' writing is in fact concerned with political rather than social matters, but in such a way as to deny 'the extraordinary nature and importance of state intervention' in the Stalin era, to 'de-demonize Stalin and his Politburo', and make their politics look like ordinary 'humdrum politics' as if the Soviet government was 'just like any other government operating in difficult circumstances'. In other words, the 'new cohort' dwell on normal political phenomena like conflicting interests and factions but, to their discredit, do nothing about the task of explaining the peculiarity of the political order that let factional struggles result in mass bloodletting. Eley finds the same fault (i.e., under-estimation of the terror aspect) to be the effect of a rush to study 'social' or 'from below' phenomena without pausing to 'theorize' the conceptual relationship between the 'social' and 'political' spheres; in the absence of a conceptual discussion, the 'new cohort' tend to slip into couching their discoveries in a vocabulary that has already been infused with the definitions of the pluralist model of politics, thus in effect making a provocative and unwarranted assertions of similarity between Stalinism and pluralist democracy.

The fourth contributor – Alfred Meyer – offers his comments from an anti-positivist stance, where debates among historians are seen as being more about the value judgements and ideological implications of scholarly works than about their factual correctness. According to Meyer, the 'new cohort' writings have been surrounded by a scholarly furore because their bottom line amounts to a proposal to reapportion the blame for the unpleasant aspects of life in Stalin's Russia. 'By showing that Stalin was not as much in control as the totalitarianism school asserted, they are to some extent absolving him from blame for some of the cruellest episodes of the Stalinist era. This does not, of course, lessen the pains of these episodes, but places the blame somewhere else.' Another point made by Meyer is about the theoretical preconceptions of the 'new cohort': they seem broadly Marxist in that they look for the causes of things in 'the socio-economic base rather than the political-ideological superstructure', but this is a Marxism stripped of its element of 'unrelenting radicalism'. The 'new cohort' are failing to ask radical questions about social institutions, and this characteristic they share with Stalinist Marxism as well as with the 'totalitarianism school'.

Another observation about the differences between 'revisionism' and 'orthodoxy' in the historiography of the Soviet 1930s is made by Geoff Eley: the terms and bitter tones in which the differences are voiced have a precedent in the debate between 'intentionalists' and 'structuralists' that has animated western historians of Nazi Germany over the past two decades. The 'intentionalists' present the history of the Nazi state as an actualisation of the ideological programme originally set out by Hitler in *Mein Kampf*. The 'structuralists' see a semi-chaotic, 'polycratic' power structure at work underneath the monolithic surface of the regime; the ostensibly radical dictatorship found a source of political stability in a symbiotic relationship with old elites and social institutions, and its decisions were made as improvised responses to new situations, bringing about a process of 'escalating radicalization' which Hitler could exploit but not really control. The 'structuralists' even have their own Young Turks who are prepared to conclude that Hitler was a 'weak dictator'. The 'intentionalists' suspect the 'structuralists' of trivialising the evils of Nazism and constructing a sort of apologetics for them. The 'structuralists' consider the 'intentionalists' to represent a conservative historicism devoted to keeping the subject insulated from the modern insights into human affairs which have been offered by social science. Eley promises gains in conceptual awareness to those historians of

Stalinism who make the effort to acquaint themselves with the controversies in the field of German history.

In her brief concluding article, Fitzpatrick answers her critics by restating her position roughly as follows. She celebrates the 'new cohort' at the expense of earlier contributions because the latter already have been assimilitated into the field while the perspectives of the 'new cohort' are *new*. Far from ignoring the terror, she and the 'new cohort' in fact very much want to study it, but not by simply repeating the old 'facts' and judgements on it. She believes the new perspectives are better off without much abstract theorising; traditional Marxism only offers the dead weight of concepts defined by Soviet historians, while western neo-Marxism, too, has a tendency to stultify innovative research by the burdens of 'semantic orthodoxy'. She does not consider the debates in the field of German history a compulsory reading, for chances are that historical scholarship in general does not make its progress by an orderly accumulation of theoretical insights. She favours 'the illusion of objectivity' over reflexive moralising as her choice of heuristic standpoint, and observes that this preference is not normally deemed by western scholars to necessitate a defensive justification. Her 'revisionism' is 'iconoclastic' rather than 'ideological'; it values experimentation with a succession of hypotheses more than a consistency of interpretation which strains to fit all facts into a single theme. Vital scholarship, she believes, is above all else a search for new patterns among the facts of a field, and it has much to gain from the periodic shake-ups of 'the kaleidoscope'; it is in this spirit of pragmatic experimentation that she proposes to 'leave out the politics' and focus on social phenomena instead, for a time.

THE DISTINGUISHING CHARACTERISTICS OF 'NEW COHORT' WRITING

The *Russian Review* articles are surprisingly unhelpful to the reader who wants to know exactly what it is that distinguishes the 'new cohort' from the rest. The 'new cohort' are not alone in posing a challenge to the totalitarian model, 'revisionist' criticisms of this model having been a long-established theme within the Sovietological field, and it is equally difficult to credit the 'new cohort' with the distinction of approaching their subject as historians rather than political scientists. *Smolensk under Soviet Rule* by M. Fainsod, *The*

CPSU by L. Schapiro and *The Great Terror* by R. Conquest[2] – to name just three well-known works that Fitzpatrick would presumably classify as belonging to the core of Sovietological orthodoxy on the interwar period – are all written in a form that looks more like historical narrative than social-science analysis; and, if there is something about the content of these books that is more ahistorical than historical, Fitzpatrick does nothing to show what it is. Indeed, her categorisation of Sovietological orthodoxy as 'political science' rather than 'history' implies a clear boundary between two academic subjects which in reality share a lot of common ground, for political science in general has always had a strong base in historical studies alongside with the philosophical and analytical-quantitative ones.

To say that the 'new cohort' are social historians rather than political historians is also confusing, for two reasons. Firstly, Fitzpatrick's references pointedly exclude the *Making of the Soviet System* by M. Lewin[3] from her definition of the 'new cohort', although this well-known collection of essays defines its subject as a 'social history' in an explicit and clear argument. And secondly, some of the writers who are included in the 'new cohort' by Fitzpatrick address the topic that is central to the political histories of the period – the party purges – without in fact paying much analytical attention to the social context in which the purges took place.[4]

So much for Fitzpatrick's definition of the difference between the 'new cohort' and the rest. But the *Russian Review* debate includes two other suggestions of how the line separating the 'new cohort' from its critics might be drawn. One suggestion is implicit in Eley's observations on the debate between 'intentionalists' and 'structuralists' within the field of German interwar history. However, here again it is quite easy to think of examples indicating that this particular battle-line is not quite the one that separates orthodoxy from revisionism in Soviet studies; not all 'new cohort' works are very 'structuralist' in their terms – e.g., *The Best Sons of the Fatherland* by L. Viola certainly is not – while the 'totalitarian orthodoxy' includes such explicitly 'structuralist' books as *The Organizational Weapon* by P. Selznick.[5] There are things to learn from the scholarly disputes surrounding the history of the Nazi state, and we shall have an occasion to explore them below, but 'structuralism' is hardly the label that is exclusive to the embattled 'new cohort' in the Soviet field.

Finally, there is the suggestion, made by the *Russian Review* editor in his preface to the debate, that '[w]hat is at issue is socialism'. In the last analysis, this is probably true, for it would be idle to deny that the descriptions and interpretations of historians have their ideological implications, or that these implications in all probability play their part in the motivations of the historians who get embroiled in heated disputes. But this is a 'last analysis' verisimilitude into which scholarly debates ought not to be reduced in a hurry. It certainly is not the case that the 'new cohort' can be readily identified by a shared belief in regard to the question of feasibility or desirability of socialism superseding capitalism; their writings tend to be too relativistic in their stance to advertise a clear ideological message, and they draw the fire of critics whose ranks seem to include a whole spectrum of political colours, judging by the attitudes that can be discerned in the respective writings of Kenez, Cohen, Meyer and Eley.

The *Russian Review* debate makes it clear that there is a sense of division between the 'new cohort' and their critics, and it sketches out the lines of attack and defense. It is, however, not so successful in establishing what it is about the content of the 'new cohort' writings that sets them apart from the rest. I shall therefore draw on my own reading of the relevant texts to identify three respects in which the 'new cohort' writings are similar to each other but different from the work of that other social historian of interwar Russia, Moshe Lewin, who has been so pointedly excluded by Fitzpatrick from her deliberations.

The first and most obvious point that can be made on reading the 'new cohort' is that all the writings include in their descriptions of the post-1929 period things that might well be regarded as positive by western readers with radical sympathies. Thus Fitzpatrick writes of mass education, social mobility, cultural revolution and a revolutionary continuity spanning from February 1917 until the consummation of the first five-year plan; Getty writes of radical tendencies within the party, which sought to bring the bureaucracy under the influence of a mobilized grass-roots democracy; Rittersporn, too, finds political forces in play that tried to grapple with bureaucratic conservatism; Manning writes of participatory management in the collective farms; Viola of working-class enthusiasm for the collectivisation compaign; and Thurston of the pleasurable as well as grim aspects of everyday life in the 1930s.[6] Lewin, by contrast, concurs with the majority of historians who see a disaster of epic proportions taking place after the defeat of the NEP alternative, which dealt a tragic blow to socialist aspirations; the collectivisation campaign re-enserfed the peasantry and in effect swamped a fragile urban culture with brutal backwardness; the industrialisation campaign negated all promise of rational economic planning by the chaotic methods of centralised command; and the Stalinist state only built a proliferation of bureaucratic institutions to stabilise the 'quicksand' society it created by its destructive campaigns.[7]

But it would be wrong simply to accuse the 'new cohort' of promoting some sort of radical nostalgia in their rendering of the 'revolution from above'. Although a small element of this might be present in some of their writings, perhaps as a sort of challenge to the conventional grey vision of a heavily etatist polity, the picture of Stalinist reality that the 'new cohort' seem to be painting is multi-coloured rather than just rosy or red. The point about the 'new cohort' picture of the Stalinist reality is that it abounds in colours and shapes that may well seem already familiar to the western reader as being present in the realm of her own life, or at least in the image she has of other historical places and times than Russia and the 1930s. The 'new cohort' write of occupational aspirations, law-and-order problems, administrative processes, citizen volunteers, political appeals to group interests, conflicts over policy issues, patriar-chal culture, popular culture, work management, education and migration[8] – i.e., phenomena which, not being in themselves unique, can be understood as sustained in their structure by a range of social behaviour and motivation that may be readily perceived by the western reader as quite normal if not always desirable. And if the social phenomena can be understood without any reference to Sta-linist terror, terror probably was not central to the social order of Stalinist Russia. It took place, but neither permeated everyday life nor defined the social totality to the extent of giving the historical period as a whole an especially peculiar, exotic, bizarre and menacing quality. The terror did not overwhelm social life – it co-existed with it.

This is a different canvas from that painted by Lewin's social history. Lewin's mastery in creating a vivid sense of social reality in his historical writing is second to none, but it aims to bring out the unique qualities of the Stalinist place and time rather than the shared ones, and it does not attempt to challenge the conventional western image of Stalinist society as terror-dominated. His emphasis tends to be on the exotic colours and configurations of the peasant and anti-peasant mentalities that had developed in the course of Russian history; here Stalinism is made to look at home in its own surround-ings while remaining visible in its most bizarre and menacing aspects. Lewin writes a history where Stalinism is re-created as a phenomenon which is no less idiosyncratic for being social in its nature, while the 'new cohort' tend to present a Stalinist reality which is social and in that sense almost normal, i.e., in important respects continuous with non-Stalinist realities.

The third characteristic of the 'new cohort' writings therefore is that, if they address it at all, they tend to present the terror as to some extent understandable in its motives, and the result of a collective process rather than Stalin's caprice. Its difference from normal political processes being one of degree rather than quality, the terror is accounted for in terms of conflicts over policy issues or responses to problems of social order which for various reasons made themselves felt with a heightened intensity within the structures of government. Behind the monolithic facade of Stalinist dictatorship there was a society the mobility and dynamism of which attained near-anarchic proportions; and this society, far from stopping short of the institutions of the state, extended its teeming ways right into them. Stalin's personal importance is de-emphasised in the 'new cohort' writings; either implicitly, by mentioning him only infrequently in the historical narratives, or explicitly, by in effect claiming, as Getty and Rittersporn do, that Stalin was just one of a number of political actors who had the stage in the dramas of factional strife.[9]

In this respect, too, Lewin's social history differs from that of the 'new cohort'. Although he does not seem in a hurry to enunciate his own explanatory version of the terror and the Stalin cult, there is enough in his published articles to suggest more a concern with filling in the social underpinnings of an absolutist dictatorship than with denying that it was an absolutist dictatorship. The historical dynamic sketched out by Lewin is one in which Stalin himself eventually becomes an institution, so that his personal motives indeed do become a determining factor in the political choices that have to be taken. While Lewin tries to de-mythologize Stalin's established status as a historical demon by providing it with sociological roots, the 'new cohort' seem to believe that the demonic character itself is something of a myth that has served to obscure relatively banal truths.

The fact that the 'new cohort' writings include some positive-sounding things in their accounts of the Soviet 1930s clearly has much to do with the heat of the criticism they attract. By indicating various continuities between Bolshevik and radical socialist impulses on the one hand and the Stalinist ones on the other, they offend the earlier 'revisionists' such as Stephen Cohen, who prefer to emphasise the discontinuities between Leninism and Stalinism.[10] And they at the same time offend the 'totalitarians' who see the continuities between

Leninism and Stalinism, but have no sympathy with them. But it would be unfair to accuse the 'new cohort' of trying to cloak Stalinist phenomena in the glow of revolutionary romance. The fundamental issue posed by the controversy surrounding the 'new cohort' writings is in my view this: whether it is appropriate for historians to ascribe normal phenomena to the Stalin period in place of emphasising the idiosyncratic and bizarre ones, or whether such ascriptions only serve to rationalize Stalinist atrocities. Connected with this is also the perennial issue posed by the relationships between historical fact, understanding and judgement.

IDIOGRAPHIC AND NOMOTHETIC APPROACHES TO HISTORICAL WRITING

Kenez criticises the 'new cohort' for reducing Stalinist politics to 'humdrum politics', denying its 'extraordinary nature', and in effect trying to 'de-demonize Stalin and his Politburo'. Outside the pages of the *Russian Review* debate, L. Schapiro comments on Fitzpatrick's *Russian Revolution* that 'it is but a pale reflection of the reality which it seeks to depict . . . Dr Fitzpatrick deals pretty lightly with these horrors.'[11] And L. Kolakowski lampoons the 'revisionist' trend in Soviet studies in a spoof article in which the history of Nazi concentration camps is described in the cool terms of economic analysis.[12] Attacks on scholarly 'revisionism' by critics who hate to see the historical horrors 'trivialized' are indeed something that the field of Soviet studies shares with that of German interwar history. Here Marxist, New Left and 'relativist' historians are charged with underestimating the reality of Nazism, so that 'the ideological and totalitarian dimension of National Socialism shrinks to such an extent that the barbarism of 1933–45 disappears as a moral phenomenon . . . it could well appear as if a new wave of trivialization or even apologetics were beginning'.[13] One critic of the social historians of Nazism devotes a whole book to this moral problem, in which she defines the correct approach to the study of the subject as one which never fails to stand witness to Nazism as 'the essence of evil, the daemon let lose in society, Cain in a corporate embodiment' because 'nothing but the most lucid consciousness of the horror that happened can help avoid it in the future'.[14]

These critics believe that, in the case of the interwar histories of Germany and the Soviet Union, historical narratives written from a detached stance as well as analyses of the social-science type are somehow inadequate to the subject and morally harmful. The 'lucid consciousness of the horror' will be dulled, it seems, if the same style of explanatory analysis is applied to the horror as to less unequivocally negative phenomena, and the reading public will be drawn into a sort of complicity by rationalisation whereby the horror becomes explained away, sterilised and acceptable. The horror is too big to be placed by social historians alongside the less horrible, more mundane, normal and understandable things of social life that also occurred in its time. It demands to be written about in narratives that bring only its unique characteristics to the fore.

The 'idiographic' mode of historical writing, which seeks to describe events in their uniqueness, has the weight of professional tradition behind it, while the 'nomothetic' mode, which focuses on explanation in terms of general relationships, or in terms of particular combinations of general phenomena, has posed a growing challenge.[15] The idiographic tradition is rooted in the terms of reference on the basis of which history became a specialised profession, namely the rejection of two features of the histories that had been written in the pre-scientific era: firstly, the desires to entertain or to teach moral lessons by stories about the past, which had tended to be too strong to leave room for concerns about factual accuracy; and secondly, the teleological vision of time which saw human affairs progressing towards a transcendental end. The professionalisation of history meant placing the methodical examination of documentary records, to establish the facts of past events, at the basis of the craft. But not only this, for the professionalised history had to offer more than simple lists of events such as had been produced by earlier chroniclers. It had to convey an understanding of the past as well, albeit an understanding that was derived from the establishment of fact rather than from theoretical speculations about human affairs. The answer lay in establishing the intentions of historical actors as fact, and in linking previously disjointed events into a coherent and understandable narrative by constant reference to these intentions. In keeping with humanistic philosophy, the historical actors were assumed to be unique individuals whose shaping of events, however, could be grasped by empathetic understanding of their intentions.

The idiographic mode of historical narrative has great strengths because it can combine the rigours of hermeneutic analysis of written documents with the readability and essential humanism of biographically-oriented description. But it is not without its weaknesses.

The first possible weakness is that the writing of an empathetic understanding into a narrative description of intentioned acts rather relies on implicit notions about human nature which may be shared by the writer, the reader and the historical actor, but which the critic might nevertheless wish to bring out for sceptical enquiry. The fluency and plausibility of an idiographic narrative sometimes seem to be based on a complicity where general truths are asserted but hidden from rational argument. Secondly, the idiographic narrative seems to emphasise the unique individuality and intentions of histori- cal actors at the expense of in effect banishing other actors into a backcloth of an irrational, unintentioned, undifferentiated and less than human 'mass'. This is a counterintuitive vision of the political world that arrived with the French revolution. And thirdly, the principle of historical knowledge that base themselves on the sym- pathetic understanding of unique individuals in stately clothes do not seem robust enough to withstand the embarassment of having to grapple with murderous politicians.

> In Nazism, the historian faces a phenomenon that leaves him no way but rejection whatever his individual position. There is liter- ally no voice worth considering that disagrees on this matter . . . Does not such fundamental rejection imply a fundamental lack of understanding? And if we do not understand, how can we write history? The term 'understanding' has, certainly, an ambivalent meaning; we can reject and still 'understand'. And yet, our intel- lectual, and psychological, capacities reach, in the case of Nazism, a border undreamed of by Wilhelm Dilthey.[16]

The historians writing in the idiographic mode tend to infuse their facts with a sense of historical insight by describing them with the help of well-placed metaphors. It is thus that they establish the particularities of the things they write about, by suggesting that they share characteristics with quite different, logically unrelated things.[17] The strategic presence of metaphorical description does not render the narratives invalid; it simply testifies to the fact that a sense of historical reality is in part created by the use of descriptive language in which metaphors have a necessary part. However, when faced with abhorrent historical facts, they tend to infuse their narratives with explanatory coherence by using the one metaphor for the characteris- ation of the leading historical actors that can describe abhorrent intentions as understood without implicating the understanding historian in outrageous sympathies: the demonic metaphor. It is exactly because we live in a secular age, in which the belief that persons may be possessed by supranatural spirits has been marginalised, that the statement 'Hitler – a demon' can work as a metaphor; it establishes both his uniqueness as a historical individual and the diabolical nature of his power, thus matching the vivid colour of the cataclysmic events with which the man Hitler was centrally involved. And once coined in its usage as the descriptive representation of Nazism, the demonic metaphor is hard to challenge, because alternative representations, far from being seen as doing justice to the fact that Hitler was probably a man, appear to do injustice to the abhorrent nature of the Nazi actions and to the suffering of their victims. 'De-demonising' explanations of the nomothetic kind, for example those that show Stalin's actions to have had rationales rooted in particular combinations of general social phenomena, look to the idiographic historians like dangerous trivialisations of the facts.

The writing that is done under the sign of the demonic metaphor inhibits scholarly discussion, for it seems to permit only one kind of response to itself, and only one type of new historical insight: it only permits further descriptions which amplify the magnitudes or intensify the colours of the abhorrent facts. Anything else seems to be casting doubt on the appropriateness of the established metaphor, and by the same token on the sense of reality that had brought the metaphor into use. The metaphor has come to stand in the way of open-ended inquiry, experimentation with interpretative ideas and the testing of truths by discursive argument; these are good enough reasons for the nomothetic school of history to persist with its challenge even in the face of abhorrent phenomena such as Nazism and Stalinism.

But the nomothetic school of historical writing has its weaknesses, too. It is based on an ontology which assumes that human affairs are subject to general scientific laws, but this is an assumption for which the social sciences have yet to furnish a conclusive proof. That is why even those historical writings that otherwise quite clearly belong to the nomothetic category steer clear of a consistent use of the hypothetical-deductive method of exposition. Rather, they present historical facts as understandable by placing them in the context of their 'specious sociocultural "present"', where the idea of general rules of combination (functions, causes and effects) is invoked by the reading of historical records as if they reflected presumed actual relationships between the phenomena of a specific time and place.[18]

These context constructions can be rendered plausible by suggestive analogies with the relationships that the readers of historical texts know from their own experience of their place and time; or by metaphorical representations; or by discursive analytical arguments of a general or comparative nature; or by a combination of all these devices. But they can never be conclusively proven to be the only valid representations of past reality.

A good piece of historical writing, however, is not that which produces an immutable knowledge of the past. There is in fact a possibility that the past becomes eminently forgettable the moment it can be filed away as immutably known, in which case the knowledge would be defeating the purpose of its production. The good piece of historical writing will be based on a careful study of the available documentary evidence, for sure; but at its best, it will also engage the reader's imagination and thoughts with the affairs of fellow humans who would have otherwise remained lifeless categories stacked behind the walls of time and place. Good historical writing, it must be said, is exclusive neither to the idiographic nor to the nomothetic mode; and therefore there is nothing intrinsically wrong about the attempts of the 'new cohort' historians to show Stalinist reality as in some respects consisting of phenomena and experiences which can be found in other times and places as well.

It is not even necessarily the case that nomothetic approaches serve to trivialise historical catastrophes such as the Nazi holocaust or the Stalinist purges. A necessary correlation between writing about widely occurring phenomena and cloaking horrors in trivial thoughts only seems to exist when it is assumed that things are momentous or trivial in themselves, in accordance with off-the-peg notions of momentousness or triviality. It was this sort of assumption that enabled L. Schapiro to pose the following question while reviewing Fitzpatrick's *Russian Revolution*: 'Is the murder of six million Jews to be assessed in terms of National Socialist overall social policy, without a hint of disapproval?'[19] He posed it as a rhetorical question permitting only a resounding 'no' as an answer. But the question does not preclude the following answer: it is certainly correct to condemn the Nazis for killing six million Jews, but they have been already condemned for it a thousand times and the ready nod of agreement elicited by the thousand-and-first condemnation is beginning to look like a conditioned response. Offering an insight into the making of Nazi social policy, on the other hand, might conceivably stimulate the reader to think before nodding, perhaps about the Holocaust and moral choice in politics as well as about social policy. The effect on the reader would not then be trivial, in which case it would be unjust to level charges of trivialisation against the historian just because she chose to research the Nazi social policy rather than Nazi killings.

THE PROBLEMS OF HISTORICAL JUDGEMENT

Another assumption that is reflected in Schapiro's rhetorical question is that a historical knowledge of the Stalin era is inadequate if it does not also pronounce an explicit moral judgement on Stalin. Fitzpatrick, on the other hand, makes explicit her belief that understanding how things happened and developed is a separate cognitive activity from judging them, and that the effort to understand is sufficient unto itself, i.e., it does not need a moralising ingredient to become a valid pursuit. Schapiro's assumption of inseparability of knowledge from morals is rendered plausible by the fact that, in the conversations of everyday life, it is common to hear the statement 'it is quite understandable that he should fail to turn up' as saying 'he should be excused for failing to turn up'; here 'understanding' denotes the acceptance of a dubious action after due consideration whereas 'not understanding' would mean a rejection of it, at least provisionally. Fitzpatrick, on the other hand, might feel able to retort that no-one is accusing Dostoevsky of condoning murder, although he wrote an understandable account of how Raskolnikov had become determined to kill his victim. The writer in fact should be credited with helping to enhance readers' moral sensibility, exactly because he showed the killer's mind to be human rather than demonic, and in so doing presented for fresh examination by the readers the nature of moral choice. There is something to be said for the difference between judging and understanding, even in the face of things which ought not to attract positive judgements; in addition to which, it might be observed that the people in society who like to pronounce judgements already outnumber those who enjoy the effort to understand, and if academic writers do not separate the one from the other in order to concentrate on the business of understanding, it is difficult to see who will.

But not even Fitzpatrick would probably wish to subscribe to the view that historical actors should be altogether exempt from being judged by moral criteria. Schapiro might have been controversial if he insisted that every new insight into Stalin's Russia must include a renewed condemnation of the dictator's crimes, but he was probably expressing a consensual view in so far as he claimed that the passage of time does not release past men of power from being held morally accountable for their acts. It is, in fact, an important task of historians to discourage present and future politicians from thinking that they do not need to have due regard for the harmful effects of their power, because history will eventually supply an apologia for them.

Addressed as they are mainly at the forms of collective life at the grass-roots and middle-management levels, the 'new cohort' writings tend to provide circumstantial evidence that some of the Stalinist policies were couched in terms which were not without their popular appeal, thus in effect raising the possibility that they were the product of shared perceptions and reasons rather than of Stalin's personal designs. But the presence of collectively shared, social phenomena surely does not exonerate a politician, let alone a dictator, from responsibility for the damage caused by his decisions. Even if some of his perceptions and responses did originate in his social environment rather than in his own mind, it would be quite appropriate to expect a person in his elevated position to be more far-sighted and wiser than many of his contemporaries, and therefore also relatively independent in his mind of opinion bandwagons. He may not have been all-powerful, but he was in a better position than anyone else within the system to influence things for the better when they were going wrong. The 'new cohort' rumour that Stalin was a human politician, i.e., that his motives may have been complex and his control over circumstances less than perfect, only adds urgency to the task of finding the criteria for a coherent evaluation of his actions; but this is something that has so far been conspicuous by its absence from the 'new cohort' contributions.

It seems not much to ask of a politician that he should treat power as a means to the public good rather than just to personal ends. Unfortunately, however, this basic requirement in itself does not offer a workable criterion for historical evaluation, for there are many notions of the public good while reliable and conclusive proofs of personal motive are few. One way of circumventing this problem is to identify a particular objective as the most urgent in view of objective circumstances, and then to evaluate Stalin's actions in terms of rationality of response to prevalent conditions. Thus Stalin has been evaluated as a 'moderniser' whose main historical role was to build up the capacity of the state to defend itself in a technologically advanced warfare.[20] From this perspective, Stalin has been given some credit by historians who list the achievements of the crash industrialisation to contrast them with the backward state of the economy in the previous decade, and with the hypothetical implication of the disastrous course that the war would have taken in the following decade had a more moderate industrialisation programme been pursued. He has also been criticised from the same 'modernisation' perspective – by historians whose analysis of the facts suggests that the Stalinist policies were not the best possible ones for the economy, that they incurred unnecessary costs and provided the war effort with an industry which was not its optimal servant.[21]

A key to the health of this particular evaluative discourse is the degree to which it is possible for historians to gain access to the 'objective circumstances' independently of the definitions of them provided by the Stalinist government. Perhaps this is in some degree possible, in regard to some economic variables. But there are unlikely to be many variables which are independently measurable and directly relevant to a near-universal notion of rationality. Outside the realm of narrow economism, it seems an attractive solution to evaluate Stalinist actions in terms of rational response to objective conditions, taking, however, into account also the definitional limits of rationality inherent in the interpretative discourse within which the economic decision-making was taking place.[22]

But herein also lies a route to a chilling apologia on Stalin's behalf, for it is possible to use the combination of positivist and relativist insights in such a way as to rebuke all criticisms: it is possible to reject reconsiderations of objective problems, which might show Stalinist policies to have been erroneous, on the grounds that they do not take into account the then prevalent *zeitgeist*; and it is also possible to reject ideological or moral criticisms of Stalinist choices on the grounds that they ignore the dictates of objective necessity. Thus protected from 'naive' criticisms, Stalinism can be seen as the inevitable outcome of a historical union between father Zeitgeist and mother Necessity. Some historians get so carried away by the explanatory rhetoric of inevitability ('. . . and so it was inevitable that this should occur . . .') that they stop seeing the point of distinguishing between Stalinist visions and objective realities. Stalinism was what happened and it happened because it had to happen; a moral judgement on it is a sentimental luxury and a wistful consideration of alternatives to it an idle speculation.[23]

One way of satisfying both the need to explain Stalinism and the need to condemn it for the damage it caused is to introduce a distinction between those undesirable aspects of it that could be counted as the unavoidable costs of the rational policy, and those that should be counted as the excess costs of Stalin's personal drives. This, however, remains an abstract and evasive formula if it does not offer a reasoned argument on the basis of which a line between rational and irrational costs might be drawn. Those historians who wish to suspend judgement on the crash industrialisation policies while holding Stalin responsible for the excesses of state power should not refrain from offering for consideration what alternative, 'excess-free' methods were made available by historical circumstance that could have been used for the pursuit of rapid industrialisation had a wiser politician been in charge.

The evaluative cul-de-sac is in part due to the fact that the industrialisation decade has so far tended to be written about by historians as if it were a monolithic package of events, phenomena and trends, i.e., as if human affairs had fallen in a historical goose-step where each action had its meaning defined by the same thematic message about where things were going. But social life is not like that; it is made up of perceptions, attitudes, beliefs and acts which are replete with ambiguities, contradictions, 'cognitive dissonances' and possible reinterpretations; it has a multi-faceted reality which at any moment harbours a whole range of potential futures. If the past has to be imbued with a 'march of events' imagery by historical writings, then the march should be pictured on a rugged terrain with a plethora of possible routes if no certain destinations. Though undoubtedly situated in contexts which he could only partially control, the leader Stalin must be counted as responsible for the choice of each step that he took.

The question about Stalin as a 'moderniser', in other words, is no longer just one of whether the policy of crash industrialisation was as a whole a good idea in the first place, whether it was rational and vindicated by its economic achievements, although this argument will probably remain interesting enough to go on; it is also a question of observing the industrialisation campaign as a dynamic and multi-faceted process which, even within the terms of the discourses it was itself generating, kept forcing the political leader to reveal and inject his value preferences in the face of a rapid succession of wide-ranging dilemmas. Assessments of Stalin as a 'moderniser' have so far tended to obscure the fact that not all the people who regard 'modernity' as a positive thing would necessarily wish to endorse all the value preferences he revealed in the course of his participation in the process, not even all the people who were themselves willing participants of the industrialisation campaign.[24] The point is that a detailed analysis of the process should reveal not a single march of events which was either rational or irrational, but a whole lot of competing rationales, nuances of meaning and possibilities of action that the leader chose to endorse or to ignore. The making of historical judgements on Stalin from the perspectives of 'modernisation' offers a great scope for interesting arguments about both the values of modernity and the actions of the Stalinist leadership.

The focus on holding Stalin responsible for the values he preferred in his responses to conflicting pressures highlights the fact that the industrialisation campaign was above all a political process, which raises the question of the standpoint from which he should be evaluated as a politician. It no longer suffices to evaluate him as a respondent to economic problems, for economic problems have to undergo political definitions to be treated by the powers of the state. Ironically, the enormity of the human casualties of the industrialisation decade, which made it imperative for the dictator to be judged on charges of mass murder, has left pending the issue of how he should be judged by historians as a political leader.

It seems to me important that he should be judged also for his lasting contributions to politics, just as artists should be judged for their lasting contributions to art, cricketers to cricket and historians to history. This requires a definition of politics as a valuable, civilising pursuit in itself; a definition rooted in that vision of the world where conflicts of interest between individuals or social groups are inevitable but not disastrous, because politics enables agreements to be made about terms of peaceful cooperation or co-existence. The measure of achievement in politics then lies in the conflicts that have been rendered harmless and the diverse interests that have been allied with common goals, without the use of force and without reliance on that dubious sense of communality that can be sometimes fostered by creating scapegoats and bogus enemies. Whether revolutionary, reformist or conservative, all politicians can be judged on what they contributed to the noble art of fitting people in without damaging their lives; in other words, whether they served to enhance or degrade the culture of politics in their society. The Stalinist industrialisation campaign gave historians an unprecedented political process to study and evaluate; herein lies a long furrow that is yet to be ploughed.

It is unjust to accuse the 'new cohort' of historians of Stalinist apologia simply because they write of social processes in which people took part rather than of Stalin's will to power of which the people were a victim. But apologetic messages are bound to creep into histories based on treating textual records as if they testified to a logically closed discourse and a single objective reality, a world where the problems defined by a government are the real problems. Avoiding this pitfall requires a critical analysis of the categories encoded in historical documents, and that is a pursuit which not all of the 'new cohort' writings consistently make their own. For one, it certainly will not do for historians to treat their 'discovery' of 'social backwardness' and 'chaos' on the ground as if it explained the policies of the Stalinist state. 'Chaos' is probably little else than a verbal cloak for the fact that patterns of social interaction did not fit in with some pre-conceived notions of social order; and 'backwardness' is likewise something that should be studied as an ideological construct rather than taken as a self-evident and all-determining fact. At issue are the discourses within which social realities became categorically known and defined as political problems, for the ability of political actors to provide rationales for their actions is in itself no proof that objective social conditions were forcing their hand.

The analysis of the political process that was taking place at the various levels of Stalinist administration requires something of a discursive approach to historical records, which is unfortunately not encouraged by the conventions of historical narrative. A feasible compromise between these conventions on the one hand and the multifaceted nature of social reality on the other is to construct themes of exposition by concentrating on certain frequently mentioned categories ('class', 'bureaucratism', 'backwardness' etc.) and showing how they were used as a practical resource by participants in different interactional settings. But this requires either a painstaking textual analysis of a limited range of documents, or an extraction of data from a large number of documents combined with an argument which makes available for critical scrutiny the models of interactional settings within which the data are considered to have had their practical meaning. Neither of these methodologies has so far been used by the 'new cohort' historians, who on the whole seem to prefer to write about the 'from below' reality of Stalinism as if it was just a question of sifting the documented facts.

It is possible to have some sympathy with Fitzpatrick's insistence that the new field of social history of Stalin's Russia should best be developed in freedom from the burdens of 'semantic orthodoxy' such as tend to be generated by theoretically-minded Marxists and social scientists. It is probably the case that historical scholarship thrives in fields where researchers cultivate a shared sense of what constitutes a skilful handling of documentary data, but allow each other to develop different themes of interpretation; the greater the diversity of ideas the better. But Fitzpatrick is particularly interested in encouraging the development of *social* history, i.e., a field where the subject is not particular sets of events involving the lives and decisions of identifiable individuals, but the rather less tangible, though undoubtedly important, realities of social life that shape the experiences and actions of large sets of anonymous individuals. Discovering these realities in historical documents requires a rather different kind of interpretative, conceptual work than establishing what particular people did in specific points of time and place. Individuals can become known to biographers by being mentioned in archival sources and by leaving a range of personal artefacts behind; a culture can become known to cultural historians by making available its artistic products; a government becomes known to political historians by its documentation of authoritative decisions; all these fields of history surely involve distinctive conceptualisations, but it is not unduly difficult to tell biographical facts from cultural or political ones. It is not so obvious where the social historian turns to find social facts; the latter permeate most of what people do and produce, but they seldom advertise themselves without being conceptualised first.

Fitzpatrick advocates a shift of focus from politics to social history as if this was a simple question of turning from one set of available facts to another, and argues that that is the way to free historical writing from the strait-jacket of ideological categories. But she must be employing a lot of conceptualisation to see any social realities behind what is written in her documents, and to distinguish social facts from ideological fictions. Her empiricist message, however, is that she would rather not talk about her reasons for seeing one set of facts behind her data rather than another. Unlike Moshe Lewin, who, although writing in a colourfully idiographic style ('painting a social canvas'), clearly reflects a wide sociological knowledge in his treatment of religion, the peasantry, political administration etc., Fitzpatrick shows little interest in the theoretical underpinnings of describing the social life of a remote place and time. Should the 'new cohort' continue to follow her example, the danger is that their works will be appreciated not for their freedom from ideological strait-jackets, but on the contrary, simply for the anti-anti-communist connotation that is present in describing Stalinist Russia as if it was made up of normal social phenomena; or even for the apologia that is present when political atrocities get endowed with specious social reasons.

NOTES

1. *The Russian Review*, vol. 45, 1986. The contributors were Sheila Fitzpatrick, 'New perspectives on Stalinism', pp. 357–73, and 'Afterword: revisionism revisited', pp. 409–13; Stephen F. Cohen, 'Stalin's terror as social history', pp. 375–84; Geoff Eley, 'History with the politics left out – again?', pp. 385–94; Peter Kenez, 'Stalinism as humdrum politics', pp. 395–400; and Alfred G. Meyer, 'Coming to terms with the past . . . and with one's older colleagues', pp. 401–8. All further references to these authors that appear below are intended as references to these articles, unless otherwise stated in a separate note.
2. Fainsod, M., *Smolensk under Soviet Rule* (London: Macmillan, 1958); Schapiro, L., *The Communist Party of the Soviet Union*, second edition (London: Eyre and Spottiswoode, 1970); Conquest, R., *The Great Terror*, revised edition (Harmondsworth: Penguin Books, 1971).
3. Lewin, M., *The Making of the Soviet System: Essays in the Social History of Interwar Russia* (London: Methuen, 1985).
4. I believe this to be particularly true of Getty, J. Arch, *Origins of the Great Purges: The Soviet Communist Party Reconsidered, 1933–1938* (Cambridge: Cambridge University Press, 1985).
5. Viola, Lynne, *The Best Sons of the Fatherland: Workers in the Vanguard of Soviet Collectivization* (Oxford: Oxford University Press, 1987); Selznick, P., *The Organizational Weapon: a Study of Bolshevik Strategy and Tactics* (Glencoe, Illinois: Free Press of Glencoe, 1960).
6. Fitzpatrick, S., *Education and Social Mobility in the Soviet Union, 1921–34* (Cambridge University Press, 1979); Fitzpatrick, S. (ed), *Cultural Revolution in Russia, 1928–31* (Bloomington: Indiana University Press, 1978); Fitzpatrick, S., *The Russian Revolution* (Oxford: Oxford University Press, 1982); Getty, J. Arch, op. cit., Rittersporn, G., 'L'etat en lutte contre lui-meme: Tensions sociales et confits politiques en U.R.S.S. 1936–1938', *Libre*, 1978, pp. 3–37; Manning, Roberta T., 'Government in the Soviet countryside in the Stalinist thirties: the case of Belyi raion in 1937', *Carl Beck Papers in Russian and East European Studies*, no. 301, Pittsburgh n.d.; Viola, L., op. cit.; Thurston, Robert W., 'Fear and belief in the USSR's "Great Terror": response to arrest, 1935–1939', *Slavic Review*, vol. 45, No. 2, pp. 213–44.
7. Lewin, M., op. cit. All references to M. Lewin that appear below are intended as references to this volume.
8. See note 6 above, plus: Dunham, Vera, *In Stalin's Time: Middleclass Values in Soviet Fiction* (Cambridge: Cambridge University Press, 1976);

Siegelbaum, Lewis, *Stakhanovism and the Politics of Productivity in the USSR, 1935–1941* (Cambridge: Cambridge University Press, 1988). The list of works on 'social' topics could be extended by the inclusion of those written by British and European-based scholars. Fitzpatrick, however, seems to be concerned with American scholarship only, and her celebration of the 'new cohort' is delimited accordingly.

9. Getty, J. Arch, op. cit.; Rittersporn, G., op. cit.
10. Cohen, S. F., 'Bolshevism and Stalinism', in Tucker, Robert C. (ed), *Stalinism: Essays in Historical Interpretation* (New York: W. W. Norton and Co., Inc., 1977).
11. Schapiro, L., 'The Russian Revolution', *Times Literary Supplement*, 18 March 1983, p. 269.
12. Kolakowski, L., in *Survey*, vol. 21, no. 4, 1975, pp. 87–9.
13. Bracher, Karl Dietrich, *Zeitgeschichtliche Kontroversen*, quoted in Kershaw, Ian, *The Nazi Dictatorship: Problems and Perspectives of Interpretation* (London: Edward Arnold, 1985) p. 16.
14. Davidowicz, Lucy, *The Holocaust and the Historians*, quoted in Kershaw, op. cit., p. 16.
15. This discussion is heavily indebted to Iggers, Georg G., *New Directions in European Hitoriography*, revised edition (London: Methuen, 1985); and White, Hayden, *Metahistory: the Historical Imagination of Nineteenth-Century Europe* (Baltimore: John Hopkins University Press, 1973). Neither of these authors, however, place a particularly strong emphasis on the 'focus on what is unique' vs. 'focus on what is general' dilemma of historical writing, and neither is to blame for labelling the respective tendencies as 'idiographic' and 'nomothetic'.
16. Wolfgang Sauer quoted in Kershaw, op. cit., p. 15.
17. I have in mind here the narrower meaning of 'metaphor', which is distinct from other figures of speech, such as metonymy or synecdoche. See White, H., op. cit.
18. Ibid.
19. Schapiro, L., in *Times Literary Supplement*, 18 March 1983, p. 269.
20. E.g., von Laue, T. H., *Why Lenin, Why Stalin?* (London: Weidenfeld and Nicolson, 1966); or Deutscher, I., *Stalin* (Oxford: Oxford University Press, 1949).
21. E.g., Millar, James R., 'Mass collectivization and the contribution of Soviet agriculture', *Slavic Review*, December 1974; or Hunter, H., 'The over-ambitious first five-year plan', *Slavic Review*, June 1973.
22. See Nove, A., 'Was Stalin really necessary?', *Problems of Communism*, vol. 25, July-August 1976.
23. I believe the history written by E. H. Carr comes close to this position.
24. For conflicts of attitude to 'industrial culture' that existed within the industrialising establishment see, e.g., Andrle, V., *Workers in Stalin's Russia: Industrialization and Social Change in a Planned Economy, 1929–1939* (Hemel Hempstead: Harvester-Wheatsheaf, 1988) ch. 3.

3 Gorbachev's Socialism in Historical Perspective
R. W. Davies

> Perhaps one, or several, of the present or future leaders of Soviet communism may develop the will, the courage, and the political ability eventually to break through the tangle of obstacles, to revitalize the forces of liberty without stimulating them to the point where they would exhaust themselves in an attempt at revolution, and to keep the reform in domestic and foreign policy in a dynamic equilibrium without a breakdown on either side. The ultimate goal of such a course would be the return not only to Lenin but to the old socialist tradition.
>
> Carl Landauer, *European Socialism* (1959), p. 1672

During the tumultuous months of 1989 the Western view that world communism was in a profound crisis seemed to have been dramatically confirmed. Hungary and Poland moved sharply towards a multi-party system in which the Communist Party is likely to be in a minority; and their economies rapidly acquired a substantial capitalist sector. In China the dominant group in the Communist Party suppressed the democratic movement by crude force.

Socialism outside the communist world has also been in something of a crisis since the 1970s. In 1939 and even in 1965 it seemed probable – at least to most socialists – that socialism would become the dominant world system, in either its communist or its democratic socialist form, or through some kind of convergence between capitalism and socialism. But by the late 1980s most of the industrialised capitalist countries had emerged from economic crisis technologically more advanced and economically more powerful; throughout the industrialised world, which now includes former third-world countries such as Taiwan and South Korea, socialism seemed to be on the retreat.

This bleak view of the prospects for communism and democratic socialism may be a superficial extrapolation from the trends of the past two decades. It was only after many centuries of turmoil, through a long process of advances and retreats, that capitalism established itself as the dominant world economic system. Perhaps in

48

the longer perspective of the next century or two, the 1970s and 1980s may seem to be merely a period of temporary retreat in the rise of socialism. Perhaps in this perspective Soviet developments since the 1920s (or since 1917?) may seem to be a disastrous if educative false start . . .

*   *   *

It seems to me that many of the traditional socialist arguments against private capitalism remain as powerful in 1990 as they were a century ago. There is a strong practical and moral case for some kind of socialist world order. Most of the advanced countries continue to be class-divided societies with extreme inequalities of wealth and power. The rest of the world remains impoverished, and now also bears the burden of a crippling debt to the advanced capitalist countries. Moreover, industrialisation has brought with it grave ecological problems on a world scale. Can these problems be solved, and the world economy prosper, without some kind of national and international planning and regulation of the activities of supra-national companies?

It is in this context of uncertainty about the future of human society, acute and obvious in the communist world, but also chronic in the non-communist world, that we should think about the grand programme of political and economic reform launched by Gorbachev and his colleagues. Soviet 'new thinking' since 1985, at first vague and hesitant, has involved a startling transformation of ideas, in internal as well as in international affairs. So far the economy has in practice largely remained unreformed, and the first steps towards reform have plunged the economy into a deeper crisis. But some elements of a new model of socialism have emerged which in major respects contradicts not only the traditional Soviet model but also the visions of the socialist future depicted by Lenin and even by Marx.

The present paper explores this new Soviet model of socialism in the context both of the history of socialist thought and of the traditional Soviet model.

SOCIALISM BEFORE 1917

Precursors of modern socialism may be found in Plato's *Republic* and Thomas More's *Utopia*, and in the visions of the future of Gerrard

Winstanley and the seventeenth-century English Levellers. But the term 'Socialism' was apparently first used by Robert Owen in 1827, and it was in nineteenth-century Europe that socialism became a popular political creed.

There are many socialisms. But in the nineteenth century the various models of the future society usually embodied three major principles: common ownership; democratic management; and equality. Views differed sharply on what these principles would mean in practice. For Fourier, Owen and Proudhon the ideal economy consisted of cooperatives or companies owned and managed by those who worked in them; socialism involved producers' democracy. They conceded that the different cooperatives or companies would have to associate with each other in order to meet national needs. But their principal concern was, as William Morris put it, to arrange for the 'unit of administration to be small enough for every citizen to feel himself responsible for its details' (1889).

Other socialists were much more concerned to ensure that the anarchy of capitalism should be replaced by the integrated management of production and distribution for the social good. One of Saint-Simon's disciples called for 'general forethought', which amounted to a kind of comprehensive planning:

> society must be organised according to general forethought and must continually be guided, as an entity and in all its parts, by such forethought.

Much later in the century Bellamy defended central direction by 'a single syndicate representing the people', and even compared the future economy to a 'disciplined army under one general'. Marx also of course took it for granted that the future socialist or communist economy should be planned comprehensively, and described a rough economy-wide planning system in *Critique of the Gotha Programme* (1875).

In general, those who stressed the need for comprehensive planning tended to favour state ownership. While Marx and Engels believed that the state as a coercive mechanism would wither away during the transition to socialism, they also emphasised that during the transition period it would be necessary to 'centralize all instruments of production in the hands of the state' (1848). It is true that Saint-Simon, Marx and Bellamy all firmly believed that socialism would be democratic; Engels referred to 'the free and equal association of the producers'. But it is perhaps fair to say that this wing of the socialist movement tended on the whole not to be worried about the power that would be vested in the controllers of a planned society. Saint-Simon happily envisaged that the economy would be run by the technical elite. Marx clashed with Bakunin, who accused him of failing to realise that workers in power would set themselves above the ordinary workers. According to Bakunin, a socialist state would be 'nothing but a barracks . . . where regimented working men and women will sleep, work and live to the beat of a drum; where the shrewd and educated will be granted government privileges'. And William Morris denounced Bellamy's Utopia as 'State Communism, worked by the vast extreme of national centralisation'.

On the issue of equality there was little disagreement. All socialists believed that the new order would embody much greater equality than all previous societies, and many advocated complete equality. Marx distinguished between the higher phase of communist society, and the lower phase, which he termed socialism. In the higher phase, the product would be distributed according to need; in the lower or socialist phase, there was not yet an abundant supply of goods, and the product was distributed unequally according to work done. But even in this lower socialist phase the inequalities due to exploitation would already be eliminated. In general, nineteenth-century socialists placed a great deal of emphasis on the more equal redistribution of social wealth as a cardinal merit of socialism.

All these rival views were current in the pre-revolutionary Russian socialist movement. There was a more or less common international appreciation among socialists of the issues – and the unsolved problems – of the future socialist society.[1]

So far I have not mentioned the market. With hardly any exceptions, both the 'cooperative' and the 'planning' wings of socialism assumed that markets would no longer be required in a socialist society. Fourier stressed that his new society would eliminate the commercial machinations of the merchants. Marx held that money would be eliminated even under socialism; it would be replaced by labour tokens, which entitled the producers to draw on the common stock in accordance with the work they had contributed. Bellamy had a similar scheme for the distribution of the product. And even at the beginning of the twentieth century Kautsky assumed that, while money would continue, exchange of goods would be replaced by some kind of planned distribution. His contemporary Bernstein, for all his revisionism, assumed that there would be one producers' association for each industry, so that 'the coercive laws of competition' would be eliminated; competition would be suppressed and replaced by monopoly.

Theodor Hertzka's 'Freeland' (1886 and 1890) was a rare exception. Here the self-managed firms were held together by the market:

> The price of all the products of work, determined through competition, rules in a quite automatic fashion the in- and outflow of labour forces, always according to the measure of need for the products of the different branches of work.[2]

Hertzka was a precursor of Heimann and the market socialists of the 1920s, who were in turn followed by Lange, Dickinson and others in the 1930s. These market models of socialism were designed in response to von Mises' famous attempt to demonstrate that administered socialism was unworkable. Some variants of the model assumed that market prices formed by competition would guide the socialist firm; others assumed that the state would fix prices equal to those which would have emerged on a free market. In some models, investment as well as both production and consumption was determined by the market; in others it was determined by the planners centrally.

Thus the view that the market would continue under socialism did not become widespread in the West until the 1920s. One of the main arguments in favour of socialism was that it would eliminate the waste, chaos and fluctuation with which the capitalist market was always associated. Before the First World War nearly all socialists assumed that this would involve the elimination of the market itself.

THE TRADITIONAL SOVIET MODEL

The Soviet model of the socialist economy rejected or drastically modified all three major principles of the predominant nineteenth-century vision of socialism: common ownership, democratic management and equality.

For Soviet communists common ownership ultimately meant state ownership. In the brief period of rethinking before his death Lenin spoke of socialism as a 'society of civilised cooperators'. But even during the New Economic Policy the standard Bolshevik assumption was that state ownership was the highest form of common ownership.

By the 1930s this assumption had become a dogma. Under Communism all ownership would be state ownership, and when the state had withered away this higher form of ownership would simply be renamed 'public ownership' (*obshchenarodnaya sobstvennost'*).

Together with their support for state ownership, Soviet communists very strongly emphasised the crucial importance of central planning in a socialist economy. Planning was of course particularly essential in Soviet Russia, because a semi-industrialised peasant society had to be brought up to the technical and productive level of the industrialised powers. But planning would also be required during the transition from socialism to communism. Planning was the antithesis to the anarchy of the capitalist market.

During the New Economic Policy some economists favoured flexible forms of planning, and until 1928 everyone assumed that plans must be made compatible with market equilibrium, and with a non-coercive economic relationship with the peasantry. But all communist economists assumed that this was a transitional stage; eventually planning would replace the market, and product-exchange would replace trade. The universal validity of planning seemed to have been clearly demonstrated when the whole capitalist world plunged into economic crisis and mass unemployment on an unprecedented scale in 1929–31.

This stress on the importance of planning was accompanied by the virtual elimination of self-management or producers' democracy from the Bolshevik programme. The story is complicated. As early as the spring of 1918, Lenin insisted that 'one-person management' in industry and elsewhere must replace committee management; and that managers must be appointed rather than elected. In 1920 this view was enforced in industry against the opposition of the trade unions and the party members then responsible for the general administration of state industry, and in 1921 it was finally enshrined in party doctrine with the defeat of the workers' opposition. Lenin argued that one-man management was essential for efficiency; the Soviet proletariat must learn from the capitalist trusts. In the ensuing decades, limited schemes for self-management and the election of foremen and managers occasionally re-emerged, particularly during the first five-year plan. But self-management virtually disappeared from Soviet socialism between 1921 and 1970.

The Soviet model exercised considerable influence on West-European socialism, which was in any case already inclined by the 1930s and 1940s to a state-oriented or bureaucratic concept of socialism. In

Britain after the Second World War, the Labour government assumed that socialisation meant nationalisation, and the trade unions agreed with the view of the politicians that nationalised industries should be run by appointed managers rather than by a board elected by the workers.

Until 1931 the third principle of nineteenth-century socialism – redistribution in the interests of greater equality – continued to be upheld in the Soviet Union, both in doctrine and in practice. The party and the trade unions acknowledged that during the transition to socialism it was necessary to retain some differentiation of wages in accordance with skill, and with the intensity and difficulty of work. But even in the course of the 1920s wage differentials between and within industries were slowly narrowed. It should be noted, however, that this greater equalisation did not apply to the emerging ruling elite: their material privileges more or less steadily increased from 1918 onwards. Party members were subject to a maximum wage (the *partmaksimum*); but leading party officials had access to special housing, medical and recreational facilities.

The great public break with the socialist egalitarian tradition came in June 1931, when Stalin in his address to business managers condemned petty-bourgeois egalitarianism, and insisted that greater differentiation of incomes was essential to the efficient construction of a socialist society. The *partmaksimum* was abolished in the following year.

We noted earlier that the post-revolutionary Soviet Communists, like the pre-war socialists, assumed that the market would be eliminated with the establishment of socialism. But this view was modified considerably, both during the New Economic Policy and in the Stalin Period. During NEP in the 1920s, it was assumed that the market economy would continue throughout the transition to socialism, and many leading party members took it for granted that the transition would take several decades. With the 'great break-through' of 1929, the end of the market seemed at last to be in sight; and the next few years saw the establishment of a centrally-planned or administrative-command economy. By 1934, however, the administrative-command model of socialism had been significantly modified. In several important respects the economic system established under Stalin was not the moneyless product-exchange economy envisaged in 1930.

First, most collective-farm and state-farm peasant households worked their own personal plot, and could own their own cow and poultry. After obligations to the state had been met, both the household and the collective farm to which it belonged were permitted to sell their produce on the 'collective-farm market', which was in effect a free market in which prices were regulated by supply and demand.

Secondly, outside the large forced labour sector, with certain restrictions employees of the state were free to change their job. A very imperfect market for labour existed throughout the Stalin period and after; wages and other material inducements played an important role in persuading people to work in priority sectors. These arrangements are in sharp contrast to the Chinese economic system, where even today the rights of workers in the state sector to change their jobs are very limited.

Thirdly, from the end of 1934 the rationing of food and consumer goods in state and cooperative retail trade was abolished (it was resumed during the Second World War until 1947, and on a local basis in the 1970s). Consumers were able to choose among such products as were available. This was, however, a very limited 'market', because prices were fixed by the state. Fourthly, various forms of illegal 'second' or black-market economy formed an inherent part of the system.

The Soviet model of socialism introduced in the 1930s was certainly an administrative-command economy managed from the centre; and this model has remained in force until now. But it made significant though limited concessions to the operation of market forces.

TOWARDS A NEW MODEL OF SOVIET SOCIALISM

The crucial feature of Gorbachev's reforms, which astonished almost every Western student of Soviet affairs, is the twin emphasis on democratic and economic reforms. Until the spring of 1989, Chinese economists argued that political democratisation was not crucial for economic reform. Other economists have even insisted that the democratic rights of workers and other citizens should be positively discouraged; they stood in the way of economic efficiency in pre-Thatcher Britain and their absence was an important factor in the progress of such countries as South Korea. But after the Chinese political crisis of the spring of 1989, Gorbachev's call for socialist democracy seems wise as well as more humane.

The Role of the Bureaucracy

All Soviet reformers, moderate and radical, left-wing and right-wing, strongly believe that the centralised bureaucratic political and administrative structure is a major conservative force and a major obstacle to reform. But what is the social nature of the Soviet system created in the Stalin era and continued by Brezhnev, the system which Gorbachev termed 'the administrative-command system for the party-state management of the country'?

The predominant official view is that Soviet development in the 1930s and 1940s, in spite of the inhumanities and social defects, represented a move towards socialism. Thus Academician G. Smirnov, director of the Institute of Marxism-Leninism, argued that Soviet society was a form of socialism: the masses were 'striving' for socialism, and there were no exploiting classes. He acknowledged, however, that the system might be described as 'early socialism', 'barracks socialism', 'state socialism' or 'deformed socialism'.[3]

Other leading figures go much further, and argue that the bureaucracy, at least until 1985, had usurped political power as a social group, or was even an exploiting ruling class.[4] In 1988–9 this view gained increasing support. It is significant that Academician Zaslavskaya, who in the past described Soviet society in terms of a complex inter-relation of groups, in December 1988 declared that the 'nomenclature stratum' were well on the way to being a class.[5]

Gorbachev and his advisers have not taken a firm line on this question. On numerous occasions Gorbachev has attacked the crippling conservatism of bureaucrats, and made it clear that this is a widespread social phenomenon. Thus at the party central committee plenum in October 1987 he recounted with approval a detective story in which a party cell had justifiably wanted to dismiss an official, but 'the whole "*nomenklatura*" from top to bottom came to the defence of this "*nomenklaturshchik*"'.[6] And in October 1988, at a central committee conference on agriculture, Gorbachev's approval for sweeping attacks on the bureaucracy was made clear by his intervention in a delegate's speech:

> [V. I. Guseinov] Specialists and leaders from the farm to the Ministry are a special kind of cog (*vintik*) in the administrative-economic apparatus, are the conservatives in *perestroika*.
> [M. S. Gorbachev] They aren't cogs, but big bolts.[7]

In the course of the past two or three years, privileges afforded to high officials in the form of special shops, medical services and housing have been confronted by a rising tide of public hostility. They were a major issue in the elections of March 1989, and played a significant role in the electoral defeat of many party officials. This general hostility to privileges was at first resisted by the Politburo, but recently Gorbachev and his supporters have been much more favourable towards the attack on privileges. They have been pushed in this direction both by public opinion and by the bitter resistance of many conservative officials to political and economic reform, which has more and more turned the struggle for reform into a struggle against the whole bureaucracy. At the Congress of Soviets in June 1989 Gorbachev proposed that a Commission of the Supreme Soviet should be set up 'to carry out a kind of general inspection (*'reviziya'*) of all concessions and privileges', and Prime Minister Ryzhkov added teeth to this proposal:

> In this connection [he reported] the leadership of the country makes the proposal that, on the basis of the principles of social justice, the differences which exist in the level of maintenance of sick people in different medical establishments should be eliminated; this refers particularly to the sanatoria and rest-homes of government departments, including the Fourth Chief Administration attached to the Ministry of Health of the USSR. (*Applause*).[8]

On the other hand, Gorbachev also believes that a new generation of efficient administrators should be properly rewarded for their work. In September 1988 he told representatives of the media:

> Wage war on bureaucrats. But at the same time bear in mind that revolutionary renewal will not work without a good body of cadres (*kadrovyi korpus*) which has accepted the ideas of *perestroika* or has developed and established itself in the process of *perestroika*.[9]

Whether the democratisation of the Soviet Union will produce a society without a ruling class is a matter for future political struggle.

From the Administrative System to the Market

The supporters of *perestroika* almost all believe that the elimination of the administrative-command system, with or without the overthrow of the bureaucracy as a class, necessarily involves a much greater role for the market. At the Twenty-Seventh Party Congress in February 1986 Gorbachev merely spoke cautiously of the need to strengthen 'commodity-money relations'. At that time many Western specialists believed that he merely intended to increase the role of *khozraschet* within the command economy. But by 1989 he was unambiguous:

> a decisive direction of the economic reform must be to establish a full-blooded socialist market. The market is not of course all-powerful. But humanity has not worked out another more effective and democratic mechanism for managing the economy. The socialist planned economy cannot do without it, comrades. This must be recognised.[10]

And V. A. Medvedev enthusiastically declared:

> The market – if speculative distortions are eliminated – is one of the greatest achievements of human civilisation.[11]

How much should be planned by the state, and how much left to the market, is so far quite unclear. Some enthusiasts for the market would go as far as Mrs Thatcher, or even Milton Friedman. One author proposed that medical treatment should be the subject of an annual contract between patient and polyclinic, paid for by the personal income or insurance of the patient. Similarly, housing financed by the state or the municipal authorities should be available only to those with special needs. According to this author, this drastic cut in state welfare provision would not be a departure from socialism, 'only from the socialism which Stalin thought up'![12] In contrast, V. A. Medvedev insisted that the economy needs a strong centre to manage the market, citing Alec Nove in his support.[13] Ryzhkov takes a similar line:

> I am firmly convinced that the market will be able to develop successfully in the new system of economic management and will serve the good of human beings only if we create an effective economic mechanism to control it, securing the reliable defence of the interests of the citizens from market spontaneity.[14]

On several occasions Gorbachev has also rejected the extreme ideas of the market economists, including proposals to close down all loss-making farms immediately, and to get rid of shortages on the retail market simply by letting prices rise till supply equalled demand.[15] Gorbachev intends that the state should continue its role both as a provider of social services and as the general regulator of the economy. But he has not committed himself to the continuation of any direct administration of production and investment by the state. At the Congress of Soviets he outlined quite limited functions for the state:

> [State management] will be freed from the functions of direct interference in the operational administration of economic units and concentrated on the establishment of general normative frameworks and conditions for their activity. Its natural spheres will remain: the key directions of scientific and technical progress; the infrastructure; the defence of the environment; securing that people are adequately supported socially; the financial system, including its instruments of taxation; and economic legislation, including legislation against monopoly and its negative consequences for society.[16]

From State Ownership to Common Ownership

Together with the rejection of the bureaucratic command structure in favour of the market, the new model of socialism has also abandoned the assumption that state ownership is the highest form of common ownership. Instead, state, cooperative and even individual ownership are deemed to be of equal status in the socialist economy; the choice between them should be decided by practical experience.[17] On one occasion Gorbachev even asserted that 'the main criterion of the socialist nature of any social forms, institutions or transformations . . . is in the answer to the question: are human beings the means or the ends?'[18] This is a dangerous statement: any capitalist government might assert that its society was socialist by this criterion. At the Congress of Soviets, Gorbachev offered a more exacting criterion:

> We are in favour of the creation of flexible and effective social relations in regard to the utilisation of social wealth; each form of property should demonstrate its power and its right to existence in the course of lively emulation and just competition. Only one

condition is required: that exploitation and the alienation of the worker from the means of production should not be permitted.[19]

Self-management and Self-finance

This brings us to the important question of 'self-administration' or 'self-management' (*samoupravlenie*), a term used to mean something like 'producers' democracy'. Throughout the 1970s Soviet industry devoted a great deal of attention to arrangements by which teams (*brigady*) of workers in state factories elected their team-leaders (*brigadiry*) and worked with some collective autonomy.[20] Then in 1983 a 'Law on Labour Collectives' declared that 'the decisions of meetings of the labour collective . . . are binding on members of the collective and the management of the enterprise'. This provision was hedged with qualifications, and was hardly carried out at all in practice.[21] But these experiments in 'self-management' were a remarkable departure from the previous theory and practice of Soviet socialism. They were advocated by prominent supporters of reform such as Kurashvili (in the Institute of State and Law), Agenbegyan and Zaslavskaya (from the Novosibirsk group) and L. A. Gordon (from the Institute for the History of the International Workers' Movement). We do not yet understand the political processes behind the scenes at the top which enabled these measures to go forward in a time of apparent stagnation, albeit in truncated form.

Kurashvili consistently argued that the economic independence of enterprises should be coupled with their democratic management by those who worked in them.[22] In the first two years after the appointment of Gorbachev as party general secretary, support for self-management and support for the socialist market economy grew in tandem. The economic reform adopted in July 1987 was a convoluted compromise between different views, and self-management appeared very prominently in it. The Law on the State Enterprise declared both that the enterprise must be self-financing, and that the labour collective was the master of the enterprise. The Law also firmly stated that the Council of the Labour Collective (STK) in each enterprise 'decides all production and social questions'.[23]

Self-management by the labour collective is supposed to be consistent with 'one-person management' by the director of the enterprise. The labour collective decides basic strategy, and the director and his staff then administer this strategy in detail without interference from the STK. Draft legislation on the division of authority between the

STK and the managers of the enterprise strongly emphasises that ultimate authority is intended to rest with the labour collective.[24] The relationship between STK and enterprise director has been described as analogous to the relationship in a capitalist economy between a ship's owner and its captain.[25] How authority should be distributed between management and the self-managing labour collective has been widely but inconclusively discussed.[26]

The principle of self-management restores a crucial aspect of the nineteenth-century concept of a socialist society. And in pragmatic terms it is a powerful force against the command system. The party and government officials who manage the command system derive their power from their ability to interfere in the activities of enterprises, and from their control over the appointment and dismissal of managers. The new rights of the labour collectives fundamentally challenge this authority.

Apart from broad statements of principle, the future relationship between the state, the management of the enterprise and the labour collective is quite uncertain, and is the subject of ferocious experimentation. The favourite scheme in 1989 was *arenda* – the renting-out of the enterprise as a whole to its labour collective, and of sub-units within the enterprise to those who work there.[27]

In all its various forms, self-management combined with self-finance has been applied in practice only in a minute number of enterprises: but several crucial problems have already emerged.

First, as Yugoslav experience has shown, there is a strong tendency for the labour collective to distribute all the net earnings of the enterprise as wages, leaving as little as possible for investment. Soviet protagonists of self-management have accordingly proposed a variety of share schemes to counteract this tendency. Shares in the enterprise are issued to those who work there, so that they will have a stake in its future. In most of these schemes, workers derive a substantial part of their income from the shares, which also provide a large supplement to their pensions. Shares have to be cashed when the workers leaves the enterprise or when the pensioner dies.[28]

Secondly, should self-financing self-managed enterprises be required to conform with the USSR-wide legislation on wages and working conditions in state enterprises? One school of thought strongly criticises national wage-scales as responsible for enforcing equal payments for unequal work, and insists that every enterprise should make its own arrangements. Fedorov, the director of the famous eye-surgery cooperative, even denounced national wage-scales as 'a kind of atavism of slave society'.[29] One author went so far as to claim that it was that Stalin's *anti*-egalitarian reforms of 1931 which led to the introduction of the system of wage-scales which resulted in egalitarianism.[30] Other writers strongly defend the retention of the national wage-scales, as an essential means of providing a guaranteed minimum; but they also believe that considerable variations in schemes for wage payment should be permitted, according to the decision of the enterprise itself.[31]

A third problem seems much more difficult to cope with. If self-management is coupled with share ownership, workers will be disinclined to move to another factory or industry. And the labour collective may well be unwilling to declare their fellow-workers redundant – they are after all share-holding joint 'owners'. Can a system of self-management be designed which is compatible with the mobility of labour?[32]

But it is a fourth difficulty which is the overwhelming practical obstacle to successful experimentation: the continuation of the command system. Both wholesale and retail prices are still fixed from above; most production decisions are dictated by state orders; and most supplies are obtained through the central supply system. Enterprises deal not with the market but with the administered plan. This introduces a great deal of arbitrariness, to put it mildly, into the earnings of enterprises. Managers and workers depend for the level of their earnings not only on their own activities but also on the higher authorities.

This undermines the argument that workers should accept financial sacrifices so as to make 'their own' enterprises profitable. In Noril'sk, a coal-mine was put on a self-financing basis and as a result the job-rates (payment per unit of output) were slashed. The miners, supported by informal groups and by some party members, occupied the mine for five days. The mine management and the Ministry insisted that there was no source available to finance the previous level of wages, and a letter from the Council of Ministers and the All-Union Council of Trade Unions uncompromisingly declared that 'the fault for what happened wholly rests with a small group of irresponsible agitators, whose aims have nothing in common with the interests of the collective'. Throughout the dispute, all the administrators assumed without question that the prevailing prices, profits deductions and sales conditions could not be changed.[33]

Self-management on this basis will naturally be seen by the workers merely as a means of enforcing state exploitation. In a recent interview, V. I. Shimko, head of the social and economic department of the party central committee pointed out that on some recent occasions collectives had demanded that wage increases should be paid from state reserves: 'on this basis serious conflicts develop between the labour collective and the administration'.[34]

Equality

In the late 1950s and early 1960s Khrushchev somewhat reduced the differentiation of incomes generally; and then in the 1970s the gap in earnings between most professionals and the less-skilled further narrowed.[35] Most reformers now argue that these egalitarian trends were one of the causes of economic stagnation. They believe that earnings should be differentiated more sharply, and purport to believe that this is compatible with socialism. While privileges based on office should be swept aside, they should be replaced by differentiation of earnings based on the value of the work as measured on the market. In his report on the occasion of the anniversary of Lenin's birth, V. A. Medvedev emphasised that 'the differentiation of incomes will obviously increase . . . Demagogic calls for equalising the incomes of everyone and everything are alien to socialism'.[36] This view is shared by most leading intellectuals. Igor Klyamkin declared that greater differentiation of earnings in accordance with efficiency would be a major ingredient of the forthcoming 'spiritual revolution'.[37]

The present reforms resume Stalin's drive against 'egalitarianism' (*uravnilovka*). But in the vast literature about Stalin published since 1986, his anti-egalitarian drive launched in 1931 is almost invariably passed over in silence. In an era of widening *glasnost'*, this subject has become a new 'blank spot' about the past.[38]

What greater differentiation of incomes could mean in practice was indicated by Academician Zaslavskaya. Rejecting the 'popular Soviet view' that income as high as 2000 rubles per month must be 'dishonest' (average earnings are about 210 rubles), she suggested that the ceiling for earnings should be 10,000 rubles.[39]

The call for greater income differentiation has not gone unchallenged. V. Z. Rogovin has sturdily defended the cause of greater equality;[40] and at a round-table organised jointly by the industrial newspaper and the research institute of the Academy of Social Sciences speakers called for improved wages and services for ordinary workers, and the imposition of a maximum wage.[41]

The plans to increase income differentiation have met with widespread public opposition. Klyamkin admitted that 'millions of people' believed that progress should be accompanied by greater equality: 'Khrushchev did not adopt the policy of overcoming the gap in wages accidently – he followed mass expectations'.[42] In this respect a large section of the Soviet public still adheres to the pre-1931 concept of socialism.

THE FUTURE OF SOVIET SOCIALISM

In April 1987, in one of the first frank public discussions about the future of socialism to have taken place in the Soviet Union since the 1920s, L. A. Gordon suggested four possible scenarios: first, and most desirable, radical economic reforms combined with democratisation; secondly, the continuation of directive planning combined with the authoritarian political regime, cleansed of their worst features; thirdly, democratisation without radical economic reform; fourthly, radical economic reform without democratisation.[43] At the end of 1989, all these scenarios are still claiming their right to perform on the Soviet stage. A moderate variant of the first scenario predominates: major strides have been taken towards democratisation, and the reform programme presented by Abalkin in November 1989, if put into effect, would certainly change the economic system fundamentally. The second scenario still has many advocates: at the conference to which Abalkin presented his programme many industrial managers and officials supported a call for social order and the return to greater centralised control of the economy.[44] The third scenario is roughly what existed at the end of 1989: democratisation and *glasnost'* had far outpaced economic reform. And a remarkable feature of 1989 was the unexpected emergence of the fourth scenario, in spite of the repression in Tiananmen Square: a number of reformers strongly advocated the assumption of authoritarian presidential powers by Gorbachev as the only means to bring about a radical change in the economic system.[45]

By the end of 1989 the dominant trend of opinion among reformers went much further than the government reform programme, and advocated a 'full-blooded' variant of the first scenario, in which nearly all economic decisions are taken on the market, and a variety of different forms of ownership, including capitalist ownership, are permitted. The case for the market economy was presented by Selyunin in a well-known article published in May 1988. On his account the history of Russia since the sixteenth century was the story of the struggle between the emerging market economy and the repressive state; economic progress occurred only when the market was free from the depredations of the state.[46] At that time a leading Soviet historian reported that 'the notion has suddenly become widespread that there was a "Stolypin alternative" in the history of Russia, and that this would have spared it from revolutionary upheavals and sacrifices'.[47]

Stolypin sought to establish peasant capitalist agriculture within the framework of a capitalist system; and there is no doubt that a substantial number of Soviet reformers believe that the Soviet Union should be transformed into a capitalist democracy. This view was expressed much more openly in the course of 1989, and became popular among a large section of the intelligentsia. At the Congress of Soviets the chairman of the Moscow Trade Unions, V. S. Shcherbakov, accused the 'radical' group of Moscow deputies of supporting 'purely market relations, the transfer of state enterprises into private hands, the creation of a free market for labour – can't they think up anything more suitable?'[48] This was an exaggerated characterisation of the Moscow group as a whole, and of the larger 'inter-regional' group of deputies to which they now belong, but it accurately described a very important trend among the economic reformers. These reformers take the view which has now become government policy in Hungary and Poland – capitalism is the only alternative to state socialism, and most industries should be privatised.

Privatisation on any substantial scale would be technically very difficult to achieve in the Soviet Union, with its vast industries and its lack of any capitalist class; and in any case the idea is still very unpopular among the population at large. So the plan for a transition from socialism to capitalism is put forward with some circumspection. Gavriil Popov, now an influential vice-chairman of the inter-regional group of deputies, argued at the Congress of Soviets in June 1989:

> The experience of developed capitalist countries shows that economically developed countries have a state sector of about 30–40 per cent. Taking into account our traditions and the interests of social control in the hands of the state, it is sufficient to keep 50 per cent of the economy. The remaining 50 per cent must be transferred to cooperatives and to the private, individual sector.[49]

In June 1989 this seemed a radical proposal. But a few months later he claimed much more bluntly at a conference held under the auspices of the party central committee that the forces of production even in more advanced countries were not sufficiently developed to enable them to progress without private ownership. According to Popov's casuistic argument, if the Soviet Union followed a Marxist approach, it would bring its relations of production into line with its forces of production, which were insufficiently advanced to be organised as social production (by permitting private ownership).[50] As for agriculture, 'we must do what was done by the unforgettable Stolypin; we must introduce *otrubs* and *khutors* [peasant family farms separated from the village commune]'.[51]

Academician Shatalin was even franker. He explained that 'at the time when they were distracted by nationalisation the French and the English even socialised motor-car and aircraft firms'; and he declared that 'progress in Britain is associated with the conservative Thatcher', praising her success in 'denationalising practically everything'. According to Shatalin, only the infrastructure such as roads and telephones should be in the hands of the state, though the cooperative sector should also be of major importance.[52]

For the time being the 'privatisers' have concluded that any substantial move towards privatisation is impossible owing to popular hostility to capitalism. 'One should not be frightened of private ownership, there is nothing terrible in it,' Shatalin assured the central committee conference in October, 'But it is not appropriate today to propose it as a programmatic task.'[53] Instead, they hope that the renting-out of enterprises and the introduction of share-holding will produce the same result. Share-holding by workers in an enterprise can be, as we have seen, an aspect of self-management. But if shares can also be owned by other enterprises, or by individuals, such joint-stock arrangements could be a major step towards private ownership. 'After all', Shatalin ingenuously remarked at the central committee conference, 'the issue of shares also leads to private ownership.' And Nikolai Shmelev, another influential economist, explained that from the point of view of economic technique, 'there is no difference between a joint-stock [or share-holding – the word *aktsionernoe* is the same in Russian] socialist enterprise and an association of shareholders [a joint-stock company] in the West, or between their managers'.[54]

Many proposals have been made which involve the issue of shares not only to those working in the enterprise but also on some kind of share market or stock exchange. According to one proposal, the leases (*arenda*) of enterprises should not be signed with their labour collectives, but offered on a competitive basis, so that they go to 'entrepreneurial leaders with intitiative'.[55] The schemes under way to involve foreign capital in Soviet enterprises could be an even more effective move towards capitalism.

During 1989 significant preparations were made for converting state industry into rented-out joint-stock companies. In June a significant clause was quietly slipped into a general policy resolution of the Supreme Soviet:

> Conditions shall be created for the formation of a socialist market, including a market for shares [*tsennye bumagi*] and for investment resources.[56]

During the autumn a committee of the Supreme Soviet chaired by P. Bunich prepared a wide-ranging Law on Renting-Out [*arenda*]. This envisaged that state enterprises would be rented out, usually but not necessarily to the workers at the enterprise, and that this would be combined with forms of share ownership. The Law would thus permit both self-managed enterprises and enterprises managed by a lessee separate from those who work in it. In the case of small enterprises, Bunich rhetorically asked: 'Why should not a private individual become a lessee and take on, say, fifty associates to work for him?'[57]

Whether the new arrangements become a bridge to self-managed socialism or to the establishment of a large private sector in the economy depends on the strength of the self-management arrangements. During 1989 criticism of self-management (or producers' democracy) became much stronger. In the party theoretical journal, A. Nekipelov, of the Institute of the Economics of the World Socialist System, suggested that self-management by labour collectives would prevent the efficient transfer of capital and labour between industries, and therefore undermine the attempt to form a socialist market; the alternative would be to establish a market for labour as well as goods, and to link the earnings of *managers* to profits.[58] Another writer claimed somewhat prematurely that 'party policy is oriented on the development of a real market, including a market for capital and labour', and in this context frankly repudiated self-management:

> How justified are the attempts to introduce self-management here,

particularly when economic regulators are not yet operating? After all the needs of democracy and economic efficiency often fail to coincide, and even contradict each other. So far not even one country has made production democracy work. The whole world is following a different path, developing business administration on the basis of one-person management.[59]

Speaking to the USSR Factory Directors' Club in May 1989, Academician Aganbegyan frankly declared:

> From my point of view, the election [of directors] was inspired by the wish to activate the workers. But the further we go, the more obvious are the negative sides of this system . . . I think that in a few years we will have to reconsider the Law on the State Enterprise and give up election in its present form.[60]

More recently, workers' self-management was severely restricted in a number of ministries by a Council of Ministers' decree, leading to 'a very negative reaction by the population'.[61]

Hostility to self-management will undoubtedly be reinforced by the advice from the numerous Western firms and management consultants which are being employed to improve Soviet business efficiency. George Soros, head of the Soros Foundation which has financed many projects in eastern Europe, commented after a recent visit to the USSR:

> The reformers want to abolish these privileges [of *nomenklatura* personnel, etc.], and they also want to maintain an egalitarian approach to wages and prices, which is incompatible with economic reform. They embrace the concept of self-management – long after it has proved unworkable in Yugoslavia – but they are unwilling to reward entrepreneurial ability and risk-taking.[62]

On one scenario, then, the backlash against the election of managers and against self-management by labour collectives could result in the emergence of state firms which closely resembled private-capitalist firms, operating on a free market and rented-out to a management which was not elected by or even controlled by the work-force. Simultaneously, small- and medium-scale capitalist firms could be legalised, along the lines envisaged by some influential reformers. Soviet socialism would then incorporate a very large element of capitalism. Until a year or two ago, Trotsky's prediction in *Revolution Betrayed* that state bureaucrats might be transformed into private capitalists seemed to have been completely falsified by history. Even with the scenario we have outlined, it would still not be correct in detail, because a new generation of specialists and others would lease the state firms. Nevertheless Trotsky's prediction has unexpectedly turned from a wild misjudgment into an imaginative prophecy.

In contrast to the 'radical' pro-capitalist economists, a significant group of prominent intellectuals strongly supports workers' self-management, and regards it as compatible with economic reform. I have already mentioned the very active group of students and teachers at Moscow University which is preparing detailed draft regulations on self-management. Other intellectuals support a very broad concept of workers' management and workers' democracy, encouraged by the rehabilitation of Shlyapnikov and the Workers' Opposition of 1920–1. Thus one writer on labour problems has called for the formation of local, republican and USSR-wide Councils of Labour Collectives which would examine key social issues in the national-economic plans, national investment policy and difficulties in the election of managers; the aim should be to transform workers into 'actual co-owners of production'.[63] A long article in the popular weekly *Ogonek* described the Soviet period of history in terms of the suppression of the rights of the working-class, and argued that the working class and the intelligentsia should cooperate together to drive out the bureaucrats. According to the author, 'the fate of the workers and the intelligentsia is indivisible'; their cooperation is possible because of the close ties of the intelligentsia with the working class which already exist (*sic*).[64]

There is no doubt, however, that the 'workers' democracy' trend is less influential among intellectuals than the 'free-market' or so-called 'radical' trend. And the 'workers' democracy' trend is also weaker in the sense that its specific proposals for the reform of the economy as a whole are considerably vaguer than those of the 'radicals'. But the intellectual arguments of the supporters of workers' democracy have been reinforced by the emergence of independent working-class political and economic activity in the Soviet Union, the embryo, perhaps, of an independent working-class movement. According to a Soviet survey, between 1985 and 1988 the number of strikes greatly increased. They were often a response to managerial attempt to cope with the first stages of economic reform by increases in job-rates, compulsory overtime, and administrative pressure to put brigades or enterprises on a self-financing basis. Some strikes were in protest against the failure to elect managers democratically.[65] In the spring of 1989 the Central Committee official Shimko also reported the development of 'open conflicts and mass actions', including strikes. He attributed them particularly to wage disputes and to the transfer of enterprises to full *khozraschet* and to *arenda*. Frequently new arrangements for determining wages were introduced without consulting the labour collective; STKs were sometimes passive and fitted in with the management. Shimko admitted that the protests often received wide support:

> Extremist elements actively use the threat of strikes. But we must observe that the healthy part of the working class is also included.[66]

Even before 1985 attempts were made to set up independent working-class organisations.[67] In the course of 1985–8 informal workers' clubs were established in a number of towns and factories, and, following a case of the unjust dismissal of a worker reported in the Young Communist newspaper, some of the clubs formed a joint inter-urban workers' club. By the beginning of 1989 this met quite regularly to discuss the experience of self-management.[68] By the summer of 1989 it had members in twenty-three towns, though it involved only 600–700 people altogether.[69]

By the summer of 1989 there were two distinct but overlapping trends within this embryonic working-class movement: first, to secure real powers at their place of work for ordinary workers, and secondly, to defend and advance the material interests of the workers within a factory or industry, or in the working class as a whole, in face of the privileges of the management and the state bureaucracy.

Both these trends were present in the large-scale miners' strikes of the summer and autumn of 1989, which forced the workers as a social force on the attention of Soviet intellectuals and Western commentators, who had largely ignored the earlier developments. The strikes involved several hundred thousand miners in the Kuzbass in Siberia, in the Donbass region, and in Vorkuta in the North.

Their starting-point was the failure of the authorities to remedy long-standing grievances about food, housing and working conditions. As the strikes developed the workers' demands were increasingly directed against the bureaucracy. During the strikes newly-elected strike committees, independent of the control of the trade unions, assumed considerable authority both in the mines and in the mining towns. Many members of the strike committees were elected to the Councils of Workers' Collectives. Something like a genuine if fragile workers' democracy had come into being. The miners' representatives sought to combine workers' democracy with economic reform: they called for the autonomy of the mines under the control of the workers, and for their right to sell freely part of their own output.[70] But as yet no satisfactory reformed national economic framework existed within which the mines could operate.

During and following the strikes, two rival political tendencies have sought to capture the workers' movement and wield it in their own interests. First, the Russian nationalists, together with the official trade unions, have organised workers' movements. The first major 'workers' front' of this kind met in Leningrad in June 1989; and then on September 8–9 the constituent congress of the United Front of Working People of Russia (the OFT, from its Russian initials) assembled in Sverdlovsk. The Congress fiercely attacked 'the ill-considered economic policy which has opened the way to gaining non-working incomes via the pseudo-cooperatives, and has oriented state enterprises on profit and not on the satisfaction of the needs of the working people and the urban population'. It also called for elections to the soviets based on the work-place rather than the place of residence, and for a currency reform directed against the holders of large amounts of illegally-acquired money.[71]

There is no unanimity in the OFT and similar organisations. Many of its members sincerely advocate workers' democracy. But one extreme wing is strongly tinged with anti-semitism.[72] It is fair to say that the whole organisation is conservative in the sense that it wants to retain the present 'command-administrative' economic system, albeit with greater rights for workers. Reflecting these views, Ligachev, at the plenum of the Party central committee of 19–20 September 1989, condemned those who are 'in favour of moving towards capitalism and bourgeois democracy, of introducing private property into the economy and a multi-party system into the political system'.[73]

The 'radical' supporters of private property and the free market are also making strong efforts to win over the workers' movement. When a new miners' strike broke out in Vorkuta in November 1989, representatives of the inter-regional group of deputies and of the cooperatives attempted to win their support. The cooperatives made an agreement with the miners to help them establish trading cooperatives and a cooperative bank, so as to enable them to sell the 20 per cent of above-plan output which the mines are now entitled to dispose of freely.[74] The evolution of Solidarity in Poland shows that a workers' movement in a bureaucratic regime can be transformed into a movement supporting evolution towards capitalism: in the course of his visit to Britain in December 1989, Lech Walesa declared that a large part of Polish industry needed to be privatised.[75]

Neither the Russian nationalists nor the 'radical' economists are endeavouring to combine economic reform with workers' management. For the moment, at least, however, this remains the official policy of Gorbachev and his associates. Speaking at the plenum of the Ukrainian party central committee in September 1989, Gorbachev insisted that '*perestroika* is the renewal of socialism, not the dismantling of it . . . a revolutionary transformation, eliminating the deformations of socialism, but not the restoration of capitalism'. Its basic principles included 'social ownership of the means of production', 'the real transformation of working people into the masters of all social production', and 'entrepreneurship, emulation, and bold initiative combined with a planned approach'.[76] Under pressure from conservatives on the one hand and 'radical' advocates of a move towards capitalism on the other, will Gorbachev be able to maintain this socialist position?

Nor is there yet any clear outcome of the struggle against egalitarianism. It is true that the initial stages of reform have already resulted in sharp increases in income differentiation. But this was not so much the deliberate result of the anti-egalitarian policy of the authorities, as the unintended result of the inflation resulting from the initial stages of reform. The establishment of cooperatives in conditions of repressed inflation enabled many cooperative members to acquire large incomes. Simultaneously, according to a Gosplan survey, the growing inflationary pressures have particularly hit the lower-paid groups. On the other hand, in spite of its strong declarations in favour of greater income differentiation, the Soviet government has prepared a series of measures which will increase the incomes of pensioners and the lower-paid; it has also prepared a draft law on personal income-tax which would somewhat reduce lower rates of tax and increase higher rates.

*   *   *

To sum up. The nature of the future socialist society in the USSR will be disputed not only between conservative supporters of the administrative system and enthusiasts for a rapid move towards a free market. The third factor is the question of how far the bureaucratic system will be replaced by new forms of production democracy, how far by a mere imitation and adaptation of the capitalist enterprise. This is partly an intellectual dispute, in the sense that all groups of reformers have to work out how to carry out their variant of reform in practice. But it is also a social and political struggle, the outcome of which is quite unclear. The fate of all the classic principles of socialism – equality, as well as common ownership and self-management – has not yet been determined. Even in outline, the Soviet model of socialism for the twenty-first century has not yet emerged.

NOTES

Preliminary versions of this paper were presented at a conference in the University of Hokkaido in July 1989 and at the annual conference of CREES, University of Birmingham, in June 1989. The author is grateful to the participants in these conferences, and particularly to Drs N. Shiokawa, E. Ambartsumov, and J. Cooper, and Professor P. Hanson, for their helpful comments.

1. On Russian socialist views of the future, see R. Stites, *Revolutionary Dreams: Utopian Vision and Experimental Life in the Russian Revolution* (1989).
2. On Hertzka and similar thinkers, see A. Chilosi, 'The Right to Employment Principle and Self-Managed Market Socialism', *EUP Working Paper* 86/214 (European University Institute, Florence, 1986).
3. *Politicheskoe obrazovanie*, No. 1, 1989, pp. 13–14.
4. For the debate among historians on this question, see my *Soviet History in the Gorbachev Revolution* (1989), ch. 7.
5. *Izvestiya*, 24 December 1988.
6. This speech was first published in *Izvestiya TsK*, No. 2, 1989.
7. *Pravda*, 14 October 1988.
8. *Izvestiya*, 31 May, 8 June 1989. The Fourth Administration is responsible for privileged medical facilities for officials.
9. *Izvestiya*, 16 September 1988.
10. *Izvestiya*, 31 May 1989.
11. *Kommunist*, No. 17, 1988, p. 17.
12. *Nedelya*, No. 21, 1989 (A. Venednitskii, a correspondent of the journal *Tekhnika i nauka*); in the same issue the influential economist Petrakov took a somewhat similar view.
13. *Kommunist*, No. 17, 1988, p. 17.

14. *Izvestiya*, 8 June 1989.
15. *Pravda*, 31 March 1989; *Izvestiya*, 31 May 1989.
16. *Izvestiya*, 31 May 1989.
17. See for example Gorbachev's statement to a central committee plenum, *Pravda*, 16 March 1989.
18. *Pravda*, 16 November 1988 (speech in Orel).
19. *Izvestiya*, 31 May 1989.
20. See *Soviet Studies*, vol. 39 (1987), pp. 205–28 (J. C. Moses) and D. Lane, *Soviet Labour and the Ethic of Communism* (1987), pp. 182–213.
21. See D. Lane (ed.) *Labour and Employment in the USSR* (1986) pp. 239–55 (E. Teague), and *Soviet Studies*, vol. 37 (1985), pp. 173–83 (D. Slider).
22. *Sovetskoe gosudarstvo i pravo*, No. 6, 1982, pp. 38–48 (B. P. Kurashvili). Kurashvili's views are further discussed by R. Amann in *Detente*, No. 8 (Winter 1987), 8–10.
23. The provisions of the Law are discussed by S. I. Shkurko in *Sotsialisticheskii trud*, No. 4, 1989, pp. 45–7; Shkurko argues that this provision should be qualified so as to make it clear that the Council of the Labour Collective cannot take decisions outside its competence, for instance disposing of resources which are not available.
24. See *Sotsialisticheskii trud*, Nos. 3, 1989, pp. 42–6, and 5, 1989, pp. 58–61; these drafts, published in the official organ of the State Committee on Labour and Social Questions, were prepared by 'the temporary scientific collective of students, postgraduates, research workers and teaching staff of Moscow State University'!
25. *Sotsialisticheskii trud*, No. 5, 1988, p. 68.
26. See for example *Voprosy ekonomiki*, No. 5, 1989, pp. 60–1 (A. G. Kulikov).
27. For the proceedings of a conference on *arenda* see *Voprosy ekonomiki*, No. 3, 1989, 35–53.
28. For examples of the share arrangements, see *Sotsialisticheskii trud*, No. 5, 1989, pp. 15–22 (L'vov engineering corporation 'Konveier'), and more generally ibid., No. 4, 1989, pp. 3–6 (Bunich, chair of the scientific council on *khozraschet*).
29. *Nedelya*, No. 22, 1989.
30. *Sotsialisticheskii trud*, No. 12, 1988, 78 (R. Khasbulatov).
31. See for example *Ekonomicheskaya gazeta*, No. 21, 1989 (L. Kunel'skii).
32. The Hertzka self-management model of 1886–90 assumed free mobility of labour, so that any worker had the right to be taken on by any firm, but it is difficult to think of a practicable version of this (see *Journal of Comparative Economics*, vol. 10 (1986), pp. 237–54 – A. Chilosi).
33. The story is told from the administration point of view in *Ekonomicheskaya gazeta*, No. 16, 1989.
34. *Ekonomicheskaya gazeta*, No. 19, 1989.
35. Simultaneously, however, the privileges in real terms of the highest levels of officialdom substantially increased.
36. *Pravda*, 22 April 1989.
37. *Novyi mir*, No. 2, 1989, p. 236.
38. There is a slightly astonishing exception. In *Nedelya*, no. 21, 1989,

A. Venednitskii, citing the long passage about egalitarianism in Stalin's interview with the German writer Emil Ludwig (*Sochineniya*, vol. xiii (1949), 119), claims that this is an example of Stalin's hypocrisy:

> By the way the great nourisher of socialism [i.e. Stalin] was in words also against any equalisation . . . In words he was also, as we would say now, in favour of *perestroika* . . .
> The tyrant was not stupid: he knew well what he had created, and he did not hurry to create what he had promised in words.

39. *Ekonomika i organizatsiya promyshlennoi proizvodstva* (hereafter *EKO*), No. 10, 1988, pp. 93–4.
40. See, for example, Rogovin's reply in *Druzhba narodov*, No. 10, 1988, pp. 181–8, to the heated attack on him by G. Lisichkin (ibid. No. 1, 1988).
41. *Sotsialisticheskaya industriya*, 18 April 1989 (speeches by E. Zhil'tsov, a professor at Moscow University, and P. Savchenko of the Institute of Economics). Zhil'tsov cited the example of China, claiming that the top-bottom wage gap was between 5:1 and 7:1.
42. *Novyi mir*, No. 2, 1989, p. 236.
43. *Voprosy filosofii*, No. 11, 1988, pp. 51–3. This contribution had been revised before publication, as it mentioned Nina Andreeva's letter of March 1988.
44. See *Literaturnaya Gazeta*, 2 November 1989.
45. For the debate about the 'iron hand', see *Literaturnaya gazeta*, 16 August (I. Klyamkin and A. Migaryan), 20 September (L. Batkin) and 17 September 1989 (survey of readers' letters).
46. *Novyi mir*, No. 5, 1988, pp. 162–89 (V. Selyunin).
47. *Voprosy istorii*, No. 3, 1988, p. 22 (V. P. Danilov).
48. *Izvestiya*, 4 June 1989.
49. *Pravda*, 11 June 1989.
50. *Pravda*, 11 November 1989.
51. *Pozitsiya* (Tartu), No. 1, October 1989.
52. *Literaturnaya gazeta*, 11 October 1989.
53. *Pravda*, 30 October 1989.
54. *Vechernyaya Moskva*, 23 March 1989.
55. *Voprosy ekonomiki*, No. 3, 1989, pp. 45–6 (V. Volkonskii, Central Mathematical Economics Institute TsEMI), p. 13 (L. Nikiforov and V. Rutgaizer).
56. *Pravda*, 25 June 1989.
57. See the interview with Bunich in *Ogonek*, No. 47, 1989.
58. *Kommunist*, No. 7, 1989, pp. 15–22.
59. *Literaturnaya gazeta*, 19 April 1989 (L. Shevtsova).
60. *EKO*, No. 9, 1989, p. 77.
61. See speech by A. A. Sobchak at the central committee economists' conference, *Pravda*, 30 October 1989.
62. *New York Review of Books*, 1 June 1989.
63. *Moscow News*, No. 45, 1988 (V. Perlamutrov of TsEMI).
64. V. Kostikov, 'A Hero not in a Poster', *Ogonek*, No. 17, 1989, pp. 26–30.

65. *Voprosy ekonomiki*, No. 4, 1989, pp. 120–9 (E. Leont'eva, a correspondent of the industrial newspaper *Sotsialisticheskaya industriya*); this informative article explains that the Institute of Sociology, the Centre for the Study of Public Opinion, the State Committee for Labour, the trade unions, the State Committee for Statistics and the research institute of the Ministry of Internal Affairs all fail to study social conflicts; one person is engaged in this in the Institute of the International Workers' Movement (she does not mention the KGB . . .).
66. *Ekonomicheskaya gazeta*, No. 19, 1989. For evidence, based on a survey in Khar'kov, that the economic bureaucracy has tended to take over the STKs, regiment them artificially, or turn them into a 'talking-shop', see *Voprosy ekonomiki*, no. 5, 1989, p. 79 (V. Glushenko).
67. See *Voprosy ekonomiki*, No. 4, 1989, p. 121 (E. Leont'eva).
68. *Sotsialisticheskii trud*, No. 3, 1989, pp. 68–73.
69. *Literaturnaya gazeta*, 13 September 1989.
70. A careful account of the Kuzbass strikes may be found in *Znamya*, No. 10, 1989 (Yu. Anenchenko).
71. *Literaturnaya Rossiya*, 13 October 1989.
72. In *Nash sovremennik*, No. 8, 1989, M. Antonov presents the views of this wing of the movement with some verve.
73. *Pravda*, 22 September 1989.
74. Rival accounts of these attempts to influence the strikers appear in *Literaturnaya gazeta*, 15 November 1989 (A. Buturlin, a deputy procurator) and 29 November 1989 (V. Tikhonov, head of the cooperatives).
75. BBC2 TV, 12 December 1989.
76. *Pravda*, 30 September 1989.

4 The Tsar, the Emperor, the Leader: Ivan the Terrible, Peter the Great and Anatolii Rybakov's Stalin

Maureen Perrie

In his book *The Making of the Soviet System*, Moshe Lewin refers to a 'significant phenomenon in Stalinism: the return of the modernizing Soviet state under Stalin to the models and trappings of earlier tsardom'. In particular, he notes 'the changeover of historical antecedents from Stepan Razin and Pugachev, leaders of peasant rebellions, to Ivan the Terrible and Peter the Great, respectively the most absolutist of the tsars and the first emperor'. 'This spiritual conversion,' Lewin continues, 'was rooted in a set of striking parallels in the social setting and political situation created in the 1930s.' Stalin's 'revolution from above' was similar to those of Ivan the Terrible and Peter the Great. Peter's programme of forced industrialisation, subjugation of the peasantry and bureaucratisation bore a marked resemblance to Stalin's policies.[1] Both Ivan and Peter created new elites which were dependent on and subservient to the ruler alone; Stalin did the same. Under later tsars, the autocratic system became institutionalised; Stalin resisted such tendencies within the Soviet system, and launched the purges in order to prevent processes of political 'normalisation' from taking hold.[2] It is therefore not accidental, in Lewin's interpretation, that Stalinist historiography should have idealised Ivan the Terrible and Peter the Great. The role of these early tsars was more similar than that of the later ones to Stalin's role; the regime sought legitimisation in elements of the tsarist past 'which best suited the new situation and the self-image of the new leader: the great tsars, builders and despots, Ivan the Terrible and Peter the Great, seemed to fit the bill'. Stalin himself, Lewin further suggests, had some kind of 'deep psychological need' to find such historical antecedents, and 'might have felt a genuine affinity with those great predecessors'.[3]

Lewin, of course, is not the only writer to have commented on the parallels between these three figures. Comparisons of Ivan, Peter and Stalin, indeed, have become almost a cliché of Soviet journalism in the era of *glasnost'*.[4] In his novel, *The Children of the Arbat*, which is set in 1934, Anatolii Rybakov presents us with a fictional Stalin who is heavily influenced by an analogy between himself and the two tsars. Rybakov's Stalin admires Ivan and Peter as great statesmen, who had demonstrated their strength by their ruthless elimination of political rivals. By such methods they had not only maximised their own power, but also gained the love and respect of their people. Soviet historiography denigrated the role of individuals: but Rybakov's Stalin seeks to justify his own concept of leadership by having Russian history rewritten to give due prominence to individual rulers such as Ivan and Peter.[5]

Rybakov's imaginative reconstruction of Stalin's thought processes is very plausible. In this essay, however, I propose to examine it critically. In the first part, I shall trace the treatment of Ivan and Peter in Soviet historiography of the Stalin period and attempt to estimate how far it was influenced by Stalin's personal views of the tsars. In the second part, I shall explore the relationship between the 'cult of personality' and the 'myth of the tsar'.

*   *   *

Ivan the Terrible and Peter the Great were undoubtedly the most controversial figures in pre-revolutionary Russian historiography. The early part of the reign of Ivan IV (1533–84) saw the Russian conquest of the Tatar khanates of Kazan' and Astrakhan' on the Volga, and a series of administrative and judicial reforms. Ivan embarked upon the Livonian War (1558–81) in the hope of gaining Russia a foothold on the Baltic; but after a number of initial successes, the tsar's armies became bogged down in protracted, costly and ultimately unsuccessful campaigning. In 1565 Ivan created his notorious *oprichnina*, a part of the country which was directly under his own control, leaving the rest (the *zemshchina*) to his council of boyars (noble counsellors). The *oprichnina* territory was administered by the *oprichniki*, the tsar's personal bodyguard, who in practice launched a reign of terror against the inhabitants of the *zemshchina*: the term '*oprichnina*' then came to be used for the

oprichniki and their methods as well as for the territory they controlled. The worst atrocity perpetuated by the *oprichniki* was the
massacre of the people of Novgorod in 1570, an act which was
apparently motivated by the tsar's suspicion that the city had treason-
ous links with Poland. The *oprichnina* was abolished in 1572, following its failure to prevent the burning of Moscow by the Crimean
Tatars in the previous year.

Most nineteenth-century Russian historians, following the example
of N. M. Karamzin, expressed moral outrage at Ivan's terror. But the
'statist' school of Russian historiography, headed by S. M. Solov'ev,
provided a justification for the tsar's policies. In their eyes the
oprichnina contributed to the building of the autocratic state by
weakening the old hereditary aristocracy and promoting in their
place the new class of military servitors who provided the social basis
for tsarism. For Ivan's critics such as N. M. Kostomarov, however,
the Terrible Tsar was responsible for introducing the harshest and
most repressive features of the autocratic system into Russia. At the
end of the nineteenth century, S. F. Platonov offered an economic
variant of the 'statist' justification for the *oprichnina*: that its main
aim was to destroy the landholding of the old aristocracy by resettling
the new service nobles on their confiscated estates. This approach
appealed to the first generation of Russian Marxist scholars. M. N.
Pokrovskii, who until his death in 1932 was the leading Soviet
historian, asserted that small-scale service landholding was more
advantageous than the large hereditary estates, and that the *oprichnina* therefore furthered Russia's economic progress.[6]

Peter the Great (1689–1725) pursued similar foreign policy objectives to those of Ivan IV, but with greater success. The threat from
the south – from the Crimean Tatars and their Turkish backers – was
contained, while victory over Sweden in the Great Northern War
(1700–21) secured Russian expansion on the Baltic, symbolised by
the foundation of the new capital, St Petersburg. Peter built up the
Russian army and navy, with the help of new technology as well as
personnel imported from the West. To supply the armed forces with
metal, a great new iron industry was developed in the Urals. Much of
the workforce for this industry, and for construction projects such as the
building of St Petersburg, comprised the forced labour of peasants, who
bore increasingly heavy burdens of serfdom and taxation. In Peter's
concept, the whole of society, including the nobility, had to serve the
state. The boyar council was abolished, and Peter ruled directly with
advisers appointed by himself. The creation of the Table of Ranks in

1722 further weakened the hereditary aristocracy by making state service rather than birth alone the main qualification for social status.

Peter and his achievements were greatly admired by proponents of the eighteenth-century Russian Enlightenment, and in the early nineteenth century he was a hero both to the conservative adherents of Official Nationalism and to the more radical Westernised intelligentsia. The Slavophiles, by contrast, provided a Romantic critique of the Petrine reforms, which in their eyes had destroyed the organic harmony of Muscovite culture by introducing alien Western values of rationalism, legalism and compulsion. In the second half of the nineteenth century, Solov'ev defended Peter for his contribution to the growth of the Russian state, while his pupil V. O. Klyuchevskii provided a more nuanced assessment, bringing out the contradictions in Peter's achievement. The liberal historian P. N. Milyukov was even more critical, stressing the wastefulness and cost of much of Peter's activity, and condemning the compulsory methods by which the reforms were imposed. Some of these themes were continued by Pokrovskii. In his view Peter's use of forced labour and insistence on state regulation of the economy limited the growth of commercial capitalism and led to the collapse of much of the new industry soon after Peter's death.[7]

Pokrovskii's revolutionary iconoclastic stress on impersonal economic forces, rather than the role of personalities, dominated Soviet historiography throughout the 1920s.[8] In the course of the 1930s, this approach came increasingly under attack, and a new emphasis was placed on the contribution of individuals such as Ivan and Peter. How far did Stalin personally influence the 'rehabilitation' of these two tsars?

Stalin's first recorded references to Ivan and Peter occurred in the context of the party debates about industrialisation in the late 1920s. In a speech on the economy in 1926, he drew a distinction between the type of industrialisation which was proposed for the Soviet Union and the development of manufacturing in general. To illustrate this distinction, he observed that Ivan the Terrible could not be regarded as an 'industrialiser', although the rudiments of manufacturing had emerged during his reign. Not even Peter the Great, in Stalin's view, deserved to be called Russia's 'first industrialiser': a true industrialisation policy involved the development of heavy industry, production of the means of production, and especially machine-building, in order to guarantee not only economic growth, but also economic independence.[9] In 1928, however, Stalin was willing to concede that a

parallel did exist between the Bolsheviks' attempt to overcome
Russia's backwardness and the economic policy of Peter the Great:
'When Peter the Great, having to deal with more developed countries
in the West, feverishly constructed factories and mills to supply the
army and strengthen the defence of the country, this was a unique
attempt to break the constraints of backwardness.'[10] He hastened to
add, however, that none of the dominant classes of pre-revolutionary
Russian society had been capable of overcoming economic backwardness: this task could be correctly identified and resolved only by
the dictatorship of the proletariat in the course of socialist
construction.[11]

It was perhaps Stalin's own comparisons between Soviet and
Petrine industrialisation that led the German writer Emil Ludwig, in
an interview with the Soviet leader in December 1931, to ask whether
he saw any similarity between himself and Peter the Great, and
whether he considered himself to be continuing Peter's policies.
Stalin's reply was categorical: 'Not in any way. Historical parallels
are always risky, and this particular parallel is meaningless.' Ludwig
was not satisfied: 'But surely Peter the Great did a great deal for the
development of his country, and to bring Western culture to
Russia?'[12] Stalin in his reply stressed the upper-class character of the
national state which Peter created, and distinguished it from the
internationalism of the workers' state which he himself served:

Yes of course, Peter the Great did a lot for the elevation of the
landowning class and the development of the embryonic merchant
class. Peter did very much for the creation and strengthening of the
national state of landowners and traders. One must also say that
this elevation of the class of landowners, and the assistance he gave
to the embryonic class of traders and the strengthening of the
national state of these classes took place at the expense of the
enserfed peasantry, who were flayed thrice over by them.[13]

'As for me', Stalin continued modestly, 'I am only the pupil of Lenin
and the aim of my life is to be his worthy pupil.' His own task, Stalin
said, was to elevate another class, the working class, and to
strengthen the socialist state and hence the international labour
movement. 'You see,' he concluded, 'that your parallel is inappropriate.' 'As for Lenin and Peter the Great,' Stalin added, 'then the latter
was a drop of sea-water, while Lenin was an entire ocean.'[14]

Ludwig persisted, however, asking Stalin whether his recognition of the role of historical figures did not contradict Marxism. Stalin responded with an exposition of his understanding of the Marxist position: that individuals could and did make history, in so far as they correctly understood the circumstances in which they found themselves, and how to change these circumstances. Ludwig remained unconvinced, observing that his professors in Germany had taught him that Marxism denied the role of heroes. These professors, Stalin retorted, were not true Marxists, but vulgarisers of Marxism.[15]

This exchange was to prove to be an ominous one. In 1934 an official attack was launched on those Soviet historians whose understanding of the Marxist position on the role of the individual in history was closer to that of Emil Ludwig's professors than to that of Comrade Stalin. The teaching of history in Soviet schools was said to be too abstract and schematical, stressing socio-economic formations rather than the chronological sequence of events, facts and the characteristics of historical figures. Stalin's interview with Ludwig was cited as an example of 'how true Marxists understand the role of the individual in history'.[16] Ivan and Peter were not, however, mentioned as examples of historical figures whose role should be stressed in the proposed new textbooks. The only individuals named in the *Pravda* editorial were Bolotnikov, Razin and Pugachev – leaders of popular revolts in the seventeenth and eighteenth centuries whom Stalin had also mentioned in his interview with Ludwig – and Catherine the Great, the Empress who had suppressed the Pugachev revolt.[17]

In 1936 the persistence of 'anti-Marxist, anti-Leninist views' and 'harmful tendencies' in Soviet historical scholarship was blamed on the influence of the late M. N. Pokrovskii and his 'school'.[18] Pokrovskii's mistakes were said to include an underestimation of the role of the individual in history; and among the individuals he had denigrated was Peter the Great. But ironically it was not Stalin but his renowned opponent Bukharin (himself to fall victim to the terror in 1938) who publicly initiated Peter's rehabilitation. In a lengthy attack on Pokrovskii, Bukharin accused him of 'fear of giving true recognition to the relatively progressive historical activity of Peter the Great (in contrast to Marx and Engels, who recognised the positive significance of the Petrine reforms, which destroyed "barbarism")'.[19]

In 1939–40 a two-volume denunciation of Pokrovskii's views, in the form of a collection of articles by various authors, was published under the authoritative imprint of the Institute of History of the Academy of Sciences of the USSR. By this time, according to the preface to the first volume, many representatives of Pokrovskii's 'school' had been exposed as 'Trotskyite and Bukharinite hirelings of Fascism' whose 'harmful and counter-revolutionary work' had been conducted even within the walls of the Institute of History.[20]

In his article in the first volume of this collection, K. Bazilevich criticised Pokrovskii for failing to give due recognition to the role of the individual in history. Pokrovskii had argued that the very different personalities of the three sixteenth-century tsars – Ivan IV, Fedor Ivanovich and Boris Godunov – had not been reflected in policy differences. Pokrovskii had described Ivan as a 'hysterical blockhead (*samodur*), concerned only with his own ego, and unwilling to consider anything other than his precious ego, having no political principles nor social obligations'. In reality, however, Bazilevich asserted, Ivan was 'one of the most talented and educated representatives of his class'.[21] Bazilevich offered a positive assessment of the *oprichnina*:

> the long struggle of the autocracy, expressing the class interests of the nobility, against the boyars, who attempted to restrain the development of the centralised state, culminated in the *oprichnina*, which imposed a homogeneous order over the entire territory of the country and further strengthened autocratic power.[22]

But since Pokrovskii himself had seen the *oprichnina* as a progressive force in Russian history, Bazilevich could only quibble with him about its character: Pokrovskii had wrongly depicted the urban traders as allies of the nobility against the boyars; and by implying that the threat to the monarchy from the boyars was already largely overcome by the mid-sixteenth century, he had cast doubts on the historical necessity of the terror.[23]

In her introductory article to this volume, A. Pankratova compared Stalin's views on the role of the individual in history with Pokrovskii's. Like the author of the *Pravda* editorial of 1934, she cited Stalin's reference to Bolotnikov, Razin and Pugachev, in his conversation with Emil Ludwig, as an example of the 'profound and concrete nature' of Comrade Stalin's views of the historical role of individuals.[24] But she also quoted the casual comments which Stalin had made about Peter the Great in the same interview, describing them as 'a model of concrete historical analysis and assessment of historical figures', and as a 'scholarly, concrete and profound Marxist-Leninist evaluation'.[25] By way of contrast, she cited Pokrovskii's view of Peter in his popular textbook *Russian History in its Most Concise Exposition*:

> Peter, designated 'the Great' by sycophantic historians, shut his wife in a convent in order to marry Catherine, who had previously been the maidservant of a certain pastor (a Lutheran priest) in Estonia. He tortured his son Alexis with his own hands, and then ordered him to be secretly executed in a dungeon in the Peter-Paul fortress. We have already noted how he suppressed rebellions. He died (in 1725) from the consequences of syphilis, after infecting his second wife as well.[26]

'Thus,' Pankratova concluded, 'Pokrovskii did not give a Marxist-Leninist evaluation of Peter's character, and did not demonstrate his progressive role, as Lenin and Stalin did.'[27]

In the article devoted to Peter in the second volume of the collection, B. B. Kafengauz also criticised Pokrovskii for his negative depiction of the great tsar's character. Citing Stalin's interview with Ludwig, Kafengauz identified Peter as one of those individuals who could indeed change history because they understood it correctly.[28] Pokrovskii had been wrong to criticise Peter's industrialisation policy; unlike Comrade Stalin (in his speech of 1928), Pokrovskii had failed to give due recognition to Peter's attempt to overcome Russia's chronic economic backwardness.[29] But where Stalin in his interview with Ludwig had drawn attention to the exploitation of the enserfed peasantry in the Petrine state, Pokrovskii had virtually ignored the plight of the peasants and their anti-feudal protests.[30]

In *Children of the Arbat*, Rybakov makes his Stalin praise both Ivan and Peter as great statesmen, and criticise Pokrovskii for presenting all Russian historical figures as untalented nonentities.[31] The author thereby implies that the new images of Ivan and Peter that emerged in Soviet historiography in the later 1930s were personally dictated by Stalin. But it is difficult to accept this. Certainly there is evidence of Stalin's sanction for the stress on the role of the individual in history which appeared in 1934 (the resolution of 16 May 1934 'On the teaching of civil history in Soviet schools' was published over his signature). And it is entirely plausible that, as Rybakov suggests, this new emphasis was motivated not so much by concern for the educational needs of Soviet schoolchildren as by Stalin's preoccupation with his own historical reputation (and with that of Lenin, on whose posthumous cult his own living one was modelled).[32] There is, however, no evidence that Stalin was a great admirer of Ivan and Peter at such an early date as this. The favourable comments about Ivan which Rybakov attributes to Stalin in 1934 were based, as we shall see below, on Stalin's conversation of 1947 with the film director Sergei Eisenstein. The only guidance which his published works provided for a 'Party line' on Ivan the Terrible in the 1930s was his somewhat negative comment of 1926 that Ivan was not an industrial-iser. Rybakov's Stalin describes Peter in 1934 as a great ruler who had created a new Russia. He cites Pokrovskii's words about Peter which Pankratova was to criticise in 1939, and he remarks indignantly that Pokrovskii had failed to notice that Peter had transformed Russia.[33] But the real Stalin's few public comments about Peter, as we have seen, fall well short of the unqualified praise which Rybakov attributes to his fictional counterpart.

But if Stalin did not give direct guidance to the historians concern-ing the rehabilitation of Ivan and Peter, there were plenty of indirect signs which pointed them in that direction. The official attack on Pokrovskii indicated that those historical figures whom he had deni-grated should now be praised; and Bukharin had specifically ident-ified Peter's activity as 'relatively progressive'. The historians' task was undoubtedly made easier by the availability of apologias and justifications for both Ivan and Peter in pre-revolutionary histori-ography. Some older scholars whose careers had been eclipsed in the years of Pokrovskii's dominance may genuinely and sincerely have espoused views sympathetic to Ivan and Peter.[34] Others no doubt had more opportunist reasons for denouncing Pokrovskii's influence. More importantly, perhaps, the professional historians could hardly avoid noticing the analogies between Stalin's terror of 1936–8 and the repressions of his tsarist predecessors, and it seems clear that they found it prudent to tailor their interpretations accordingly. In the new *History of the USSR* textbook for university students, published in 1939, we can clearly detect echoes of contemporary events.

The chapter on 'The beginning of the transformation of the Rus-sian state into a multi-national centralised state in the 16th century', written by S. V. Bakhrushin, devoted due attention to Ivan's person-ality, and provided a generally positive assessment of his character:

No-one denies the great and strong intellect of Ivan IV . . . He was well educated for his day . . . and possessed literary talent . . . He was an outstanding strategist and a capable leader of military actions. Ivan the Terrible correctly understood the requirements of domestic and foreign policy and marched unswervingly towards his goal. In his aspiration to consolidate strong central power and in his plans with regard to the Baltic littoral he demonstrated his far-sightedness, and in this respect his activity was positive.[35]

Admittedly, Ivan was cruel. But his cruelty could be explained. It 'developed in the circumstances of his struggle against the boyars'. There were Western analogies: Louis XI of France fought to eradicate the remnants of feudal fragmentation with 'no less cruelty' than Ivan IV. Ivan's ruthlessness was a legitimate response to subversion: 'In many cases his cruel actions were provoked by the stubborn opposition of the great feudal lords to his endeavours and by outright treason on their part.' And the end justified the means: 'Ivan the Terrible recognised the necessity of creating a strong state and did not hesitate to take harsh measures'.[36]

Peter too was given a generally favourable assessment in the textbook. In the chapter by V. I. Lebedev on 'The military-bureaucratic Empire of Peter I', the tsar's active nature and inquiring mind were stressed, and he was described as 'the most talented and energetic representative of the ruling class of his time'.[37] If in the textbook's treatment of Ivan's *oprichnina* we can detect an implicit parallel with Stalin's terror, for Peter's reign the equivalent analogy was the case of Tsarevich Alexis, Peter's son by his first marriage. Alexis was 'the centre of a conspiratorial conservative opposition, plotting to carry out a palace coup and murder Peter'; he sought refuge abroad with the Holy Roman Emperor, Charles VI; when persuaded to return to Russia he was found guilty of participating in a conspiracy against his father, and condemned to death. 'Thus,' the author commented, 'in his struggle for the creation of a mighty national state, Peter did not spare even his own son.'[38] Attentive readers will recall that Peter's killing of his son had been criticised by Pokrovskii in the passage cited by Pankratova.

By the end of the 1930s, therefore, the 'cult of personality' had put its mark upon the historians' depiction of the two tsars. Both were explicitly identified as 'great men' of the Russian past. More specifically, parallels with Stalin were implicitly acknowledged, and their repression of political opponents was justified in the name of the overriding interests of the state. But even at this date the characters of Ivan and Peter were not entirely idealised. Readers of the student textbook were informed that 'The psychiatrist Kovalenskii came to the conclusion that Ivan IV suffered from psychopathological perversions', and that 'The depravity and drunkenness to which he was unrestrainedly devoted aged him prematurely, and he died well short of the fullness of his years'.[39] Significantly, these two sentences were omitted from the second edition of the textbook which was published in 1947.[40] Peter's personality too was sanitised between 1939 and 1947. In the first edition he was described as 'abrupt and coarse'; he 'combined the talent of an organiser, strategist and diplomat with the brutality of a crude serfowner'.[41] These phrases, together with references to Peter's drunken and blasphemous orgies, were dropped from the second edition.[42]

Comparison of the treatment of Ivan and Peter in the first and second editions of this history textbook indicates that between 1939 and 1947 there was a significant move towards the idealisation and simplification of the images of the two tsars. By the end of the Second World War, Ivan and Peter had been elevated to the status of Russian national heroes.

Even before the outbreak of hostilities, the growing international tension of the late 1930s had led to a search for patriotic hero-figures in the Russian past. This tendency was particularly obvious in the cinema, the most influential popular art form of the period. The first part of the feature film 'Peter the First', with a screenplay by A. N. Tolstoi, was released in 1937 (and its second part in 1939); Eisenstein's 'Alexander Nevskii' (the thirteenth-century conqueror of the German Teutonic Knights) appeared in 1938; and Pudovkin's film about Minin and Pozharskii, the victors over the Polish invaders of the early seventeenth century, in 1939. The personification of nationalism in the figures of 'great men' of the past lent itself to wartime propaganda purposes. In his famous speech in Red Square on the twenty-fourth anniversary of the Revolution, with the Germans only forty miles from Moscow, Stalin invoked the inspiration of 'our great ancestors': the medieval princes Alexander Nevskii and Dimitrii Donskoi; Minin and Pozharskii; the eighteenth-century general Suvorov; and Kutuzov, who had defeated Napoleon.[43] Ivan and Peter were not included in this pantheon of pre-revolutionary military leaders, but during the war a whole series of novels, plays and films, as well as works of popular historical biography, glorified the first tsar and the first emperor.[44]

By the time that the second edition of the textbook *History of the USSR* was published, a public indication had appeared of Stalin's personal attitude towards Ivan. The first part of Eisenstein's film, 'Ivan the Terrible', released in 1945, had won a Stalin Prize. In 1946 the second part of the film was suppressed. Part One had dealt with the early part of Ivan's reign, including his conquest of Kazan'; Part Two covered the period of the *oprichnina*. A Central Committee resolution of 4 September 1946 accused the director of 'ignorance in his depiction of historical facts, presenting Ivan the Terrible's progressive force of *oprichniki* as a band of degenerates on the lines of the American Ku-Klux-Klan, and Ivan the Terrible, a man of strong will and character, as weak and irresolute, something like Hamlet'.[45]

In February 1947 Eisenstein and Cherkasov, the actor who played the part of Ivan in the film, were summoned to the Kremlin to discuss with Stalin and his henchmen Molotov and Zhdanov the director's request to be allowed to remake the banned work. Stalin's opening comments on Ivan repeated the points which had been made in the Central Committee resolution on the film: that the *oprichnina* was depicted like the Ku-Klux-Klan and that Ivan himself was shown as an irresolute Hamlet-like figure. In reality, Stalin remarked, 'Tsar Ivan was a great and wise ruler'. Ivan was ruthless, and it was legitimate for Eisenstein to have shown his ruthlessness, but the director had failed 'to show why IT WAS NECESSARY TO BE RUTHLESS'. There followed Stalin's notorious comment that:

> One of Ivan the Terrible's errors was that he failed to knife through five large feudal families. Had he wiped out these five families, there would have been no Time of Troubles [the civil war of the early seventeenth century – M. P.]. But Ivan the Terrible executed someone and then he felt sorry and prayed for a long time. God hindered him in this matter. Tsar Ivan should have been even more resolute.

Stalin offered various other *obiter dicta* about Ivan the Terrible: Ivan had anticipated Lenin by introducing a monopoly on foreign trade; a unified state was necessary in order to prevent new attacks by the Tatars; Malyuta Skuratov (the most vicious executioner among the *oprichniki*) was 'a great military leader and died the death of a hero in the war against Livonia'; and in the film 'the oprichniks during their dances look like cannibals'.[46]

The intellectual climate of the immediately post-war years in the Soviet Union was one of xenophobia and anti-Westernism, and of anti-semitism loosely disguised as anti-'cosmopolitanism'. The influence of these current concerns can be detected in the criteria which Stalin employed in his comparison between Ivan and Peter the Great.

Peter I, he conceded, 'was also a great sovereign, but he was too liberal in relation to foreigners, opened the gates too wide and let foreign influence into the country, having allowed Russia to become Germanized'. By contrast, 'Ivan the Terrible's wisdom was that he championed the national point of view. He did not let foreigners in – he safeguarded the country against penetration by foreign influences'. 'Ivan the Terrible,' Stalin repeated, 'was a more national, more prudent tsar. He didn't let foreign influences into Russia. But "Petrukha" [Peter the Great] flung the gates wide open into Europe and let in too many foreigners.'[47]

There can be little doubt that the second part of Eisenstein's film was suppressed because, in the words of the director's biographer, 'Eisenstein's portrayal of repressions and the loneliness of the tyrant who destroyed all his comrades in arms evoked sinister analogies'.[48] The film director Mikhail Romm, who was present at a preview of the film, has insisted that Eisenstein's behaviour on that occasion left no doubt that he had consciously intended *Ivan the Terrible Part Two* to be an attack on Stalin.[49]

Rybakov in his novel *Children of the Arbat* puts into his fictional Stalin's mind in 1934 a paraphrase of the real Stalin's remarks of 1947. Ivan was a great ruler who had expanded Russia's boundaries, established a monopoly on foreign trade, and introduced into Russian politics the principle that everything must be subordinated to the interests of the state. The boyars had opposed his creation of a mighty centralised Russia, and therefore '*Groznyi*'s mistake was not that he executed the boyars, but that he executed too few of them, that he did not entirely destroy the four [sic] great boyar clans. The ancients were more far-sighted in this respect, they destroyed their enemies unto the third and fourth generations, cleanly and permanently.'[50]

Stalin's bizarre defence of Ivan as an outstanding ruler whose only faults were his excessive clemency and piety has rightly been frequently cited as a revealing insight into Stalin's own mentality. But it must be placed in the appropriate context. By dating it to 1934, Rybakov implies that Ivan's terror was an inspiration and model for the Great Purges. The correct date of 1947 puts it in a somewhat different light: it was a retrospective justification for the *Ezhovshchina*, formulated in response to Eisenstein's implied criticism of Stalin himself as a psychopathogical tyrant. And far from imposing his own eccentric views of Ivan upon the professional historians, Stalin may have borrowed his arguments from them. As we have seen, Bakhrushin in the 1939 edition of the university textbook had already explained why it was necessary for Ivan to be ruthless. And Academician Wipper, in his much praised wartime biography of Ivan, had defended the tsar against the charge of over-suspiciousness of treason: on the contrary, Wipper wrote, Ivan was too trusting and underestimated the real dangers which he faced.[51]

Our review of Stalin's public utterances about Ivan and Peter between 1926 and 1947 thus indicates that it was only in the post-war period that he expressed his admiration for Ivan; and that his views of Peter's greatness were always hedged with qualifications (although these varied with circumstances: in 1931 he criticised Peter for creating a 'national' state; in 1947 he attacked him for being insufficiently 'national'). We must therefore question how far these two tsars served as models for Stalin's political practice of the mid-1930s onwards, as Rybakov suggests.

*　　*　　*

Both Lewin and Rybakov contend that the cult of personality was modelled on the trappings and pomp of tsarism. Lewin argues that the official cults of both Lenin and Stalin represented a deliberate attempt by the regime to harness the traditional Russian 'myth of the tsar' to its own requirements; and he raises the interesting question of whether these attitudes were invoked by Stalin and his officials because of some deep psychological needs of their own; or as a response to what they – perhaps wrongly – believed to be popular attitudes.[52] Rybakov's Stalin reflects that Caesar and Napoleon both had to make themselves emperors out of 'historical necessity', and comments that

> Supreme power must be ROYALLY (*tsarstvenno*) majestic; it is only such power that the people will worship and obey; only it can instil in them trepidation and respect.[53]

It is doubtful, however, how far the cult of personality was modelled on tsarist precedents. The official ideology of autocracy put its stress on tsarism as an institution; the monarch was revered because of his office rather than because of his personality (in Weberian terms, his authority was traditional rather than charismatic). Also, as Robert Tucker has persuasively argued, the direct and immediate model for the Stalin cult was the posthumous cult of Lenin; and the Lenin cult in its turn can be almost entirely explained in terms of the traditions of Bolshevism, without any need to resort to the invocation of a recrudescence of Old Russian autocratic and religious ideologies.[54] And a comparison of the Stalin cult with the cults of the leaders in Fascist Italy and Nazi Germany suggests that the phenomenon may owe as much to the internal dynamics of twentieth-century European totalitarianism as to those of Russian tsarism.

Both Lewin and Rybakov, however, identify Ivan and Peter as exceptional figures within the tsarist tradition. Lewin suggests that these two rulers, in particular, were incorporated into the cult of personality because their bids to establish their personal power within the framework of autocracy provided the closest tsarist parallels to Stalin's rule.[55] Rybakov indicates that Stalin was attracted by Ivan and Peter because he regarded them not just as monarchs, but also as leaders who destroyed their opponents. Rybakov's Stalin reflects on the nature of leadership, and the Leader's need for freedom of action:

To whom was Lenin indebted? To the London and Geneva emigres? To whom was Peter indebted? To Menshikov? To Lefort? The hereditary character of his power does not affect the essence of the matter. In order to rise to the status of a leader, a monarch has to destroy an entourage which has become accustomed to see him as a puppet. So it was with Peter, so it was with *Groznyi*.[56]

Thus hereditary power in itself was not enough to make a monarch a leader, in Stalin's view: strength of character was also required:

The Petrine epoch was one of the most brilliant in Russian history; it reflected his vivid personality. The reign of Alexander III was the dullest; it fully matched his personal nonentity.[57]

There is however no basis in Stalin's writings or other public utterances of the 1930s for the views of Ivan and Peter as political leaders which Rybakov attributes to him, and we therefore have no grounds to accept Rybakov's suggestion that Stalin consciously modelled himself upon them.

But there is a further aspect of Ivan and Peter that attracts Rybakov's Stalin: both had a popular reputation as 'good tsars,' which Stalin believes to have been created by their persecution of the boyars. Stalin tells the Old Bolshevik official Budyagin (a fictional character in the novel):

> We must stand aside and give way to personnel from the ordinary people. At the head of the state the people wants to see its own sons, and not new upstarts, new nobles. The Russian people does not like nobles. The history of the Russian people is a history of struggle against the nobility. The Russian people loved Ivan the Terrible and Peter the Great, that is precisely those tsars who destroyed boyars and nobles. All peasant movements from Bolotnikov to Pugachev were movements for the good tsar and against the nobles.

And Budyagin interprets Stalin's words as follows: 'old cadres like Budyagin are the new nobles. It is they whom the people no longer want'.[58]

Thus Rybakov's Stalin not only plans his purges to rid himself of rivals and establish himself as a true Leader in the mould of Ivan and Peter, but he also hopes thereby to gain the love of his people as a 'good tsar' who destroys his boyars. There is however no evidence that the real Stalin thought of Ivan and Peter as 'good tsars': his only recorded comments about the tsarist mentality of the Russian peasantry related to Razin and Pugachev, the leaders of the major popular uprisings of the seventeenth and eighteenth centuries respectively. 'You should never forget,' he told Emil Ludwig in 1931, 'that they were tsarists: they acted against the landowners, but for the "good tsar". For that was their slogan.' 'As you see,' he added, 'an analogy with the Bolsheviks is quite inappropriate.'[59]

Regardless of Stalin's own intentions, however, one of the most intriguing parallels with Ivan and Peter lies precisely in this area of popular attitudes towards the ruler. It is this aspect of the historical analogy which I should like to explore in the final part of this essay.

First of all, we should ask whether Rybakov's Stalin was correct in his assertion that the Russian people loved Ivan and Peter. Certainly Soviet scholarship of the Stalin period presented them as 'good tsars' who were generally depicted positively in folklore. After Stalin's death, however, much of the criticism of the idealisation of Ivan the Terrible in Soviet historiography focussed on his presentation as a 'people's tsar'.[60] Subsequently some Soviet scholars (most notably the historian A. A. Zimin) argued that the folklore about Ivan was predominantly hostile towards him.[61] These conflicting interpretations of Ivan's popular image both appear to have been inspired by the same neo-Slavophile or neo-Populist 'myth of the people' – an assumption that the judgements of folklore must be in some sense 'correct', and evaluate a ruler according to his true merits. More recently a Soviet philosopher has dared to suggest that the opposite may be the case, and that popular assessments of rulers may bear an inverse relationship to their deserts. Making an explicit analogy between Ivan the Terrible and 'Joseph the Bloody', M. Kapustin observes that 'the masses had a semi-disdainful attitude to "kindly tsars" (like Fedor Ioannovich and Boris Godunov), but revered the "dread" ones with holy terror'.[62] As I have argued elsewhere, Russian folklore does present us with the apparent paradox that the popular image of a bloody tyrant such as Ivan the Terrible is generally a sympathetic one.[63] The same is true, to a lesser extent, of Peter the Great – and also of Stalin.

In Russian popular mentality, responsibility for the problems and plight of the ordinary people was traditionally attributed to their immediate overlords: the local landowners and officials. The tsar was assumed to share his humble subjects' hatred of these figures. To a certain extent, this was a defensive psychological device for the legitimation of popular protest: by attributing their own values to the ruler, the peasants could justify attacks on local exploiters as 'rebellions in the name of the tsar'.[64] When the real tsar's actions failed to correspond to this expectation (as was all too frequently the case), the myth of the ruler could still be preserved. The tsar could be seen as a boyar himself, who had treacherously seized the throne; and Russian history in the seventeenth and eighteenth centuries spawned a whole series of pretenders claiming to be the 'true tsar' who would replace the reigning usurper. Even when the reigning monarch was recognised as a 'true tsar', he could be viewed as the tool or puppet of the boyars (Razin's rebellion of 1671–3 aimed to free the tsar from the clutches of his evil boyars). But on the rare occasions when the actual behaviour of a ruler could be interpreted as persecution of the boyars (as was the case with both Ivan and Peter), the 'monarchist illusions' of the people were reinforced.

In Russian folklore Ivan the Terrible and Peter the Great are generally depicted as 'good tsars'. In a number of folktales Ivan befriends a humble hero, and aids and abets his efforts to outwit or revenge himself upon a corrupt and avaricious boyar. Many of the same motifs are associated with Peter the Great. There are also works of folklore which depict repressions by Ivan and Peter against innocent victims with whom the performers sympathise. But even here the tsars are not explicitly criticised. The blame for Ivan the Terrible's massacre of the people of Novgorod in 1570 is laid on evil informers who falsely accused the citizens of treason. In the song in which Ivan condemns his son to death, the villain of the piece is the *oprichnik* Malyuta Skuratov, who is over-zealous in carrying out his master's orders. In these cases, Ivan's image corresponds to the stereotype of the tsar as the dupe or hostage of his boyars. This image is also associated with Peter the Great, although Peter can also be depicted more negatively, as a boyar tsar, or even (by the schismatic Old Believers) as the Antichrist.[65] But within half a century of Peter's death, even Old Believers could contend that one of his most repressive acts against their co-religionists, the execution of the rebel *strel'tsy* in 1698, had been inspired by false denunciations by the boyars.[66]

There are therefore two versions of the folk myth of the good but harsh tsar associated with Ivan and Peter. In the first version, the tsar's harshness is directed only against 'evil boyars' who oppress the people and therefore deserve their cruel punishment. In the second, repressions against innocent victims occur only when the tsar is misled by his evil boyars. Both of these versions – the tsar as scourge of the boyars; and the tsar as hostage of the boyars – can also be found in unofficial Soviet views of Stalin.

Some explanations for the terror of the 1930s try to exempt Stalin from any responsibility or blame. During the Stalin period itself there were many people in the Soviet Union (most notably, of course, the victims of the purges themselves) who recognised that innocent victims were being accused and shot. But the illusion of Stalin's goodness was preserved by the myth that he did not know what injustices were being perpetrated by his subordinates.[67] A variant on this theme was that Stalin did know about the terror, but genuinely believed that the accused were guilty, because he had been deceived by evil alien elements such as Ezhov and Beriya, who had infiltrated their way into the NKVD leadership in order to destroy the best people in the Party. According to Roy Medvedev, such attitudes were particularly common after the Twentieth Party Congress in 1956, when Khrushchev in his 'secret speech' denounced the crimes of Stalin.[68] The 'Beriya version' has persisted into the Gorbachev era. A letter to the literary journal *Znamya* in 1987, protesting against the publication of Alexander Tvardovskii's poem 'By Right of Memory', attacked the author for suggesting that Stalin was responsible for all the 'mistakes and errors' which had occurred under his rule – the 'violations of socialist legality and democracy', and the 'repressions against innocent citizens' were in reality 'the black deeds of the gang of Beriya and others'.[69] Roy Medvedev recognises a parallel with the older concept of the ruler as the hostage of his boyars when he describes the explanation that Stalin was ignorant of the terror as 'only a new version of the common people's faith in a good tsar surrounded by lying and wicked ministers'.[70]

A recent contributor to *Izvestiya* has referred to a second version of the myth of Stalin as a 'good tsar': the image of Stalin as the scourge of the boyars. He expounds a 'folk explanation' of Stalin's repressions: 'They say he wiped out the authorities, chopped the heads off his "boyars". And he did right, because it was from them, the "boyars", and not from the tsar that all the evil came.' 'Do not imagine,' he adds, 'that in our enlightened century our highly educated people are alien to such an explanation. Believe me, I have heard and even argued with advocates of the "folk version".'[71]

The author does not elaborate on the content of this 'folk version' of the repressions. Certainly the arrest and execution of so many Old Bolshevik members of the Central Committee and Politburo in the 1930s could have been interpreted as the tsar's punishment of his 'boyars'. This seems to be what Rybakov has in mind when he makes Stalin tell Budyagin that a purge of the 'new nobles' would have popular support. But in the popular mind Stalin also appears to have been viewed as the scourge of corrupt and degenerate officials at a lower level: the local authorities with whom the ordinary people came into daily contact.

Such attitudes were noted by the American journalist Hedrick Smith in the 1970s. Smith quotes a number of Soviet informants who admired Stalin not only as a successful military commander and state-builder, but also as a strong leader who imposed labour discipline and kept local officials under control.[72] 'The intelligentsia may dream of democracy,' a state farm accountant told him:

but the huge mass of the people dream of Stalin – his strong power. They are not reactionary but they are being mistreated by their petty bosses, who cheat and exploit them, suppress them. They want a strong boss to 'put the shoes on' the petty bosses. They know that under Stalin [economic] conditions were not as good, but the state farm directors and other officials were not robbing them under Stalin, were not mocking then. There was a check on local authorities.[73]

Similar attitudes have been recorded in the Soviet press in the *glasnost'* era, although commentators have been quick to point out that they represent a retrospective idealisation of the Stalin period, and should be seen primarily as a form of protest against the corruption and abuses of the 'era of stagnation' under Brezhnev.[74] In this respect, there is another clear parallel with the popular images of Ivan and Peter, whose idealisation in folklore as the scourge of the boyars can also be seen in large part as a response to the series of weak rulers who succeeded them.

Thus when Rybakov's Stalin hints to Budyagin that by destroying the 'boyars' he can, like Ivan and Peter, not only rid himself of his rivals, but also gain the love of the people, he appears to have been proved correct. As we have seen, there is no evidence that the real Stalin calculated the effect of his actions in precisely this way; but it appears that a reinforcement of traditional Russian attitudes towards a 'strong' ruler was one of the unintended consequences of the purges.

* * *

Historical parallels – as Comrade Stalin said to Emil Ludwig – are always risky. And they are risky not least because historians seldom agree on their interpretations of events and processes. But whether we regard them as heroes or villains, the careers of Ivan the Terrible, Peter the Great and Stalin undoubtedly present us with many intriguing similarities. Rybakov's implied explanation of these parallels is that Stalin consciously modelled himself on his tsarist predecessors: the *Ezhovshchina* resembled the *oprichnina* because Stalin willed it so. Even if there were evidence to support this hypothesis, however, it would be rather too simplistic to satisfy the serious historian.

Moshe Lewin also implies that Stalin's personal sense of affinity with Ivan and Peter played a part in his reversion to patterns of the past; but Lewin places this in the framework of a more sophisticated analysis which includes within its purview 'the historical-cultural traditions of the country, in particular those represented by the peasantry'.[75] But Lewin is understandably reluctant to accept that the cult of personality was a reflection of the backward mentality of the peasants: he rightly attributes the responsibility for its creation to Stalin and his entourage.[76] The unofficial perceptions of Stalin which we have discussed in this essay, however, clearly have more in common with traditional stereotypes of the 'good tsar' than with the image of the leader projected by the official Stalin cult. To that extent, the striking parallels which we have noted in popular images of Ivan, Peter and Stalin must be seen as an expression of continuity in the structure of Russian mentality.

NOTES

1. Moshe Lewin, *The Making of the Soviet System: Essays in the Social History of Inter-War Russia* (London, 1985) pp. 272–3.
2. Ibid., pp. 277–9.
3. Ibid., p. 307.
4. In addition to works cited elsewhere in this essay, see V. Kobrin, 'Posmertnaya sud'ba Ivana Groznogo', *Znanie – sila*, 1987, no. 8, pp. 54–9; V. Selyunin, 'Istoki', *Novyi mir*, 1988, no. 5, pp. 180–7; and N. Eidel'man, '"Revolyutsiya sverkhu" v Rossii', serialised in *Nauka i zhizn'*, 1988, nos. 10–12, 1989, nos. 1–3, especially 1988, no. 10, pp. 100–5, and no. 11, pp. 109–18. I am grateful to friends and colleagues, and especially to Bob Davies and Julian Cooper, for kindly drawing my attention to references to Ivan and Peter in the current Soviet press.
5. Anatolii Rybakov, *Deti Arbata; roman* (Moscow: Moskovskii rabochii, 1988) pp. 179–80, 184, 240–3.
6. For reviews of Russian and Soviet historiography of the reign of Ivan the Terrible, see Leo Yaresh, 'Ivan the Terrible and the *Oprichnina*', in C. E. Black (ed.), *Rewriting Russian History; Soviet Interpretations of Russia's Past* (London, 1957) pp. 224–41; Richard Hellie, 'In Search of Ivan the Terrible', in S. F. Platonov, *Ivan the Terrible* (Gulf Breeze, Florida, 1974); Hugh F. Graham, editor's introduction to R. G. Skrynnikov, *Ivan the Terrible* (Gulf Breeze, Florida, 1981); and the polemical work by the Soviet *émigré* writer Alexander Yanov, *The Origins of Autocracy: Ivan the Terrible in Russian History* (Berkeley, 1981).
7. For a thorough review of Russian and Soviet historiography of Peter's reign, see Nicholas V. Riasanovsky, *The Image of Peter the Great in Russian History and Thought* (Oxford, 1985).
8. On Pokrovskii's career, see George M. Enteen, *The Soviet Scholar-Bureaucrat: M. N. Pokrovskii and the Society of Marxist Historians* (London, 1978); and J. D. Barber, *Soviet Historians in Crisis, 1928–32* (London, 1981). A valuable general account of the politics of Soviet historiography is Konstantin F. Shteppa, *Russian Historians and the Soviet State* (New Brunswick, 1962).
9. I. V. Stalin, *Sochineniya*, T.VIII (Moscow, 1952), pp. 120–1.
10. Ibid., T.XI (Moscow, 1949), pp. 248–9.
11. Ibid., p. 249.

12. Ibid., T. XIII (Moscow, 1951), p. 104.
13. Ibid., p. 105.
14. Ibid.
15. Ibid., pp. 105–6.
16. *Pravda*, 16 May 1934, p. 1 ('O prepodavanii grazhdanskoi istorii v shkolakh SSSR').
17. Ibid. ('Za vysokoe kachestvo sovetskoi shkoly').
18. *Izvestiya*, 27 January 1936, p. 3 ('V Sovnarkome Soyuza SSR i TsK VKP(b)').
19. Ibid., p. 4 (N. Bukharin, 'Nuzhna li nam marksistskaya istoricheskaya nauka?').
20. *Protiv istoricheskoi kontseptsii M. N. Pokrovskogo. Sbornik statei. Chast' pervaya* (Moscow and Leningrad, 1939) p. 3.
21. K. Bazilevich, '"Torgovyi kapitalizm" i genezis moskovskogo samoderzhaviya v rabotakh M. N. Pokrovskogo', ibid., p. 154.
22. Ibid., p. 155.
23. Ibid., pp. 151–2.
24. A. Pankratova, 'Razvitie istoricheskikh vzglyadov M. N. Pokrovskogo', in ibid., p. 54.
25. Ibid.
26. Ibid., pp. 54–5.
27. Ibid., p. 55.
28. B. B. Kafengauz, 'Reformy Petra I v otsenke M. N. Pokrovskogo', in *Protiv antimarksistkoi kontseptsii M. N. Pokrovskogo. Sbornik statei. Chast' vtoraya* (Moscow and Leningrad, 1940) pp. 172–5.
29. Ibid., pp. 155–60, 174.
30. Ibid., pp. 165–7, 175.
31. Rybakov, *Deti Arbata*, pp. 240–3.
32. Ibid.
33. Ibid., p. 241.
34. Alexander Yanov somewhat unfairly attributes to Russian historians of both the pre-revolutionary and Soviet periods a slave mentality which worships the state and leads to the justification of tyranny: Yanov, *The Origins of Autocracy*, esp. p. 300.
35. *Istoriya SSSR. T. I. S drcvncishikh vremen do kontsa XVIII veka. Pod red. V. I. Lebedeva, B. D. Grekova, S. V. Bakhrushina.* (Moscow, 1939), p. 390.
36. Ibid., pp. 389–90.
37. Ibid., p. 643.
38. Ibid., pp. 644–5. Nicholas Riasanovsky notes that in the final (1938) version of A. N. Tolstoi's play about Peter, Alexis was transformed from the 'poignant tragic protagonist' of earlier versions into 'a conspiratorial collaborator of foreign enemies who deserved death': Riasanovsky, *The Image of Peter the Great*, p. 282.
39. *Istoriya SSSR*, T. I, pp. 389, 390.
40. Compare *Istoriya SSSR*, T. I, Izdanie vtoroe (Moscow, 1947), pp. 343–4.
41. *Istoriya SSSR*, T. I [1939 edn], pp. 643, 644.
42. Compare pp. 642–5 of the 1939 edition with pp. 580–4 of the 1947

edition. The chapters about Ivan and Peter were written by the same authors (Bakhrushin and Lebedev respectively) in both editions.

43. I. V. Stalin, *Sochineniya*, T.2 [XV], ed. R. H. McNeal (Stanford, 1967) p. 35.
44. For example, plays about Ivan by A. N. Tolstoi and V. A. Solov'ev, a novel by V. Kostylev, and popular biographies by S. V. Bakhrushin, I. I. Smirnov and R. Yu. Wipper; the films, play and novel about Peter by A. N. Tolstoi, and a popular biography by V. V. Mavrodin.
45. 'O kinofil'me "Bol'shaya zhizn"'', in *O partiinoi i sovetskoi pechati: sbornik dokumentov* (Moscow, 1954) pp. 575–6.
46. R. Trofimov, ed., 'A Conversation with Stalin, Molotov and Zhdanov about Eisenstein's "Ivan the Terrible" (Part Two). Transcript by Sergei Eisenstein and Nikolai Cherkasov', *Moscow News*, 1988, no. 32, pp. 8–9.
47. Ibid. The transcript was accompanied by an article by V. Kobrin, a specialist on the reign of Ivan the Terrible, criticising the historical accuracy of Stalin's comments: 'Stalin and the Tsar', ibid., p. 9.
48. R. Trofimov, 'Formidable Shadows of 1947', ibid., p. 8.
49. M. Romm, *Besedy o kino* (Moscow, 1964), pp. 90–91.
50. Rybakov, *Deti Arbata*, pp. 240–1. The content of the conversation was available to Rybakov at the time of writing of the novel in the briefer version provided by Cherkasov's memoirs: N. K. Cherkasov, *Zapiski sovetskogo aktera* (Moscow, 1953) pp. 379–81.
51. R. Wipper, *Ivan Grozny* (Moscow, 1947) pp. 146, 159–60. (This is an English translation of the 1944 Russian edition.)
52. Lewin, *The Making of the Soviet System*, pp. 16, 275–6.
53. Rybakov, *Deti Arbata*, p. 240.
54. Robert C. Tucker, *Stalin as Revolutionary, 1879–1929: a Study in History and Personality* (London, 1974), pp. 279–88.
55. Lewin, *The Making of the Soviet System*, pp. 277–8, 307.
56. Rybakov, *Deti Arbata*, p. 184. Menshikov and Lefort were favourites of Peter the Great, both 'new men' (of humble and foreign origin respectively) who owed their careers to Peter's patronage.
57. Ibid., p. 243.
58. Ibid., pp. 179–80.
59. Stalin, *Sochineniya*, T.XIII, p. 113.
60. See especially the debate held in the Institute of History in Moscow in May 1956 to discuss S. M. Dubrovskii's attack on the popular biographies of Ivan by Bakhrushin, Smirnov and Wipper: see S. M. Dubrovskii, 'Protiv idealizatsii deyatel'nosti Ivan IV', *Voprosy istorii*, 1956, no. 8, pp. 121–9; M. D. Kurmacheva, 'Ob otsenke deyatel'nosti Ivana Groznogo', ibid., no. 9, pp. 195–203; V. N. Shevyakov, 'K voprosu ob oprichnine pri Ivane IV', ibid., no. 9, pp. 71–7.
61. Maureen Perrie, *The Image of Ivan the Terrible in Russian Folklore* (Cambridge, 1987) pp. 21–7.
62. M. Kapustin, 'Diagnoz – tiraniya', *Nedelya*, 1989, no. 12, pp. 14–15.
63. Perrie, *The Image of Ivan the Terrible*, esp. ch. 3. This view is also held by several present-day Soviet scholars.
64. Daniel Field, *Rebels in the Name of the Tsar* (Boston, 1976); Maureen

Perrie, 'Folklore as Evidence of Peasant *Mentalité*: Social Attitudes and Values in Russian Popular Culture', *Russian Review*, vol. 48 no. 2 (April 1989), pp. 119–43.

65. See, for example: Perrie, *The Image of Ivan the Terrible*; Riasanovsky, *The Image of Peter the Great*, pp. 74–85; V. K. Sokolova, *Russkie istoricheskie pesni XVI–XVIII vv.* (Moscow, 1960), pp. 21–81, 201–54; V. K. Sokolova, *Russkie istoricheskie predaniya* (Moscow, 1970) pp. 49–96.

66. A. I. Klibanov, *Narodnaya sotsial'naya utopiya v Rossii: period feodalizma* (Moscow, 1977) pp. 156–8.

67. Roy A. Medvedev, *Let History Judge: the Origins and Consequences of Stalinism* (London: Spokesman Books edn, 1976) pp. 289–90; Alexander Solzhenitsyn, *The Gulag Archipelago*, vol. 2 (London: Fontana edn, 1976) pp. 316–17.

68. Medvedev, *Let History Judge*, pp. 298–9. Khrushchev argues that this version was fuelled by the arrest and execution of Beriya soon after Stalin's death in 1953, when the Party leadership itself blamed Beriya for all the abuses committed by Stalin: *Khrushchev Remembers*, vol. 1 (London: Penguin Books edn, 1977), pp. 377–8.

69. 'Chitateli o poeme A. T. Tvardovskogo "Po pravu pamyati"', *Znamya*, 1987, no. 8, p. 232.

70. Medvedev, *Let History Judge*, p. 290.

71. Yurii Feofanov, 'Gruzchik Ivan Demura v skheme Niny Andreevy', *Izvestiya*, 19 April 1988.

72. Hedrick Smith, *The Russians* (London: Sphere Books edn, 1976) pp. 300–5.

73. Ibid., p. 302.

74. See especially Igor' Bestuzhev-Lada, 'Pravdu i tol'ko pravdu', *Nedelya*, 1988, no. 5, p. 15. Bestuzhev-Lada's discussion of various categories of defenders of the 'cult of memory' of Stalin is based on an analysis of letters written in 1963 to the editorial board of *Nedelya* (the weekly supplement to *Pravda*) in protest against the publication of Evtushenko's poem 'The Heirs of Stalin'. Similar attitudes have been expressed in readers' protests against the more recent publication of literary works critical of Stalin, Rybakov's *Children of the Arbat* and Tvardovskii's *By Right of Memory*: see *Literaturnaya gazeta*, 19 August 1987, p. 4; and *Znamya*, 1987, no. 8, pp. 227–36. In both cases, however, pro-Stalin responses came from only a small minority of correspondents.

75. Lewin, *The Making of the Soviet System*, p. 274.

76. Ibid., pp. 275–6.

5 The Omnipresent Conspiracy: On Soviet Imagery of Politics and Social Relations in the 1930s
Gábor Tamás Rittersporn

In August 1941 a young NKVD officer was taken captive by the Germans. He pretended to be a peasant's son who had studied agronomy and mathematics, before being 'mobilised' to work in the political police in the spring of 1938, at the age of twenty-five. He also pretended to having rendered some services to German intelligence in Riga in 1940. His interrogators were impressed by his willingness to cooperate and to present himself in a favourable light.[1] They were equally impressed by his manifestly sincere conviction that there was hardly any sphere of Soviet society where conspiracies were not present in the 1930s. In some respect the young man was far from being poorly informed. Apparently assigned to the surveillance of Komintern officials and foreign Communists in Moscow, he possessed pertinent information about people who must have been unknown even to police cadres, if they were not specialised in his field.[2]

Nevertheless, the interrogators could not help wondering if he was able to distinguish his undeniable familiarity with certain facts and rumours arising out of the NKVD's obsession with the ubiquity of spies and plotters.[3] Indeed, the young man reported a profusion of conspiracies in educational institutions, enterprises and offices as well as in the highest spheres of government in the 1930s. He even presented a chart of the complicated relations among secret organisations of 'leftist' and 'rightist' groups that included defendants in the show trials, commanders of the army and leading officials of the Komintern and the NKVD.[4] Despite his eagerness to seek the favour of his interrogators, he was ready to enter into dispute with them when they objected to his tendency to see spies in entire ethnic groups, and especially when they reminded him that they knew better who had been working for German intelligence in the Soviet Union: so much that he continued to stick to his opinion concerning an alleged German spy, insisting that he was better informed about the real state of affairs behind the régime's façade.[5]

The young officer's propensity to see a complicated web of conspiracies at the centre of Soviet politics had obviously more than a few things to do with his training at the NKVD and proceeded from a consciously cultivated spy mania in the secret police. Nevertheless, everything points to the assumption that Soviet citizens of the epoch were inclined to lend credit to the régime's propaganda about the subversive activities of plotters and foreign agents. Captured officers seemed to believe that there was something behind the accusations against the high command in 1937.[6] At the start of the war, ordinary citizens were ready to accept the idea that the 'whole of our country is full of spies' and to attribute the disastrous military situation to 'high treason' and 'wrecking' in leading circles.[7]

In the course of the 1930s, political and even social relations came to be understood increasingly in terms of conspiratorial intrigues. Plots and wrecking became central paradigms by which the régime sought to explain political processes and social conflicts, and official as well as popular milieux were disposed to suspect the work of subversive machinations behind the apparently inexplicable turmoil that turned into an unmanageable daily reality and represented a permanent threat to the security of virtually any Soviet citizen.

*　　*　　*

It became routine for the Soviet authorities to ascribe the régime's difficulties to 'subversive' activities of 'conspirators' during the collectivisation and industrialisation drives. Well-publicised show trials were staged between 1928 and 1931 to demonstrate that the hardships of the period originated in the 'wrecking' of 'plotters' among managerial and technical cadres and among members of the scientific and planning establishments.[8] Anti-saboteur campaigns focused on specialists who were identified as leftovers of the Old Régime, and when the last show trial of this wave took place in April 1933, against the background of famine and intense intra-Party conflict and in the wake of a major crisis of collectivisation and industrialisation, its defendants were once again Soviet and foreign engineers.[9]

The identity of the 'wrecker' changed, however, in a matter of less than four years. A new imagery of the 'enemy' emerged by the early months of 1937 which applied to veteran members of the Party, to high-ranking officials and to practically all cadres. This imagery could be disregarded as the propaganda of a completely perverted régime, were it not that it reflected real problems of the system and something of the way they tended to be seen in leading circles and by the population, and explained a good deal of the régime's perversity.

It became increasingly doubtful after the early 1930s that the hardships the public had to endure were temporary and incidental, and that people alien to the régime could alone be blamed for them. This fiction seemed all the more difficult to maintain since it was hardly possible to separate the adversities of daily life from the operation of governmental mechanisms which turned out to be unmanageable. The official discourse acknowledged that collectivisation and industrialisation had increased the 'strength and authority' of the Party and state apparatus 'to an unprecedented degree' and that 'everything or almost everything' depended therefore on the way officeholders fulfilled their 'decisive [and] exceptional' rôle. It had to be admitted, however, that this state of affairs did not mean that the apparatus worked in a uniform, regular and controllable manner. Hence strict measures were necessary to ensure the implementation of the Party's 'political line'.[10] This line ceased to be the object of open contestation by the early years of the decade, but the functioning of the administration, the attempts by top bodies to regulate it and the response of the apparatus to such attempts were far from making the régime's policy clear and unambiguous.

Governmental mechanisms had a strong tendency to work in an unpredictable way and, whatever the 'Party line' happened to be, there was every chance that it would be altered through the daily operation of the apparatus. Virtually all important decisions about industrial and agricultural policy or about the screening of Party membership were implemented in such a manner that the outcome had little to do with the originally envisaged effects. If officials bothered to carry out major directives, they concentrated their efforts mainly on producing immediate and spectacular results which often did not amount to more than the appearance of the projected changes. Far from improving the work of Party bodies and rationalising management and production, nation-wide campaigns disorganised the administration and the economy and aggravated social tensions.[11] This phenomenon had nothing to do with alternative programmes of reform-minded cadres, or oppositional movements within the apparatus. Officials routinely misused their powers in order to make a show of success, and in many cases they hardly had a choice, confronted as they were by the indifference or hostility of the masses, by inadequate resources and by the prospect of censure, dismissal or penal sanctions if they could not produce at least the semblance of results or find scapegoats for failures.

The behaviour of officials did not deviate from the norms set by higher bodies, including the centre, whose incompetent or contradictory measures, scapegoating of subordinates and 'hostile' elements, and triumphal reports on dubious successes were merely imitated by the apparatus. However sincere Moscow's warnings against abuses and excesses might have been, insiders had no reason to take them too seriously. Measures to alleviate tensions in the countryside even included a rather parsimonious amnesty for some categories of peasants who had been exiled or imprisoned for their alleged or real resistance to collectivisation, and a symbolic amnesty for officials condemned mainly for their liberal attitude during the ruthless food procurement drives of 1932 and 1933.[12] But a multitude of instructions and injunctions concerning the sowing and harvesting campaigns and the delivery of agricultural products showed that there was no illusion in high places about the cooperativeness of the population: if results were to be obtained, it had to be put under pressure by grass-roots cadres who were themselves under the threat of penal sanctions.[13]

Moscow had every reason to issue repeated calls for restraint in the prosecution of petty rural officeholders[14] who were frequently put on trial by higher-ups if something went wrong with farming and food procurements. More often than not, however, the latter acted in the spirit of directives of the Central Committee and the government which pressed for quick results and emphasised the personal responsibility of all cadres for the success of the agricultural campaigns.[15] In the same way, it was vain to enjoin local authorities to moderate their zeal in purging the Party and to refrain from persecuting people merely because of their social origin, if the move came some months after a vigilance drive in the name of the Central Committee which had dispatched lists of 'unmasked' people whose 'guilt' was nothing more in most cases than their social origin or their past.[16] Official spokesmen admitted that wholesale repression discredited the régime and that the authority and efficiency of penal provisions would be compromised if used in an inflated and irregular way.[17] Nevertheless, harsh measures against the masses and junior officials seemed justified by instructions which mobilised the judiciary to 'contribute to the successes' of agriculture, industry and transport and to detect 'hostile' intentions behind failures and professional errors.[18]

A paradoxical situation developed in which the activities of individual officeholders often deviated from or were in conflict with policies decided by the central authorities, yet were in harmony with a general pattern of action that was hardly ever compatible with the political line fixed by the centre. The paradox was intimately related to the contradictory political objectives of the régime: ensuring order among the masses as well as social peace, regular and controllable functioning of the administration and its 'decisive and exceptional' rôle. Maintaining order and the preeminence of the apparatus implied the delegation of large powers and created the danger of transgressions and social tensions. On the other hand, control meant curtailing the authority of officialdom, which tended to encourage popular insubordination, as in the case when Moscow publicly condemned the first excesses of collectivisation and triggered a series of riots.[19] When the top bodies tried to regulate the administration's working, they were in fact trying to do away with the logic which their own actions had established and which inevitably reappeared in the operation of the apparatus. A solution to this problem could hardly be found if the dominant position of the Party and state apparatus in society was to be maintained.

Something had to be done, however, since the activities of officialdom manifestly disorganised the régime and brought a deterioration in its relations with the rest of society. The agricultural administration's habit of furnishing false data made a fiction of economic planning, as did the tendency of industrial management to meet plan targets through manufacturing defective goods, raising prices or refusing to fabricate badly-needed products.[20] There could be no question of running a self-contained and highly centralised apparatus if it refused to cooperate with control agencies and, despite repeated warnings, dismissed officials who had been nominated by top bodies.[21] Not even the appearance of a legal order could be maintained where officials extended their powers, especially when they inflicted unauthorised penalties on the population through local ordinancies incompatible with statute law.[22] And the state's legitimate monopoly on violence was under serious threat when the régime proved unable to define which officials were e   tled to carry out arrests, and when regional administrations had to be reminded that the supreme governing body had the prerogative to take the ultimate decision about the execution of death sentences.[23]

There could be no secret about the involvement of ranking cadres and Party veterans in the disorganisation of the system's functioning. Authoritative statements emphasised that officials, often high dignitaries with 'well-known merits in the past', were responsible for the irregular and uncontrollable working of governmental mechanisms, and warned that intractable 'bigwigs' would be demoted, dismissed and punished 'without respect of personalities'.[24] Actions were taken against a number of transgressing officeholders but, instead of looking for the origins of their misdeeds in the administration's working, there was a notable tendency to attribute them to 'criminal' intentions and to the allegedly 'alien' social origin of the culprits.[25] Already, during the collectivisation, excessively harsh measures as well as reluctance to apply such measures were ascribed to 'deviationist' or 'hostile' practices of cadres.[26] In this respect, threats to censure distinguished officials merely for their abuses represented a remarkable innovation. Nevertheless, when it came to singling out a Central Committee member, the propaganda did not dwell on his presumed faults. It highlighted his alleged association with 'class enemies' and called for vigilance against 'kulaks' and 'Trotskyists'.[27]

The persistence and ubiquity of official abuse does not allow one to explain it as a transitory phenomenon, and the tensions it provoked within the régime were more than rivalry between centre and periphery. Even top officials had good reasons to feel insecure in face of charges against unruly 'bigwigs', because malpractice and the ensuing conflicts had broad implications for every echelon, in all agencies and in all branches of the apparatus, just as transgressing officials and their allies were likely to be found everywhere. The interaction of agencies in a huge governmental mechanism, and the wide networks of solidarity among cadres spread abuses throughout the apparatus, and the Party-state itself organised officials in groups and coteries which had members, patrons and associates on different hierarchical levels and in many institutions and localities. Any office-holder was likely to participate in a systematic and organised obstruction of openly uncontested policies, and almost any cross-section of the apparatus behaved like a clandestine political opposition, with the sole aim of securing the careers of the incumbents of responsible positions.

Inclined to equate their career with the strengthening of the régime, officeholders were unlikely to grasp the political implications of this state of affairs, and were not disposed to see the disorganising effect of their activities, especially since they followed a pattern that characterised the working of the highest bodies. Obstruction of the régime's policies was as inseparable from the ordinary functioning of the administration as were periodic attempts to check officialdom, and refusal to submit to control agencies was as necessary in order to remain in responsible positions as it was necessary to ensure the regular and controllable operation of governmental mechanisms. The more it became indispensable to fight official abuse, the more such abuse became an integral part of the everyday realities of the system, and the more difficult it became to recognise its manifestations as results of the ordinary functioning of the régime and its relations with the rest of society. Officialdom saw itself as the best representative of the interests of the working masses. This was not conductive to the realisation that the practices of the administration stemmed from unpopular policies. To admit that uncontrollability and abuses were inseparable from the régime's normal universe would cast doubt on the *raison d'être* of the administration as an agency invested with the prerogative to direct and supervise the system's functioning and its own working. These circumstances made it difficult to avoid attributing the régime's problems to the machinations of people alienated from or hostile to the system.

There was already a remarkable tendency in the 1920s to avoid searching for the origins of the administration's intractability in the fact that it was accountable only to itself. Characteristically, the consequences of this state of affairs were debated mainly in terms of an analogy with the French Revolution, and even oppositionists were reluctant to acknowledge that the system had not evolved according to the promises of October.[28] Besides the scapegoating of 'bourgeois specialists', the late 1920s also saw the criminalisation of fractional activities in the Party, and alleged deviations from the sinuous 'General Line' were identified with a negative stereotype which ended with the top leadership creating the image of an organised 'Right Opposition' which never existed in reality.[29] A succession of Party purges accustomed the membership to suspect wrongdoing by 'class-alien elements',[30] and this certainly helped to strengthen the conviction of cadres that the régime's ills had hardly anything to do with the mode of operation of the apparatus. This conviction must have been shaken by attacks against 'bigwigs, braggarts and petty tyrants' and on 'their disregard for the decisions of higher bodies'.[31] But the 'discovery' in June 1936 of widespread 'subversion' by former oppositionists must have reassured officials that the origins of the régime's problems would not be sought in the everyday work of the administration. Very soon, however, the pretexts of 'Trotskyism' or 'sabotage' could also be used to clamp down on cadres who had never belonged to the opposition, and whose eventual 'wrecking' consisted only in their working in accordance with the usual pattern of the apparatus.[32]

Difficult to believe as it seems today, the monstrous accusations of 'subversion', 'high treason' or 'conspiracy' against leading officials were not necessarily incredible in the 1930s, especially for insiders of the administration. They were likely to remember strictures like those of a secret circular of late 1927 that complained about the surfacing of confidential Party and government instructions in foreign capitals shortly after their enactment, a circular that also happened to find its way abroad. At the time the leaking of state secrets was attributed to oppositionists, and apparatchiki might also have known about an unsuccessful attempt to set up an oppositional 'bloc' in 1932. It was this 'bloc' that was referred to when the 'Trotskyist' threat was 'rediscovered'.[33] In all probability it was only from hearsay that most officials could learn something about Trotsky's attempts to mobilise followers in the early 1930s by sending postcards to the USSR.[34] On the other hand, a multitude of official documents and declarations mentioned 'anti-Party' groups of militants who were highly critical of the policies prevailing in the first years of the decade and among whom figured a certain number of leading cadres and former 'deviationists.[35] In one form or another, insiders were likely to have been acquainted with the call of one of these groups to remove the 'grave-digger of the Revolution', Stalin, or with rumours about the dissatisfaction of certain delegates of the Seventeenth Party Congress with Stalin and their intention to replace him.[36] And accustomed to reason according to the principle of analogy that was a cornerstone of the period's legal practice,[37] officeholders might be tempted to explain the régime's repressed problems in terms of similar phenomena.

Beyond these circumstances, the credibility of charges against 'wrecking' and 'conspiring' officials was certainly reinforced by the experience of those who were involved in the political processes of the 1930s. Many of them would have known about obscure manoeuvres, like an abortive attempt of the secret police in 1933–4 to stage a show trial.[38] They might wonder if similar machinations were behind the manifestly contradictory moves that followed Kirov's murder, when for about three weeks the authorities could not decide if the assassin had acted alone or in concert with a White plot or with the former Left Opposition, and nevertheless ordered the execution of dozens of people on the basis of a law that was promulgated in three versions within a week. Since it was finally decided that the murderer belonged to a 'leftist conspiracy', the mass shootings could not be taken even for retaliation, since their victims had been identified as White Guards. Insiders may have been even more bewildered by the inconsistency of the version implicating the Left Opposition, whose former leaders were originally cleared from suspicion and nonetheless slated for banishment, and ended up at a trial at which they were condemned to heavy prison terms, although they were not found guilty of being involved in the alleged plot.[39]

'Revelations' about 'conspiratory machinations' in high places were not entirely unbelievable for people who had some reason to suspect obscure intrigues among top policy-makers, and the number of such people must have been considerable in an apparatus that experienced notable political turnabouts at the time when organised 'wrecking' was 'discovered' in the Party-state. Changes in industrial policy could not go unnoticed for cadres who had been accused of 'sabotaging' Stakhanovism, before being officially cleared from suspicion[40] at the moment when 'Trotskyist subversion' became a major theme of the propaganda. A year after the noisy vigilance campaign that followed Kirov's assassination, it was decreed unlawful to discriminate and fire people solely on the grounds of an 'alien' or 'suspect' background and, in a striking departure from past practice, the Central Committee warned that the fact of having concealed one's social origin was not necessarily a sufficient reason for expulsion from the Party.[41] While these moves hardly squared with the drive against 'hidden Trotskyists', officeholders could see an obvious contradiction between the line mobilising merely a hunt for ex-oppositionists, and efforts to draw a profile of the 'enemy' that could apply to everyone answerable for any failure of the administration.

Constantly under the threat of finding themselves cast as scapegoats by those higher up the hierarchy, grassroots cadres were not necessarily reluctant to accept the idea that their superiors acted with ulterior motives. And, increasingly exposed to punishment for any deficiency in their administrations, leading officials were by no means impervious to the reasoning that the actions of unruly subordinates had brought about their misfortunes and that these actions proceeded from harmful intentions. Nevertheless, the metaphors of 'wrecking' and 'conspiracy' denoted more than pervasive suspicion within the apparatus. They expressed something that was well beyond the régime's official self-image: the fact that the political process consisted of behind-the-scenes intrigues to manipulate governmental mechanisms, and potentially unmanageable chain-reactions of manoeuvres and counter-moves with unforeseeable consequences. Ever since the 1920s Soviet politics had been characterised by intricate covert manoeuvring in the highest milieux.[42] But a new situation arose in the wake of collectivisation and industrialisation, when the 'decisive and exceptional' rôle of the administration and the extraordinary breadth of officialdom's responsibilities had a strong tendency to make obscure machinations of the entire apparatus inseparable from the régime's policies.

The only legitimate agency of decision-making and action, the Party-state ensured its predominance through trying to assume the direction of all essential activities of society. The everyday functioning of the administration had an immediate impact on the political process, even if this was by no means clear for those who happened to be involved in the petty intrigues of this or that institution, agency or locality. Irregular and uncontrollable working patterns brought disruptions whose agents were genuinely subversive from the point of view of the régime's quasi-military ideal of order, and the disorganisation and social conflicts their actions brought about represented a real threat to the efficiency, popularity and stability of the system. Attempts to impose control were in fact efforts to do away with politics as it had come to be practiced by the 1930s. The failure of these attempts was an integral part of the political process and liable to appear as the result of 'wrecking' and 'conspiracies', especially since control was entrusted to the very administration whose ills were to be cured and officialdom was not inclined to see these ills in the fact that it was accountable only to itself.

The system's logic appeared in the imagery of 'sabotage' and 'plots', so much so that it is questionable if insiders were able to keep entirely away from rationalising the régime's internal conflicts through the representation of a 'struggle' with 'enemies'. It is beyond reasonable doubt that this imagery was cynically manipulated by top politicians, who directly participated in the fabrication of 'proofs' against high-placed 'plotters',[43] and it is more than probable that a great number of dignitaries imitated their example at lower levels of the hierarchy. But even these people seem to have acted in order to avert something that appeared to them as the threat of potential 'conspiracy', be it in the form of their censure by dissenting militants or their attempted ouster at the Seventeenth Congress, in the form of the sheer existence, even at their places of exile and detention, of old oppositionists,[44] or in that of unpredictable machinations by rivals under the pretext of the 'fight' against 'subversion'.

While Bukharin could not help wondering if the high leadership believed Kamenev's 'monstrous [and] mean accusations' against him, he had no doubt about Kamenev's culpability, and reckoned with the possibility that Tomsky was also 'enmeshed' in his 'plot'.[45] People did know that they were not 'enemies' or 'conspirators'. On the other hand, they knew how disorderly the functioning of the régime was, and they also had information about all sorts of irregularities and abuses. The secretive character of dealings within the Party-state made the position and activities of one's colleagues uncertain, and therefore virtually anything could be supposed about anyone, especially about *a priori* 'suspect' people. like former oppositionists. These circumstances must have weighed heavily when a commission of the Central Committee found convincing statements by detainees against Bukharin and Rykov, and decided 'unanimously' to refer their affair to the secret police because of their alleged connivance with 'plotters'.[46]

Few members of this commission could have been unaware of the way in which such confessions were obtained. One of these people, P. P. Postyshev, was amongst those regional leaders whose apparatus suddenly 'discovered' that 'terrorist acts' had been in preparation against them at the time of the Kirov murder by 'counter-revolutionary groups' whose alleged participants were pressed to admit their 'guilt'.[47] Another member, V. Ya. Chubar', suspected a 'torrent of slander and intrigues by enemies of the people' when his turn came in the wake of denunciations he himself had helped to set in motion.[48] A third participant, R. I. Eikhe, headed a region that had distinguished itself in the launching of the purge: he too was presumably in danger after the 'evidence' given by the victims of a show trial.[49] He did not seem to doubt that people arrested with his sanction were 'real Trotskyists', even when he was already in the hands of the NKVD, though he maintained that their confessions against him had been dictated by 'conspiratorial' intentions and that other 'proofs' of his 'guilt' were 'dirty falsifications' of the interrogators.[50] His conviction was shared by a purged candidate member of the Politbureau, Ya. E. Rudzutak, who wanted to inform the Central Committee that 'there is in the NKVD an as yet unliquidated centre skilfully fabricating cases and forcing innocent people to admit crimes they did not commit'.[51]

It is hardly surprising if cadres 'discovered' that ' . . . what appeared . . . before to be occasional shortcomings in the work of the Party apparatus . . . were [in fact] a systematic subversive work conducted over the years [to achieve] the political corruption of the apparatus . . . [and] its transformation into a blind instrument . . . '.[52] Everything points to the assumption that, unable to deny their share of responsibility in measures contributing to the deterioration of the living conditions of the population, fallen officials were probably sincerely claiming to be ignorant of 'the behind-the-scenes life' of their 'unmasked' superiors and 'blind executants of the whole work of wrecking'.[53] Inexplicably contradictory directives became easily understandable as parts of the 'sabotage' that might be suspected even behind the overburdening of the courts by the purge.[54] Omnipresent as it appeared, 'subversion' was imputable to any officeholder, and since cadres were under heavy pressure to reveal culprits in their ranks, they did their best to deflect the offensive onto the most vulnerable: against people whose office or affiliations became *a priori* 'suspicious' in the new conditions and, as usual, against people whose past or personal relations furnished pretexts to designate them as 'hostile elements'.[55] Everyone could become 'suspect' virtually for anything, and the circumstances were ideal for settling old accounts, regardless of the consequences and often perhaps in anticipation of intrigues by rivals.

The manipulation of the purge and its unexpected turns had every chance to appear as the work of 'conspiracies', the more so since there was no difference between the muddled and confusing schemes to single out 'enemies' and the usual machinations of the apparatus. As zealous purgers were no less exposed to arrest than officials reluctant to hunt down 'wreckers', devout implementation of the rather uncertain 'line' was as likely to arouse suspicion as attempts to protect hard-pressed associates. Both tendencies could be detected in the actions of the high leadership, therefore people had good reason to feel reassured that they were following Moscow's policies, even if they happened to deviate from them at any particular moment. The understanding of the struggle against the régime's ills in terms of fighting 'subversion' amounted to taking the problems of the system for their solution. No wonder then that these problems were only aggravated in the wake of the purge. The threat intensified the activity of solidarity networks among cadres whose attempts to save each other reinforced the imagery of omnipresent 'plots'.[56] The overenthusiastic hunt for 'enemies' was often nothing more than the application of policies according to the momentary career interests of officials who purged the institutions under their jurisdiction in order to prove their political trustworthiness.[57] Energetic 'cleansing' could also be taken for 'wrecking', especially after January 1938 when the decimated Central Committee warned that the campaign was distorted by 'hostile' manoeuvres.[58]

There was scarcely any need to convince the population about the existence of 'subversive' activities among higher-ups. Allusions to acts of 'sabotage' by grassroots cadres were already multiplying in letters of complaint from peasants and workers at a time when the propaganda was still concentrating its fire merely on 'hidden Trotskyists'.[59] Routinely comparing their superiors to gendarmes or to the bosses of the Old Régime, and indignant to see that they were often shielded from prosecution by local potentates even when guilty of obviously criminal offenses,[60] ordinary citizens were inclined to suspect the authorities of the basest machinations. The masses were ready to attribute all the hardships of their working and living conditions to premeditated wrongdoing by officeholders, and even to demand the shooting of their 'wrecking' superiors.[61] The show trials seemed to suggest that 'it is impossible to trust Party members', though people could also believe that purged 'conspirators' wanted to 'liberate' peasants and workers.[62] Rumours about intricate scheming among top leaders[63] indicate that the turbulent events of 1936–8 convinced the public that everything was possible in high places. Where people were under constant threat of becoming victims of unpredictable reversals in the struggles between their superiors, and believed every Party member was a police spy, that 'the country is ruled by a small bunch of people',[64] politics could easily be seen in terms of conspiratorial intrigues.

Officialdom was also disposed to see clumsy 'cabals' among the population and was obsessed with its potentially 'hostile' acts. When, in the wake of the first 'revelations' about the 'Trotskyist threat', a group of workers wrote to a regional secretary that Kirov could be murdered only because of people like the managers of their factory, the addressee noted on their letter that it represented 'the enemy's method of discrediting the leadership'.[65] There was a remarkable tendency to look for 'subversive' intentions behind the reluctance of the masses to comply with official orders, especially in the rural world where the judiciary was regularly reminded that even negligent work could conceal 'wrecking' or 'counter-revolutionary' acts.[66] One of the most widespread manifestations of popular unruliness, theft of public property, was also declared a 'counter-revolutionary' crime and ascribed to 'enemies of the people'.[67]

Officialdom felt beleaguered by a hostile population whose unpredictable moves motivated local cadres to impose punishments for the use of 'indecent expressions' by their 'subjects' and to restrict their right to assemble or to enter and leave villages.[68] Received ideas about proletarian virtues prompted questions about the supposedly 'class-alien' origins of 'counter-revolutionary attitudes' among workers, for whom close surveillance was nevertheless strongly recommended in order to prevent their political troublemaking.[69] Kirov's assassination revealed a dark hatred toward high dignitaries: people often rejoiced at the killing and prophesied that others would follow, including that of Stalin.[70] In the following weeks an attempted murder of Stalin was persistently rumoured, so that the public believed that he had died when Kuibyshev's death was announced in a Leningrad theatre.[71] But it was far more than megalomaniac fear that dictated a nation-wide clampdown on 'counter-revolutionary expressions in connection with comrade Kirov's assassination'.[72] The population's respect for the system's most publicised symbol was in question, even ultimately, its loyalty to the state, especially in view of the pervasive war psychosis of the period and apparently frequent manifestations among the masses of a willingness to oppose the régime in case of armed conflict.[73] Simple citizens formed the overwhelming majority of the purge victims, subjected to wholesale repression in an increasingly chaotic and murderous attempt to root out the omnipresent danger of popular insubordination that coalesced with centrally-sponsored drive of the wholesale purge of 'former kulaks, members of anti-Soviet parties, White Guards, gendarmes and officials of tsarist Russia, bandits, returned émigrés, participants of anti-Soviet organisations, churchmen and sectarians [and] recidivist criminals'.[74]

There were many possibilities of 'unmasking enemies' among the masses. Nothing was easier than 'cleansing' *kolkhozes* and enterprises from people of allegedly 'kulak' background or from sons and daughters of 'class-alien elements', though such actions – whose victims were sometimes denounced to the police – could also hit 'disorganisers' of production who had a 'corrupting' effect on work discipline.[75] The number of these 'enemies' could be high since, taking advantage of the disarray of the purged apparatus, peasants worked less and less in the *kolkhoz,* illegally enlarged their household plots and avoided paying taxes and making compulsory food deliveries.[76] As the purge unfolded, workers began to defy cadres under the pretext that they were potential 'wreckers' and more and more often absented themselves from the enterprises.[77] Characteristically, calls intended to mobilise the judiciary to fight these practices pretended that they were encouraged by 'enemies of the people', and stopped short of imputing 'sabotage' to workers.[78]

The purge ended with a mobilisation drive to enforce harsh disciplinary and penal measures against workers and peasants.[79] No wonder then that a poll among wartime refugees showed that they were more likely than other social groups to characterise their work environment as 'hostile' or 'frightening'.[80] No wonder also that the powers-that-be felt threatened by the reaction of the masses who, when the war came, could feel betrayed by 'parasitic' bosses whose determination to save only their own skins seemed to confirm forebodings about the disastrous consequences of 'wrecking' and 'plots' of higher-ups.[81]

* * *

The imagery of omnipresent 'subversion' and 'conspiracy' denoted a dark feeling of suspicion and threat among leaders and led. This feeling did not necessarily appear as fear from a specific danger, and the underlying experience of anxiousness varied according to age, personal background and social status.[82] It nevertheless permeated the relationships of social categories to each other and to the régime. As social groups define themselves in their relations to each other and to the state, the representation of ubiquitous 'wrecking' and 'plots' revealed a strong inclination of officialdom and the masses alike to identify themselves as potential victims of impenetrable machinations.

Given the omnipresence of misgovernment and official abuse as well as that of the social tensions and political conflict they were inseparable from, the imagery of ubiquitous 'subversion' was by no means ungrounded. It seems difficult to escape the conclusion that the unpredictable, incomprehensible and treacherous daily reality of the system turned out to be a universe of omnipresent conspiracy. From the point of view of those who were inclined to see concerted action by a monolithic Party-state as the *primum movens* of the period's turmoil, it was natural to attribute every event and every twist and turn of the sinuous political line to the machinations of an all powerful centre and its supreme leader, whereas the work of a multitude of competing forces could be suspected by those who had doubts about the régime's ability to control and regiment everything.

In both cases, the representation of 'wrecking' and 'plots' located a paradigmatic feature of the entire system in merely one or some of its parts. The allegorisation of an ineffable evil that came to possess the life-world of every social category, the projection of the régime's elusively hostile universe in identifiable deeds and agents, tallied with traditional popular beliefs.[83] But such a projection could never have taken the form of 'sabotage' and 'conspiracies' without the régime's unwillingness to explain its problems in terms of the administration's ordinary working and social conflict, and it could hardly ever have had murderous consequences without officialdom's attempt to exorcise the system's ills through the use of an apparatus that happened to provoke and embody them. Collective representations of the omnipresent conspiracy were captive of the everyday reality of a system that became colonised by the Party-state's political practice and discourse.[84]

NOTES

The author wishes to express his gratitude to the Alexander von Humboldt Foundation whose generous support made this research possible.

1. Political Archive of the Foreign Office, Bonn (hereafter *PA,AA*) Abteilung Pol. XIII, Akten betreffend GPU-Funktionär Shigunow, pp. 175755, 176008, 176019, 176023, 176026–7.
2. Ibid., pp. 175760, 175770, 175779, 175796, 175925.
3. Ibid., p. 176023.
4. Ibid., pp. 175761–3, 175862, 175885, 175888.
5. Ibid., pp. 176009, 176022.
6. *PA, AA*, Abteilung Pol. XIII, Allgemeine Akten 12, Teil II, DIX 221: 'Vernehmung . . .', 23 September 1941, p. 2; Abteilung Pol. XIII, Allgemeine Akten 14: Document 409, p. 2. See also R. V. Ivanov-Razumnik, *Tiurmy i ssylki* (New York, 1953) p. 277 where, writing during the war, the author evokes 'Tukhachevskii's well-known conspiracy' and T–4908 of the Trotsky Papers about Moscow rumours of the summer of 1937 concerning the 'military plot'. (Quoted with the permission of the Houghton Library.)
7. *PA, AA*, Abteilung Pol. XIII, Allgemeine Akten 13, DIX 322: No. 147 149, 211, 213; Federal Archive, Koblenz (hereafter *BA*) NS 8, 226, p. 35.
8. K. Bailes, *Technology and Society under Lenin and Stalin* (Princeton 1978) pp. 69–121; H. H. Schröder, *Industrialisierung und Parteibüro*

kratie in der Sowjetunion (Berlin, 1988) pp. 216–30.
9. H. Kuromiya, *Stalin's Industrial Revolution* (Cambridge, 1988) pp. 292–4; Bailes, p. 280; Schröder, pp. 317–23.
10. *XVII S'ezd VKP (b)* (Moscow, 1934) pp. 33–5, 48, 532–3, 600–01; *KPSS v rezoliutsiiakh i resheniiakh s'ezdov, konferentsii i plenumov TsK,* vol V (Moscow, 1971) pp. 152–4, 159–160.
11. J. A. Getty, *Origins of the Great Purges – The Soviet Communist Party Reconsidered, 1933–1938* (Cambridge, 1985) pp. 58–91; L. H. Siegelbaum, *Stakhanovism and the Politics of Productivity in the USSR, 1935–1941* (Cambridge, 1988) pp. 99–144; G. T. Rittersporn, *Simplifications staliniennes et complications politiques* (Paris, 1988) pp. 49–69.
12. *Sobranie zakonov i rasporiazhenii Raboche-Krest'ianskogo Pravitel'stva SSSR* part I (hereafter *SZ*) (1934) pp. 465–6, (1935) pp. 613–14, 674–5.
13. *Sovetskaia iustitsiia* (hereafter *Slu*) (1934) No. 8, p. 3, No. 9, p. 25, No. 17, p. 22, (1935) No. 4, p. 17, No. 27, p. 2; *Sotsialisticheskaia zakonnost'/Za sotsialisticheskuiu zakonnost' (SZak)* (1934) No. 4, pp. 36, 39–41, No. 5, p. 11, No. 7, p. 37, No. 8, pp. 3, 31–2, No. 9, p. 44, No. 10, pp. 1–2, 28–30, 34, No. 11, pp. 48–9, No. 12, p. 48, (1935) No. 10, p. 64, *Ugolovnyi kodeks RSFSR* (hereafter *UK*) (Moscow, 1937) pp. 132, 138.
14. *Slu* (1934) No. 13, p. 13, (1935) No. 2, p. 2, No. 13, p. 5, No. 31, p. 15 (1936) No. 13, p. 5; *SZak* (1934) No. 10, p. 35 (1935) No. 5, pp. 58–9.
15. Smolensk Archive (hereafter *WKP, RS, 116/154e*) WKP 84, p. 42, WKP 176, p. 181, *WKP* 186, pp. 178–80.
16. *Bol'shevik* (hereafter *B*) (1936) No. 13, pp. 9, 12–13, No. 15, pp. 45–8; *Partiinoe stroitel'stvo* (hereafter *PS*) (1936) 8, p. 55, No. 14 pp. 52–3, 15, p. 36; *SZ* (1936) pp. 473–4; 'Ob iskliuchennykh iz partii . . . ', *Pravda* (hereafter *P*) 6 June 1936 p. 3; *116/154e*, pp. 44–9, 79–88.
17. *Slu* (1935) No. 10, pp. 1–2, No. 13, p. 5, No. 25, pp. 2–3, No. 27, p. 2 (1936) No. 6, p. 5, No. 13, p. 13, No. 27, pp. 7–8; *Szak* (1935) No. 5, pp. 7, 9–10, No. 6, pp. 5, 7.
18. *Slu* (1934) No. 19, p. 25 (1935) No. 5, pp. 24–5, No. 36, p. 3; *SZak* (1934) No. 12, p. 51 (1935) No. 2, pp. 59–60. See also note 13.
19. L. Viola, *The Best Sons of the Fatherland – Workers in the Vanguard of Soviet Collectivization* (Oxford, 1987) pp. 123–6.
20. *XVII S'ezd . . . ,* pp. 23, 153–4, 267–8, 289; 'O zapasnykh chastiakh . . .'; *P*, 16 June 1937, p. 2, 'O beloi zhesti . . .'; *P*, 17 June 1937, p. 3, 'Planovykh del mastera'; *P*, 1 July 1937, p. 3.
21. *PS* (1935) No. 13, pp. 44–5 (1936) No. 20, pp. 37–8, 47, No. 22, p. 48; *B* (1936) No. 6, pp. 76–7; 'O rabote upolnomochennykh KPK', *P*, 17 March 1936, p. 2.
22. *Vlast' sovetov* (hereafter *VS*) (1936) No. 9, pp. 8–9, No. 11, pp. 37–9, No. 16, pp. 23–4, (1937) No. 10, pp. 16–18; *Szak* (1934) No. 5, p. 11; *Slu* (1934) No. 13, pp. 9–10.
23. *Slu* (1934) No. 13, pp. 9–10, (1935) No. 16, p. 9, (1936) No. 27, p. 17, *Szak* (1934) No. 1, pp. 35–6, No. 5, p. 10, No. 7, p. 36; *WKP* 184, p. 16.
24. *XVII V S'ezd . . . ,* p. 34; *KPSS v rezoliutsiiakh . . . ,* pp. 152–3, 160.
25. *PS* (1934) No. 13, p. 3, No. 16, p. 48, No. 21, pp. 63–4, No. 22 pp. 3–4, (1935) No. 3, p. 47, No. 14, pp. 45–8.

26. R. W. Davies, *The Socialist Offensive – The Collectivisation of Soviet Agriculture 1929–1930* (London, 1980) p. 330; N. E. Zelenin, 'O nekotorykh "belykh piatnakh" zavershaiushchego etapa sploshnoi kollektivizatsii', *Istoriia SSSR* (1989) No. 2, pp. 11, 13–14; Viola, pp. 128–9.
27. Editorials *P,* June 8 and 16, 1935; *PS* (1935) No. 12, p. 10.
28. T. Kondrateva, *Bolcheviks et Jacobins* (Paris, 1989) pp. 113–70.
29. M. Reiman, *Die Geburt des Stalinismus* (Frankfort, 1979) pp. 42–70; Schröder, pp. 172–9.
30. Cf. the reasons for explusion during the 1929, 1933 and 1935 purges in Getty, pp. 47, 54, 83; Schröder, pp. 183, 345.
31. 'Kommunist i sovetskii zakon', *P,* 1 April 1936 p. 2, editorial, *P,* 9 May 1936.
32. Rittersporn, pp. 103–8, 120–31.
33. Reiman, pp. 244–5. For the 'bloc' see Getty, pp. 119–22; *Id.,* 'Trotsky in Exile: The Founding of the Fourth International', *Soviet Studies* (1986) No. 1, pp. 28–9; P. Broué, 'Trotsky et le bloc des oppositions de 1932' *Cahiers Léon Trotsky* (1980) No. 5, pp. 5–37.
34. Trotsky Papers, T-10248 (quoted by the permission of the Houghton Library).
35. R. W. Davies, 'The Syrtsov-Lominadze Affair', *Soviet Studies* (1981) No. 1, pp. 29–50; Schröder, pp. 320–2.
36. *Izvestiia TsK KPSS* (1989) No. 6, pp. 103–6; *Istoriia KPSS* (Moscow, 1963) p. 486; Schröder, pp. 325–6. For data casting doubt on rumours about the Seventeenth Congress, see *Izvestiia TsK KPSS* (1989) No. 7, pp. 114–21.
37. P. H. Solomon, *Soviet Criminologists and Criminal Policy* (New York, 1978) pp. 22–6.
38. For the relevant documents see *PA, AA* Botschaft Moskau, A 14d, Verhaftungen bei Controll Co.; Abt. IV Rußland, R15, Verhaftungen bei Angestellten der Controll Co. m. b. H. in Sowjetrußland and Strafverfolgung, Begnadigung, vol. 4.
39. Getty, *Origins* . . . pp. 209–10; G. T. Rittersporn, 'Soviet Politics in the 1930s', *Studies in Comparative Communism* (1986) No. 2, p. 112.
40. F. Benvenuti, 'Stakhanovism and Stalinism, 1934–38', *CREES Discussion Papers,* Series SIPS, No. 30, pp. 40–7; Siegelbaum, pp. 117–20, 127–35.
41. See note 16.
42. R. Service, *The Bolshevik Party in Revolution* (London, 1979) pp. 175–99; Reiman, pp. 118–71.
43. *Izvestiia TsK KPSS* (1989) No. 4, pp. 49, 51–5; pp. 71, 73–4, 76; No. 8, pp. 91–2; No. 9, pp. 36–9, 42.
44. Ibid. (1989) No. 5, p. 72; No. 6, pp. 112–15; No. 9, pp. 35–6.
45. See his letter to Voroshilov in D. Volkogonov, 'Triumf i tragediia', *Oktiabr'* (1988) No. 12, pp. 118–19.
46. *Izvestiia TsK KPSS* (1989) No. 5, pp. 79–81, 84.
47. See two documents quoted to this effect in Volkogonov, pp. 52–3.
48. Ibid., p. 159.
49. Rittersporn, *Simplifications* . . . , pp. 121–3.
50. Volkogonov, p. 161; *Izvestiia TsK KPSS* (1989) No. 3, p. 141.

51. Volkogonov, pp. 161–2; *Izvestiia TsK KPSS* (1989) No. 3, p. 142. The two editions reproduce this document and Eikhe's letter in slightly different wording.
52. *WKP* 392, pp. 96–7; *WKP* 103, p. 126.
53. *WKP* 109, pp. 67, 72; *WKP* 321, pp. 194–5.
54. *WKP* 103, p. 133, *Slu* (1937) No. 8, pp. 11, 16; No. 23, pp. 37–8.
55. Rittersporn, *Simplifications* . . . , pp. 173–91.
56. 'Dela sverdlovskogo obkoma', *P*, 22 May 1937, p. 4; 'K chemu privodit politicheskaia slepota', *P*, 31 May 1937, p. 2; 'Dela krasnoiarskogo kraikoma', *P*, 11 July 1937, p. 2; 'Vragi i ikh pokroviteli', *P*, 17 July 1937, p. 3; *B* (1937) No. 14, pp. 5–8; *PS* (1937) No. 15, pp. 40–3; *WKP* 111, pp. 229, 151–2, 176; *WKP* 163, p. 131, *WKP* 321, p. 165.
57. Rittersporn, *Simplifications* . . . , pp. 191–2.
58. *KPSS v rezoliutsiiakh* . . . , pp. 303–12.
59. *WKP* 195, p. 182; *WKP* 197, pp. 77, 89, 230; *WKP* 355, p. 220.
60. *WKP* 195, pp. 52, 182; *WKP* 197, pp. 77, 89, 230; *WKP* 201, p. 246; *WKP* 355, p. 187.
61. *WKP* 195, pp. 21–3.
62. *WKP* 87, p. 6, *WKP* 199, pp. 46, 55.
63. See e.g. *PA, AA,* Botschaft Moskau, A2c Innere Politik der UdSSR (Verwaltung . . .): the embassy to the Foreign Office, 28 September 1936; Pol. Abt. V. Po. 5 Ukraine, Innere Politik . . . , vol. 1: the Kiev consulate to the embassy, 1 April 1937, pp. 1–2; Botschaft Moskau, A4 Militär- und Marineangelegenheiten, vol. 6: telegrams of the embassy to the Foreign Office, 11 and 12 June 1937; Pol. Abt. V Po. 5 Rußland, Innere Politik . . . , vol. 3: 'Lagebericht', 7 July 1937, p. 3, vol. 5: v. Tippelskirch to v. Welck, 10 January 1938; Pol. Abt. V Po. 7 Ministerien, Rußland: v. Tippelskirch to Schliep, 1 August 1938.
64. *WKP* 87, p. 7; *WKP* 199, p. 72.
65. *WKP* 355, p. 114.
66. *Slu* (1934) No. 8, p. 3 (1935) No. 11, p. 33, No. 20, p. 24; *SZak* (1934) No. 4, p. 41, No. 11, p. 48, No. 12, p. 48 (1935) No. 2, p. 63; *UK* pp. 135, 138–9.
67. *SZ* (1932) pp. 583–4; *Slu* (1935) No. 5, pp. 2–3, No. 13, p. 3; *SZak* (1937) p. 3; I. V. Stalin, *Sochineniia*, vol. XIII (Moscow, 1951) pp. 207–12.
68. *Slu* (1935) No. 13, p. 5; *VS* (1936) No. 16, p. 24; *SZak* (1938) No. 3, p. 125, No. 6, p. 12.
69. *WKP* 87, p. 7; *WKP* 109, pp. 19, 21, 36.
70. *WKP* 109, p. 73; *WKP* 252, pp. 37–40; *WKP* 316, pp. 6–7; *WKP* 352, p. 115; *WKP* 415, pp. 22, 132; *RS* 921, pp. 133, 294.
71. *PA, AA,* Abt. IV Ru. Po. No. 3, Rußland, Personalien . . . vol. 5: the Leningrad consulate to the embassy, 26 January 1935.
72. *Slu* (1935) No. 18, p. 10.
73. *RS* 921, pp. 294, 300; *WKP* 199, p. 46; *WKP* 362, p. 340; *PA, AA* Botschaft Moskau, A2 Innerpolitische Verhältnisse . . . vol 8: the Kiev consulate to the embassy, 10 April 1935; Botschaft Moskau A2a, UdSSR – Parteiwesen: 'Politischer Bericht', 4 July 1935, pp. 2–3; Botschaft Moskau A24e, Zweifelhafte Persönlichkeiten . . . vol. 2: letter in Russian received on 30 December 1936; Botschaft Moskau, A39b Jahres-

und Halbjahresberichte . . . Charkow: the consulate to the embassy, 12 January 1937, p. 11 and 10 June 1937, p. 14; *BA*, NS 43, 17, p. 533.
74. For the relevant directive dated July 1937 and stipulating that the 'most hostile . . . [of these] elements' had to be shot while others were to be sentenced to long terms of detention, see *Izvestiia TsK KPSS* (1989) No. 10, pp. 81–2.
75. See e. g. *WKP* 516, pp. 2–77, in particular pp. 12–13, 22, 27, 39, 41, 45, 47, 55, 57.
76. *VS* (1938) No. 10–11, pp. 52–3, editorials, *P*, 17 April and 12 August 1938; *Istoriia KPSS*, t. 4, kniga 2-ia (Moscow, 1971) p. 428; *Istoriia SSSR s drevneishikh vremen do nashikh dnei*, vol 9 (Moscow, 1971) p. 352.
77. Editorials, *P*, 29 April, 11 May, 24 June, and 14 and 25 August 1937; *SZ* (1937) p. 246; *B* (1937) No. 16, p. 19, No. 19, p. 7.
78. *Slu* (1938) No. 17, pp. 10, 12; *B* (1938) No. 23–4, p. 10; 'Lishit' lodyrei . . .', *P*, 14 December 1938, p. 3; 'Komandiry proizvodstva i trudovaia distsiplina', *P*, 25 December 1938, p. 2.
79. Rittersporn, *Simplifications* . . . , pp. 296–8.
80. A. Rossi, *Generational Differences in the Soviet Union* (New York, 1980) pp. 216–19, 228–30.
81. *PA, AA*, Abteilung Pol. XIII, Allgemeine Akten 13, DIX 322: No. 120.
82. R. W. Thurston, 'Fear and Belief in the USSR's "Great Terror": Response to Arrest 1935–1939', *Slavic Review* (1986) No. 2, pp. 213–34; R. A. Bauer, A. Inkeles, C. Kluckhohn, *How the Soviet System Works* (Cambridge, Mass., 1956) pp. 178–9; A. Inkeles, R. A. Bauer, *The Soviet Citizen* (Cambridge, Mass, 1959) pp. 23, 108, 245; Rossi, pp. 184, 186, 217, 229, 239, 324.
83. M. Lewin, *The Making of the Soviet System: Essays in the Social History of Interwar Russia* (New York, 1985) pp. 275–6, 310.
84. For a similar impact of élite concepts and practices on popular beliefs and behaviour see N. Cohn, *Europe's Inner Demons* (London, 1975) pp. 225–55; R. Kieckfeber, *European Witch Trials* (London, 1976) pp. 73–92.

6 Soviet Peasants and Soviet Literature
Alec Nove

One could write a whole book about the so-called *derevenshchiki* (village writers), authors who, often themselves of peasant origin, have the peasant cause close to their hearts. Misha Lewin is no more of peasant origin than I am, but his own interest in the fate of the peasantry has inspired some of his best pages, and it is a pleasure and an honour to contribute to celebrating his achievements. This contribution is not as long or as scholarly as its author would like, but time, alas, is a scarce commodity, even after retirement.

In my view, the literature on peasants can be divided broadly into two parts, corresponding to two distinct periods, which in turn correspond to what was and is permissible. The first is typified by critical comments on the state of the peasants today, or in the day the sketches or stories or reportage were written. The second looks back at history, especially collectivisation and the *raskulachivanie* (the dispossession of the *kulaks*).

It all began with V. Ovechkin and his astonishing (for its time) *Rayonnye budni* ('Daily Life in the Country'), published in 1952.[1] The astonishing thing is its date: Stalin was still on his throne. Yet here was a bitter criticism of the so-called Borzovs, thick-necked table-thumping party secretaries for whom the state's needs are everything, peasant interests nothing. He followed it with *Trudnaya vesna* ('A Difficult Spring'), raising the question of what a good and well-meaning party secretary *ought* to be doing. By then Khrushchev was in the saddle, and agriculture became high-priority. Unfortunately, Khrushchev's methods involved campaigns run by local party officials, often in disregard of peasant interests and even of common sense. There were the virgin lands, two-stage harvesting, maize, the fight against grasses, peat-compost pots, and so on. To their discredit, the specialist journals, economic and agrarian, praised official policy and published very little critical material. To their credit, the *derevenshchiki* did. The literary journals became the primary published source on what was going wrong.

Indeed, Alexander Yashin boldly satirised the rural party itself, in

121

his *Rychagi* ('Levers'), published in *Literaturnaya Moskva* (2nd series) in 1956. A group of people is shown in relaxed conversation, freely criticising various errors and omissions, but as soon as they are called to order in their capacity as members of the village party group they at once make routine speeches in what the French call *langue de bois*. His short story *Vologodskaya svad'ba* ('A Vologda Wedding'), published in 1962, painted a realistic picture of village life in northern Russia, to the evident annoyance of officialdom.

Officialdom also had every reason to be annoyed by the talented Fedor Abramov. Already in 1954 he wrote highly critically of the false and over-favourable representation of the peasantry in works published since the war.[2] His excellent short story *Vokrug da okolo* ('Here and There') raised basic questions about the position of the peasant in the *kolkhoz*, and about the *kolkhoz* management vis-a-vis party officials; thus the peasants found good reasons for not partici- pating in haymaking unless and until they were promised a larger share of the hay (though the bureaucrats did not allow for this), and the low status of the passportless peasant was, for the first time, openly commented upon. Abramov later wrote some first-class novels on rural themes (eg *Bratya i sestry* ('Brothers and Sisters'), *Dve zimy i tri leta* ('Two Winters and Three Summers')), and died in 1983 a highly respected writer.

Also noteworthy in the Khrushchev years was the work of Efim Dorosh, especially his *Derevenskii dnevnik* ('A Country Diary'), which appeared in 1958, and which presented a bold challenge to bureaucratic campaigning methods, pointing to their negative effects both on efficiency and on the peasants as human beings. These and other authors showed up various excesses of official zeal, such as ploughing up growing clover in order to be able to report a reduction in the area of sown grasses, even though there was no alternative use for that land. The disease was described as *vodka i svodka*, the latter being the term describing the report sent upwards.

Of course Solzhenitsyn cannot be classed as a *derevenshchik*, but the publication in 1963 of his short story *Matryonin dvor* ('Matryo- na's Home') none the less requires a mention in the present context, for its powerful and moving picture of the peasant woman, her sufferings and her morality.

In 1966 Boris Mozhaev published his *Iz zhizni Fedora Kuzkina* ('From the Life of Fedor Kuzkin'), which got him into trouble for his too-realistic portrayal of the peasant as a man with no rights.

So it can be said that, despite censorship obstacles, the *derevensh-*

chiki did their duty, publicising many of the real problems. Sadly, their efforts proved largely in vain. Occasional good resolutions did nothing to change the *modus operandi* of rural bureaucracy. Indeed Ovechkin once attempted suicide in despair.

Gradually, even in the Brezhnev years, the problems of the village came to be discussed as such, without any 'literary' disguise. It is particularly worth praising the excellent book by Yu. Arutyunian about the Soviet peasantry in the war, which told us a great deal about their sacrifices and miserable life in 1941–5.[3] Several economists strongly criticised aspects of the contemporary scene. Needless to say, no direct attack was permitted under Brezhnev on the *sovkhoz* and *kolkhoz* system as such, but newspapers and periodicals published an increasing range of materials on various defects and distortions: poor-quality machinery, lack of spare parts, delivery of unwanted material inputs, detailed orders from above about sown area, numbers of livestock, what crops to sow and when, and so forth. The authors were frequently practical men, including farm managers. The coming of Gorbachev and *glasnost* brought with it the possibility of generalisation about the system itself. Here is just one sample of what become permissible, taken from a letter published in the paper for rural youth, *Sel'skaya molodezh'*, in December 1987:

It seems to me that some do not understand the situation that has arisen in agriculture . . . Millions of people have abandoned their villages and have gone to town, where they live in hostels, wallowing in sorrow and in drink. Those who remain in the villages are in a still worse state. The land is no longer theirs. They are not peasants any more, they are just *batraki*. Where is it known for a *batrak* to work well on someone else's land and wish to have children? What for? So they too should be *batraki*? What is the consequence of the fact that today the land is controlled not by those who work on it but by officials, bureaucrats? Our agriculture is 3–5 times behind America. I consider that the granting of land to the peasants is the most vital and immediate task. It would be as significant as were in their time the abolition of serfdom and the agrarian revolution. One must save the peasants from final degradation and rural officials from nervous and mental breakdown, or else they will fall victim to the most clumsy, chaotic and senseless agricultural policy. Whence the panic fear to resemble capitalism? Did not Marx say that private property was to be transcended not forbidden?

Meanwhile the literary men turned more to the past, to the tragic history of the peasantry under Stalin. We know that Khrushchev's 'destalinisation' never touched either collectivisation or the fate of the *kulaks*. The team headed by Danilov in the Institute of History (Ivnitskii, Bogdanov, Moshkov, Vyltsan) did try to tell the truth about these brutal times, but was silenced, and a bland version (a few excesses, but basically it was all correct and successful) was imposed by the dreary ideologist S. P. Trapeznikov. However, a few literary men were able to turn to the theme even before the coming of *glasnost*.

The first, to my knowledge, was Ivan Stadnyuk, in his novel *Lyudi ne angely* ('People are not Angels'), published in 1962. This was the more surprising because Stadnyuk appeared to be a 'stalinist', as can be seen from his basically apologetic novel *Voina* ('War'). But there he was, as early as 1962, writing of the ruthless state procurements which left the cultivators with no land. His example was not followed (or the censorship refused to allow it to be followed) for many years. The pages of Vasilii Grossman's *Vse techet* ('Everything Flows'), painting a most harrowing picture of the coercion and the famine, were published only in the West (in 1970) though 'full' publication was promised in the USSR in 1990.

S. Zalygin's *Na Irtyshe* ('On the Irtysh'), published in 1964, contained a vivid and critical view of *raskulachivanie*. Tvardovskii's *Po pravu pamyati* ('By Virtue of Memory') recalled his own family's deportation. Written in the late sixties, it was not then published; it appeared in 1987, after his death.[4]

Among novels which were able to refer to the famine and were published before *glasnost*, there was also M. Alekseyev's *Drachuny* ('The Brawlers'), published in 1982 (though the same author had earlier written favourably of collectivisation).

Typical of the *glasnost* period is not only the appearance (at last!) of specialist work by historians, and articles by many authors denouncing forcible collectivisation and the mass deportation,[5] but also the belated publication of works previously banned, such as the exceptionally vivid semi-autobiographical stories by V. Tendryakov.[6] Tendryakov describes *raskulachivanie* and the famine in some shatteringly realistic pages. One must also welcome the publication of Andrei Platonov's *Kotlovan* ('The Pit'), set at the time of collectivisation.[7]

By 1989 there was almost a consensus: collectivisation was brutal and coercive, *raskulachivanie* deprived the village of able and energetic peasants, the famine carried off millions of lives – and it was a man-made famine. A few voices still argued that in the circumstances it had been a necessary or inescapable tragedy.[8] But to pursue this argument would take us wide of the theme of the present paper.

I will end with a brief analysis of two authors' views of what had occured in those years: B. Mozhaev and V. Belov.[9] To their credit, they do paint a realistic picture of the sufferings of the peasantry in the thirties and subsequently. However, when it comes to discussing 'who is to blame', they both want to succumb to the temptation of blaming it on – the Jews. Thus, Mozhaev specifically assigns responsibility to Trotsky, Kamenev and Kaganovich, though the first two have evident alibis.[10] Belov did note that it was Stalin who was in power, but stated that 'in my opinion Trotsky's ideas triumphed after 1928. Unbearable taxes and levies, confiscation . . . , repression, arrests, shootings, this is what Trotskyism [sic] meant for millions of peasant families! . . . In my view the chief Trotskyist was Stalin'.[11] In his novel he adds another (Jewish) villain, Yakovlev, who was indeed commissar for agriculture in 1930. While showing Stalin to be hostile to the peasants, he leaves the reader with the impression that Stalin was subject to some sort of blackmail on the part of those (Trotskyists?) who knew of his past links with the *Okhrana*, the tsarist secret police, and that they somehow used this power to make Stalin take an even more harsh line than that suggested by Yakovlev. One of Belov's characters suggests that the inspirers of revolution and counter-revolution are of some 'special breed', and that the struggle was not in fact a class struggle at all, but 'national or maybe religious. We are divided and they rule. And anyone who comes to know this, believe me, will again be shot'. Collectivisation was imposed by whom? 'Who directs all this devil's sabbath? Who has conquered our country? . . . Are we again under the yoke?'[12] It is in such a context that the reader sees graphic descriptions of the processes and brutalities of *raskulachivanie*.

Protests against such an interpretation have come from I. Klyamkin, and also from A. Turkov.[13] But Belov sticks to his guns. In his latest *Novyi mir* story he seems to be suggesting that collectivisation had been forced on Stalin by some sort of undefined judaeomasonic conspiracy.

Far be it from me to assert that this is typical. There is a lively debate, including in academic circles, on such matters as 'were there real kulaks in 1928?',[14] how many died in the famine,[15] and much else. There is, however, a neo-Slavophil current which, while blaming

Stalinism for destroying traditional peasant culture, seek to affix blame on *inorodtsy* (aliens), a tendency from which Solzhenitsyn is not altogether free.

However, one can only welcome the greater freedom of expression, whether this be by economists, literati, officials or the peasants themselves. There is no more need to disguise critical thoughts in Aesopian language. Those who believe that the future lies with private family farming can freely say so, and argue with those who hold different views. There is no 'party line' any more. For this at least we should be thankful.

NOTES

1. *Novyi mir*, 1952, No. 9.
2. *Novyi mir*, 1954, No. 3.
3. *Sovetskoe krestyanstvo v gody velikoi otechestvennoi voiny* (Moscow 1970).
4. *Znamya*, 1987, No. 2.
5. For example, R. Medvedev in *Sobesednik*, 1988, No. 18; Yurii Afanasiev in *Literaturnaya Rossiya*, 17 June 1988; G. Shmelev in *Oktyabr*, 1988, No. 2.
6. *Novyi mir*, 1988, No. 3.
7. *Novyi mir*, 1987, No. 6.
8. Notably I. Klyamkin in *Novyi mir*, 1987, No. 11.
9. For example, their works published in *Don*, 1987, No. 3 and *Novyi mir*, 1987, No. 8, and Belov's extraordinary series *Kanuny* in *Novyi mir*, 1987, No. 8; 1989, No. 3.
10. In his postface in *Don*.
11. *Pravda*, 15 April 1988.
12. *Novyi mir*, 1989, No. 3, pp 12, 24, 27.
13. *Druzhba narodov*, 1988, No. 4.
14. See the debate between Danilov and Tikhonov in *Istoriya SSSR*, 1989, No. 3.
15. *Voprosy istorii*, 1989, No. 4 (letter from V. Tsaplin).

7 Masters of the Shop Floor: Foremen and Soviet Industrialisation
Lewis H. Siegelbaum

Addressing the Eighth Congress of Trade Unions in December 1928, M. I. Tomskii, the soon-to-be-ousted chairman of the trade unions' central council, referred to a recent incident at the Leningrad Skorokhod shoe factory. There, a foreman had been shot and killed by a worker. This act, he said, might be attributed to the 'abnormal' and 'hooligan' nature of the worker, but such an explanation was too simplistic and clichéd. In his view, what was responsible for this and similar 'unhealthy and shameful' occurrences of recent times was the 'uncultured' and 'rude' behavior of foremen and the unions' failure to intervene in relations between foremen and workers.[1]

Tomskii's interpretation appears well-founded. Over the previous few years, the press had reported numerous instances of foremen establishing or perpetuating 'old régime' relations with workers. They demanded bribes in the form of money, vodka and sexual favours in return for preferential job assignments; they compelled workers to work on the side for them, using the factory's equipment; they placed their unqualified relatives in high wage-skill categories; they threatened workers with demotion or dismissal if the latter complained or in other ways challenged their authority, and in several cases, made good their threats. Far from attempting to put a stop to these outrageous acts, some factory and shop committee chairmen willingly served as accomplices.[2] Some workers were moved to respond in kind. The incident at Skorokhod was only one of several reported by the press.[3]

At the same time, however, the press had been critical of other actions by foremen, actions that belie their image as the tyrants of the shop floor. From Kolomna it was reported that before Easter and other holidays, foremen assigned workers to better paying and easier tasks, that, being 'insufficiently independent in their relations with workers', they were indulgent with them and were thus guilty of 'tailism'.[4] At Krasnoe Sormovo, foremen were said to be too lenient with absentees, compensating them with overtime work, while at Krasnaia Oborona in Moscow, they took a 'conciliatory' attitude toward drunkenness among workers.[5] Workers in their turn could be indulgent toward foremen. At a production conference in the Stenka Razin glassworks (Nizhnii Novgorod *guberniia*), workers argued that it was not the foremen but the higher administration that was responsible for the high proportion of defective goods.[6] And in a letter to *Trud*, a worker from Krasnoe Sormovo defended a foreman against the charge of carelessness, claiming that all the sins of the administration were wrongly placed on him.[7]

How are we to reconcile these two diametrically opposed images of foremen? If it was not merely a function of different personality types, we must seek to explain why foremen were brutes toward workers in certain circumstances and their allies in others. To do this, we first need to appreciate the intermediate position that foremen occupied in the Soviet industrial hierarchy.

Like their counterparts in the capitalist world and in Russia before 1917, Soviet foremen were Marx's 'sergeants of an industrial army.' They were the 'non-coms' who partially bridged the gap between management and rank-and-file workers, between 'the demands for maximum output and the need to maintain social relations with those under [them], between accommodation and legitimation'.[8] From the dawn of the factory age, which in Russia's case can be dated from the 1880s, foremen both facilitated the formal subjection of labour to capital and made difficult management's real control over the labour process. Only with the managerial revolution of the late nineteenth and early twentieth centuries could supervision be placed on a more rational basis. Instead of foremen's determination of job tasks, skill levels and appropriate pay, 'the skilled engineer was now actively involved – as pacemaker and technical supervisor – in the work of management'.[9]

This revolution did not triumph everywhere or soon. Worker resistance, both active and passive, slowed it down, as did the costs involved in expanding the white collar work force. Yet, from the employers' point of view, the advantages of adopting bureaucratic and technical forms of control increasingly outweighed their problems. Those firms that adopted rationalisation measures often gained a competitive edge that spurred on others to imitate and experiment with their own. All the while, the functions, flexibility and authority of foremen in the Western industrial nations were being reduced. They too became subjected to a division of labor that parcellised their responsibilities, at the same time as it narrowed the interstices between management and labor.

Explaining why no such fate befell Soviet foremen in the inter-war period is the central *problématique* of this article. That Soviet industrialisation deviated from capitalist experience in this respect may seem surprising, given the extensive borrowing of Western models of management and technology.[10] It was not for lack of trying that the Soviet authorities failed to put foremen and their relations with workers on a more 'modern' footing. Like their Western counterparts, Soviet foremen found themselves, at least in the early stages of industrialisation, 'between Taylorism and technocracy'. They, and the workers they supervised, were also subjected to the political imperatives demarcated by the Communist party. The survival of foremen's traditional powers therefore suggests that what Michael Burawoy has called 'the politics of production', not only had a different outcome in the USSR, but were played by different rules.[11]

THE FOREMAN'S EMPIRE CHALLENGED

'Foreman' is a notoriously difficult term to define, mainly because the difference in function between those bearing the title and other supervisory personnel is often purely semantic. The problem of definition is compounded by the existence of different degrees of hierarchy within separate branches of industry, or, depending on the size of an enterprise and its constituent shops, within the same industry. Thus, a shop foreman in one enterprise could be referred to as a shop supervisor in another; a gang boss in construction or mining might be an overseer or assistant foreman in a larger metalworks shop, whereas in smaller establishments, a less elaborate hierarchy may not permit such intervening categories between foremen and manual workers.[12]

While by no means peculiar to Soviet Russia, the terminological confusion in that country has certain unique features owing to the survival of indigenous pre-capitalist or at least pre-industrial terms ('elder,' *nadsmotrshchik, desiatnik, prorab*), those borrowed from other languages (*master, ober-master, shteiger*), and certain generic and syncretic terms, usually of military provenance, which took on peculiar meanings in the Soviet industrial context (*brigadir, podmaster, kadr spetsialist, malyi komandir*, and even *srednyi administrativno-tekhnicheskii personal*). The coexistence of all these terms,

each with their own specificities and nuances, reflected the multitude
of organisational patterns, managerial strategies and ideological constructs that bore on both the formal definition of foremen's responsibilities and their real power on the shop floor. It is also worth noting
that terminology had an important relational dimension. For
example, whether foremen were to be classified among engineering-
technical personnel (ITR) seems to have depended on the referent
group. If it was only technicians and engineers, then foremen were
excluded; but in distinguishing them from manual workers, foremen
were often included among the 'specialists'.

At the risk of overgeneralizing, it can be said that as of the
mid-1920s, foremen occupied the lowest rung on the managerial
hierarchy, being subordinate to shop supervisors (*nachal'niki tsekha*)
and exercising full (*polnopravnye*) powers of supervision over manual workers. This arrangement formally owed its existence to the
'Bolshevik' principle of *edinonachalie*, but in fact was little different
from the pre-revolutionary factory régime.[13] Even if foremen were
typically nominated by the trade unions' factory committees, the
qualities of a good foreman in a Soviet enterprise were identical to
those that comprised competence before the revolution.

Essentially, he – there very few forewomen even in industries with
a predominantly female workforce – had to match job tasks (*nariady*)
to available workers, ensure that the appropriate equipment was in
working order and that supplies of power, tools, spare parts and raw
and semi-finished materials were adequate, understand technical
processes sufficiently to be able to impart his knowledge to new
workers or trainees and evaluate the performance of his charges, and
mete out sanctions to workers who violated labour discipline and
rewards to those who overfulfilled their quotas. Notwithstanding the
creation of planning departments, labour economics sections and
rates and norm bureaus within some Soviet enterprises, the overwhelming majority of foremen were expected to fulfill all of these tasks.

In doing so, they could rely on intermediaries who combined
manual labour with supervision and usually received some compensa-
tion over and above their nominal wage. Traditionally known in
manufacturing industry as *masterovye*, these skilled or senior workers
took the title of *brigadiry*, a term that is probably of civil war vintage.
In mineral and peat extraction as well as the construction industry,
where the labour force was more fluid and seasonal, the pre-
revolutionary term, *starshii*, persisted as did the group of workers, the
artel', over which the elder presided. Agreements between foremen

and elders were commonly on a task rather than time basis, the task being known as *akkordnaia rabota*. Wages were paid to the artel and distributed by the elder out of the common 'pot'.[14]

Although foremen enjoyed broad discretion and in the eyes of many workers appeared to be a law unto themselves, they were in act restrained by rules and procedures to a degree that was unknown before the revolution. For a start, there was the enterprise triangle, consisting of management, the party cell and the trade union committee. One of the functions of the latter two was to head off trouble between workers and line supervisors by inviting and investigating complaints and sponsoring production conferences at which grievances could be aired. While many a party organiser and trade union committee chairman colluded with management, this was not always the case. Mention should also be made of the enterprise Rates and Conflict Commissions (RKK) and arbitration boards which routinely took up alleged violations of collective agreements, and of worker-correspondents who shed the light of publicity on the misconduct of foremen and other shop floor personnel.[15]

Even more of a constraint were the bureaucratic procedures that foremen had to follow in carrying out their daily functions – confirming the list of workers reporting for work, recording on the work order the amount of work done and the time it required, and assigning skill levels (*razriady*) to workers and tasks in accordance with industry-wide manuals. Of course, the latitude for circumventing such procedures and doctoring the records could be considerable. But from the mid-1920s, Soviet foremen were confronted with a still more serious challenge to their autonomy and status. This was scientific management, or in its Soviet version, NOT, the scientific organisation of labour.

Typically, NOT has been regarded by Western scholars as a means of increasing pressure on workers to speed up their pace of production, which correspondingly provoked intense opposition among the older, highly-skilled stratum. This was the case, but NOT had a broader agenda and its opponents were not exclusively skilled workers. Most closely identified with Alexei Gastev and the Central Institute of Labour (TsIT) over which he presided, NOT actually encompassed a range of principles and procedures that extended far beyond the activities of that body and its provincial affiliates. As Samuel Lieberstein noted over a decade ago, NOT seemed to provide a pragmatic recipe for overcoming Russian backwardness, a relatively painless way of catching up to and overtaking the advanced capitalist countries.[16] As such, it was embraced by many engineers and the planning establishment with a passion reminiscent of a cult or religion. Its totems – precision of measurement and technique, standardisation, and specialisation – were the constituent elements of a productivist utopia that was the very antithesis of Soviet reality.

Instead of relying on rule-of-thumb methods to determine how machines should be used and what could be gotten out of them, NOT offered the 'passport,' a card attached to each machine on which was written its specifications, optimal speed of operation, and so forth. Instead of basing output norms on approximations of workers' everyday performance (or worse still, what was needed for workers on piece rates to exceed the wages of those paid on an hourly or shift basis), it introduced and celebrated time and motion analysis via the stop watch and camera. And, in place of on-the-job training or that offered by the factory apprentice schools, it redefined and simplified occupations so that they could be learned in two-month courses run by the Central Institute of Labour.

NOT, then, constituted an ambitious program that entailed not only the reorganisation of labour, but that of management as well. Indeed, the latter was a prerequisite for the former and nowhere more so than at its lower levels. It was, after all, foremen who had employed rule-of-thumb methods in determining how machines should be used, what constituted appropriate output norms, and how workers should be trained. Consequently, it was foremen whose job profile was to be radically redefined.

INSTRUKTAZH AND *USTANOVKA*

To take up the matter of training first, Gastev was fond of quoting from his spiritual mentors, Taylor and Gilbreth, to the effect that 'the main difficulty in applying the scientific organisation of labor consists in the struggle against old methods of training'. Writing in early 1924, he recalled that 'When Taylor began to apply his ideas of organising a functional system of management, he immediately came up against the lack of appropriately trained foremen . . . . He himself began to prepare and teach foremen who could work according to his plan'.[17] If Taylor and his disciples found American foremen lacking in this respect, their Soviet counterparts were worse. Gastev repeatedly railed against the 'harsh bellowing', 'overbearing' attitude and 'boasting' of foremen, which, he claimed, masked their lack of talent.[18] What was required was to train foremen in the art of instruction – *instruktazh* – the key to which was the correct positioning (*ustanovka*) of workers.

These terms were a kind of incantation for Gastev. No aspect of TsIT's work consumed as much of his attention as the production of instructional cards to be used by 'instructors' in training workers. By employing such cards, Gastev insisted, what would otherwise have taken five to seven years of traditional apprenticeship or at least a year in a factory apprentice school, could be accomplished in a few months and at a fraction of the cost.[19] The argument was sufficiently convincing to garner for the Institute's share company (named, incidentally, 'Ustanovka') contracts from the Commissariat of Labour and several unions for the training of some 10,000 unemployed workers in the metal trades. By the early 1930s, TsIT's instructional cards or those based on its methods had become an important feature of the Soviet industrial scene. Summing up fifteen years of the Institute's activities, Gastev could claim (in 1936) that some 20,000 instructors, controllers and consultants had used the cards to train over 500,000 skilled workers in more than 200 occupations.[20] Unquestionably, many of these 'instructors' were foremen, who themselves had been trained at TsIT 'bases.' But not only foremen were encouraged to administer *instruktazh*. Brigade leaders were as well, and, in the guise of *sheftsvo* and Izotovite schools, so too were skilled workers.[21]

The standardisation and democratisation of vocational training, based on engineers' appropriation of technical specifications and job profiles, constituted a potential threat to the foremen's empire. That the threat was never actualised can be explained by several factors. First, *instruktazh* was administered selectively, concentrating on semi-skilled assembly-line work in the metal trades, certain occupations in the textiles industry and construction work. Even in these occupations, the turnover of workers was so great, that training was done, as it were, on the run. Second, there was a great deal of confusion over what the appropriate specifications for new – often imported – machines should be, and a dearth of competent technical personnel to interpret and enforce them. As new technologies were introduced, debates about the appropriate division of labour erupted. This was particularly the case in the mining industry, where engineers and administrators went back and forth on the question of subdividing or combining occupations. Some argued that the decomposition of the miner's craft made it easier to train newcomers; others insisted that when workers combined several tasks stoppage time was reduced.[22]

But perhaps most important of all, *instruktazh* failed to take hold because it presupposed the cooperation of foremen in the emasculation of their powers. They simply had nothing to gain by conveying standardised instructions to workers, especially as those instructions often did not reflect the (chaotic) reality of the shop floor. In any case, loss of control over the training of new workers jeopardised the standing of foremen with respect to all their charges. Pressed from above by the technical rationality of engineers and from below by 'upstart' brigade leaders and shock workers, foremen did their best to keep both at bay.

That they enjoyed a measure of success is evident in the revision of vocational training programs in the 1930s. This had less to do with the application of *instruktazh* and *ustanovka*, than with the urgent need to produce skilled and especially semi-skilled workers by whatever methods. The narrowing and shortening of the factory apprentice school curriculum in 1933 and the even more abbreviated technical minimum courses that were introduced in the same year reflected official impatience with *both* traditional apprenticeship and TsIT's methods. In the event, the new courses actually strengthened the hand of the foremen.[23] The scheme for technical minimum courses was devised by the Council of Labour and Defence and monitored on the national level by the industrial commissariats. But it was individual enterprises that ran the courses (or in some cases 'circles') and foremen who taught them.[24] When, in 1935, state technical examinations were administered to over 800,000 workers employed in 255 'leading occupations', foremen comprised the main group within the skills commissions that devised the examinations and assessed workers' performance.[25] Similarly, with respect to the craft, railroad and factory training schools that were set up in 1940 to train labour reservists, the curriculum was almost entirely practical, and, appropriately enough, foremen comprised 86 per cent of the staff.[26]

The survival of apprenticeship, even in its truncated and bureaucratised form, meant that foremen remained arbiters of workers' advancement through the ranks (*razriady*). They had primary responsibility for determining who qualified for each skill level and, indeed, for interpreting what constituted skill. They retained this power not despite the multiple social and economic dislocations accompanying industrialisation, but because in such circumstances, someone had to give instructions to workers and grade their performance. Since, in Kendall Bailes' piquant phrase, engineers 'fled from production' if they could, trade unions could no longer impose their own rules, and the workers' own traditional networks had been sundered or driven underground, it was left to foremen to mediate between the utopian targets and behavior prescribed by higher authorities and the existing work culture. The implications of this relationship for the determination of output norms and the enforcement of labour discipline were profound. But before turning to these matters, we might consider what it took to become a foreman during these years and who served in this capacity.

TRAJECTORIES OF SOVIET FOREMEN

No category of industrial personnel grew as fast in the early 1930s as did foremen (see Table 7:1). While the number of workers in large-scale industry nearly doubled between 1929 and 1934, there were still relatively twice as many foremen supervising them at the end of this period than at its outset.[27] Despite the attention that Soviet and Western historians have given to questions of social background and mobility, it is difficult to be precise about the process by which foremen were recruited. At best, we can trace three trajectories.

One was via formal education in which the *rabfaks* and industrial *tekhnikums* played the major role. That is, some of the workers who

TABLE 7.1 *Numbers of managerial and engineering-technical personnel in large-scale industry*

	October 1929 No.	%	April 1930 No.	%	November 1933 No.	%	1933/30
Directors and Assistants	–	–	8,507	9.5	16,926	5.4	198.9
Admin./Prod. specialists	–	–	56,835	63.2	197,569	63.3	347.6
Scientific-lab. personnel	–	–	4,605	5.1	13,714	4.4	297.8
Foremen	18,695	22.6	20,814	23.1	83,846	26.9	402.8
TOTAL	82,689	100	89,911	100	312,055	100	347.1

SOURCE A. E. Beilin, *Kadry spetsialistov SSSR, ikh formirovanie i rost* (Moscow, 1935) pp. 122, 216.

had been selected for promotion via education as well as students from other social backgrounds left these institutions or graduated to become foremen rather than proceeding on to VTUZy and an engineering degree.

A second path was charted by a decree of September 1933 stipulating that graduates of higher and secondary technical institutions 'must pass through the school of lower administrative-technical personnel (foreman, sub-foreman, shift engineer, etc.)'.[28] Intended to give young engineers some supervisory experience as well as to professionalise foremanship, this decree proved difficult to enforce and does not appear to have been widely observed. 'I at least have not seen such foremen,' reported a construction trust official, who attributed their absence to young engineers' preference for planning departments and their reluctance to 'dig around in the earth in primitive conditions'.[29] As late as June 1941, the cadre department of the Commissariat of Heavy Machine Construction regarded the appointment of engineers and technicians to foreman's responsibilities as 'insufficient in the extreme'.[30]

As is evident from Table 7.2, the vast majority of foremen did not become so as a result of formal specialised education, but were rather *praktiki*. Three out of four foremen in November 1933 had been workers, 54 per cent of whom were promoted from the bench during the first five-year plan.[31] Scattered data suggest that most had considerable production experience, primarily in the skilled trades. Thus, only 11 per cent of foremen surveyed in Moscow had less than seven years of production experience, as contrasted with nearly 40 per cent of workers nationwide who had less than two years' experience as of

TABLE 7.2 *Educational background of foremen in large-scale industry (in %)*

Date	No. of Foremen	Higher Education Complete/Incomplete		Secondary Technical Complete/Incomplete		Praktiki
Oct. 1929	18,695	2.7	1.2	6.2	1.8	88.1
April 1930	20,814	3.4		7.8		88.8
Nov. 1933	83,846	1.2		4.9		93.9
Nov. 1939	212,613	1.7		9.4		88.9
Jan. 1941	138,363	3.0	0.7	7.5		88.8

SOURCES for 1929, M. Firin, 'K voprosu o probleme kadrov', *Ratsionalizatsiia proizvodstva* (1930) No. 9–10, pp. 48–50; for 1930 and 1933, Beilin, *Kadry spetsialistov*, pp. 216, 222; for 1939 and 1941, *Industrializatsiia SSSR, 1938–1941 gg., Dokumenty i materialy* (Moscow, 1973) pp. 218, 276.

1933.[34] At the Il'ich Metallurgical Factory in Mariupol', only one of 95 foremen had less than five years' experience as of 1932, whereas 58 had more than ten, most of it as workers in the same factory.[33] Another study, from 1934, found that the proportion of foremen who were under 23 years of age ranged between 4.2 per cent and 11.1 per cent, compared to 5-6 per cent for engineers, 15 per cent for economists, and 35 per cent for technicians. The corresponding proportion of workers was 41 per cent.[34] In other words, to the extent that respect on the shop floor was a function of skill, experience and age, many foremen were in a position to demand it.

During 1935, thousands of workers who had received a grade of 'excellent' on the state technical examinations were promoted to foremen. Thereafter, Stakhanovites constituted the main pool of recruits.

What training these workers received either before or after their promotion consisted of either TsIT's short-term courses or, from 1936, the more elaborate Master of Socialist Labour course. The latter entailed two years of study and was specifically designed to 'raise the cultural-technical level of workers to that of ITR [engineering-technical personnel]'.[35] While in terms of specialised education, the course was said to approximate what was offered in the *tekhnikums*, the narrowness of its curriculum did not permit those who completed it to enter a secondary educational institution without additional study.

It did, however, enable foremen to become shift engineers and shop supervisors. For, just as thousands of Stakhanovites were promoted to the ranks of foremen, so, partly as a result of the Great Purge and partly through 'natural' attrition, many who had preceded them to this position moved higher up the industrial hierarchy. This ratchet effect, accelerated by the Great Purge, may explain why, by 1941, the production *stazh* (and probably the age) of foremen was considerably less than what it had been in the mid-1930s. Whereas by the latter date, those with ten or more years of production experience comprised 35.7 per cent of foremen, almost exactly the same proportion (35.8 per cent) had less than five years' experience.[36] It also would tend to account for the increased presence of women in the profession (see Table 7.3). Here, though, the critical factor was not so much the Great Purge as the feminisation of the industrial working class, a process that was intensified in the late 1930s and early 1940s by the build-up of the Red Army.

To conclude, the foremen of the 1930s were mainly 'yesterday's

TABLE 7.3 *Social background, Party saturation and gender foremen in large-scale industry*

Date	Foremen	Party Members and Candidates (%)	Komsomolites (%)	Workers (%)	Women (%)
Oct. 1929	18,695	33.5	–	72.1	–
Nov. 1933	83,846	34.8	–	76.8	1.7
Jan. 1941	138,363	29.8	8.2	–	10.3

SOURCES For 1929 and 1933, Beilin, *Kadry spetsialistov* pp. 222, 237; for 1941, *Industrializatsiia SSSR, 1938–41*, pp. 277–8.

workers', in many cases quite literally so. More specifically, and not unlike their counterparts in the industrialised West, they were drawn overwhelmingly from the working class, lacked formal technical education and were predominantly male. Whether in other respects a particular strategy was pursued in selecting foremen, for example, on the basis of their nationality or Party membership, is impossible to say with any degree of certitude. While the proportion of foremen who were Party members was approximately twice that of workers in general, the lack of systematic data on party membership among the strata from which foremen were recruited (e.g., brigade leaders, shock workers, those in the higher skill grades, Stakhanovites) make any correlations on this score speculative. Certainly among Stakhanovites, who were not necessarily in the top *razriady* but appear to have constituted the main pool of recruits for foremanship in the late 1930s, Party saturation did not come close to what it was among foremen.[37]

In contrast to contemporary and even earlier Western experience, foremanship in the USSR tended not to be a terminal appointment. The barrier between foremen and higher echelons of the industrial hierarchy remained bridgeable in the 1930s, making foremanship a way station on the path of upward mobility. This would explain in part the continued predominance of *praktiki* among shift and shop supervisors, shop technicians, and even enterprise directors.[38]

Can we therefore conclude that by promoting workers who had already displayed a degree of reliability (by joining the Party, rate-busting, sharing the 'secrets' of their trade, serving as worker-correspondents or trade union activists), the Party was shoring up its and management's authority on the shop floor? The simple answer is that it seems likely. But what kind of authority did foremen have and how did they use it? What countervailing pressures existed to complicate the strict line of authority from the director's office down to the work bench? These are the questions to which we must now turn, focusing on the two most conflictual aspects of shop-floor relations, output norm determination and labour discipline.

'SCIENCE' VS. FOREMEN

Earlier it was argued that the threat to foremen posed by NOT was more apparent than real with respect to vocational training. There was, however, another aspect of the scientific organisation of labour that most definitely challenged foremen's power. This was the determination of output norms based on the technical capacities of machines and time and motion study of individual workers. Introduced in the mid-1920s in connection with the drive for increased productivity, technical norm determination had the double purpose of revealing potential output and, because norms were linked with wages via the piece rate system, of stimulating workers and management to reach that potential.

The role of TsIT in promoting technical norm determination was clearly important. It organised conferences to discuss and advertise the use of chronometry, analysed procedures pioneered in the West, conducted its own laboratory experiments, and provided training for norm setters. And when, in 1927, a Central Council on Technical Norm Determination was formed, its bureau included Gastev, Ia. M. Punskii, and other leading lights from TsIT.[39]

But within industrial enterprises, the main burden of formulating and defending such norms fell to the Technical Norm Bureaus, or TNBs, and their diminutive staff of norm-setters. These were the organs, clothed in the mantle of 'science,' that were supposed to eventually eliminate the notional targets established by foremen on the basis of past experience, negotiation with *artel'* or brigade leaders, or simple observation (*glazomer*). These were the organs, therefore, that threatened to expropriate what had become a traditional function of foremanship, depriving foremen of a great deal of their manoeuverability.

Labour economists, trade union officials and other advocates of technically-based norms repeatedly asserted that foremen had a vital role to play in the process. They would serve, so the argument ran, as consultants to the TNBs and instructors in new production methods revealed by the TNBs to be more efficient. They, no less than norm setters and workers themselves, had a stake in discovering the 'correct', scientifically determined norm for each job.[40]

For their part, foremen were under no illusions about what the new organs meant. Norms coming down from an office that was not party to informal negotiation with workers were bound to be higher than those set by foremen. Since foremen had to see to it that norms were fulfilled – no matter what their origin or method of determination – it was in their interest to create a 'reserve' in case of unforeseen shortages of materials, breakdowns and stoppages. Moreover, 'tight' (*zhestkie*) norms exacerbated tensions and disgruntlement on the shop floor. This is why foremen took a characteristically uncooperative attitude toward technical norm determination and the TNBs, or, to cite one of many euphemisms that were employed in the press, 'fail[ed] to appreciate their importance'.[41]

Not surprisingly, workers were mistrustful of TNBs and their work. 'The chronometrist must approach the worker tactfully so as not to make him nervous and intentionally or unintentionally distort the production process', advised *Trud*.[42] The problem, however, was not the behaviour of chronometrists, but the close association of their work with increased output norms. When time studies were conducted openly, workers intentionally slowed down; when attempts were made to conceal such monitoring of work methods, 'disturbances' (*volnenie*) occurred.[43] Gastev's recommendation that output norms should be based on not only the best worker but the 'super-best' (*sverkh-luchshii*), and that other workers should be trained so that they *eventually* would be able to fulfill such norms, could not have helped.[44]

A curious alliance was thus forged between foremen and a substantial part of the industrial working class over the issue of norms. Curious, because the arbitrariness and favouritism displayed by foremen in setting norms and assigning them to individual workers had been – and would continue to be – a common complaint among workers. But the contradiction is probably more apparent than real. Workers favoured by foremen were not alone in feeling threatened by the new system. As agitated as many workers were about foremen's license, the prospect of norms being determined and periodically revised upwards by TNB 'bureaucrats' was still more objectionable. The arguments used in defense of TNBs – that they were completely impartial, that they concerned themselves 'not with the individual worker – Ivanov, Petrov, Sidorov – but workers in general', and that their decisions were based on scientific principles would hardly have met workers' objections.[45] While foremen were generally accessible to workers, norm setters were not. While, as we have seen, foremen were overwhelmingly male and had their roots in the working class, the social origins and sexual composition of norm setters were more mixed and their authoritativeness was therefore more questionable. Even if foremen were prone to dish out abuse in the form of curses and fists, it was a menu with which workers were familiar. That of norm setters was mystifying, and therefore less palatable. Associated with the upward pressure on norms and the downward pressure on rates and living conditions, norm setters were frequent targets of *spets*-baiting in the late 1920s.

This is not to idealise foremen-worker relations, or to deny that in certain instances, workers could forge alliances with engineering staff against foremen's arbitrariness.[46] It is rather to suggest that for many workers, foremen's manipulation of norms was the lesser of two evils. For a brief period during the first five-year plan, some workers seized the opportunity to avoid both. Organising themselves as production collectives and communes, workers, primarily in the metalworks and textile industries, were able to institute self-management which included – at least in some cases – the self-determination of rates and norms.[47] It may well have been the assumption of these functions by the Baltic Shipyard's Bakunin commune that induced one of its members to boast that 'Now, brother, we don't toady. Nobody sucks up to the foreman'. By the same token, such syndicalist tendencies weighed against the collectives and communes in the eyes of higher authorities, and explain in part why they were disbanded in the course of 1931–2.

As it turned out, the technically-based norms of the TNBs did not manage to displace those based on foremen's estimations. For this, there were many reasons: the incompetence of norm setters who by and large were *praktiki*, the vast number of norms to be revised (several tens of thousands in large enterprises), the addition of 'laid on' (*nakladnoe*) time to take account of the unfamiliarity of equipment and problems in intra-enterprise routing, intimidation by workers, and especially during the first five-year plan years, inter-enterprise competition for skilled workers.

But even where such norms were applied, foremen were able to mitigate their effects. For example, they employed the 'pencil', that is, the registration of non-existent work, which in some railroad repair shops could represent a quarter of the workers' wages.[48] More commonly, they arbitrarily raised rates for particular jobs. 'Let's say

one piece of repair work costs 10 rubles', recalled an informant of the
Harvard Interview Project. 'I would raise it to 15 by adding some
artificial cost to the transport of goods which they could not check up
on. And so the worker would overfulfill [sic] his norm by 150%.'[49]
For workers in the highest skill categories, these additional earnings
(*prirabotki*) could amount to as much as 180 per cent of their base
rate as established in collective wage agreements.[50] The same effect
could be achieved by ascribing work performed on an overtime basis
to the normal shift or paying out bonuses to workers even when they
did not fulfill their norms.[51] Finally, by juggling work assignments so
that all workers occasionally performed tasks with 'looser' norms or
at higher skill levels, foremen could anticipate and preempt workers'
complaints. As another informant put it, 'I could "set up" a situation
in which a worker could achieve a higher norm than usual by giving
her easier work or arranging her material in advance. This was the
way it was usually done in all fields'.[52]

It is unlikely that foremen could have engaged in such sleights-of-
hand without at least tacit approval from higher management. For, in
the context of taut planning and massive labour turnover, not only
foremen but shop supervisors, technical directors and directors found
the TNBs to be millstones around their necks. The reserves of
productivity that foremen accumulated relieved some of this pressure, providing enterprise management with a degree of flexibility in
its struggle to keep up with periodic revisions in centrally-determined
plans.[53]

This tug of war between management and Commissariat officials
over technical norms began to shift in favour of the former in 1933, a
year of great crisis and much second thinking by the political leadership. Having earlier been persuaded by Gastev and other NOTists to
install a system of management based on functional principles and a
minute division of labour in the textile and construction industries, the
Commissariats found that the former encouraged the avoidance of
personal responsibility (*obezlichka*, one of the cardinal sins discussed
by Stalin in his 'New Conditions, New Tasks' speech of June 1931)
and the latter bred chaos. When enterprises were ordered to phase
out certain functional departments (rationalisation bureaus, planning
sections, and where appropriate, capital construction offices) and
trim the staff of others, directors seized the opportunity to reduce the
size of their TNBs and their capacity to formulate technically based
norms.[54]

Although some directors were accused of going too far, as NOT's influence waned, so did official faith in technics and, in particular, technical norm determination. Stalin's abandonment of technology in favour of cadres deciding 'everything' marked the culmination of the shift in official attitudes.[55] At an industrial conference in May 1935 – the same month in which Stalin exchanged formulas – Ordzhonikidze attacked 'the technical norm determination to which we are accustomed' as 'not fit for the devil', and his deputy, Piatakov, was no less critical.[56]

The victory of enterprise management, however, proved to be short-lived. The eclipse of technically-based norms did not give managers a free hand, but rather ushered in Stakhanovism, the exemplars of which outdid anything norm setters could have imagined. Stakhanovism immensely complicated foremen's lives. Failure to adequately service a Stakhanovite or enable an ambitious worker to become one could have serious consequences, including criminal prosecution. Yet, if a foreman chose to protect himself in this manner, he risked creating imbalances in the delivery of supplies, overloading machinery and neglecting his other duties.[57]

One way of reading Stakhanovism is to see it as an attempt by the party leadership to pry a portion of the working class away from the rest and at the same time to sever its dependence on foremen and other supervisors. To the extent that such a strategy existed and was successful, the result was doubly ironic. Not only did many Stakhanovites eventually become foremen, but, owing to the peculiar circumstances of the late 1930s and early 1940s (to be discussed below), they were vested with powers that strengthened the dependency relationship between them and their subordinates.

FOREMEN AND LABOUR DISCIPLINE

The problem of labour discipline was not peculiar to the 1930s, but the dimensions it assumed during that decade were sufficient to cause much alarm among trade union, state and party officials. Violations of labour discipline covered a multitude of sins – lateness, absenteeism, frequent job changing, the misuse of equipment, idling on the job, refusal to carry out instructions, attacks on unpopular workers and managerial-technical personnel – and stemmed from a variety of causes.[58] There is no doubt, though, that the shortage of labour, which the key industrial sectors experienced as a chronic phenomenon after 1929, severely hampered efforts to combat such behaviour.

Trade union, Komsomol and Party committees developed a number of strategies to improve the standard of labour discipline. The organisation of collective responsibility via socialist competition, shock brigades and cost-accounting brigades was one. Visits to the homes of offenders, production-comrades courts, boards of disgrace (*chernye doski*), and denunciations in factory newspapers was another. A third, aimed at reducing labour turnover, was to offer incentives to workers to sign contracts committing them to remain at their jobs for several years, a scheme that went by the revealing name of *samozakreplenie*. Finally, the provision of special services and goods to outstanding workers was intended at least in part to spur others to emulate their example.

These techniques had some success in socialising the new industrial labour force, but the persistence of 'flitting', 'sponging', and other forms of 'petty bourgeois spontaneity' – by no means limited to new workers – provoked sterner measures. There is no need to rehearse the legislation that was aimed at increasingly restricting workers' mobility and freedom of action within their places of work.[59] For our purposes, it is sufficient to note that the effectiveness of such legislation critically depended on its enforcement by enterprise management. And there was the rub. As managers have discovered the world over, fining, demoting, and dismissing workers have limits beyond which the fragile cooperation and consent of workers becomes jeopardised. But beyond this general rule, the imposition of such punitive measures in circumstances of a chronic labour shortage and super-ambitious production targets threatened to deprive Soviet enterprises of their most vital resources, labour power.[60]

These considerations, perfectly rational from the perspective of individual enterprise directors, in fact vitiated the impact of the coercive legislation. Vesting in enterprise management the power of enforcement, political authorities repeatedly condemned its preference for 'the path of least resistance'. It is in this context of conflicting pressures and demands with respect to labour discipline that we can analyse the role of foremen.

On 3 January 1933, *Trud* reported that two workers had been arrested for stabbing and seriously wounding a shock worker who had been promoted to foreman at the Sacco and Vanzetti machine construction factory in Stalingrad. The account of this incident was as emblematic as were those from the late 1920s to which reference was made at the outset of this paper. Whereas foremen's rude behaviour was cited in those accounts as provocation for attacks on them, in this case, the culprits were described as 'truants, loafers and bodgers' (from 'class alien' backgrounds, to boot!) who had been dismissed by the exemplary foreman in accordance with the decree of 15 November 1932. That law called for the dismissal, confiscation of ration coupons and removal from enterprise accommodation of workers who had been absent from work for as little as a single day.

The decree itself and the campaign surrounding it suggest both the desperation and powerlessness of the régime in its efforts to deprive workers of the leverage they enjoyed on the shop floor. For it is clear that foremen were at best highly selective in enforcing the decree's provisions, and that in evading responsibility, had numerous collaborators within the factory adminstration. This point may be illustrated by citing the procedures used at the Khar'kov Locomotive Engine Works and recommended for adoption by other factories. At the beginning of each shift, the time keeper presented the foreman with a list of absentees. Every three days, the foreman reported to the shop supervisor, who, after investigating the reasons for absences, forwarded the names of those absent without excuse to the factory's service department. The department would then remove the offenders from their apartments and withdraw their ration books.[61]

There were numerous ways of sabotaging this process and all seem to have been employed. Foremen could retroactively inform time keepers that absences were authorised or simply strike certain names from the list. Shop supervisors could similarly amend the lists they turned over to the service department. Finally, even those workers dismissed from one shop could be rehired by another without losing their entitlement to rations or accommodation.[62]

Simple humanitarianism should not be ruled out as a motivating factor here. Excuses that outside investigators considered illegitimate or questionable, such as the loss of a pass to enter the factory, illness in the family, or difficulty with housing authorities, may have been viewed otherwise by supervisors. But, it was not only or necessarily feeling and sentiment that ruled the 'informal organisation' constructed by foremen and other factory personnel.[63] Charged with the task of keeping production flows moving, they could ill-afford the loss of workers whom they had trained and with whom they had developed mutual understandings about effort and reward. By the same token, workers who did not share such understandings probably did not benefit from foremen's indulgence.

In any case, the campaign to combat absenteeism died a quiet death in 1933. Had the régime overreached itself or were its priorities changing? Even while the campaign was in full swing, a new one was emerging. This was to make full use of the work-day. The new campaign corresponded to the increased emphasis on the 'mastery of technology', which itself reflected the shift to a more intensive strategy of industrial expansion. It included criticism of foremen for concealing stoppages, failing to organise in advance the delivery of blueprints, tools and spare parts to the shop floor, and allowing workers to wander about the factory, thereby 'transforming the shops into boulevards [and] passage ways'.[64] One proponent of *uplotnenie* even went so far as to warn that 'along with workers who violate labour discipline, it is necessary to hold responsible the foremen who permit the violations'.[65]

But it is obvious that the main targets of the campaign were workers, and that criticism of foremen was intended to steer them in the direction of becoming true *nachal'niki*. 'Without the knowledge of the *desiatnik*, no worker is to be moved', proclaimed a joint Sovnarkom-Central Committee resolution of May 1933 that sought to sort out the mess in the Donbass coal industry. 'He attaches (*prikrepliaet*) workers to their places and machines.'[66] In the factories, various schemes were developed for keeping workers at their benches. At the Leningrad Bol'shevik factory, passes were used; different coloured flags could be hoisted over the bays at the Kaganovich Ballbearings Factory in Moscow to alert foremen or mechanics to problems; and at the Marti factory, 'S' tokens (for *skvoznoi prokhod*) were distributed to managerial and technical personnel as well as Party and union officials, while workers had to obtain ordinary tokens from foremen if they had to relieve themselves or were sent on an errand.[67] Meanwhile, foremen were acquiring the accoutrements of managerial personnel – telephones to connect them with dispatchers, desks, time account clerks, and salaries that were well above the average wages of workers and often higher than what technicians, economists and other staff personnel earned.[68]

All of this was part of the articulation of a strictly hierarchical factory régime to replace the Taylorite functionalist model which had fallen into disrepute. At its lowest level, the régime now included brigade leaders, who were given formal responsibility for the fulfillment of the production tasks assigned to the brigade and the maintenance of labour discipline among its members. Above them stood section and shift foremen possessing general supervisory, instructional and punitive powers with respect to all workers in their section or on their shift, and responsibilities for the proper use of all materials and equipment at their disposal. And so it went on, to senior foremen, unit and shop supervisors, all laid out in model statutes drafted by a conference of directors, chief engineers, *glavk*, trust and commissariat officials for different branches of heavy industry.[69]

The extent to which such prescriptions improved enterprise administration and labour discipline is difficult to determine. Certainly, compared to the primeval chaos of the early 1930s, industry as a whole performed more efficiently. But this undoubtedly had much to do with the settling-in of workers, the stabilisation of the situation in the countryside and the corresponding improvements in food supply. Moreover, clear-cut lines of authority did not in and of themselves guarantee that 'commanders' or workers would observe the rules. Informal shop-floor negotiation achieved what conformity to formal procedures could not, namely, mutual accommodation between workers and their bosses.

This is precisely why Stakhanovism was so threatening, and why many foremen and workers at least initially resisted it. Stakhanovism shook up the shop-floor pecking order and the mutual understandings on which it was based. Some workers, resentful of the special treatment given to Stakhanovites and fearful of the consequences their records would have for output norms, sabotaged their work. Others, seeking the material rewards that went along with Stakhanovite status, denounced foremen and other supervisors for not providing the prerequisites. Stakhanovites, protected by local Party officials and access to the press, often exposed foremen's shortcomings.

As we already have seen, the favouritism exercised by foremen was endemic; what Stakhanovism did was not only to raise the ante but, in an important sense, to turn the tables on foremen by calling into question their competence and status. After all, the vast majority of innovations in work methods were attributed to workers rather than their supposedly more knowledgeable bosses. It (or rather the progressive piece-rate system) also enabled the innovators and many who emulated their example to earn far more than what foremen normally received.

Not surprisingly, foremen often figured among those prosecuted for crimes against the Stakhanovite movement. Of twenty-one people convicted of such crimes by the Ivanovo People's Court up to March 1936, four were foremen and another seven were adjusters; among the cases that were referred to the Supreme Court of the RSFSR by district and regional courts in January and February 1936, 20 per cent involved brigade leaders or foremen, as compared to only

11.5 per cent involving shop supervisors and department personnel.[70] Charges against foremen typically concerned failing to service Stakhanovites, arbitrarily cutting their rates, and 'disorganising production'.

Yet it did not take long for Stakhanovism to be tamed, that is, to become routinised and 'contaminated' by the very practices it was supposed to overcome. As trade union officials inflated the number of Stakhanovites, Stakhanovite status became devalued; in many enterprises, even occasional overfulfillment of output norms was sufficient for a worker to be considered a Stakhanovite. Stakhanovite periods (*polosi*) inevitably turned into storming sessions and were just as inevitiably followed by slumps in activity. Factory directors discovered that they could use Stakhanovites as expediters, while at the same time avoiding the general application of Stakhanovite methods.

The failure of Stakhanovism to significantly curtail managerial indiscipline was one of the factors that led to the undoing of many managers during the Great Purge of 1937–8. However, the weight of state repression now fell most heavily on enterprise directors and higher personnel rather than low-level cadres. True, in the context of heightened class vigilance, the class alien backgrounds of some foremen and their past slights against individual workers were sufficient to evoke accusations of wrecking. But, at least in published reports of *aktiv* meetings, foremen were more often among the accusers than the accused.[71]

The Great Purge proved to be a boon to many foremen who became the prime candidates to replace their bosses further up the industrial hierarchy. For those who remained or became foremen, the Purge had another and less appealing consequence, namely, the disorganisation of production and a serious decline in labour discipline. References to the paralysis of industrial cadres and the fact that 'backward' and 'unconscious' elements among the workers were taking advantage of it appeared throughout 1937.[72] Aggregate figures on absenteeism provide only a dim reflection of the problem, no doubt because managers were reluctant to record workers as absent. Still, the recorded rate in 1937 was higher than for any year since 1932.[73] The situation seems to have been particularly serious in the mining industry where directors insisted that if they dismissed workers for lateness and unexcused absences, they would find employment at neighboring mines. It was an old excuse, but probably a valid one. As if the clock had turned back to the early part of the decade, the old scheme of *samozakreplenie* was dusted off, now by the newly appointed Commissar of Heavy Industry, L. M. Kaganovich.[74]

Even when workers were on the job, they were not necessarily at work. If, as was claimed in 1939, Krivoi Rog iron ore miners had become accustomed to working three or four hours per day and no more, then we should not be surprised that figures for the first half of 1938 show them spending only half of their nominal work time productively.[75] Elsewhere, the situation was only marginally better. In the rolling mills of the nation's steel industry, downtime accounted for 23 per cent of work time in the last six months of 1937.[76] With war clouds gathering over Europe, the laggardly pace of production in Soviet industry was even more alarming than it would otherwise have been.

This, then, was the context in which the state redoubled its effort to establish strict labour discipline. The best-known features of this effort were the decrees of December 1938, which introduced work books and extended the provisions of the 1932 law, and the criminalisation of labour truancy via the decree of 26 June 1940. Another that has received comparatively little attention was the campaign to transform foremen into the 'central figure of production'.[77] This campaign was initiated in January 1939 by the publication in *Pravda* of a series of letters from foremen complaining about their lack of authority on the shop floor. 'In our shop, the foremen are regarded merely as elder comrades,' wrote one. 'Of course, it is known that they can go to the shop supervisor and demand that someone be fired . . . But, it is also know that they themselves cannot decide this.'[78] Other letters detailed the excessive amount of time foremen spent on paperwork and fetching tools and spare parts, and their low salaries relative to Stakhanovites' wages. In earlier years, the fact that many foremen were earning less than some of the workers they supervised occasionally received critical comment in the press.[79] Now it was claimed that this anomaly was hampering the recruitment of foremen among Stakhanovites.

Some of these complaints eventually were met in a joint Sovnarkom-Central Committee resolution issued in May 1940. The resolution, 'On Promoting the Role of Foremen', applied only to factories in heavy machine construction, though it is likely that it was intended to serve as a model for other industries as well. The most significant aspect of the resolution is that it essentially repeated, with slightly greater specificity, the provisions of the model statutes drawn

up six years earlier. Just as in 1934, foremen were now given authority to hire and fire workers subject to confirmation by shop supervisors, and to assign skill categories to, penalise and reward workers as
they saw fit.[80]

The resolution thus bore approximately the same relation to the
repressive laws of December 1938 (and the soon to be decreed edict
of June 1940) as the model statutes did with respect to the legislation
of 15 November 1932. Both were attempts to extricate the régime
from a vicious cycle of its own making. As Donald Filtzer has
perceptively noted, 'where the policies of the régime threatened to
disrupt the functioning of the economy, the rule was either to ignore
the law or, if that was impossible, get around it as best one could'.[81]
The statutes and the 1940 resolution in effect acknowledged that
foremen could do just that without too much risk of punishment. In
short, by the decade's end, foremen were as they had once been –
masters of the shop floor.

CONCLUSIONS

The second and most egregiously Stalinesque edition of the *Bol'shaia
Sovetskaia Entsiklopediia* distinguished foremen in socialist enterprises from their counterparts under capitalism. In the former, they
were said to be 'the direct organiser of the productive process'; in
the latter, 'the steward of the proprietor'.[82] The distinction obscures
as much as it reveals. As Daniel Nelson, David Montgomery and
other American labour historians have pointed out, foremen were
powers in their own right in turn-of-the-century factories; worker's
hatred of them was at least as much a function of their arbitrariness as
it was of their 'stewardship' of capital's interests.[83] Indeed, it was
their lack of control over foremen that convinced many employers to
experiment with scientific management or at least to systematise
some aspects of their operations. These thrusts were often parried in
the same way that Soviet foremen warded off the impact of NOT. But,
inexorably, foremen were losing their discretionary power to personnel departments, quality control inspectors, and feed and speed men
on the one hand, and the maze of seniority and trade union rules,
enforced by shop stewards, on the other. By mid-century, foremen in
the industrialised West were routinely being referred to as the
'stepchildren of industry', and 'marginal' and 'forgotten' men.[84]

The basic conclusion of this paper is that at least up to the Great

Patriotic War, Soviet foremen retained most of the power they had had at the outset of industrialisation. There are three principal reasons why this was so. First, the thinning of the ranks of skilled, experienced workers via promotion or mobilisation for collectivisation and the suppression of traditional mechanisms for adaptation to an industrial environment (e.g., the *artel'*) ensured foremen of a major role in training and otherwise breaking-in the mass of new workers. The fact that the régime increasingly opted for on-the-job training – itself a response to the critical shortage of skilled workers – enhanced foremen's position in this respect.

Second, the resistance of enterprise management and workers to external intervention in the setting of output norms left foremen much room for adjusting and evading these procedures to suit the highly fluid circumstances of the shop floor. The absence of effective trade-union representation, institutionalised seniority rules or shop steward advocacy obviously contributed to foremen's ability to juggle workers, to play some off against others and distribute bonuses as favours. This is not to suggest, however, that foremen were dictators who could operate according to whim. What was lacking in terms of formal countervailing forces was to some extent compensated by the prevailing shortage of labour, the survival of informal bonds among workers (about which we need to know a great deal more), and the ever-present possibility of worker resentment being unleashed against bosses in general. This possibility became a reality during the years 1936–8.

Third, foremen retained their power at least to some degree because for both practical and ideological purposes – the two are not easily disentangled – it suited the régime for them to have it. Foremen had several qualities that appealed to the political leadership. They came from the right class. True, many perpetuated the traditions of *masterovshchina* – the extraction of favours, alcoholism and rudeness. But such forms of behaviour were well on their way to becoming endemic to Soviet (male) culture, and in any case, could be excused as part of the rough-and-tumble of shop floor life.

Obviously, these factors did not weigh equally throughout Soviet industry. Foremen's power varied from one branch of industry to another depending on the skill, gender, nationality and age of the work force and of foremen themselves, as well as differences in technology. Establishing these correlations for different industries should be high on the agenda of future research.

But in the final analysis, it was what foremen were not, as much as what they were, that secured their position within the industrial hierarchy. They were not, nor did they have pretentions to be, 'bigwigs', their realm was contained by the shop floor and their mastery over it did not constitute a political threat. The coalitions they entered into with workers were of a purely negative kind and could not be translated into opposition to the factory regime itself.

All of this may help to explain the extraordinary toast that Stalin made in October 1937, that is, in the midst of the Great Purges. Addressing a gathering of factory directors, engineers, foremen and Stakhanovites from the metallurgical industry, the old *praktik* characterised the tens of thousands of 'small and middle-level leaders' as 'modest people' who 'do not thrust themselves forward' and 'are hardly noticed'. 'But', he went on, 'it would be blindness not to notice them, since on these people depends the future of production in our entire economy . . . and the fate of our economic leadership'.[85] Indeed it would.

NOTES

1. *Trud*, 13 December 1928, p. 2.
2. See, for example, *Fabzavkom* (supplement to *Trud*) (1924) No. 2, p. 2, No. 4–5 p. 11; *Trud*, 15 July 1927, p. 3; 7 August 1927, p. 6; 8 March 1928, p. 3; 27 April 1928, p. 3; 28 April 1927, p. 3; 11 May 1928, p. 3; 21 June 1928, p. 3; 29 June 1928 p. 6; 13 July 1928, p. 5.
3. *Trud*, 16 September 1927, p. 5; 10 May 1928, p. 3; *Voprosy truda (VT)* (1929) No. 1, p. 21.
4. *Trud*, 15 July 1927, p. 3.
5. *Trud*, 28 December 1928, p. 3.
6. *Trud*, 29 July 1927, p. 4.
7. *Trud*, 7 August 1927, p. 6.
8. See respectively K. Marx, *Capital*, vol. I (New York, 1967) p. 424 and J. Melling, '"Non-Commissioned Officers": British Employers and Their Supervisory Workers, 1880–1920', *Social History* (1980) No. 2, p. 193.
9. J. Foster, *Class Struggle and the Industrial Revolution* (London, 1974) p. 227.
10. R. Bendix, *Work and Authority in Industry* (New York, 1963) pp. 206–211.
11. Michael Burawoy, *The Politics of Production* (London, 1985).
12. S. Grabe and P. Silberer, *Selection and Training of Foremen in Europe* (Paris, n.d.) p. 4 refers to a Dutch report listing more than 100 titles given to people performing foremen's functions, whereas in Britain the

title 'foreman' was used on four different levels in industry, from leading hands to superintendents. See National Institute of Industrial Psychology, *The Foreman: A Study of Supervision in British Industry* (London, 1951) pp. 86–98.

13. For foremen's role in pre-revolutionary factory life, see, inter alia, R. Zelnik, ed., *A Radical Worker in Tsarist Russia, the Autobiography of Semen Ivanovich Kantachikov* (Stanford, 1986) pp. 18–19, 53, 55, 61, 63, 73–4, 88–9; P. Timofeev, 'What the Factory Worker Lives By', in V. E. Bonnell (ed.), *The Russian Worker, Life and Labor under the Tsarist Regime* (Berkeley, 1983) pp. 85–90, 93–5, 98, 101–8; R. Glickman, *Russian Factory Women, Workplace and Society, 1880–1914* (Berkeley, 1984) pp. 142–3, 211–12; and S. Smith, *Red Petrograd* (Cambridge, 1983) pp. 39–41, 64, 119, 136. The transition from the revolutionary upheaval of 1917–18 when many workers elected new foremen to the mid-1920s remains to be explored.

14. On the artel, see H. Kuromiya, 'The Artel and Social Relations in Soviet Industry in the 1920s', paper presented to NEP Conference at Indiana University (2–5 October, 1986).

15. A member of the collegium of NKTrud RSFSR counted 23 channels through which labour disputes could be handled. See *Trud*, 14 January 1928, p. 2.

16. S. Lieberstein, 'Technology, Work and Sociology in the USSR: the NOT Movement', *Technology and Culture* (1975) No. 1, p. 49.

17. A. K. Gastev, *Trudovye ustanovki* (Moscow, 1973) pp. 308–9; *Trud*, 4 March 1924, p. 2.

18. *Trud*, 29 February 1924, p. 2; 6 March 1924, p. 2; 30 March 1924, p. 3.

19. *Trud*, 19 April 1928, p. 2. See also *Organizatsiia truda* (1933) No. 6, pp. 3–4.

20. This was a modest claim, for according to the Commissar of Labour, 750,000 workers had been so trained by 1932. See S. Fitzpatrick, *Education and Social Mobility in the Soviet Union, 1921–1934* (Cambridge, 1979) p. 200.

21. See, for example, *VT* (1933) No. 6, pp. 34–6; *Voprosy profdvizheniia* (*VP*) No. 11, pp. 57–8.

22. L. H. Siegelbaum, *Stakhanovism and the Politics of Productivity in the USSR, 1935–41* (Cambridge, 1988) pp. 58–63. Foremen, who continued to assign workers at each shift's *nariad*, remained oblivious to the issue, that is, until the advent of Stakhanovism, after which they had to pick up the pieces, so to speak. See also H. Kuromiya, 'The Commander and the Rank and File: Managing the Soviet Coalmining Industry, 1928–1933', pp. 17–19, paper presented to SSRC Seminar on Soviet Industrialization (Ann Arbor, Michigan, April 22–4, 1988).

23. Fitzpatrick, *Education and Social Mobility*, p. 226; M. Anstett, *La formation de la main d'oeuvre qualifiée en Union Soviétique de 1917 à 1954* (Paris, 1958) pp. 106–14; *Industrializatsiia SSSR, 1933–1937 gg., Dokumenty i materialy* (Moscow, 1971) pp. 434–6.

24. Granick, *Management of the Industrial Firm in the USSR* (New York, 1954) p. 119; *Za promyshlennye kadry* (1936) No. 2, pp. 7–8; J. Scott, *Behind the Urals* (Bloomington, Ind., 1972) p. 174.

154   *Stalinism: Its Nature and Aftermath*

25. *Industrializatsiia severo-zapadnogo raiona v gody vtoroi i tret'ei piatiletok, 1933–1941 gg.*, *Dokumenty i materialy* (Leningrad, 1969) p. 432; *Za Industrializatsiiu (ZI)* 4 January 1935, p. 4; and *VP*, (1934) No. 3, pp. 12–21 for public technical exams which served as a model for the state technical minimum scheme.
26. *Industrializatsiia SSSR, 1938–1941 gg.*, *Dokumenty i materialy* (Moscow, 1973) p. 263.
27. The proportion of foremen to workers was 2.2 per cent, ranging from 1.8 per cent in machine construction to 4.0 per cent in coal mining. See A. Khavin, 'O mastere', *ZI*, 11 January 1935, p. 3.
28. *Sbornik vazhneishikh zakonov i postanovlenii o trude* (Moscow, 1958) p. 123.
29. *Sovet pri narodnom komissare tiazheloi promyshlennosti SSSR, Pervyi plenum, 10–12 maia 1935 g.* (Moscow–Leningrad, 1935) p. 252.
30. *Industrializatsiia SSSR, 1938–41* p. 281.
31. *ZI*, 11 January 1935, p. 3.
32. Ibid; *Professional'naia perepis', 1932–1933 g.* (Moscow, 1934) p. 17.
33. *VT* (1933) No. 1, p. 60.
34. *VP* (1934) No. 12, p. 66; *Professional'naia perepis'*, p. 17.
35. M. Lazvin, 'Kursy masterov sotsialisticheskogo truda', *Stakhanovets* (1939) No. 8, p. 28, and *Industrializatsiia SSSR, 1933–37* pp. 503–4.
36. *Industrializatsiia SSSR, 1938–41*, p. 274.
37. Siegelbaum, *Stakhanovism and the Politics of Productivity*, pp. 121–2.
38. The proportion of *praktiki* among each was respectively 60.6 per cent, 58 per cent and 76.5 per cent. See *Industrializatsiia SSSR, 1938–41*, p. 276. In the Ruhr already before 1914, 'a position as Steiger or Meister represented the ultimate achievement, not the beginning, of a career'. E. G. Spencer, 'Between Capital and Labor: Supervisory Personnel in Ruhr Heavy Industry Before 1914', *Journal of Social History* (1975), p. 181. For career patterns of foremen in other European countries, see Grabe and Silberer, *Selection and Training of Foremen in Europe*, pp. 42–51, and in the United States, E. S. Cowdrick, 'Foreman Training in American Industry', *International Labour Review* (1933) No. 2, pp. 207–19.
39. See I. H Siegelbaum, 'Soviet Norm Determination in Theory and Practice, 1917–1941', *Soviet Studies* (1984) No. 1, pp. 49–50.
40. *Trud*, 15 July 1927, p. 3; 27 April 1928, p. 3; *VT* (1932) No. 10, pp. 14–16.
41. *Trud*, 15 July 1927, p. 3; 11 January 1929, p. 5; *VT* (1929) No. 12, p. 63; *VT* (1931) No. 3–4, p. 32; *VT* (1933) No. 6, pp. 73–4. See also *VP* (1933) No. 11, p. 23 for the injunction that 'the foreman and the norm setter must not represent themselves as polar opposites'.
42. *Trud*, 6 March 1928, p. 1.
43. P. B. Zilbergleit, *Proizvoditel'nost' truda v kamennougol'noi promyshlennosti* (Khar'kov, 1930) pp. 33, 39; *Trud*, 16 March 1928, p. 4. See *Trud*, 8 January 1929, p. 2 wherein it was reported that secret time study had provoked at least thirteen disturbances in 1928.
44. *Trud*, 15 May 1928, p. 1. O. A. Ermanskii, a labour physiologist and advocate of setting norms on the basis of optimal expenditures of energy,

characterised Gastev's recommendation as typifying the 'capitalist principle'. Most trade unionists attending the conference at which these proposals were advanced were critical of both. See *Trud*, 18 May 1928, p. 5.

45. See *Trud*, 6 January 1928, p. 4. These assurances were given in response to a Kolomna factory worker who referred to the TNB as an 'eyesore'.

46. For evidence of such alliances, see D. Shearer, 'From Functionalism to Shop Autonomy, Changes in the Structure of Work and Management in Soviet Machine Building Factories, 1926–1934', paper presented to SSRC Seminar on Soviet Industrialization (Ann Arbor, Michigan, April 22–4, 1988).

47. L. H. Siegelbaum, 'Production Collectives and Communes and the "Imperatives" of Industrialization in the USSR, 1929–1931', *Slavic Review* (1986) No 1, p. 75. For the boast referred to above, see the epigraph of this article.

48. *Trud*, 27 April 1928, p. 3. This was also the case among *desiatniki* in the coal mining industry according to *Udarnik* (1932) No. 2, pp. 15–16.

49. Harvard Interview Project on the Soviet Social System, Interview No. 99, pp. 8–9. See also No. 456, p. 10.

50. *VT* (1931) No. 3–4, p. 32; *VP* (1934) No. 3, pp. 40-43.

51. *VP* (1935) No. 2–3, pp. 57–63, No. 5–6, p. 47; Harvard Interview Project, No. 99, pp. 8–9.

52. *VP* (1934) No. 3, pp. 35–45, No. 4, p. 47, No. 10, pp. 59–64; Harvard Interview Project, No. 1106, p. 13.

53. For directors' defense of flexibility, see *Soveshchanie khoziaistvennikov, inzhenerov, tekhnikov, partiinykh i profsoiuznikh rabotnikov tiazheloi promyshlennosti, 20–22 sentiabria 1934 g.*, (Moscow, 1935) pp. 223–6.

54. For one such directive to the coal mining industry, see *Industrializatsiia SSSR, 1933–37*, pp. 245–6. According to the head of the Commissariat of Heavy Industry's Labour Department, the number of norm setters had declined by one-and-a-half times in 1933–4 because directors 'misunderstood' the directive. See *Soveshchanie khoziaistvennikov*, p. 227.

55. I. V. Stalin, *Sochineniia*, R. McNeal (ed.), vol. I [XIV] (Stanford, 1967) pp. 56–64.

56. *Sovet pri narodnom komissare*, pp. 172–4.

57. Siegelbaum, *Stakhanovism and the Politics of Productivity*, pp. 164–8.

58. See V. Andrle, 'How Backward Workers Became Soviet: Industrialization of Labour and the Politics of Efficiency under the Second Five-Year Plan, 1933–1937', *Social History* (1985) No. 2, pp. 147–69.

59. For an excellent treatment of this legislation, see D. Filtzer, *Soviet Workers and Stalinist Industrialization* (Armonk, N.Y. 1986) pp. 107–15, 233–53.

60. Filtzer is right to emphasise these circumstances as enabling workers to maintain control of the labour process, even if he exaggerates the degree of control by, among other things, ignoring the role of foremen.

61. *VP* (1933) No. 4, pp. 45–6.

62. *Trud*, 10 February 1933, p. 3; 12 February 1933, p. 3; *VP* (1933) No. 5, pp. 45–7, No. 7, p. 75; *VT* (1933) No. 4, pp. 61–4.

63. For the distinction between formal organisation governed by 'logic' and

informal organisation based on 'feeling and sentiment', see the seminal article by F. J. Roethlisberger, 'The Foreman: Master and Victim of Double Talk', *Harvard Business Review* (1945) No. 3, pp. 290–2.

64. *VP* (1933) No. 3, pp. 31–3, No. 13, p. 60; and for quote ibid. (1934) No. 7, p. 50.
65. *VP* (1934) No. 7, p. 50.
66. *Trud*, 22 May 1933, p. 1; See also *VP* (1933) No. 7, pp. 3–11.
67. *VP* (1933) No. 11, p. 76, (1934) No. 7, pp. 50–1.
68. *VT* (1933) No. 5, p. 67; *VP* (1933) No. 11, p. 76; TsUNKhU Gosplana SSSR, *Zarabotnaia plata inzhenerno-tekhnicheskikh rabotnikov, sluzhashchikh i uchenikov v sentiabre-oktiabre 1934 g.* (Moscow, 1936) pp. 6–51.
69. *Soveshchanie khoziaistvennikov*, pp. 343–70.
70. *Sotsialisticheskaia zakonnost'* (1936) No. 3, p. 7; *Sovetskaia iustitsiia* (1936) No. 8, pp. 4–5.
71. *Pravda*, 26 March 1937, p. 3; *ZI*, 4 April 1937, p. 3; 10 April 1937, p. 2.
72. See *Pravda*, 24 June 1937; *ZI*, 5 May 1937, p. 2; *Stakhanovets* (1937) No. 8, p. 20.
73. J. Barber, 'Labour Discipline in Soviet Industry, 1928–1941', paper presented to the Twelfth AAASS Convention (Philadelphia, November 1980) Table B.
74. *Pravda*, 4 January 1938, p. 2.
75. Filtzer, *Soviet Workers and Stalinist Industrialization*, p. 168; *Planovoe khoziaistvo* (1938) No. 1, p. 63.
76. *Planovoe khoziaistvo* (1938) No. 2, p. 63.
77. *Mashinostroenie*, 2 November 1938; *Pravda*, 8 January 1939, p. 2. See also P. A. Morozov, *Master, polnopravnyi rukovoditel' uchastka*, (Moscow, 1949).
78. *Pravda*, 6 January 1939, p. 2.
79. See, for example, *ZI*, 4 October 1936, p. 2; 28 August 1934, p. 3.
80. The resolution is in *Industrializatsiia SSSR, 1938–41*, pp. 121–5.
81. Filtzer, *Soviet Workers and Stalinist Indusrialization*, p. 246.
82. *Bol'shaia sovetskaia entsiklopediia*, 2nd ed., vol. XXVI (1954), p. 456.
83. D. Nelson, *Managers and Workers* (Madison, 1975) pp. 34–54; D. Montgomery, *The Fall of the House of Labor* (Cambridge, 1987) pp. 115, 129–130, 204–5; W. H. Lazonick, 'Technological Change and the Control of Work: The Development of Capital-Labour Relations in US Mass Production Industries', in H. F. Gospel and Craig R. Littler (ed), *Managerial Strategies and Industrial Relations* (London, 1983) pp. 125–9. It is interesting that whereas US labour historians tend to stress foreman-worker antagonism around the turn of the century, their British counterparts stress mutual accommodation. For an example of the latter, see C. Littler, *The Development of the Labor Process in Capitalist Societies* (London, 1982) pp. 86–7.
84. See Roethlisberger, 'The Foreman: Master and Victim of Double Talk', p. 284; Th. H. Patten, Jr., *The Foreman: Forgotten Man of Management* (New York, 1968); L. Baritz, *The Servants of Power* (Middletown, Conn., 1960) pp. 182–4.
85. *Pravda*, 31 October 1937, p. 1.

8 Upward Social Mobility and Mass Repression: The Communist Party and Soviet Society in the Thirties

Hans-Henning Schröder

The years of industrial construction gave Soviet society its form and created the basis of the system of political rule normally referred to as 'Stalinism'. There were above all two processes that moulded the character of Stalinist society: the wave of upward social mobility initiated by industrialisation and the mass repression with which a hypertrophied police apparatus took action against supposed enemies. It is scarcely possible to separate these two processes from each other.

The change of economic policy, that is, the acceleration of the expansion of industry which was pushed through in 1928–9 and the forced collectivisation of agriculture, set in motion a profound change in social structure. Many peasants left their villages and found work in construction or in industrial enterprises. The composition and behaviour of the Soviet workforce changed rapidly. At the same time the apparatuses of state, economy and Party were extended, and hundreds of thousands of manual workers and low-grade white-collar workers acquired the possibility of upward social mobility. This profound social and economic change also had consequences for the Party, which had to accommodate itself in all haste to new conditions, and also had an effect on the relationship between political leadership and management.

There were already conflicts in the course of pushing through forced industrialisation, not only within the Party leadership – Bukharin, Rykov and Tomskii standing on this issue against Stalin's Party supporters – but also between the parts of the Party that wanted to accelerate industrialisation and those experts in the planning and economic apparatuses who considered that they could not support

157

this forcing of the speed.[1] At the beginning of 1928 the Party leadership made public its disagreement with the 'bourgeois specialists': in a large-scale trial a series of mining experts from the Donets basin were accused of sabotage and 'parasitic activity'. The first trial was followed by further ones up to 1931, accompanied by a broad political campaign which attempted to mobilise the Party and the workers against the 'parasites' in management.[2] Publicly-expressed opinion and the mood on the shop-floor turned against the 'bourgeois specialists'. Management and economic planners came under pressure. In this way scapegoats for faulty economic developments were named and at the same time the economic leadership was induced to give way to the demands of the Party leadership for the acceleration of industrialisation.

The Shakhty trial, as the proceedings against the mining engineers became known, also initiated a change in the policy towards cadres and higher education. The political leadership recognised that there was a lack of experts for the rapid expansion of industry and introduced a reform of training, in the course of which the number of specialists was to be hurriedly increased, while, at the same time, the specialists were to be 'proletarianised' and closely tied to the Party.[3] Technical colleges and institutions of tertiary education were hastily reorganised, new ones were founded, student numbers were increased and the duration of study was reduced.[4] There was an increase in the numbers of workers and children of workers who studied. In 1932–3 the proportion of proletarian students in the total student body was 50 per cent, in technical colleges as high as 64 per cent.[5] The work of the Communist Party and its youth organisation was intensified, and there was a clear increase in the proportion of Party and Communist Youth members in tertiary education institutions. In 1928 65.5 per cent of students were not members, but only 47 per cent were not by 1933. 22.5 per cent of students belonged to the Party, 30.5 per cent to the Komsomol.[6] The reorganisation of technical colleges and the institutions of tertiary education, the permeation of the student body with workers and Party members, all served the purpose of building up for industry and the economy a cadre of politically loyal experts with specialist qualifications. Admittedly this programme came too late for the years of the first five-year plan, the initial phase of forced industrialisation – and that is an indication of the unplanned and precipitate way in which the change in economic policy was introduced. The new generation of loyal, proletarian specialists was only available to enterprises after a period of two or three years – and then they were at first lacking in practical experience.

However, industrial expansion demanded in the short term an increase in management and technical personnel at all levels. Technical colleges and institutions of tertiary education were unable to produce the required number of qualified personnel. Thus the supplementary cadre plan of 1930 provided for the filling of this gap by *vydvizhenie*, that is, the promotion of manual workers and low-level white-collar workers.[7] The consequences of this for specialists' qualifications is shown in Table 8.1. At the end of the first five-year plan the leading personnel of Soviet industry were significantly underqualified. There was a lack of trained specialists, their numbers having risen in absolute terms but having perceptibly declined in

TABLE 8.1 *Numerical growth and qualification of technical engineering and economic specialists in Soviet industry, 1929 and 1933*

Branch of industry	specialist personnel 1929 absolute level of education (%)				specialist personnel 1933 absolute level of education (%)			
	absolute	tertiary	tech. coll.	practician	absolute	tertiary	tech. coll.	practician
coal mining	10,086	15.9%	21.5%	62.6%	23,708	11.1%	12.5%	76.4%
steel industry	8,736	19.2	23.5	57.3	23,544	18.4	15.4	66.2
mechanical engineering	23,555	27.5	29.1	43.4	74,335	19.6	19.5	60.9
chemical industry	4,859	45.2	31.9	22.9	18,102	25.3	19.9	54.8

	increase in numbers of specialists (1929=100%)	filling of posts by appropriately qualified personnel, 1933:	
		graduates of tertiary institutions	technical college leavers
coal mining	235.6%	30.5%	21.7%
steel industry	315.6	50.6	28.6
mechanical engineering	269.5	51.05	31.05
chemical industry	372.5	34.6	38.8

SOURCE A. E. Beilin, *Kadry spetsialistov v SSSR - ikh formirovanie i rost* (Moscow, 1935) pp. 212 f. 1929: VSNKh figures, 1933: a Central Committee, VKP and TsUNKhU survey.

relative terms. The lion's share of personnel was made up of 'practicians', that is, upwardly mobile individuals without formal qualifications.

In view of the demands made on leading personnel by imported technologies, perspective planning and the modern organisation of production, the low qualification of managerial cadres was bound to create major problems. On the other hand the assignment of 'practicians' to leadership positions must be seen as part of the upward social mobility that determined social development in the phase of forced industrialisation and that tended to integrate large parts of the workforce into the system. This upward mobility reached huge proportions. In the period between 1928 and 1933 alone, about 770,000 Party members from proletarian backgrounds are supposed, according to Soviet sources, to have moved up socially – either through *vydvizhenie* in the apparatuses of state, Party and economy, or through training in technical colleges or institutions of tertiary education.[8] These details do not include non-Party people, let alone those from white-collar backgrounds, so that the total number of those who moved into, or were prepared for, leading positions must be much higher than the figure quoted.

If the wave of upward social mobility within the apparatuses of state, Party and economy was one factor that changed society and stabilised the political system, then the second was a fundamental change in structure of the workforce. Within a few years, between 1928 and 1932, the number of people employed in the non-agricultural sector doubled.[9] In large-scale industry the number of workers rose from 2.69 million in 1928 to 5.15 million in 1932,[10] in the building trade from 361.9 thousand in 1928 to 1.496 million in 1931.[11] Altogether in the course of the first five-year plan about 11 million people began work in the non-agricultural sector.[12] In 1932 about half the workers in large-scale industry – 2.5 million – were new arrivals in their enterprises, that is, had entered in 1928 or later. The majority of these 'new workers' came from agriculture. They were former peasants who came from the village into large enterprises, whether directly or by way of the building trade and seasonal work. It was especially the influx of the years 1931 and 1932 that was recruited predominantly from this group.[13] The hasty expansion of workforces and the influx of inexperienced workers who had grown up in a peasant milieu and were not used to the industrial work-process produced considerable problems. The average level of qualification of the Soviet workforce sank, while the number of cases of indiscipline at the workplace rose. Lack of knowledge and lack of care led to faulty production and damage to machinery. The new workers' lack of social anchorage, their low level of wages, problems of supply and the shortage of housing caused the rates of turnover to rise steeply: workers changed from one place of employment to another in a haphazard way.[14]

The Communist Party was unprepared for the problems that arose in the context of forced industrialisation – the shortage of experts, the expansion and disintegration of the working class, the increasing mobility of society and growing difficulties in the production and supply sector. The Party had to be re-equipped both politically and organisationally. Up until 1928 the Party apparatus had fought against an 'opposition' that spoke out in favour of speedy industrialisation, but now it had to carry the line on forced industrialisation into the Party organisations based in individual enterprises and villages. The Party leadership now advocated a policy which was bound to seem exaggerated and unrealistic to many functionaries at all levels. Thus in 1929–30 political change was first carried through by means of a revision of the membership, as also by the propagation of a newly-invented image of the enemy – that of 'right deviation' or of 'right deviation in practice.'[15] But considerable personnel and organisational problems appeared as well. On the one hand collectivisation made necessary an expansion and stabilisation of the pitifully weak Party organisations in rural areas; on the other hand the expansion of the workforce required a strengthening of the Party organisations within enterprises. Moreover, because of the lack of cadres and the scepticism of the experts and the leadership personnel it was only possible to accelerate industrialisation by mobilising the Party apparatus. The Party organisations within enterprises were now urgently occupied by economic tasks for which they were not equipped, while their real work in the realm of politics and ideology was no longer done. While economic decisions were politicised and economic rationality moved increasingly into the background, the Party lost its 'political' character: it became a mere instrument for carrying through an exaggerated policy of industrialisation.

An expression of this development was the reorganisation of the Party, which was carried through in 1929–30, and its mobilisation for the policy of forced industrialisation. The apparatuses of the Party committees were reconstituted and made more specialised; the Party organisations in enterprises and administrative offices were reformed, and their work reorganised under the slogan 'Front for Production'. At the same time a recruitment campaign was initiated, which in a few years drew more than two million new members into the Party.

The intensification of Party work in the economic realm and the rapid growth in the number of workers made an increase in Party cadres necessary. The first step towards this was a broad-based recruitment campaign. For the tenth anniversary of the October Revolution in October 1927 a recruitment campaign was organised, which between October 1927 and April 1928 drew 123,167 production workers into the Party.[16] But that was just the beginning. In November 1928 the Central Committee decided to raise the proportion of production workers in the Party to 50 per cent. To this end the formalities of admission were simplified for workers 'from the workbench', and the admission of non-workers reduced to a minimum.[17] The regional Party organisations were urged by headquarters to hasten the recruitment of proletarian Party members. Between December 1927 and April 1930, over 600,000 production workers were admitted into the Party; in 1931, of 997,398 new members, 629,803 were workers; in the first quarter of 1932 there were 233,859 new members, among them 158,434 workers.[18] In all, between 1927 and 1932, the number of party members grew by 2,400,000 – from 1,147,074 to 3,555,338.[19] The proportion of workers 'from the workbench' rose from 28.6 per cent (1927) to about 40 per cent (1928) and then stagnated, while that of white-collar workers sank from 41 per cent (1927) to 26.9 per cent (1932).[20] The Party thus completely changed the composition of its membership in a few years. The great mass of Party members of 1933 had not experienced the internal discussions and Party life of the twenties, they had barely the fundamentals of political knowledge and had no independent conception of what socialism could be. On the other hand the Party leadership now had a reserve of proletarian cadres on which it could fall back as the apparatuses were expanded and permeated with loyal personnel. Admittedly, the mass influx of new members also led to organisational problems: registration fell behind, and it was often not possible to integrate new members into the work of the Party.[21]

The increase in membership made necessary a reform of the Party organisations at the base, something that was in any case required in view of the new and extended tasks involved in pushing through and completing the process of industrialisation. The organisational network was expanded. The number of Party cells rose from 38,783 in 1927 to 139,000 in 1933.[22] In large enterprises cells were organised for the individual sections of the plant, in part also for the members of different shifts. The network of cells belonging to a particular enterprise was led by a Party Committee.[23] The purpose of the reform was to shift the main focus of Party work directly into the production process, and to gear the activity of the cells to the meeting of production targets and the acceleration of the pace of industrialisation.[24]

In order to activate the great mass of members and integrate them into the work of the Party organisation of the particular enterprise, a new subdivision was introduced besides the vertical, hierarchical division between, for example, the enterprise Party Committee and the cell of an individual section of the plant: there was now a horizontal subdivision according to 'sectors', which looked after particular specialist fields – production, recruitment, the trade union, women's questions etc. – and which were to be anchored at every level in the vertical subdivision up to that of Party Committee.[25] However, the web of vertical and horizontal structures that now arose in many places often overtaxed Party organisers.

The enterprise Party Committees were, it is true, relieved of some of their duties and could concentrate on management and administrative work, but the communication between sectors and Party cells soon proved to be impracticable: the organisation was complicated and it was scarcely possible to direct it.[26] All the same, the reshaping of the base organisation did lead to a temporary activation of many Party members and, because it was scarcely possible to keep a check on such a complex structure, permitted certain freedoms at the base.

The reform of the Party base was supplemented by a reorganisation of the apparatus at middle and upper level. The staff of the Party Committees, which was unspecialised and weak in terms of personnel, rapidly proved incapable in the context of forced industrialisation of fulfilling its tasks with regard to economic management and administration.[27] The goal of the measures introduced in 1929 was to differentiate the apparatuses of the Central Committee and regional Party Committees so that they would be in a position to influence effectively the process of industrial and socialist construction. To this end the existing departments were restructured according to 'functional' criteria. There were now four departments, of which one, the 'Orgotdel', was concerned with personnel and with the organisational management of the Party apparatus; the second with personnel policy in state, economy and unions; the third, the Department of Culture and Propaganda, with education, the press, political instruction and the personnel involved in this work; and finally the fourth,

the Department of Agitation and Mass Campaigns, with the organisation and supervision of campaigns and mass organisations.[28]

Each of these four – in addition there were some technical departments concerned with archives, administration of security matters,
etc. – drew together all powers in one 'functional' area, from the
allocation of personnel and the running of organisational matters to
the resolution of individual issues of substance. This subdivision of
the apparatus certainly represented a step forward by comparison
with the preceding situation, but at the same time the foundations of
new problems were laid. The splitting-up of areas of competence; the
fact that there was no central allocation of personnel; and the
functional subdivision of realms of management authority were all
bound to make tight leadership of the Party from above more
difficult.

The reorganisation of the apparatus and the base organisations of
the Party, and the large influx of members led to a mobilisation of the
Party and an activation of many Party members, but could not
prevent Party work from becoming ever more disorganised. This was
also a consequence of the increasing unplannedness of the expansion
of industry and of the accelerated social change. A whole society had
begun to move, and regional mobility, like upward social mobility,
took on enormous proportions.

Even Party members were seized by this movement. The Party
statistics for the year 1931, in which membership rose from 2.057
million to 2.883 million, record that 507,000 members changed loca-
tion and regional organisation, of whom only 497,000 'arrived': ten
thousand were lost. A further 90,000 were deleted from the lists since
nothing was known of their whereabouts.[29] These data illustrate the
desperate state of Party registration, overtaxed as it was by fluctuation and mass influx. The confusion in the Party apparatus was also
to be seen in the unplanned deployment of regional Party cadres,
who were continually being relieved of their duties and given different
ones instead.[30] This, combined with their low qualifications and the
'functional' structure of the apparatuses, created great strains. Personnel budgets were inflated, responsibility was distributed in an
unclear way, leadership methods were bureaucratic in the 'chancery
style' and discipline was not highly regarded.[31]

The reorganisation of the apparatus and the base organisations of
the Party, and the large influx of members led to a mobilisation of the
Party and an activation of many Party members, but could not
again. As early as 1932 the Central Committee set about simplifying

enterprise base organisations and structuring responsibilities in a clearer way. At first an attempt was made to improve Party work in the enterprise by merging and enlarging the sectional cells and strengthening them with experienced Party workers.[32] Finally, at the Seventeenth Party Congress in 1934, a regulation was passed which made the enterprise Party organisation tighter and easier to supervise.[33] The Party apparatus, too, was partially restructured as early as 1932,[34] and in 1933 was complemented by a parallel apparatus in the agricultural sector, the 'Political Sections'.[35] The establishment of these special sections was intended to make it easier for the Central Committee to push through its directives at the base, since the regular Party apparatus often enough failed to transfer them, or only did so in a distorted fashion. Lastly, the Seventeenth Party Congress decided to abolish the 'functional' structure and to organise 'integrated branch-of-production sections'. In the place of departments which were responsible for a single function (agitation, organisation etc.) in all areas of society, the Central Committee now formed ones which took over all functions in individual areas: one section for agriculture, one for industry, one for the transport sector, one for planning, trade and finance, one for politics and administration, one for culture and propaganda and finally one for Party organisation.[36] The apparatuses of the regional Party Committees were restructured in a similar way. The reshaping and simplification of Party organisation was accompanied by a purge that began in 1933 and which by the beginning of 1935 had removed about 17 per cent of candidates and full members.[37]

The reform of Party organisation that took place in the years 1932–4 reflects a political change that was ushered in by Stalin's Six Points speech of 1931, turning away from a policy that relied on mass mobilisation and initiatives from the base, to an emphasis on leadership from above and the construction of more strongly authoritarian structures of management. This went in parallel with the introduction of new principles in economic management and more cautious planning for the period of the second five-year plan. In particular a certain realism was to be seen in the individual year-plans.[38] The first three years of the new five-year plan, 1934, 1935 and 1936, were characterised by a rapid growth of industrial production, the gradual recovery of agriculture, and excessively high investments. The great industrial construction projects of the first five-year plan were concluded, and new enterprises began production. Productivity rose as the influx of new workers declined and the 'old' workers gradually gathered experience and acquired technical qualifications. Wage differentials and the Stakhanov movement took care of incentives, both moral and material ones. After these 'three good years' there was a collapse of growth in 1937–8, which was ascribed to the diversion of resources into the armaments sector, but which seems to have been a consequence of the mass arrests in the economic apparatus. Finally, the third five-year plan, which had to be broken off in 1941, provided again for very high rates of growth. Nevertheless, the increasing danger of war made greater efforts in armaments necessary. This adjustment, in combination with the after-effects of mass repression, led to an irregular development; there were temporary crises, especially in the fuel sector and in smelting.[39]

Social change slowed down in the second five-year plan. The number of workers and white-collar workers in large-scale industry had nearly doubled between 1929 and 1932 – it had risen from 3.36 million to 6.48 million – but between 1932–5 only a comparatively moderate growth to 7.06 million was recorded.[40] After the 'great leap forward', the years of 'bacchanalian' planning (1928–32), the phase up to the beginning of the war was rather a period in which social structures were consolidated and forms of political control were solidified, although the development of industry was still proceeding very rapidly. Nevertheless, within the leadership strata the mass arrests of those years led to displacements. There was a generational change in the apparatus of political, economic and military leadership.

Mass arrests, Party purges and the extensive ritualisation of politics determined the political climate of the years 1933–41. A clear symptom of internal Party development was the decline in membership numbers at this time. Between January 1933 and January 1938 the Party lost 46 per cent of its numbers – 1,635 million members and candidates. Since the admission of new members was discontinued from January 1933 and only resumed in November 1936, and since a mere 40,000 people entered the Party between December 1936 and the end of 1937,[41] these are actual losses. A small proportion of them had natural causes (death through illness, old age), but the great mass of leavers had resigned or were expelled. The large membership losses were due to the repeated purges of the thirties: the Party purge (*chistka*) of 1933, which dragged on into 1935,[42] the verification (*proverka*) of Party documents, which was presumably planned in October 1934 and then put into action in May 1935, and the reallocation of Party membership cards that took place in the first half of 1936.[43] In parallel to the continued purges of the Party, the People's

TABLE 8.2   *Membership figures for the VKP (b) 1927–41 (full members and candidates)*

Year	absolute	in % (1933=100%)	annual losses	losses as % of 1933 total
Jan. 1927	1,212,505	–	–	–
Jan. 1933	3,555,338	100.0%	–	–
Jan. 1934	2,701,008	75.97	–854,330	24.0%
Jan. 1935	2,358,714	66.3	–342,294	9.6
Jan. 1936	2,076,842	58.4	–281,872	7.9
Jan. 1937	1,981,697	55.7	–95,145	2.7
Jan. 1938	1,920,002	54.0	–61,695	1.7
Jan. 1939	2,306,973	64.9	–	–
Jan. 1940	3,399,975	95.6	–	–
Jan. 1941	3,872,465	108.9	–	–

SOURCE   T. H. Rigby, *Communist Party Membership in the USSR 1917–1967* (Princeton, 1968) p. 52.

Commissariat for Internal Affairs (NKVD) intensified its acts of repression, which were directed against the whole of society and cannot always be clearly distinguished from the Party purges – although, as is often overlooked, these are different processes. The campaign of repression, which found expression in show trials and mass arrests, reached a climax in the years 1937 and 1938 under People's Commissar Ezhov.

The three membership revisions of the years 1933–6, which removed about 1.6 million people from the Party, were, for both organisational and political reasons, carried out by Party headquarters. After the mass influx of new members in the first five-year plan and the repeated reforms of the Party apparatus, the registration of members had become an unholy mess, with the result that it was necessary to draw up a new list of members and revise the membership files and the Party cards that had been issued.[44] In addition, the mass admissions had washed into the Party numerous politically ignorant or entirely passive members, who were now expelled.[45] Nevertheless the element of political discipline must not be overlooked. The Party purge of 1933, initiated in view of the serious crisis of 1932, which evidently triggered off considerable dissatisfaction within the Party, was directed against those members who opposed the directives of the leadership.[46] The murder of the Leningrad Party Secretary S. Kirov in December 1934 added a new element to the membership revision: former opposition leaders, among them Zinoviev and Kamenev, were arrested in connection with the assassination and given prison sentences.[47] In a 'Closed Letter' the Central Committee called for increased watchfulness, and above all for the exposure of former opposition figures. Local organisations reacted to this with a wave of denunciations.[48] The verification of Party documents that followed thus took place in a climate that was determined by suspicion and fear. This did not, however, make a significant difference in terms of numbers. Many more than half the Party expulsions of the years 1933–7 took place before 1935: 850,000 in 1933, 340,000 in 1934.[49] In the following years the numbers fell: to 280,000 in 1935, 90,000 in 1936 and to between 60,000 and 100,000 in 1937.[50] The 'politicisation' of the Party purges did not therefore lead to their extension. The great mass of expulsions took place in connection with the problems of political organisation in the years 1930–3.[51]

There are scarcely any reliable details about which groups within the Party were most affected by the membership revision. The statistics of the Leningrad Party may possibly give some indications (see Table 8.3). Same caution is necessary in evaluating these data. To begin with, the incompleteness of the details for 1933 is something of a problem, so that the rates of loss for the years 1933–7 are uncertain.[52] Especially in the case of the cohorts of Party entry for 1928–32, the proportion of people expelled may be much higher than is here shown. A further cause of uncertainty is to be found in the fact that nothing is known about the reasons for leaving the Leningrad area organisation.[53] In a period of high regional mobility it is impossible to be certain whether departure from the region means expulsion or simply a move to new employment, and among the older generation of Party members a higher mortality rate is to be expected. Nevertheless, when comparing the generational cohorts of the beginning of 1937 and of the beginning of 1940, one's eye is caught by the fact that the generations entering up to 1919 suffered especially in the years 1937, 1938 and 1939, while the generations of 1925–32 were largely spared in this period. The mass expulsions of the years 1933 and 1934 tended therefore to affect primarily the Party base and the younger members, while the purges of the years 1937–9 had a different tendency: they were evidently directed at members who had been in the Party for a long time, of whom many occupied responsible positions in the apparatuses of state, Party and economy.[54]

TABLE 8.3 *Distribution of Party members (full members) in the Leningrad area according to duration of membership*

Year of entry into Party	Distribution of Party members					
	in Jan. 1933 absolute	in Jan. 1937 absolute	in % of 1933	in Jan. 1940 absolute	in % of 1933	in % of 1937
before 1917	870	812	93.3	612	70.3	75.4
1917	2,479	2,006	80.9	1,490	60.1	74.2
1918		2,930		2,364		80.6
1919	12,791*	5,140	90.2*	4,199	74.4*	81.6
1920		3,476		2,959		85.1
1921				931		
1922	2,594**	1,921	74.0	691****	62.5**	84.4
1923						
1924		5,859		5,096		86.9
1925–7	39,685***	28,185	85.7***	24,845	75.4***	88.1
1928–30	41,485^{55}	33,134	79.9	29,837	71.9	90.0
1931–32	52,691	43,758	83.0	40,180	76.2	91.8
	(152,594)					
Total	199,760	127,221	63.6	137,224	68.6	107.8

* 1918–20
** 1921–23
*** 1924–27
**** 1922–23

SOURCE *Leningradskaya organizatsiya KPSS v tsifrakh 1917–1973* (Leningrad, 1974) pp. 87 f.; the admission years 1933–40 are not taken into account here; cf. similar developments in Belorussia, *Kommunisticheskaya partiya Belorussii v tsifrakh 1918–1978* (Minsk, 1978) pp. 112 f.

There are grounds for supposing that there is a connection between this and the wave of repression of those years.

The mass arrests of the thirties are only indirectly connected with the Party purges. The mass expulsions of the years 1933–4 took place in the context of the attempts to overcome the organisational chaos of the period of the first five-year plan. It was only in the following years, when the number of Party expulsions became significantly fewer, that the organs of the NKVD, the executors of state power, began to carry out increased numbers of arrests, which reached a climax in 1937–8.[55]

The security organs – until 1934 the OGPU, which was then incorporated into the NKVD – had played a subordinate role in the NEP. The security organs only became a political factor with the

transition to the policy of forced industrialisation and the implementation of forced collectivisation. The OGPU played a part in the
'parasites campaign': authorised representatives of the OGPU supervised collectivisation, special troops of the OGPU broke the resistance of peasants. The expenditure for OGPU/NKVD in the state
budget, which had remained largely constant between 1923–4 and
1926–7, began in 1927–8 gradually to rise and by 1937 was nine times
as high as the sum for 1928.[56] The influence of the political police,
which had built up a prisoner economy of its own by 1929–30, grew in
many areas of society. The number of prisoners in the system of
'corrective labour camps' is disputed. The majority of authors assume
a figure of 2–2.5 million prisoners for the years 1931–2, but the
estimates for 1940 vary greatly: they range from 3.5 to 13.5 million.[57]
Although reliable figures are unobtainable, it cannot be disputed
that, in the thirties, the OGPU/NKVD built up a complex system of
camps which held several million prisoners.

The first wave of mass arrests took place in the context of
collectivisation. It was peasants above all who were affected, but also
'bourgeois specialists'. These measures served to push through the
policies of industrialisation and collectivisation, but at the same time
marked out scapegoats for the economic crisis for which the Central
Committee was actually responsible. After the implementation of
Stalin's industrialisation policy, repression was evidently restricted;
the rights of the security organs seem to have been curtailed in the
years 1933 and 1934.[58] Then there came a change with the Kirov
murder, which was followed immediately by the trial of Zinoviev and
Kamenev, combined with further forms of repression, among others
the deportation of former aristocrats from Leningrad.[59] After this
'Kirov wave' the activity of the security organs again declined.
Between July 1935 and August 1936 there were neither spectacular
trials nor unusually large-scale mass arrests. Then in August 1936[60]
there began the first great show trial of this period, the legal action
against the 'Trotskyite-Zinovievite Centre'. The accused, among
them Zinoviev and Kamenev, were condemned to death. Further
trials were being prepared while this one was still running, and
former oppositional figures were arrested in large numbers. At the
end of September 1936 Yagoda was replaced as Commissar for
Internal Affairs by Ezhov. Repression now swiftly gained in range
and intensity. In October three groups of 'saboteurs' were discovered
in the economic leadership. In January 1937 a new group of former
oppositional figures, among them Sokol'nikov, Piatakov and Radek,

were prosecuted under the heading 'Anti-Soviet Trotskyite Centre', which ended for most of the accused with the death sentence.

In the meantime the majority of section leaders in the NKVD had been arrested and replaced. The machinery of repression now got under way. The command structure of the Red Army was broken and a large proportion of the military leadership personnel thrown into prison; the Leningrad Party organisation lost the mass of its cadres, among them also large sections of local economic management. Similarly in the summer of 1937 one regional Party organisation after another was smashed, the leading Party officials arrested, many shot. Even members of the Central Committee and of the Soviet leadership, the people who worked in the Central Committee apparatus and the People's Commissariats, were not spared. The leadership cadres of the unions, the Komsomol and the economic management were decimated too. In March 1938 a further spectacular trial took place. In the dock stood, amongst others, Bukharin, Rykov and Rakovskii, beside Yagoda – a curious combination. All except one of the accused were condemned to death. Meanwhile the arrests continued. A turning-point seems to have been reached only after Ezhov had been replaced by Beriia. The NKVD apparatus was once again reorganised, Ezhov's colleagues being for the most part arrested. After that the number of arrests evidently declined, current cases were in part dismissed, prisoners awaiting trial were released.

The repression of the years 1934–8 – the 'Kirov wave' at the beginning of 1935 and the 'Ezhovshchina' of 1936–8 – evidently affected all realms of Soviet society. Details about population losses are only gradually becoming available. According to the Director of the National Economy Archive of the USSR, V. V. Tsaplin, who has analysed material from the census of 1937, between 1927 and 1938 7.9 million people died of hunger or were killed in labour camps, and a further 2 million emigrated.[61] Included in these figures are the peasants who died of hunger in connection with forced collectivisation, but also people who in the course of the waves of arrests ended up in the camps and died there of undernourishment and overwork. It is not easy to determine from the hitherto available sources which groups of the population were especially affected by the arrests. Nevertheless, we possess partial data which allow us to draw certain conclusions. Thus the victims were particularly numerous among those Party members who were prominent in public life. Of the 1966 delegates to the Seventeenth Party Congress of 1934, only ninety-five (4.8 per cent) can be identified at the Eighteenth Party Congress of

1939. According to details given in Khrushchev's secret speech of 1956, 1108 of the 1966 delegates, i.e. 56.3 per cent, were arrested in the phase of mass repression. It was a similar story in the Central Committee: of the 139 members and candidates of the Central Committee elected at the Seventeenth Party Congress, 115 (82.7 per cent) were missing at the Eighteenth Party Congress; of these the NKVD had, according to Khrushchev, liquidated ninety-eight (70.5 per cent).[62] The Congress incorporated the great mass of upper and middle management of the Party – including members and candidates of the Central Committee and the Central Control Commission, regional and area Party secretaries, the secretaries of the national Communist Parties, 140 town and urban district secretaries, fifty secretaries of Party Committees of individual enterprises, 120 district Party secretaries, and in addition 168 people working in political departments in rural areas and in transportation.[63] One can therefore start from the assumption that the cadre of Party officials was smashed.[64]

However, the group who graduated from tertiary education in the years 1928–7 does not appear to have suffered to the same degree. If one compares the numbers of graduates with the census of specialists of January 1941, one arrives at the picture given in Table 8.4. The generation of specialists trained in the period of the five-year plan was evidently only slightly affected by the acts of mass repression. If one takes into account that the figures for specialists for 1941 do not include qualified people working in the NKVD, the Party and the

TABLE 8.4　　*Graduates 1928–37, and specialists as listed in the census of January 1941*

period	number of tertiary level graduates (not military academies) (1)	specialists, 1.1.1941. who graduated 1928–1937 (not military, NKVD, Party apparatus) (2)	difference	level of 1941 as % of number of graduates
1928–32	198,700	152,200	46,500	76.6%
1933–37	369,900	266,350	103,550	72.0
1928–37	568,600	418,550	150,050	73.6

SOURCES　(1) *Kul'turnoe stroitel'stvo SSSR* (Moscow, 1973) p. 270 (2) *Industrializatsiya SSSR 1938–1941 gg.* (Moscow, 1973) p. 270; the absolute figures are calculated from the total information and percentages.

military, then the rate of loss of graduates is even lower. This group did not therefore belong in the first instance to the victims of repression, but rather benefited from it through upward social mobility.

Statistical information about the generation born in 1906 provided by the Soviet demographer B. C. Urlanis points in a similar direction.[65] The members of this generation, among whom L. I. Brezhnev belonged, were eleven years old at the time of the Revolution, twenty-two at the beginning of forced industrialisation. At the time of the 'Ezhovshchina' they were thirty-one or thirty-two, i.e. they belonged to the generation that only advanced into positions of responsibility during the course of the thirties. The mortality rate of this age-cohort rose in the years 1931–3, the values were higher than those that were to be expected for twenty-five to twenty-seven year-olds[66] – a consequence of forced collectivisation and famine. For the years 1934–9 Urlanis then provides the information given in Table 8.5. The mortality rate of the generation of 1906 shows no significant change in the years of the second five-year plan. There are no demographic consequences of the phases of intensive repression, i.e. the 'Ezhovshchina'. That is to say that the operations of the NKVD – at least as far as the generation of 1906 is concerned – were limited in scale; the majority of the incidences of death had natural causes.[67]

TABLE 8.5 *Incidences of death in the years 1934–9 of members of the generation born in 1906*

year	men	women	together
1934	10,000	9,000	19,000
1935	9,000	8,000	17,000
1936	9,300	9,600	17,400
1937	9,600	8,000	17,600
1938	9,600	8,000	17,600
1939	9,500	7,500	17,000

SOURCE B. Urlanis, *Istoriya odnogo pokoleniya* (Moscow, 1968) pp. 200 f.

Even if one considers the mortality of the total population in the thirties it does not appear that the repression had any demographic effect – by contrast with collectivisation, which led to a clear increase in mortality, as demonstrated in Table 8.6. One must certainly take note of the fact that the census of 1939, the official population figures and the official registration data, which the quoted authors take as

TABLE 8.6   *Estimates of the mortality rate in the Soviet Union 1930–38 (incidences of death per 1000 inhabitants)*

year	Lorimer	Prokopovic	Kulischer	Martschenko	Biraben
1930	28.2	20.4	20.4	20.4	19.8
1931	28.5	–	–	21.0	26.6
1932	34.5	–	–	21.6	23.2
1933	27.0	–	–	100.7	32.5
1934	24.3	–	–	16.1	34.4
1935	22.5	16.3	16.3	18.0	16.4
1936	20.6	17.1	18.4	21.0	18.2
1937	18.6	16.7	17.9	19.0	17.6
1938	17.8	17.8	17.8	–	17.6

SOURCES   I am grateful to S. G. Wheatcroft for drawing my attention to this data, which he has collated and subjected to critical examination: F. Lorimer, *Population of the Soviet Union* (Geneva, 1946) pp. 134 f.; S. N. Prokopovic, *Russlands Volkswirtschaft unter den Sowjets* (Zürich, New York, 1944), pp. 21, 33; E. Kulischer, *Europe on the Move. War and Population Changes 1917–1947* (New York, 1948) p. 80; B. Marotschenko, 'Soviet Population Trends 1926–1939' (mimeographed, New York, 1953) pp. 13, 22; J. N. Biraben, 'Essai sur l'évolution demographique de l'URSS', *Population* 13, 1958, no. 2 (b), pp. 29–62.

their starting-point, are not incontestable. But none of the authors has been able to provide grounds for believing that the mortality rate rose in a significant way in 1937–8. The 'Ezhovshchina' evidently took place on a scale that did not influence the movement of the population as a whole.

There is, however, another demographic approach to the population losses of the phase of repression. If one correlates the data of the 1939 census on the distribution of the population according to age and sex one arrives at the results given in Table 8.7. What is striking about this table is a demographic anomaly: if one compares the proportion of men in the age-group between forty or forty-nine to that in the group aged between fifty and fifty-nine the former is significantly lower, although in theory the male deficit increases with age. In this case war and civil war must in the first instance be deemed responsible, but that applied also to the age-groups of thirty-five to thirty-nine and fifty to fifty-four. It is however also conceivable that those aged forty to forty-nine, who in 1937–8 made up the great mass of personnel at the middle and upper levels of leadership, were especially strongly affected by acts of repression. The figures for the

TABLE 8.7 *Proportion of men in the age-cohorts of the Soviet population on 17.1.1939 (in % of the number of women of the corresponding age-group)*

age-group	
0–9	101.6%
10–14	99.4
15–19	97.5
20–24	99.4
25–29	93.2
30–34	90.9
35–39	83.0
40–44	78.5
45–49	78
50–54	81.8
55–59	81.6
60–64	77.5
65–69	74.3
70 and older	66.5
average	91.96%

SOURCE Census data, corrected by F. Lorimer, *Population of the Soviet Union* (Geneva, 1946) p. 143.

age-group twenty to thirty-four in this table could be used to confirm the data of Urlanis, namely that the generation of 1906 was not significantly affected by repression, and similarly the thesis of S. Fitzpatrick, who shows that graduates of the years 1928–37 were only peripherally affected. This agrees also with the deduction to be made from the Leningrad Party statistics that it was the 'old' Party members from the time of Revolution and Civil War who were 'purged'.

There is certainly something speculative about these data, but, drawn together, they would permit the hypothesis that the repression of the years 1936–8, which is often confused with the Party purges of 1933–6, by no means affected the whole of the population. The human losses of this phase are far fewer than those of forced collectivisation, which are generally reckoned at 5–6 million. Those affected were evidently above all the stratum of established functionaries in Party, state, economy and military, and it is this stratum that was essentially broken. A new generation advanced into their positions. The arrests and death sentences disorganised the economy, the administration and the army; they determined the political culture and unsettled the population, which learnt to abstain from any kind of initiative, whether or not of a political nature. Stalin and the rest of the Party leaders had thereby finally established their dominance: a new generation that only knew the Revolution by hearsay had advanced into the key positions of the economy and the state. The process of restructuring the social and political system, which had begun at the end of the twenties, had reached a preliminary conclusion.

The question why the Soviet state took action against leading people who worked in it must probably still remain open. If the Party membership revisions of 1933–6 can still be explained rationally, the reasons for the acts of mass repression at the beginning of 1935 and in 1936–8 are not easy to comprehend. The removal of desperately-needed specialists in the army, the administration, the Party and the economy, people whose absence must be made responsible for the crisis in economic growth at the end of the thirties, as also for the failure of the Red Army in 1941, must appear absurd. The images of the enemy propagated during the years of 1936–8, the association of 'Trotskyism' and 'fascism', and moreover the groundless accusations on which the show trials were built, reveal no coherent political concept. Thus it is only possible to suggest hypotheses as to the motives and mechanisms of the 'Great Purge'. The majority of authors make Stalin personally responsible for the waves of repression. They argue that he was concerned to destroy all potential rivals and all autonomous forces which might have threatened his position of absolute power. Such a view then often also leads to the assumption that the course of the 'Great Purge' from the Kirov murder to the removal of Ezhov followed a grand plan.

On the other hand, some authors see in the sequence of waves of repression a mechanism at work in which were expressed on the one hand the self-interest of the security organs and on the other a multiplicity of conflicts – between Party headquarters and local Party offices, between rival groups in individual provinces, between specialist and political apparatuses. For example, the American historian Getty interprets the liquidation of the area Party apparatuses as an attempt by the Party headquarters to cut back the independence of local apparatuses and finally to shape in a more effective way the process of leadership by the headquarters.[68] Other factors which led to the intensification of repression are presumably connected with the mass psychosis, the climate of fear and suspicion that was produced in the public realm. Clearly the majority of functionaries were afraid of not measuring up to the publicly-laid-down norms of 'watchfulness' if they did not relentlessly pursue the exposure of 'enemies'. The wave of denunciations which swept through the country and the Party certainly contributed to the increase in the number of arrests. It seems plausible to suppose that in such a climate of political hysteria it was possible for a policy of irrational terror to develop whose intention was no longer clearly recognisable. As against the 'intentionalists', who interpret the policy of repression as a strategy planned from above, there are those historians who stress that Stalin's repression was a process, and in constructing an explanation draw not only on Stalin's calculations but also on socio-cultural factors.

The stabilisation of the system of political rule and the replacement of the 'old' leadership stratum with a new one, the result of the wave of repression of the years 1936–8, had created a socio-political framework to which the Party leadership tried to do justice at the Eighteenth Party Congress of 1939 by means of a new reorganisation of the apparatus and a change in recruitment policy. The restructuring of the Party organisation and the reform of the apparatus, which ran parallel to a regional and administrative reform, had in the first instance technical reasons. It was a question of eliminating the dysfunction of the Party and state apparatus by means of organisational changes. Areas, regions and districts were made smaller and divided up in a clearer way, while the number of People's Commissariats of the Union was raised from fourteen to thirty-four.[69] The Party organisation was adapted to the new structure of administration. Furthermore the 'integrated branch-of-production sections' that had been created in 1934 were abandoned, since the Party apparatus when structured in this way strove to take the place of the economic apparatus and thus caused considerable confusion.[70] Only the agricultural section and the educational department survived, since the Soviet authorities did not have at their disposal administrative bodies capable of operating satisfactorily.[71] For the rest the Central Committee set up three departments: a cadre administration, an administration for agitation and propaganda, and a department for organisation and instruction. These three departments were to exist at area and district level, and in addition, in the case of area committees, there was to be an agricultural department. Further, there were organised below Central Committee level military departments for all committees, which were to arrange mobilisation, conscription, etc.[72]

The reorganisation of the Party apparatus illustrates the change in its function. In the initial phase of forced industrialisation the Party leadership had urged the whole organisation to push through the leadership of the Party in all realms of state and economy and to have an influence over every single decision. After the old Party cadres had been decimated, after economic and social control had shifted in many areas to the NKVD, the tasks of the Party were once again reduced – reduced to the establishment of legitimation by means of schooling and agitation, and the training and allocation of cadres. The structure of the Party apparatus was now adapted to this narrower field of activity.

In the context of the adaptation of the Party statutes to the new situation, the party leadership set the direction by abolishing 'mass purges' and setting down on paper the rights of members – the expression of criticism, the right to vote and eligibility for office, the right of appeal, etc.[73] Even if the criticism of 'mass purges' can in theory only be applied to the period 1933–6, Zhdanov made it clear that it was a question of the practice of the years 1937–8, when Party members were, without closer investigation, branded as 'enemies of the people' and then often arrested.[74] The Eighteenth Party Congress marked a clean break here, although admittedly it had limited value since the Central Committee had already made similar noises in the February-March plenary of 1937 and in the January plenary of 1938,[75] without the arrests being reduced in any way.

Nevertheless, the Party Congress *did* make a clear change by turning away completely from the traditional recruitment patterns of the Party. Up to January 1933, when the admission of new recruits was discontinued, the Party leadership was concerned above all to attract workers, if at all possible those 'from the work-bench'. Within the framework of recruitment campaigns, large numbers of workers were drawn into the Party. The regulations governing admission made the entry of workers easier and that of peasants and white-collar workers more difficult. An end was now put to this tradition. All applicants were treated equally, irrespective of their social origins. All had to present three guarantors of three years' membership and had to go through a one-year period of candidature.[76] There were no longer special rights for workers. Zhdanov described the traditional norms that had given advantage to members of the working class as obsolete on the grounds that the 'victory of socialism' had eliminated class differences and brought the classes closer to each other.[77]

The change in admission regulations led to a landslide displacement of the social composition of newly-recruited Party members: white-collar workers streamed into the Party, manual workers were now only a minority.[78] This is very clear from the admission policy of the Leningrad area organisation, which in 1939–40 took in increased numbers of white-collar workers and students instead of falling back on the reservoir of Leningrad industrial workers (see Table 8.8). As early as 1938 the proportion of workers among the new recruits fell significantly and the percentage of white-collar workers shot up. Then in 1939 and 1940 white-collar workers and students made up nearly two-thirds of the new candidates, the workers no more than a fifth. This displacement is significant for the change in the way the Party saw itself between 1930 and 1940. If, during the years of forced industrialisation, it had been a motor of radical social transformation, driving forward industrial construction and organising a wave of upward social mobility, it represented after the change of generation and the period of repression nothing more than an organisation of the

TABLE 8.8   *Occupations of newly-admitted candidates in the Leningrad area 1930–40*

year	total candidates admitted	of whom: workers	peasants, kolkhozniki	artisans	white-collar workers	lower-grade staff	students
1930 abs.	50,872	43,972	3,722	26	1,639	78	182
in %	100%	86.4%	7.3%	0.05%	3.2%	0.15%	0.35%
1931 abs.	84,017	69,619	9,580	321	2,772	–	–
in %	100%	82.7%	11.4%	0.4%	3.3%	–	–
1932 abs.	51,445	43,798	5,348	–	1,685	–	346
in %	100%	85.1%	10.4%	–	3.3%	–	0.6%
1933–35	---------------------------------- no admissions ----------------------------------						
1936–37 abs.	1,003	767	4	2	205	–	14
in %	100%	76.5%	0.4%	0.2%	20.4%	–	1.39%
1938 abs.	13,335	6,777	824	–	5,734	–	–
in %	100%	50.8%	6.2%	–	43.0%	–	–
1939 abs.	37,603	8,324	2,940	798	22,514	167	2,769
in %	100%	22.1%	7.8%	2.1%	59.8%	0.4%	7.3%
1940 abs.	15,983	2,769	2,288	315	9,037	24	1,519
in %	100%	17.3%	14.3%	2.0%	56.5%	0.15%	9.5%

SOURCES   *Leningradskaya organizatsiya KPSS v tsifrakh 1917–1973* (Leningrad, 1974) pp. 112, 114, 116; percentages calculated by the author; cf. details for Belorussia with just the same tendency: *Kommunisticheskaya partiya Belorussii v tsifrakh 1918–1978* (Minsk, 1978) pp. 52 f.

180   *Stalinism: Its Nature and Aftermath*

establishment. Social change had come to a halt, the generation of Khrushchev and Brezhnev had advanced into the leadership stratum. The Party was now a party of the social 'status quo' as, since 1928-9, it had been one of the political 'status quo'.

NOTES

1. R. V. Daniels, *The Conscience of the Revolution* (Cambridge, Mass., 1960) pp. 322-60; E. H. Carr and R. W. Davies, *Foundations of a Planned Economy* (Harmondsworth, 1974) vol. 1, pp. 918 f., vol. 2, pp. 58-9; S. F. Cohen, *Bukharin and the Bolshevik Revolution* (Oxford, 1980) pp. 276 f.; P. A. Diaconoff, 'Gosplan and the Politics of Soviet Planning, 1929-1932', unpublished PhD thesis, University of Michigan, 1979, p. 84; K. E. Bailes, *Technology and Society under Lenin and Stalin* (Princeton, 1978) pp. 19-20; N. Lampert, *The Technical Intelligentsia and the Soviet State* (London, 1979) pp. 38 f.
2. For the Shakhty affair and the 'anti-parasites' campaign, see the titles referred to in note 1; R. Conquest, *The Great Terror* (London, 1968) pp. 549 f.; R. A. Medvedev, *Let History Judge* (New York, 1972) pp. 111-13. See also N. Krylenko, *Klassovaya bor'ba putem vreditel'stva* (Moscow-Leningrad, 1931).
3. See S. Fitzpatrick, *Education and Social Mobility in the Soviet Union 1921-1934* (Cambridge, 1979) pp. 133 f.; *KPSS v rezolyutsiyakh i resheniyakh* (Moscow, 1971) vol. 4, pp. 91, 111 f., 334 f., 443; F. N. Zauzolkov, *Kommunisticheskaya partiya – organizator sozdaniya nauchnoi i proizvodstvenno-tekhnicheskoi intelligentsii SSSR* (Moscow, 1973) p. 80; H. Schröder, 'Wirtschaftsleitung und Parteibürokratie in der Sowjetischen Industrie 1928-1932' in *Järbücher für die Geschichte Osteuropas (JGO)* NF 29, 1981, pp. 537-68; 550 f.
4. Fitzpatrick, p 188; *Sotsialisticheskoe stroitel'stvo SSSR* (Moscow 1934) pp. 406-7; A. E. Beilin, *Kadry spetsialistov v SSSR-ikh formirovanie i rost* (Moscow, 1935).
5. Ibid., p. 75.
6. Ibid., p. 311.
7. *Plan obespicheniya narodnogo khozyaistva kadrami spetsialistov (1929-1933)* (Moscow 1930) pp. 45 f.; Schröder in *JGO* NF 29, 1981, p. 550.
8. Party archives, quoted in I. A. Yudin, *Sotsial'naya baza rosta KPSS* (Moscow 1973) pp. 129 f.
9. *Sotsialisticheskoe stroitel'stvo 1934*, pp. 310 f.
10. Ibid., pp. 306 f.; 323.
11. *Trud v SSSR* (Moscow 1932) p. 76; in each case at the beginning of the year.
12. *Sotsialisticheskoe stroitel'stvo 1934*, pp. 7, 310 f.

13. See *Profsoyuznaya perepis' 1932–1933* (Moscow 1934) p. 94 f.
14. S. Schwarz, *Labor in the Soviet Union* (New York, 1952) pp. 16–17, 86–92; Z. L. Mordukhovich [Mokhov], *Na bor'bu s tekuchest'yu rabochei sily* (Moscow 1931). Cf. A. Z. Khain and V. Khandros, *Kto oni – novye lyudi na proizvodstve* (Moscow 1930); J. Scott, *Behind the Urals* (Bloomington, 1973) pp. 74–75; H. H. Schröder, *Industrialisierung und Parteibürokratie in der Sowjetunion* (Berlin, 1988) pp. 291–305.
15. Schröder, pp. 172–9; E. H. Carr and R. W. Davies, vol. 2, pp. 80–81; M. Reiman, *Die Geburt des Stalinismus* (Frankfurt, 1979) pp. 145 f.; Daniels, pp. 322–69; Cohen, pp. 270 f.; N. Ezhov, L. Mekhlis and P. Pospelov, 'Pravyi uklon v prakticheskoi rabote i partiinoe boloto', *Bol'shevik* (1929) No. 16, pp. 39–62; T. Szamueli, 'The Elimination of Opposition between the Sixteenth and Seventeenth Congresses of the CPSU', *Soviet Studies*, Vol. XVII (1965–6), pp. 318–38.
16. *Pravda*, 13 November 1927, p. 1; *KPSS v rezolyutsiyakh*, vol. 3, p. 543; *Izvestiya TsK VKP*, 1928, no. 24, p. 4.
17. *KPSS v rezolyutsiyakh*, vol. 4, pp. 148–9.
18. *Partiinoe stroitel'stvo*, 1930, no. 10, p. 8; 1931, no. 13, p. 5; 1932, nos. 7–8, pp. 53 f.; no. 15, pp. 51 f.
19. Cf. *Vsesoyuznaya partiinaya perepis' 1927 g.* (Moscow 1927) pp. 3, 6; T. H. Rigby, *Communist Party Membership in the USSR 1917–1967* (Princeton, NJ, 1968).
20. *Vsesoyuznaya partiinaya perepis'*, pp. 18 f., 22 f.; *Partiinoe stroitel'stvo*, 1932, no. 9, pp. 50 f.
21. Kaganovich, *XVI s'ezd VKP* (Moscow-Leningrad, 1931) pp. 18 f.
22. *BSE*, vol. XI, pp. 535 f.; Kaganovich, *XVII s'ezd VKP* (Moscow 1934) pp. 555, 557.
23. *Pervichnaya partiinaya organizatsiya* (Moscow 1970) pp. 156–71; Schröder, pp. 135–55.
24. *Pervichnaya partiinaya organizatsiya*, pp. 156–71; *KPSS v rezolyutsiyakh*, vol. 4, pp. 158–61, 254–63; *Partiinoe stroitel'stvo*, 1929, no. 2, p. 59.
25. See L. M. Kaganovich, *Ocherednye zadachi partraboty i reorganizatsiya partapparata* (Moscow-Leningrad, 1930) p. 36; *Partiinoe stroitel'stvo*, 1929, no. 2, pp. 52, 55; 1930, nos. 3–4, pp. 63 f.
26. *Partiinoe stroitel'stvo* 1930, no. 9, pp. 27 f.
27. Cf. the criticism made of Party cadres and organisations on the occasion of the Shakhty trial, *KPSS*, vol. 4, pp. 84–93; Kaganovich, *XVI s'ezd VKP (b)* (Moscow-Leningrad, 1931) p. 82.
28. L. M. Kaganovich, *Ocherednye zadachi partraboty i reorganizatsiya partapparata* (Moscow-Leningrad, 1930) pp. 54–9.
29. *Partiinoe stroitel'stvo*, 1932, no. 9, p. 49.
30. Ibid., 1932, no. 22, pp. 24–30; 1933, no. 16, p. 39.
31. Ibid., 1934, no. 1, pp. 2 f.; Kaganovich, *XVII s'ezd*, p. 561.
32. *Partiinoe stroitel'stvo*, 1932, nos. 17–18, p. 49; *Bol'shevik*, 1932, no. 16, pp. 33 f.; *Pervichnaya partiinaya organizatsiya*, pp. 250–3.
33. *KPSS v rezolyutsiyakh*, vol. 5, pp. 169 f.
34. *Partiinoe stroitel'stvo*, 1932, no. 9, pp. 1–3, 60 f.
35. *KPSS v rezolyutsiyakh*, vol. 5, pp. 78–89.

36. Kaganovich, *XVII s'ezd*, p. 56 f.; *KPSS v rezolyutsiyakh*, vol. 5, p. 156.
37. Rudzutak, *XVII s'ezd*, p. 287; Kaganovich, ibid., p. 552; cf *Partiinaya zhizn'*, 1947, no. 20, p. 79.
38. Cf A. Nove, *An Economic History of the USSR* (Harmondsworth, 1969) pp. 224 f.; N. Jasny, *Soviet Industrialization 1928–1952* (Chicago, 1961) pp. 120 f.; E. Zaleski, *Stalinist Planning for Economic Growth 1933–1952* (London, 1980) pp. 105 f.
39. Nove, pp. 224 f.; Jasny, pp. 120 f.; Zaleski, pp. 269 f.
40. *Trud v SSSR* (Moscow 1936) pp. 10 f.; cf data in *Industrializatsiya SSSR 1933–1937 g.* (Moscow 1971) p. 516.
41. *KPSS v rezolyutsiyakh*, vol. 5, pp. 89, 282 ff.; T. H. Rigby, *Communist Party Membership in the USSR 1917–1967* (Princeton, NJ, 1968), pp. 214 ff.
42. *KPSS*, vol. 5, pp. 89, 98 ff.; Rigby, pp. 200 ff.; V. K. Palishko, *Rost i ukreplenie partiinykh ryadov v usloviyakh stroitel'stva i uprochneniya sotsializma* (Kiev, 1979) pp. 66 ff.
43. Rigby, pp. 206 ff.; Soviet research brings together as a single event the verification and the reallocation of Party documents, cf. Palishko, pp. 66 f.
44. Rigby, pp. 200 ff.; J. A. Getty, 'Party and Purge in Smolensk: 1933–1937', *Slavic Review* (1983) 42, pp. 60–79, and the contributions by Tucker and Rosenfeldt in the same issue.
45. A quarter of the expulsions in 1933 took place because of 'passivity', Rudzutak *XVII s'ezd*, p. 287; cf *Istoriya KPSS* (Moscow 1971), vol. 4, book 2, p. 283; Schröder, *Industrialisierung*, ch. 9.
46. Ibid.
47. *Pravda*, 23 December 1934; Cf. Conquest, pp. 55 f.; *Pravda*, 17 January 1935.
48. Rigby, pp. 205 f.
49. See Rigby, p. 52; the cases in which members were lost because of natural death must be subtracted from the losses.
50. Ibid., pp. 206–12.
51. It must be borne in mind that admissions had been taking place again since November 1936; by the end of 1937 about 40,000 people had joined the Party. See Rigby, pp. 214 f.
52. For 1933 we have a breakdown for 152,594 people, whereas there was a total of 199,760 full members. Cf *Leningradskaya organizatsiya KPSS v tsifrakh 1917–1973* (Leningrad, 1974), pp. 88, 69.
53. In the years 1928–1932 in the Leningrad area, 229,931 people were admitted to the Party as candidates; 134,326 were made full members; the details of the table for 1928–32 may therefore be between 30,000 and 40,000 beneath their actual value; that means also that the majority of the 47,166 members who are not broken down according to length of party membership may belong to the generation of the five-year plan.
54. That this development was not restricted to Leningrad alone we may suspect from Zhdanov's remark at the Eighteenth Party Congress that the great mass of Party secretaries with technical or other college certificates (at district and regional level 58.9 per cent of all secretaries) had concluded their training in 1934 or later (*XVIII s'ezd VKP (b)* (Moscow 1939) p. 529); a whole new generation of young cadres had

evidently moved up. Less than 20 per cent of the delegates to the Eighteenth Party Congress had joined the Party before the end of the Civil War, whereas this proportion was 80 per cent five years before at the Seventeenth Congress. Ibid, pp. 148 f.; *XVII s'ezd*, p. 303.

55. See Zhdanov, *XVIII s'ezd*, pp. 519 f. on the connection between expulsion from the Party and arrest in 1937–8.
56. R. Slusser 'The Budget of the OGPU and the Special Troops from 1923/24 to 1928/29', *Soviet Studies*, Vol. X (1958–9), pp. 375–83; 1937 details are from A. Bergson, *The Real National Income of Soviet Russia since 1928* (Cambridge, 1961) p. 67; when judging this rate of growth it must be recalled that in 1934 the OGPU was reorganised into the NKVD, which had a considerably broader realm of responsibility (fire brigade, militia, registration offices etc.) than the earlier OGPU.
57. See S. G. Wheatcroft, 'On Assessing the Size of Forced Concentration Camp Labour in the Soviet Union, 1929–1956', *Soviet Studies*, Vol. XXXIII, 1981, pp. 265–95.
58. See Schröder, *Industrialisierung*, ch. 5.
59. R. Medvedev, pp. 162–5.
60. On the problem of repression, see Conquest and Medvedev, on which the following exposition depends.
61. V. V. Tsaplin, 'Statistika zhertv stalinizma v 30-e gody', *Voprosy istorii* (1989) no. 4, pp. 175–81.
62. Conquest, p. 471; 'O kul'te lichnosti i ego posledstviyakh. Doklad pervogo sekretarya TsK KPSS XX s'ezdu Kommunisticheskoi Partii Sovetskogo Soyuza', *Izvestiya TsK KPSS* (1989) No. 3, p. 137.
63. Ezhov, *XVII s'ezd*, pp. 303 f.
64. S. Fitzpatrick, 'Stalin and the Making of the New Elite, 1928–1939', *Slavic Review* (1979) no. 3, pp. 377–402.
65. B. Urlanis, *Istoriya odnogo pokoleniya* (Moscow, 1968) pp. 199 f.
66. Ibid.
67. For causes of death, ibid., pp. 227, 229, 233, 235. According to this source tuberculosis, injury, and diseases of the internal organs were the commonest causes of death.
68. *Slavic Review*, 42, 1983, p. 77.
69. Stalin, *XVIII s'ezd*, pp. 28 f.; Zhdanov, ibid., pp. 527 f.
70. Ibid., p. 532.
71. Ibid., *KPSS v rezolyutsiyakh*, vol. 5, p. 377.
72. Ibid., pp. 377 f.
73. Ibid., pp. 375 f.; Zhdanov, *XVIII s'ezd*, pp. 517 f.
74. Ibid., pp. 519 f.
75. Ibid., p. 524.
76. *KPSS*, vol. 5, pp. 376, 383, 384 f.; Zhdanov, *XVIII s'ezd*, pp. 514 f.
77. Ibid., pp. 516 f.
78. Rigby, pp. 223 f.

9 Construction Workers in the 1930s
Jean-Paul Depretto

The 1930s were marked by a sharp increase in major construction work,[1] but, paradoxically, we do not know much about the building workers: in spite of their numbers, they have not caught the attention of historians and have been the subject of few publications. It is not only a question of better understanding of an important section of the working class. Much more is at stake, because building sites provide a privileged view of the industrialisation of the USSR. A systematic study would allow us to consider from a fresh standpoint several questions crucial to the understanding of Soviet development: the extent of mechanisation and the relative importance of Soviet and imported equipment; the place of manual work; and the contribution of prisoners to the development of the national economy. These questions greatly exceed the framework of the present study, which is a first attempt to address just some of the problems. We will examine in turn manpower, productivity, building-site equipment, and the role of the labour camps.

MANPOWER AND PRODUCTIVITY

Our study comes up against several obstacles. First, to our knowledge there is no monograph devoted to the economic history of building in this period.[2] It should be added that, because of ideological bias, Soviet historiography almost completely ignores construction workers: they came mainly from the countryside and were not 'real workers', whereas the metal workers were considered the pure proletarians. Gol'tsman's interesting article is the exception that proves the rule.[3]

Second, sources are less abundant than for industry: the annual statistics of the thirties are sadly lacking in information on the building trade.[4] For example, *Trud v SSSR* ('Labour in the USSR'), published in 1936, gives figures relating only to the whole workforce for the period 1928–31, without distinguishing different categories.

184

We therefore had to deduce the size of the construction workforce between 1928 and 1935 from two different sources. Here the new figures published since 1956 have been of great assistance. A systematic examination of specialist technical or trade union journals would no doubt allow us to consider the question in more detail.

Third, the changing methods of classification might induce error. In 1928 the figures for the building trade included only employees involved in construction or assembly; in 1937 and 1940 they also included the workforce of 'services' attached to building sites (transport, supplies, warehouses, lodgings, catering, shopping etc.) and the workforce of the 'secondary industries': in particular quarries, sawmills and factories making bricks and concrete etc. In fact, during the first five year plan, the building sites covered some of their needs themselves, because of the retarded development of raw materials production and problems of transport – many sites were situated in pioneer territory which was either very remote or inaccessible. These secondary industries, often requiring a large and skilled workforce, were expensive.[5] The change in classification therefore resulted in a significant increase in the number of workers: 31 per cent in 1932, 51 per cent in 1940. Strictly speaking, any comparison with the year 1928 must limit itself to the workforce involved in construction and assembly.

Let us now consider Tables 9.1 and 9.2 (building employees).[6] The number employed nearly quadrupled under the first five year plan (Table 9.1, column 3). The two years which saw the greatest increase were 1930 and 1931, as was the case in industry; in 1933 the trend was

TABLE 9.1 *Personnel employed in building: annual average in thousands*

(1)		(2)		(3)		(4) (inc. apprentices)	
1928	672	1929	793	1928	630	1928	646
1932	1947	1933	1989	1932	2479		
1937	1368	1937	1875				
1940	1335	1940	1929	1940	1929	1940	1935

SOURCES (1) *Trud v SSSR* (Moscow, 1968) p. 121 (includes workers employed in construction repairs in machine-hire organisations and in inter-*kolkhoz* building organisations. (2) *Dostizheniya sovetskoi vlasti za 40 let v tsifrakh* (Moscow, 1957) p. 219 (includes not only construction). (3) *Narodnoe khozyaistvo SSSR v 1958 godu* (Moscow, 1959) p. 648. (4) *Kapital'noe stroitel'stvo v SSSR* (Moscow, 1961) p. 248.

TABLE 9.2 *Personnel employed in building (thousands)*

(1) Workers and employees: ann. av.		(2) Workers (inc. apprentices)	(3) Workers and employees: quarterly				
				I	II	III	IV
1928	723	621 625	1928	412	596	971.3	900.3
1929	917.8	752 225	1929	483.2	684.6	1234.1	1223.4
1930	1623.4	1296 200	1930	826.2	1447.8	1981.5	2059.2
1931	2548.9	1989 425	1931	1911.2	2351.3	2814.4	2993.5
1932	3125.8	2525 700	1932	2965	3147.8	3276	3156.5
1933	2361.1	1937 800	1933	2398	2153.4	2385.2	2559
1934	2532.7	2126 100	1934	2347.1	2504.2	2699	2610.9
1935	2109.6	1757 700	1935	2028.7	2040.2	2228.6	2184.1

SOURCES   (1) *Trud v SSSR* (Moscow, 1936) p. 244; *Narodnoe khozyaistvo SSSR* (Moscow, 1956) p. 190. (2) 1928–31 calculated from figures for beginning of each quarter, *Trud v SSSR* (Moscow-Leningrad, 1932) p. 76; 1932–5: *Trud v SSSR* (Moscow, 1936) p. 245. (3) Calculated from the figures for the beginning of each quarter, *Trud v SSSR* (Moscow, 1936) p. 244.

reversed, as in industry, but far more abruptly: employment dropped by nearly a quarter.[7] After that date, in marked contrast with industry, there was no lasting recovery: the boom of 1934 subsided as early as 1935. All available information is agreed on this point: the record level of 1932 was never reached again; from 1937 to 1940, the number employed remained static. In 1940 the construction and fitting industries employed a smaller work-force (by approximately one-third) than in 1932, but it was still twice as big as in 1928.

Table 9.2 (column 3) shows the quarterly variations in employment. It shows that between 1928 and 1935 there was a major transformation which the annual averages conceal, namely the reduction of seasonal fluctuations through the year.[8] Between 1928 and 1930 the figures varied greatly according to season: there was a ratio of 1:2.5 between the minimum in January–March and the maximum on 1 October or 1 November. The year 1931 marked a turning point in this respect: the ratio decreased to 1:1.7 then fell to 1:1.1, and to 1:1.2 in 1932, 1934 and 1935; it rose slightly in 1933 due to the sharp decline in the workforce between January and April. Just before the first five year plan, the construction industry obeyed the rhythms of nature: work began in spring, reached its height in the summer and stopped almost entirely in winter. Enterprises drew up seasonal contracts with teams of diggers, masons and carpenters. In the quiet season, workers would go back to their villages or ply another trade: the census of September to October 1929 found that on the building sites there were 57 per cent *otkhodniki* (seasonal workers) as opposed to 43 per cent permanent workers.[9]

The first five year plan marked a turning point. For the first time construction work went on all year,[10] with the site for the tractor factory in Stalingrad leading the way in the winter of 1929–30. In the autumn of 1929, anxiety reigned over the site: if the seasonal workers, whose contracts expired on 1 November, went home as usual, the building would not be finished by the expected date. Yet the factory had to be operational as soon as possible because an increase in tractor production was a primary objective for the authorities. It was essential to convince the seasonal workers to remain throughout the winter and so the Party committee launched a propaganda campaign ('We build socialism whatever the weather'). The site director, V. I. Ivanov, an old Bolshevik and former Baltic sailor, addressed a meeting of *starosty* (work-team foremen), explaining the superiority of tractors over working animals. He promised material advantages to those who stayed over the winter and proposed to those who so wished to allow families to come up from the country. The result was that many seasonal workers accepted the offer.[11] The example of Stalingrad subsequently spread to other sites and by the end of the first plan period, it had become the general rule for construction work to continue through the whole year.

It is easy to imagine the difficulties in bringing about such a radical change over a short period. The employees had to be given board and lodging throughout the year, the *otkhodniki* had to adapt to a complete turn-about in their way of life, and special methods had to be perfected in order to cope with the frost, such as the heating of concrete by steam or by electricity.[12]

Even if the Soviet building sites were now in operation all year round, their activities were still affected by seasonal fluctuations. For example, between the fourth quarter of 1934 and the first quarter of 1935 the volume of completed 'capital' works declined by about one half (from 6.7 to 3.4 billion rubles). The severe cold was not the only cause: in the final quarter, work rhythms were accelerated in order to finish the plan (*shturmovshchina*). January arrived: the plan for the new year had not yet been ratified and because they had not received the necessary raw materials in time, the building sites worked at a slower rate, even though the director kept the workforce in reserve

TABLE 9.3 *Rates of raw material consumption and investment in construction*

| | Consumption of raw materials in construction (Powell) | | Total net investment (Jasny) |
	1928 prices	1937 prices	1926/27 prices
1928–32	+79.8%	+74%	+130%
1932–37	+55.7%	+57.2%	+50%
1937–40	−1.4%	+1%	+0%

SOURCES N. Jasny, *Soviet Industrialization 1928–1952* (University of Chicago Press, 1961) pp. 86, 137, 444–5; *Essays on the Soviet Economy* (New York: Praeger, 1962) pp. 74–5; on the Powell series, see R. W. Davies, *Capital investment and capital stock in the USSR 1928–1940: Soviet and Western estimates*, CREES Discussion Papers (University of Birmingham), SIPS no. 22, 1982, pp. 10–11 and table 1.

for future needs. This is why the number of workers diminished by only 21 per cent between October 1934 and January 1935, although the amount of work halved: thus, productivity was lower in winter.[13]

We have already noted the variations in the number of building workers: a marked increase during the first plan, followed by a drop between 1932 and 1937–40. How do we explain this movement? In a given sector, the development of employment depends on a parallel development in demand and productivity. Here we come up against statistical problems, since estimates diverge on the increase in building costs. It is therefore difficult to trace the changes in the real volume of work in the 1930s. Powell has calculated an index for construction work for the period 1927/8–58, based on the quantities and the value of raw materials used each year. Jasny, on the other hand, has tried to measure the growth rate of total net investment (building, including installation costs, and tools). These estimates give only an approximate idea of the operations of the building trade, but the results obtained are very similar, except in the case of the first plan where there is a significant divergence.

From this it is clear that building development was at its most rapid during the first plan period, but that growth continued through the second plan, before stagnation settled in 1937–40. Between 1932 and 1937 the volume of work increased by about one half. And yet the number of workers had diminished between 1932 and 1937–40. This is what leads us to a consideration of productivity in the years

TABLE 9.4   *Growth of productivity in the building trade**

1928–32	+4%
1932–7	+83%
1937–40	+32%

*Productivity is measured as the value of construction and assembly work (in comparable prices) divided by the number of labourers employed. Employees in 'secondary production' are included in this calculation, not those in services.

SOURCES   *Narodnoe khozyaistvo v 1956 godu* (Moscow, 1957) p. 41; *Dostizheniya sovetskoi vlasti za sorok let v tsifrakh* (Moscow, 1957) p. 218; *Kapital-'noe stroitel'stvo v SSSR* (Moscow, 1961) p. 252.

1928–40; Table 9.4 reproduces the figures published in the USSR after 1956.

. These figures cannot be taken at face value. In 1935 the trade union journal emphasised the fact that 'during the first plan no methods for calculating productivity were even drawn up', hence the divergence in estimates: in some cases the increase does not exceed 1–2 per cent, in others it reaches 15–16 per cent. But whatever estimate is used, the result is always the same: what appears is a sharp contrast between two periods, more clearly than in industry. According to official records, productivity practically stagnated during the first plan; in fact, it probably went down considerably (–21 per cent between 1929 and 1932 according to Jasny). This drop further accentuated the swollen figures connected with the development of major building sites; in turn, the arrival *en masse* of a new workforce had negative effects on productivity. Later the movement was reversed: progress was rapid from 1932 to 1936;[15] more was built with a smaller workforce.[16]

PRIMITIVE TECHNIQUES

How can the bad results of the first plan be explained? First, as Rakovsky indicated, the building sites suffered from bad planning and economic imbalances: 'A large proportion of construction is begun not only without work drawings, but also without any overall plan. When the plan arrives, it then becomes necessary to change everything, or even to start all over again.'[17] V. Kravchenko

witnessed such realities at the end of 1931, when the regional committee of the Party sent him to enquire into the situation at Nikopol,
where the construction of a metallurgical combine was dragging on.
The new works director, P. Brachko, who welcomed him onto the
site, complained that plans were forever changing.[18] At the end of
1934, the government had to forbid starting construction projects
without ratified plans and finance; apparently this problem was still
not solved by early 1936, since an editorial in the journal *Plan*
mentioned the 'defective state' of projects and finances.[19]

Second, raw materials were lacking. On 17 July 1930, the industrial
daily *Za Industrializatsiyu* indicated that capital construction in the
Russian republic received only half of its raw materials. This lack was
aggravated by the inefficiency of transport. Every delivery arrived
later, to the extent that, according to a spokesman from the Supreme
Council of National Economy (VSNKh), this delay became an integral part of planning.[20] Hence the running of the sites was irregular
and interruptions frequent. In 1935 Ginzburg estimated that 10 per
cent of working time was lost due to these interruptions; figures are
even worse for 1937, between 20 per cent and 35 per cent, depending on
the site.[21]

Third, on all the big building sites of the first plan (the hydroelectric power station on the Dniepr, the tractor factories at Stalingrad and Chelyabinsk, Magnitogorsk) the turnover of workers was
very high as a result of working and living conditions: insufficient
food, basic housing and cold. At a time when there was a desperate
shortage of qualified workers, this turnover only hindered the training of employees and had a detrimental effect on productivity.[22]

Finally, Soviet industry was not in a state to supply the equipment
necessary for construction work. The authorities preferred to draw a
veil over this: the statistics of the 1930s exhibit an exceptional
diffidence. Since 1956 the veil has been partially lifted. At the end of
1930 the sum total of machinery was derisory: there were no bulldozers or mobile cranes, there were only 170 excavators and 300
mechanical diggers for the whole of the USSR.[23] Moreover, this
equipment was of foreign origin. The foreign trade statistics show
that from approximately 1926–7 the Soviets imported machinery,
with imports reaching their height in 1932 before falling back to a
very low level. In 1932 the USSR produced no bulldozers or mechanical diggers; the production of excavators began only in 1931 (there
were two prototypes) and reached eighty-five units in 1932. Taking

foreign purchases into account, the country then had a total of 450 excavators at its disposal.[24]

The few machines that were produced were under-used because of the bad organisation of work and the low technical level of the workforce. During the first year (late 1927 to late 1928) at Dneprostroi (the site for the Dnepr hydroelectric power station), half the cranes were used to pick up the other half which the workers had loaded badly and knocked over! At Kuznetsk, earth was transported in wheelbarrows, while the conveyor belts remained idle as no one knew how to use them. During the first quarter of 1932, the coefficient of use of machinery in the seven trusts of Soyuzstroi did not exceed 18.1 per cent on average; the situation did not seem to improve during the following year. According to a general survey of building site equipment, 30–40 per cent of the machines were either idle or being repaired at the end of the first plan period.[25]

All this explains the negligible levels of mechanisation of work on the building sites during the first plan.[26] In 1930, a Soviet newspaper made this severe observation: 'The mechanisation of construction work this year is in ruins: there are no measures which can be taken today radically to alter this situation'.[27] In fact, in 1932 excavators were responsible for only 15 per cent of earthworks; loading and unloading was generally undertaken by hand; the movement of materials on site was only 30 per cent mechanised; hand- and wheelbarrows were mainly used instead. In the absence of cranes, the authorities encouraged recourse to simple lifting mechanisms which could be made on site: some high furnaces were installed with the help of masts, winches and hoists. Lorries and tractors played only a secondary role; horses assured essential deliveries and local peasants were mobilised to this end.[28]

To one degree or another the setting-up of building sites was difficult everywhere.[29] When the first part of the Gor'kii car plant was being set up in August 1929, the site had only eight excavators at its disposal; 70 per cent of the earthworks were undertaken by hand.[30] At the tractor factory site in Stalingrad in the summer of 1929 'mechanisation was almost non-existent. There were only some gallow hoists, some concrete mixers and a few other basic machines'.[31] At the site for the Magnitogorsk combine, preparatory work began in March 1929. In November 1929, the site boasted one concrete mixer and one breaking mill which had to be used for everything. Most of the time, the raw materials had to be hauled up onto the scaffolding by hand. In 1929 and from January to September 1930, earthworks were entirely manual; the first excavators did not arrive until October 1930. From then on the level of mechanisation rose rapidly: 23.5 per cent in the fourth quarter of 1930, 80–85 per cent in 1931–2, as opposed to 30 per cent at the chemical combine sites at Berezniki and Solikamsk in the Urals. The first two high furnaces, in 1931–2, were assembled with the aid of machinery.[32] One could easily mention many such examples: on the dyke at Dneproges the workers, wearing rubber boots and holding each other by the shoulder, trampled the concrete down with their feet; vibrators were still being developed and tested.[33] In 1933, a German specialist wrote with reference to Uralmash, which entered service on 17 July, that the factory had been constructed 'almost entirely without machines by unqualified workers'.[34]

Thus the building sites offered an amazing spectacle: the construction of modern industry relied above all on manual work, or more exactly on arduous physical labour and on the energy of animals! In spite of subsequent official statements, this situation was not due to the fact that building site directors chose manual work in preference to the use of machinery;[35] it was the result of the difficulties which beset the building sites. There were shortages of everything so that, in order to advance the work and to meet the demands of the authorities, there was no other solution than to increase the number of workers, even at the expense of productivity, not to mention the quality of work.[36]

There was nothing easier than to recruit *en masse*, since the Russian villages offered abundant reserves of cheap labour and many projects required above all great physical force. In this way a lot of country people went to sign on and a popular saying sums up their memory of the first plan: 'digging holes' (*ryt' kotlovany*); this can still be traced in literature.[37] Soviet authors take delight in evoking the arrival, either alone or in teams, of these rustic workers, sometimes accompanied by their families. They brought with them their horses and tools: for the carpenters, an axe and a saw, for the earthworkers (*grabari*) an ordinary shovel and a barrow to transport the earth (*grabarka*).[38] A qualified worker, F. Slesarev, has left a colourful description of these over-populated, crowded work sites. It was at the beginning of the construction of Uralmash:

So many people had arrived at once that there was hardly room to breathe on the site . . . Throughout these years, the site presented an unforgettable spectacle. As fitters, we often worked at a high level and remember it as a great ants' nest, always in constant motion. Looking around, we could see the green barrier of the forest on one side and, around our workshop, enormous yawning holes, mounds of upturned earth, tree stumps, stones, wood and bricks all piled up. And all around we could see a troubled sea of people, busily moving about . . . At that time, everything was done by hand.[39]

What a contrast with the sites which S. Z. Ginzburg visited in Germany in 1932:

I was struck by the small number of workers and engineers. No bustle and no noise, but rather methodical work. The site seemed to be advancing very slowly. However, coming back a week later, I realised that the work had advanced significantly . . . Raw materials were brought onto site in limited quantities, for a week at the most, and they were deposited in areas designated in advance. Bricks were not unloaded loose, but one by one or in packs.[40]

Did the predominance of manual work persist after 1932? Here again, the state of the sources does not permit a categorical answer. Ginzburg attributes the increase in productivity during the second plan principally to advances in mechanisation.[41] In fact, excavators carried out 43 per cent of earthworks in 1937, and 60 per cent in 1940, as opposed to 20 per cent in 1934; progress was also made in cement-mixing and stone-breaking. In 1936 Soviet industry produced 573 excavators, 6.7 times more than in 1932. In ten years (1930–40), the total number of machines increased rapidly, while still remaining modest in absolute terms: in 1940 the USSR possessed 2,086 excavators, 1,100 mechanical diggers, 750 bulldozers and 1,135 mobile cranes, and the use of horses declined in favour of motor vehicles.[42] The progress made must not, however, be exaggerated, as witnessed by the authorities' anxieties in 1935–6. At the end of 1935 a conference on construction, which brought together 350 of the top directors, took place in Moscow;[43] the conference heard reports from V. I. Mezhlauk, chairman of Gosplan, and from Ginzburg, head of construction within the Commissariat of Heavy Industry. Mechanisation occupied a prime place among the subjects discussed. Ginzburg criticised the craftsman-like building methods and emphasised that machines were still being badly used; if productivity had increased during 1935, it was from the 'exceptionally low' level of the preceeding years.

Where 100 workers were needed in the United States, the USSR employed 155.[44]

This conference led to the preparation of an edict on 'improvement in construction and the lowering of costs' (on 11 February 1936).[45] Observing that productivity was 'generally low', the decree called for a move from the 'cottage industry of the partisans' war [*sic*] to a major construction industry'; point 4 accentuated the 'maximal mechanisation of construction',[46] and fixed objectives for 1936. To what extent were these measures adhered to in fact? It is difficult to say. Ginzburg offers the 1935 conference, and the decisions which followed it, as a turning-point, appealing to the increased productivity in 1936–7 and from 1937 to 1940.[47] And yet in analysing the failure of the investment programme of 1937, the Soviet press complained about the small-scale methods of the construction industry and of the poor use of equipment; it also questioned the limited range of workers' salaries and the lack of stability in the work force.[48] The increase in mechanisation between 1936 and 1937 was limited. Between 1937 and 1940, the economic difficulties and the priority given to national defense provoked a decrease in production in many sectors of mechanical construction: tractors, lorries, touring cars, combine harvesters, and steam trains.[49] Machines destined for the building trade were no exception: as far as excavators were concerned, the shortfall exceeded 50 per cent against the maxima of 1936 and 1940. As a consequence, the Commissariat for Construction created in 1939 had to develop its own means of production.[50] Just before the war, despite the progress achieved since the first plan, the building trade was still backward on a technical level: the sites lacked machinery and manual work still occupied an important place.[51]

FORCED LABOUR

In analysing the evolution of employment in the building trade, we have been intrigued by the drop in the total number of employees between 1932 and 1937–40. This fall happened at a time when the volume of work was continuing to increase. Can the advances in productivity alone explain this phenomenon? Here again the uncertainty of statistics is too great to allow a categorical answer. But the limited progress in mechanisation[52] suggests another hypothesis: might this reduction in the workforce be linked to the development of forced labour?[53]

In 1918, the Cheka organised a certain number of labour camps for the imprisonment of opponents of the régime;[54] these camps of the civil war period were closed in 1922. But the Cheka (later GPU and OGPU) was authorised to maintain a small network of penitentiary institutions, of which the most renowned were the northern camps, especially those on the Solovki islands, opened in 1921–2. The highest estimates give 25,000–30,000 prisoners in 1928 under the OGPU system; the average population of the Solovki in the mid-1920s was 8,500 people. The conditions in the prisons were harsh, the governors pitiless and sometimes sadistic. But during most of the 1920s, the prisoners of the OGPU played no role in the Soviet economy: in the Solovki the condemned men only worked to maintain the camp; and even then, the political prisoners (SRs, Mensheviks, anarchists) could refuse to work. It was only in 1928 that Solovki began to undertake major works for the state.[55] If the total number of prisoners was still modest in 1928, it rose sharply during the first plan, as a result of collectivisation.[56] The resolutions and instructions of January–February 1930 in fact foresaw the isolation and imprisonment in concentration camps of *kulaks* guilty of 'terrorist acts'.[57] These prisoners were put to work: it was at this time that the important sector of forced labour was created in the Soviet economy. In no way do we pretend to offer a detailed analysis of the development of the camps and their place in Soviet society in the 1930s. Obviously, the functions of the concentration camps were many and cannot be reduced to economic considerations. Our study concerns the role assigned to the *zeks* (camp prisoners) in the completion of major works in the period 1929–41. So we will leave to one side the undeniably punitive aims of the institution, whether it be for criminals, peasants opposing collectivisation, victims of the anti-religious campaigns, members of the political opposition, representatives of national minorities, etc.

In this controversial matter, there are many unknowns: polemics have a field day in relation to the number of prisoners and the amount of production involved.[58] In the absence of official figures, researchers and witnesses offer greatly varying estimates.[59] It is of note that, for the end of the period (1939–40), the estimates by Jasny, Bergson and Wheatcroft are quite similar: between 3.5 and 5 million.[60] Unfortunately, the available sources do not allow us to construct a continuous chronological series, which prevents us from tracing the development from the end of the 1920s to the war.

Dallin and Nikolaevsky, Barton and Swianiewicz have tried to analyse the place of forced labour in Soviet industrialisation.[61] Several conclusions emerge from their work. First, the development of the camps diminished the demand for food by forcefully removing from the market a large number of potential buyers. It helped to reduce consumption, thereby benefiting investment, and lightened the weight of deprivations suffered by the free workers.

Second, at the beginning of the 1930s forced labour stimulated the mobilisation of the under-employed workforce of the Soviet countryside; it therefore facilitated the demise of rural unemployment and the USSR's entry into the era of full or even over-employment.[62]

Third, the workforce, forced to leave native villages, was directed to sectors which were considered as priorities. This gave the state several tangible advantages: the low maintenance costs allowed savings to be made on investments (though one can question the quality and productivity of the work,[63] and the costs of transport and surveillance must be taken into account); the workforce was subject to pitiless discipline and the authorities controlled its movements: at any moment they could send the workers to places where needs were being felt; they often worked in remote regions, in harsh climatic conditions, where it was difficult, if not impossible, to attract free workers: the pioneer fronts of the Great European North, Siberia and Kazakhstan.

Although this global analysis can be contested, if only on the grounds of ignorance, witnesses confirm that deportees were used in a wide variety of areas: canal-digging (from the White Sea to the Baltic and from the Moskva to the Volga); construction and maintenance of railways (for example Dudinka to Norilsk) and roads; the building of 'new towns' such as Norilsk or Magadan, including housing, factories and harbour installations; tree-felling, floating of wood and back-up activities (saw mills); the extraction of coal, limestone and gold (Karaganda, Kolyma, Vorkuta); loading and unloading of lorries, trains and boats: sugar, coal, tree trunks etc; the development of the steppe in Kazakhstan; the experimental rearing of hens on Kolyma; employment in a variety of other sectors: quarries, brick-making factories, leather works, urban cleaning, etc.[64]

In France today, forced labour in the USSR is generally known through the 'camp literature' (for example V. Shalamov, E. Ginzburg and especially Solzhenitsyn). But it must be emphasised that in the USSR, at least until 1937, there was no secret about the existence of camps; numerous official texts made reference to them. The International Commission against the concentration camp régime, created in 1950 at the bequest of David Rousset, and the Special Committee of Forced Labour (United Nations, 1951) have made many references to these documents in their publications.[65] We shall limit ourselves to a few texts.

In November 1929, E. G. Shirvindt announced the creation of 'corrective labour camps' destined for people sentenced to three years or more imprisonment. He explained unequivocally that these camps would supply a large unskilled workforce which the state badly needed in order to complete its major projects for the first plan.[66] In 1930–1 a campaign in favour of an embargo against Soviet wood imports developed in Great Britain and the United States. In replying to this campaign, V. Molotov affirmed in March 1931 that the lumbermen in the northern regions were all free salaried workers and that the wood exported from the USSR was not produced by forced labourers.[67] He did say, however, that his country used 60,000 prisoners. He gave an idyllic picture of their situation, enumerating roads and railways built by them, without forgetting the White Sea-Baltic canal.[68] In 1935, B. S. Utevskii's manual devoted to the 'Soviet policy of corrective work' recalled the same examples, taking its lead from Molotov; it also quoted a director of the OGPU, S. Firin: 'The corrective labour camps of the OGPU are pioneers in the cultural development of our remote peripheries'.[69]

We have the most information about the White Sea-Baltic (1931–3) and Moskva-Volga (1933–7) canals. The two sites are constantly quoted in connexion with prison labour.[70] When the canals were completed, *Pravda* announced the measures taken in favour of the prisoners: in 1933, 12,484 early releases and 59,516 shortened sentences; in 1937, 55,000 early releases.[71] In 1934, under the direction of M. Gor'kii, a 'brigade' of thirty-six writers (including M. Zoshchenko, V. Ivanov, V. Inber, V. Kataev, A. Tikhonov, A. Tolstoi, V. Shklovskii) published a large volume on the White Sea-Baltic canal: this apology of forced labour celebrated the re-education (the 'reforging') of prisoners by work. In 1936 I. L. Averbakh developed the same theme with reference to the Dmitrov camp (the Moskva-Volga canal).[72] Although written as propaganda, the two works are surprisingly frank: the word 'concentration camp' is used on several occasions, the *zeks* are depicted in all their diversity: robbers, prostitutes, gamblers, 'spoilers of socialist property', 'counter-revolutionaries', engineers accused of sabotage, de-kulakised peasants etc. Solzhenitsyn made great use of these two publications.[73]

Official documents and the accounts of ex-prisoners are therefore in agreement: they show that during the 1930s forced labour became of such importance that no serious analysis of Soviet industrialisation could possibly ignore it. It remains true that these sources, which are above all qualitative, do not allow us to estimate the significance of forced labour in various branches of the national economy. Jasny has made an attempt to do so with the help of a 'confidential' document which came to the West by the same means as the Smolensk archives: the document is the 'Economic Plan for 1941', which fell into German hands during the war and was then picked up by the Americans and published in the United States.[74]

This thick volume, destined exclusively for the heads of the economic administration, appears in the form of tables showing the targets to be reached in 1941: production (in value or in physical units) and works to be finished in each commissariat; the division of tasks by region; the staff and 'salary funds' anticipated in the different sectors. The document indicates neither the number of camps nor the number of prisoners, but the NKVD appears in various guises: as a customer of other enterprises (the purchaser of two turbines for the hydroelectric power station at Rybinsk, and also of ships); as an 'entrepreneur' (transport, construction work) and producer (oil, wood, furniture, spoons). By definition, such a source indicates plans and says nothing about their execution. But what we know about Soviet planning methods inclines us to think that the goals for 1941 give a clear picture of the situation in 1940.

Unfortunately, the interpretation of this information gives rise to much uncertainty. First, the plan, as it has come through to the West, is incomplete: all the tables marked 'S' (secret) are missing; moreover, it contains no information about the production of precious metals.

Second, with two minor exceptions,[75] the workforce employed by the NKVD is not shown; only the production is known. The number of forced labourers can only be guessed, with assumptions about their productivity as opposed to that of free workers: in the absence of trustworthy basic statistics, there is bound to be disagreement on this point.[76]

Third, we must take into consideration Soviet accounting practices, about which we know little, and which have been variously interpreted. This is the subject of a debate between N. Jasny and A. D. Redding. Jasny assumes that the major works carried out under the auspices of the NKVD were all completed by the NKVD.

Redding argues that the figures refer to investments funded by the NKVD and that the NKVD apportioned a small part of it to sub-contractors (for example the Commission for Construction accounted for 1.5 per cent of the total), for which it had to pay. On the other hand the NKVD worked as a sub-contractor for other organisations and these activities were attributed to the principal entrepreneur; thus a railway line built by the NKVD for the Transport Commission figured in the accounts under the 'Transport Commission' rubric.[77] Redding concludes that in ignoring this practice, Jasny has probably underestimated the role of forced labour in the construction industry.[78] Jasny concedes this point in principle, but denies that the phenomenon had any great significance.

Finally, some of the *zeks* did not work directly for the NKVD. In fact, when they were short of workers, 'ordinary' enterprises (finances permitting) could hire workers from the political police.[79] In this case, and in this case alone, the statistics counted them as salaried employees in that industry, not as NKVD workers.[80]

For all these reasons, calculations can only be approximate.[81] The principal results obtained by Jasny are summarised in Table 9.5. Two conclusions arise from it. First, construction was the most important activity of the NKVD, which in 1941 was planned to take on 17 per cent of the work: all researchers are in agreement on this point, even if the figures vary. The 1941 plan corroborates in this respect the evidence of ex-prisoners. Second, in industry as a whole, the role of the NKVD was 'almost negligible'.[82] Such a statement may be surprising: it is a result of the fact that forced labour was concentrated in a few sectors (forest work, furniture and mining). The figure given for tree-felling, a *leitmotif* in the camp literature (V. Shalamov, E. S. Ginzburg, G. Herling, K. Stainer) seems relatively modest, but it hides marked regional differences: the NKVD was completely absent from this sector in many regions of central Russia (Penza, Ryazan, Tula) – its share was only 5 per cent in Leningrad *oblast'* – but reached 26 per cent around Arkhangel'sk and exceeded 50 per cent in the Komi republic.[83] There is some doubt in relation to the mining industry. According to Swianiewicz, Jasny minimises its importance: he ignores non-ferrous metals and underestimates Soviet gold production, the extent of which is a state secret.[84] If this criticism is valid, mines move up to second place, ahead of forest work, in the economic activities of the NKVD.

In whatever sector it was used, forced labour had common characteristics. Generally speaking, the tasks were repetitive and required

TABLE 9.5 *Forced Labour*
(A) The role of the NKVD in total (planned) production in 1941

	%
Construction	17.0*
Industry:	
Wood	12.0**
Furniture	6.0*
Gold (unknown)	
Coal	2.8**
Oil	0.7**
Chromium	40.5**
Cement	1.3**
Bricks	14.0***
Fish (caught)	3.6**

* In value
** In physical units
*** In physical units for Primorskii and Khabarovskii *krai*

(B) Estimated forced labour by sector (Jasny)

	Thousands	%
Construction	1170	33.4
Industry:		
Forestry (inc. saw mills)	455	13.0
Gold	200	2.9
Coal, oil, chrome and fishing		0.7
Agriculture, shipping	150	4.3
Hire to other institutions	580	16.6
Maintenance of the camps	600	17.1

NOTE the total workforce planned for industry and construction (excluding NKVD sites and enterprises) was 14,100,000.

SOURCE N. Jasny, 'Labor and Output in Soviet Concentration Camps', *The Journal of Political Economy*, October 1951, pp. 407, 410, 417.

hardly any qualifications, but were physically harsh. In view of the lack of machines, nearly everything was done by hand: on this point all are in agreement. In *The Gulag Archipelago*, Solzhenitsyn devotes several striking pages to this subject, where the Belomor barrows recur as a *leitmotif*.[85] He frequently quotes the two works that recount the construction of the White Sea-Baltic and Moskva-Volga

canals.[86] In fact, the collective book on the Belomor canal emphasises the lack of any modern techniques. At a meeting of the site
chiefs at the beginning of the work, a conflict arose between a
prisoner, the engineer N. V. Mogilko, and two directors of the
OGPU:

'What do you want?' Kogan [site director] asked him, getting
straight to the point.

'Above all a reduction in the workforce. The workforce is more
expensive than machines. The workers should have tools in their
hands, not God knows what.' [. . .]

'At Dneprostroi', continued Mogilko, '54 engines, wagons and
caterpillars are in operation. But here?' [. . .]

Naftalii Aronovich Frenkel [chief of works] spoke:

'You can forget about those 54 locomotives and 1400 wagons. I'll
tell you straight away – no one will give them to us.' [. . .]

Kogan:

'We're not at Dneprostroi, where they were given a generous
building schedule and funds. The construction of the canal has
been given to the OGPU. And we have been told: you won't get a
kopeck of funds.' [. . .][87]

Our authors mention the existence of a machine here and there,[88] but
equipment put together on site seemed to predominate:

Methods of work were primitive: stones were carried in nets which
were emptied out onto 'Fords'. The Ford at Belomor was a heavy
platform placed on four little wheels, sculpted out of balls of wood.
This 'Ford' was drawn by two horses [. . .] On the Belomor site,
the barrow wheel was the first mechanism [. . .] The holes became
deeper and deeper. The Belomor 'Ford' and the wheelbarrow were
no longer sufficient. Cranes had to be built. The decision was made
to build derrick-cranes out of wood.[89]

In 1934, the review *Etudes* published the deposition of an ex-
prisoner which confirmed the same things: 'On the White Sea canal,
work was particularly hard because technical procedures were almost
totally lacking. Everything was done by hand.'[90] Was the same true
for the construction of the Moskva-Volga canal? The prisoners'
drawings and photographs which illustrate I. L. Averbakh's book
From Crime to Work show the presence of lorries, caterpillar

tractors, excavators, a crane, a loco-tractor.[91] Thus mechanisation seemed to have progressed, and this conclusion is compatible with everything we know from elsewhere about the second plan. But this aspect must not be exaggerated. The site was reminiscent of Belomor in more ways than one: there were long queues of women pushing wheelbarrows along planks, and earth was removed in barrows pulled by horses.

The scarcity of machines is described in all the prisoners' memoirs. On the site of the BMS metallurgical factory at Norilsk, the prisoners broke up the perpetually frozen earth with primitive tools. In 1952, they had only axes and saws to fell the trees in the taiga of Siberia.[92] In a quarry in Vladivostok, in 1939, heavy stones were transported in barrows. Evoking the construction of Magadan, Ginzburg writes: 'I too carried loads of frozen bricks, stumbling along unstable beams'.[93] M. Buber-Neumann, who was imprisoned in Kazakhstan, indicates a sizeable stock of agricultural machinery (harvesters, threshing machines, tractors, ploughs, sowers, reapers), but all the work in which she played a part was done by hand.[94] The words 'barrow, pick and shovel' recur several times in Shalamov's description of the coal and gold mines of Kolyma. Indeed one of his stories is called 'The shovel artist'.[95] 'The main road of Kolyma twists and turns over 2,000 kilometres, a road suitable for vehicles between the mountains and gorges, the poles, the rails and the bridges [. . .] The whole road had been constructed by pick and shovel, with barrows and drills . . .'[96] Nothing sums up the situation better than the nickname given by the prisoners to the wheelbarrow: *mashina OSO: dve ruchki i koleso* (the OSO machine; two sides and a wheel).[97]

All these accounts recall in a striking way that we said earlier about the big sites of the first plan, which were not much better equipped. Nikolai Petrov notes this similarity in his description of the construction of the Stalingrad tractor factory in Stalingrad: 'The only "technique" which the men had at their disposal was in no way different from the one used by the prisoners in the NKVD camps: "the vehicle with one wheel, the pick and the shovel"'.[98] For a long time specialists have emphasised that forced labour offered the advantage of not demanding modern machinery, thus allowing the state to make savings in capital.[99] In reality, the lack of material was not unique to the camps; everywhere equipment on building sites was primitive.

Industrial projects were absurdly ambitious. The result was an enormous increase in the demand for labour. It was this context which favoured the massive use of prisoners, condemned to hard labour. Conversely, we can conclude that the development of mechanisation after the war contributed in part to the reduction in forced labour which occurred in the 1950s: that, in any case, is the thesis maintained by P. Barton.[100] Should one deduce from all this that the system of concentration camps had above all an economic function and that arrests and deportations aimed above all to secure a workforce? That would doubtless be too hasty, ignoring all the political history of the period, which is still so obscure.

Let us draw our conclusions. We started out from the observation of a statistical 'anomaly': the number of workers employed in the building trade dropped between 1932 and 1937–40, without an increase in productivity sufficient to explain it. Hence the enquiry into forced labour. The results are coloured by uncertainty, especially because we are ignorant of the variations in the population of the camps between 1929–30 and 1941. However, we know that deportees were sent as a priority to major construction sites. In all probability, the reduction in the workforce in the building trade is only an apparent one and can be explained by the expansion of forced labour.

CONCLUSION

This article provides only a partial discussion, with some aspects deliberately left to one side. Our aim will have been achieved if we have shown that the themes discussed here open up rich perspectives for further study. As far as the first plan is concerned, we have placed great emphasis on the absence of machinery and the predominance of manual work. If our description of work sites is accurate, then it is of double interest: it is instructive about the condition of workers in the building trade, and it opens up a more concrete picture of the Soviet economy. Specialist works have rightly devoted lengthy articles to investments, the accumulation of capital, or the calculation of growth rates. But their authors seem to ignore the extent to which the equipment on the work sites was primitive. Can one really understand the industrialisation of the 1930s when abstracting from such material constraints?

The study of the major work sites in the 1930s leads the historian to insist on the key role of the peasants. This phenomenon prolongs a well-established tradition: under the NEP, as before the revolution, the building trade called mainly upon the *otkhod* (seasonal workers).

However, the number of workers increased so sharply during the first plan that many country people went to work in this sector for the first time in their lives: they had to learn a new trade at the same time as adapting to a new way of life. These workers from the countryside were both the builders and the first residents of the 'new towns': in 1931, the staff employed at Kuznetskstroi represented approximately 40 per cent of the population of Novokuznetsk.[101] Many of them did not stay in the building trade, the manpower of which dropped after 1932; once the building had been finished, the men were often taken on to set the factory working. The building industry served as a kind of buffer between agriculture and industry;[102] it played an essential role in the training of the industrial workforce; the new recruits acquired their first practical experience. However, because of this, the building trusts found it difficult to form and to keep a permanent nucleus of skilled workers, a weakness which was keenly felt in the industrial development of the USSR.

NOTES

1. In this text, we are dealing with industrial construction in the wide sense (factories, mine shafts, railway lines).
2. N. V. Milyakov's book *Nachal'nyi etap formirovaniya investitsionnogo kompleksa SSSR* (Moscow, 1988) came into our hands too late for us to be able to use it.
3. M. T. Gol'tsman, 'Sostav stroitel'nykh rabochikh SSSR v gody pervoi pyatiletki (po materialam profsoyuznykh perepisei 1929 i 1932 gg.)', in the collection *Izmeneniya v chislennosti i sostave sovetskogo rabochego klassa* (Moscow, 1961).
4. There are no statistics on employment and productivity in the sections on 'Construction' in *Sotsial'noe stroitel'stvo* (Moscow, 1936) and *Trud v SSSR* (Moscow, 1936).
5. See S. Z. Ginzburg, *O proshlom – dlya budushchego* (Moscow, 1983) p. 163. The author of these memoirs, a building engineer, was a deputy to G. K. Ordzhonikidze from 1929 to 1937 (working successively in the Workers' and Peasants' Inspection, at VSNKh and at the Commissariat for Heavy Industry).
6. The total figure includes workers and employees.
7. This phenomenon originated during the last quarter of 1932; after a marked drop in the first half of 1933, a revival occurred in the second half of the year. (See Table 9.2, workers and employees, quarterly averages.) Different figures, for the first quarter of 1932, are in *Narodnoe khozyaistvo SSSR* (1932) nos. 5–6, p. 232.

8. See *Trud v SSSR* (Moscow, 1936) p. 244; workers and building employees on the first of each month, 1928–35.
9. S. Z. Ginzburg, pp. 80, 146–7; M. T. Gol'tsman, p. 142.
10. S. Z. Ginzburg, pp. 87–8; M. T. Gol'tsman, pp. 147–9; V. S. Lel'chuk, *Industrializatsiya SSSR: istoriya, opyt, problemy* (Moscow, 1984) pp. 132–4; *Istoriya sovetskogo rabochego klassa* (Moscow, 1984), vol. 2, pp. 156–7.
11. See V. S. Lel'chuk, p. 133.
12. *Stroitel'stvo v SSSR 1917–1967* (Moscow, 1967) p. 71.
13. M. T. Gol'tsman, p. 150; S. Z. Ginzburg, pp. 160, 312; *Sovetskaya stroitel'naya industriya za 40 let* (Moscow, 1957) p. 45.
14. V. Il'inskii, 'Voprosy truda v stroitel'stve v 1934 g.', *Voprosy profdvizheniya*, 1935, nos. 5–6, pp. 43–4.
15. It is true that the starting-point in 1932 was very low. See N. Jasny, pp. 106, 146–8; R. W. Davies, p. 10. In 1937, productivity dropped by 2.1 per cent compared with 1936. E. Zaleski, *La planification stalinienne* (Economica, 1984) p. 320.
16. As far as employment was concerned, the second five year plan was not fulfilled, especially in construction. See E. Zaleski, p. 196.
17. Ch. Rakovsky, 'The Five Year Plan in Crisis', *Critique*, no. 13 (1981), p. 32. (Translation of an article of July–August 1930, which appeared in *Byulleten' Oppozitsii*, Nov.–Dec. 1931).
18. V. A. Kravchenko, *I Chose Freedom* (New York, 1946) p. 78. See also *Stroitel'naya promyslennost'*, 1933, no. 6, p. 3 and V. S. Lel'chuk, p. 187.
19. *Istoriya sovetskogo rabochego klassa*, p. 158; E. Zaleski, p. 312.
20. C. Rakovsky, p. 31 and T. Kirstein, 'The Ural-Kuznetsk combine: a case-study in Soviet investment decision-making', in R. W. Davies (ed.), *Soviet Investment for Planned Industrialisation, 1929–1937: Policy and Practice* (Berkeley Slavic Specialities, 1984), p. 93.
21. Nothing indicates that the figures were calculated in the same way in both cases. Sources: S. Z. Ginzburg, p. 162; E. Zaleski, p. 320 (in 1937 stoppages for an entire day alone totalled 1.73 times the number of working days) and pp. 550–3.
22. T. Kirstein, p. 91; A. D. Rassweiler, 'Soviet Labour Policy in the First Five Year Plan: The Dneprostroi Experience', *Slavic Review*, Summer 1983, p. 235; V. N. Zuikov, *Sozdanie tyazheloi industrii na Urale (1926–1932 gg.)* (Moscow, 1971) p. 167.
23. *Narodnoe khozyaistvo SSSR v 1958 g.* (Moscow, 1959) p. 467.
24. Caution is necessary since different Soviet figures are hard to reconcile. Figures taken from V. S. Lel'chuk, pp. 189–90; S. Z. Ginzburg, pp. 33, 50; *Stroitel'stvo v SSSR*, p. 32; V. N. Zuikov, p. 120.
25. A. D. Rassweiler, p. 237; *Istoriya sovetskogo rabochego klassa*, p. 156; M. T. Gol'tsman, p. 150; *Stroitel'naya promyshlennost'*, 1933, no. 6, p. 2; Zuikov, p. 120.
26. We are aware of the summary nature of the information which follows: it covers only a limited number of projects and the level of mechanisation varied greatly from one activity to another; the figures for earthworks only concern excavators (excluding, for example, water-hose

nozzles). The sources prevent any more detailed analysis.
27. *Za industrializatsiyu*, the organ of the VSNKh, quoted by Ch. Rakovsky, op. cit. (note 22), p. 31.
28. S. Z. Ginzburg, *Sovetskaya stroitel'naya industriya*, pp. 34, 53; A. D. Rassweiler, p. 233.
29. Sometimes we have been unable to decide between contradictory statements. For example Soviet accounts say that Dneprostroi enjoyed the benefit of the most modern equipment of the period: see S. Z. Ginzburg (note 5), p. 60; *Stroitel'stvo v SSSR* p. 462 (earthworks were mechanised up to 85 per cent); V. S. Lel'cuk, p. 99; A. D. Rassweiler, p. 233, insists on the contrary on the low level of mechanisation.
30. S. Z. Ginzburg, *Sovetskaya stroitel'naya industriya*, pp. 30–1.
31. S. Z. Ginzburg (note 5), p. 82.
32. *Istoriya sovetskogo rabochego klassa*, p. 156; *Stroitel'stvo v SSSR*, pp. 69, 463; V. N. Zuikov, p. 121; T. Kirstein, p. 93.
33. S. Z. Ginzburg (note 5), p. 60; V. S. Lel'cuk, p. 99.
34. Quoted in V. N. Zuikov, p. 166. See also *Istoriya sovetskogo rabochego klassa*, p. 156, for the example of Kuznetsk.
35. S. Z. Ginzburg alludes to 'anti-mechanical moods exhibited by a number of site directors'. These criticisms find an echo in the words of Ordzhonikidze at a conference on the construction industry (December 1935) which condemned these same tendencies hostile to mechanisation. *Sovetskaya stroitel'naya industriya*, p. 44, and V. S. Lel'cuk, p. 187.
36. *Stroitel'naya promyshlennost'*, 1933, no. 6, p. 3.
37. For example in V. Shukshin, 'Vybirayu derevnyu na zhitel'stvo', *Besedy po yasnoi lune* (Moscow, 1975) p. 29. Cf. A. Platonov, *Kotlovan* (Ann Arbor, 1979), a long story in which the theme of digging recurs frequently. The author precisely describes the work of labourers on the site; they use a pick and a shovel, there are no machines (pp. 21–7, 31–2, 125–6).
38. A. I. Vdovin, V. Z. Drobizhev, *Rost rabochego klassa SSSR* pp. 216–17; V. N. Zuikov, p. 137; V. S. Lel'cuk, pp. 130, 139; S. Z. Ginzburg (note 5), p. 82; the word *graber'* has virtually disappeared from current vocabulary, *zemlekop* being preferred.
39. Quoted by V. N. Zuikov, p. 137.
40. During a six-month mission (May–November), S. Z. Ginzburg (note 5), p. 69.
41. *Sovetskaya stroitel'naya industriya*, p. 125.
42. *Stroitel'stvo v SSSR*, pp. 32, 71.
43. V. S. Lel'chuk, p. 187; S. Z. Ginzburg, *Sovetskaya stroitel'naya industriya*, pp. 40–8 and op. cit. (note 5) pp. 158–66.
44. Ibid., p. 162.
45. Decree of the Council of People's Commissariats of the USSR and of the Central Committee of the Communist Party, in *KPSS v rezolyutsiyakh i resheniyakh*, vol. 6, 1933–7 (Moscow, 1985) pp. 316–31.
46. A resolution of the Sixteenth Congress (26 June–13 July 1930) was already speaking of 'maximum mechanisation' in construction (ibid., vol. 5, 1929–32, p. 152); it had few immediate consequences.

47. *Sovetskaya stroitel'naya industriya*, pp. 47–8, 53. This is very doubtful for 1937; an article by E. Vasiliev in *Planovoe khozyaistvo*, 1938, no. 8 indicates a drop of 2.1 per cent compared to 1936, cf. E. Zaleski, *La planification stalinienne*, p. 320.
48. These findings are sometimes linked to accusations of 'sabotage'. See E. Zaleski, pp. 236–58.
49. Ibid., pp. 236–58.
50. In 1936 the production of machines destined for the building trade had doubled, according to an official document of 10 November 1936, *Industrializatsiya SSSR 1933–1937 gg.* (Moscow, 1971) p. 604. Ginzburg confirms that building site equipment remained largely dependent on imports; in fact, the absolute level of the latter seems modest, in spite of the sharp increase observed in 1940 for excavators. *Sovetskaya stroitel'-naya industriya*, pp. 53–4.
51. Ibid, p. 53 and op. cit. (note 5), pp. 205, 208.
52. One should also take into account the changes which had occurred in the level of qualifications, the organisation of work and the methods of payment.
53. The following pages examine forced labour in concentration camps; exiles and forced labour by non-prisoners are excluded. The importance of the forced labour of exiles, and particularly of the *kulaks*, was perhaps far greater than has traditionally been thought. A recently declassified report of 1938 from the American Embassy in Moscow shows that at Magnitogorsk 30,000–40,000 exiled *kulaks* were forced to carry out nearly all the hard construction work, and that approximately 30 per cent of the factory staff worked under some form of constraint. See S. G. Wheatcroft, *Soviet Studies*, April 1981, p. 281.
54. For all this paragraph, see P. H. Solomon, 'Soviet Penal Policy, 1917–1934: A reinterpretation', *Slavic Review*, June 1980, pp. 200–3.
55. M. Heller, *Le monde concentrationnaire et la littérature soviétique* (Lausanne, 1974) pp. 65–6 places this turning point in 1925–6 and not in 1928. Cf. D. J. Dallin and B. P. Nicolaevsky, *Forced Labor in Soviet Russia* (London, 1948) pp. 181–2.
56. The arrest of engineers accused of sabotage also made a contribution.
57. *Istoriya SSSR* (Moscow, 1967), vol. VIII, pp. 550, 725.
58. Given the present state of documentation, the question of the economic viability of the camps is insoluble. Hypotheses on the productivity of prisoners can only be arbitrary; it would be necessary to deduct the cost of transport and surveillance. The camps used specialists who were cruelly lacking elsewhere, and the social usefulness of some of the projects is doubtful. See A. Solzhenitsyn, *The Gulag Archipelago*, vol. 2 (London, 1975) pp. 92–4; K. Stainer, *7,000 jours en Sibérie* (Paris 1983) p. 404; S. Rosefielde insists on this point in his article 'The First "Great Leap Forward" Reconsidered: Lessons of Solzhenitsyn's Gulag Archipelago', *Slavic Review* (1980) No. 4, pp. 570–1.
59. The controversy surrounding this matter, which was very lively during the cold war and subsequently dormant, was taken up again in the early 1980s, in particular in the journals *Soviet Studies* and *Slavic Review*.
60. W. Eason estimates the number of salaried workers employed by the

State at 28.8 million in 1939, excluding agriculture: A. Bergson and S. Kuznets (eds), *Economic Trends in the Soviet Union* (Cambridge, Mass., 1963), p. 84.

61. D. J. Dallin, *The Real Soviet Russia* (New Haven, 1944), pp. 194–5; Dallin and Nicolaevsky, pp. 88–92; P. Barton, *L'institution concentrationnaire en Russie (1930–1957)* (Paris, 1959) pp. 69–73, 75–7, 371; S. Swianiewicz, *Forced Labour and Economic Development* (Oxford, 1965) quoted in W. L. Blackwell, *The Industrialisation of Russia: An Historical Perspective* (London, 1970) pp. 112–15.

62. That is to say a lack of workers.

63. See the discussion of contradictory opinions on this matter in P. Barton, pp. 244–52. Cf also R. Brunet 'Géographie du Goulag', *Hérodote*, no. 47, pp. 159–61.

64. A. Solzhenitsyn, pp. 442–4, gives a much longer list; we have limited ourselves to those for which we have detailed information from the memoirs of M. Buber-Neumann, V. Shalamov, E. Ginzburg, G. Herling, K. Stainer and from P. I. Negretov, 'How Vorkuta Began', *Soviet Studies* (1977) no. 4, pp. 565–75.

65. On the CICRC see D. Rousset, *La société éclatée* (Paris, 1973), pp. 759–65; following a public session held in Brussels in 1951, the CICRC published a *Livre blanc sur les camps de concentration soviétiques* (depositions and reports). The Commission review, *Saturne*, appeared from December 1954 to January–March 1959 (19 editions); all this work is described in P. Barton, op. cit. *Le Rapport du Comité Spécial du Travail Forcé* was published by the B. I. T. in Geneva in 1953.

66. *Ezhenedel'nik sovetskoi yustitsii*, the organ of the Commissariat of Justice of the RSFSR, 28 Nov. 1929, pp. 1087–9. Sirvindt was the director of the prison camp administration. See *Bol'shaya Sovetskaya entsiklopediya* (Moscow 1935), vol. 29, article on 'The policy of corrective labour', p. 600.

67. Dallin and Nicolaevsky, pp. 274–8; *Pravda*, 11 March 1931, p. 2.

68. Ibid.

69. B. S. Utevskii, *Sovetskaya ispravitel'no-trodovaya politika* (Moscow, 1935) pp. 63–4. S. Firmin lists the following camps: Ukhta (oil and coal), Vorkuta (coal); Island of Vaigats (lead and zinc); Yugorskii Shar (exploitation of spath fluorine); Karaganda (agriculture).

70. Ibid., pp. 66–7; *Bol'shaya . . .*, p. 600; *Ot tyurem k vospitatel'nym uchrezhdeniam* (Moscow 1934) p. 10.

71. *Pravda*, 5 August 1933, 15 July 1937.

72. *Belomorsko-Baltiiskiy kanal imeni Stalina* (henceforth *BBK*) (Moscow 1934); analysis by M. Heller, pp. 104–116; I. L. Averbakh, *Ot prestupleniya k trudu* (Moscow, 1936).

73. *BBK*, pp. 251, 566–7; I. L. Averbakh, pp. 192–4; A. Solzhenitsyn, op. cit., ch. 3.

74. *Gosudarstvennyi plan razvitiya narodnogo khozyaistva SSSR na 1941 god* (Baltimore, American Council of Learned Societies Reprints, s.d.); discussed in J. Miller, *Soviet Studies*, April 1952, pp. 365–86.

75. We are concerned with the NKVD's industrial projects and the State

Organisation for Main Roads (NKVD): respectively 16,820 and 60,680 workers. These figures apparently correspond to the small contingent of free workers employed by the NKVD.

76. N. Jasny, 'Labor and Output in Soviet Concentration Camps', *The Journal of Political Economy*, October 1951, pp. 410, 412, 418; Dallin and Nicolaevsky, p. 138.
77. See D. Redding in *Journal of Political Economy*, no. 60, 1952.
78. Redding does not try to estimate the number of people deported, but agrees with Jasny that 'figures of 10–15 million are simply nonsense' (ibid.)
79. This practice is attested to by several statements by factory directors or prisoners. See V. A. Kravchenko, pp. 198–9, 285–6, 296; *Livre Blanc*, pp. 82–5; 89–90; P. Barton, pp. 65–7.
80. At least, this is Jasny's theory, which Redding follows; Dallin, however, thinks that camp prisoners were always included in work force statistics. See note 79.
81. N. Jasny, ibid., p. 407.
82. N. Jasny, ibid., p. 416.
83. N. Jasny, ibid., p. 410.
84. S. Swianiewicz, Appendices, pp. 292–6. Swaniewicz argues that mining of iron ore, platinum and phosphates should be added.
85. Op. cit. (note 61), pp. 66, 68–9, 71–3, 78–9.
86. With two exceptions, the photographs reproduced in Solzhenitsyn, op. cit., are also taken from these volumes.
87. *BBK*, pp. 176–7.
88. Ibid., pp. 318, 435, 575, 577.
89. Ibid., p. 246.
90. *Etudes*, 20 March 1934, pp. 717–8 (the author is a prisoner who managed to escape via Finland).
91. Cf. Solzhenitsyn, op. cit., pp. 84, 88–91.
92. K. Stainer, pp. 93, 215, 231–232, 255, 319–20, 338–9; on forest work, cf. V. Shalamov, *Kolymskie rasskazy* (Paris, 1982) p. 54; E. Ginzburg, *Krutoi marshrut* (Frankfurt, 1967), vol. 1, pp. 418–24; vol. 2 (Milan, 1979) p. 117; G. Herling, *A World Apart* (London, 1951) p. 41.
93. E. Ginzburg, vol. 1, pp. 349–52; vol. 2, p. 195.
94. M. Buber-Neumann, *Deportée en Siberie* (Paris, 1986) pp. 98, 105, 114, 129–31, 135, 158, 160; it was sometimes a question of supplying a machine, cf. pp. 130–1, 133.
95. Shalamov, pp. 289, 310–12, 322, 433, 438. The motif of 'wheelbarrow and shovel' is taken up by Solzhenitsyn, p. 85. Shalamov's account contradicts Dallin and Nicolaevsky, pp. 140, 145–6, on the mechanisation of gold mines.
96. Shalamov, p. 154.
97. Ibid., p. 438. See also Yu. Dombrovskii, *Fakul'tet nenuzhnykh veshchei* (Paris 1978) p. 160.: 'The prisoner was taken away and from that moment the barrow-camp began'. The same association between the labour camp and the wheelbarrow can be found in the recently published novel by V. Azaev, 'Vagon', *Druzhba Narodov* (1988) no. 7, pp.

154–5. OSO refers to the Special Board of the NKVD (*Osoboe Soveshchanie pri Narodnom Kommisare Vnutrennykh Del*) that had the right to sentence people to imprisonment.

98. N. Petrov, 'Of camels and tractors', *Critique communiste*, (1986), no. 55, p. 86. (Petrov was deported to Siberia as a 'Trotskyite' in 1937.)
99. P. Barton, p. 207; L. E. Hubbard, *Soviet Labour and Industry* (London, 1942) pp. 148–9; Dallin and Nicolaevsky, pp. 118–20. For a (rather unconvincing) critique of this theory see Jasny, op. cit., (note 78) p. 412.
100. P. Barton, pp. 265–6, 296, 351–3; *Saturne*, no. 7, pp. 16–17; no. 9, p. 31.
101. Approximately 21,000 people out of a total of 51,700, according to A. V. Volchenko, *Novokuznetsk v proshlom i nastoyashchem* (Novokuznetsk, 1971), p. 112.
102. M. Ya. Sonin estimates that during the second plan at least 2 million workers (a 'probable' figure) left the building sites for industry or another non-agricultural sector; cf. *Vosproizvodstvo rabochei sily i balans truda* (Moscow, 1959) p. 154. See also R. P. Dadykin in *Istoricheskie zapiski*, no. 87 (1971), pp. 49–50.

10 Nationality and Class in the Revolutions of 1917: A Re-examination of Social Categories[1]

Ronald Grigor Suny

SOME PRELIMINARY CONSIDERATIONS

The concepts of class and nationality have been problematic ever since they entered the broad political discourse of European intellectuals in the mid-nineteenth century. Long before they were categories employed by social scientists, their use by political activists and publicists carried with it values, expectations, and political claims that determined and limited their analytical utility. While Mill regarded nationality as positively related to the contemporary democratic struggles, conservatives of his day, like Lord Acton, feared the implications of claims to political recognition based on ethnicity and culture. In the classical Marxist tradition class was considered to be a more historically durable formation than nationality and provided both legitimacy for the socialist project and an instrument to achieve it. Not surprisingly, then, the proponents of enfranchisement of these social groups tended in their own understanding, and with the aid of committed intellectuals, to essentialise, eternalise, and naturalise the social categories whose political claims they were defending.

Ever since Stalin's early pronouncements as Commissar of Nationalities, the Soviet justifications for 'gathering' the non-Russian peoples into a new federal state have been based on the priority of the claims of class (proletarian; here read Russian) over nationality (identified with the bourgeoisie, the peasantry or simply the ethnic; here read the peoples of the periphery). Separatism, it was said, at best reflected the interests of bourgeois parties, at worst the false consciousness of people misled by Western imperialists. In stark contrast non-Marxist Western analysts, by playing down social and class characteristics and emphasising (or even exclusively focusing on) political and ideological aspects of nationalist movements, have

211

argued, sometimes explicitly, for the validity of the nationalist claim that only separation from Russia and the creation of independent nation-states could have satisfied their real aspirations.

The universality and permanence granted to class and nationality by their proponents led both Marxists and nationalists to neglect other social identities such as gender or generation and the independent claims of feminists, the young or the old. For Marxists the abolition of class differences would lead to the elimination of gender and ethnic oppression, while for the nationalists the priority of the ethnic community deflected attention from both class and gender conflicts. While the Marxist project was to transform the social order and emancipate women within it, the nationalist project in some instances had a more conservative aim, to preserve the traditional social form with its explicitly patriarchal values and power relations. In general women have been subsumed within these dominant interpretations, and though some work has been done on specific women and on women's issues a deeper investigation of the ways in which the revolutionary camps and their struggles were 'gendered' has not yet been undertaken by historians of the Russian revolutions.

In the years immediately before and during the First World War the question of national rights occupied a prominent place in the discourse of both liberals and the Left. For the leaders of the Entente Powers, most particularly Woodrow Wilson, nationality was equated with popular sovereignty and the right to self-determination. Propaganda about peoples oppressed by the Central Powers – Belgians, Alsatians, Poles, Eastern Slavs, Armenians, Kurds, and Arabs – as well as the Fourteen Points and the socialist slogan, 'The Right to Self-Determination of Nations', provided hope for Armenian victims of genocide, Polish, Czech, and Finnish aspirants to statehood, and the dozens of other nationalities that stood to benefit from the breakup of the great empires of central and eastern Europe. At the same time the overthrow of tsarism and the consequent emergence of socialists at the head of the *demokratiia* (the lower classes or 'democracy') in Russia gave the language of Marxist class analysis a power and resonance that it had never before enjoyed. While both Marxists and nationalists used their particular reading of historical evolution to define the context and the players, to win followers, and legitimise the use of violence, their respective utopias were mutually exclusive: Marxists saw the end of nationalism as contingent on proletarian victory; nationalists celebrated the vertical unity of the nation as the negation of class struggle. For non-Russians in the empire the conflicting loyalties to one's social peers and ethnic compatriots presented challenging and changing choices.

Before and during the revolution, and indeed in the analytical literature to the present time, the discussion of social categories has depended on a stark distinction between class and nationality that overlooks their complex relationship. In at least three important ways the extreme dichotomy between the exclusive claims of nationality and the priority of class should be questioned. Firstly, as many writers have pointed out, in eastern Europe and the Russian Empire class and nationality coexisted, with ethnic loyalties often preventing or delaying class solidarity, or with horizontal social links thwarting vertical ethnic integration. In particular conjunctures ethnicity and class reinforced one another and at other times undermined each other. In central Transcaucasia Georgian nobles and peasants, sharing a common ethnic culture and values based on rural, pre-capitalist traditions, faced an entrepreneurial Armenian urban middle class that dominated their historic capital, Tiflis, and had developed a way of life alien to the villagers. To the east, in and around Baku, the peasantry was almost entirely Azerbaijani, and urban society was stratified roughly along ethnic and religious lines, with Muslim workers at the bottom, Armenian and Russian workers in the more skilled positions, and Christian and European industrialists and capitalists dominating the oil industry.[2] At the same time the vertical ethnic ties that linked different social strata or classes together in a single community worked against the horizontal links between members of the same social class.

Nationality reinforced class, but at the same time national loyalties cut across class lines. A poor unskilled Moslem worker had little in common with a skilled Armenian worker apart from their memories of the massacres of 1905, whereas he had the bonds of religion and custom tying him to a Moslem peasant and, indeed, to a Moslem capitalist. Moslem workers occupied the bottom of the labor hierarchy while at the same time Moslem industrialists experienced condescension from Armenian, Russian, and foreign capitalists.[3]

A second reason for reducing the distance between class and nationality is that the intensity with which commitment to either is felt at a given time is highly contingent on the nature, depth, and ferocity of the social and political conflicts of the time. The direction from which the major danger to a social formation comes – whether from above in the form of state oppression, or below from the claims of other classes, or from outside from a foreign threat or alien ethnicity – contributes importantly to the kinds of ties that grow tighter. In the context of the Russian Empire, at least, the sense of ethnic oppression and aspirations to national recognition were reinforced by the unequal relationship between particular ethnicities and the dominant Russian nationality. The tsarist state promoted some peoples at some times (the Baltic Germans, the Armenian merchants until the 1880s) and discriminated against others (Jews, Ukrainians, Poles particularly after 1863, Armenians after 1885, Finns at the turn of the century). After 1881 the ruling nationality, the Russians, increasingly conceived of social problems in ethnic terms and saw Jewish conspiracies, Armenian separatists, and nationalists in general as sources of disruption and rebellion. Such enmity and discrimination directed against whole peoples, regardless of social status, helped erase internal distinctions of members of the ethnic group under attack and engendered support for the conceptions of the nationalists. Yet even as the nationalist construction of the ethnic enemy gained in power, the economic developmental policies of tsarism and considerations of security and profit attracted certain national bourgeoisies to try to work with the Russifying regime. Moreover, the embryonic working classes of Russia's peripheries remained ambivalent about nationalism in most cases and expressed their ethnic consciousness obliquely through ethnic socialist movements.

The development of ethnic cohesion and national awareness – not to mention political nationalism – was extraordinarily uneven in the Russian empire, connected as it was to the effects on various peoples of the general socioeconomic transformation that took place in Russia in the decades following the Emancipation of 1861. Some peoples continued to have little representation in towns (e.g., Lithuanians, Ukrainians, and Belorussians) or, if they did migrate to industrial or urban centers, tended to assimilate into the predominantly Russian work force. Their experience differed radically from those ethnicities that developed a working class of their own (Georgians, Latvians, Estonians, Jews, and to an extent, Armenians), experienced industrial capitalism more directly, and came into contact with the radical intelligentsia. Yet a third group, which included most of the Muslim peoples of the empire, had little contact with the social revolution of industrialism, relatively little urban experience, and less contact with the socialist or nationalist intelligentsia. (Here one should be careful to differentiate between Muslim peoples, some of whom, like the Azerbaijanis and the Volga Tatars, had a significant if small urban presence.) As the seigniorial economy gave way to market relations and new forms of the exploitation of labour replaced more tradition-sanctioned and paternalistic ones, those peoples that more immediately experienced industry and city life were recruited by radical intellectuals for socialist movements, but the degree and the nature of their mobilisation was affected by their ethnic as well as class sense of oppression.

Nationalists as well as socialists found it difficult to reach the peasants, and economic backwardness gave them no advantage over the socialists. Like socialism, nationalism as an intellectual and political configuration was largely an urban phenomenon, and no matter how sincerely patriots may have extolled the virtues of the peasantry, making actual converts among villagers proved to be as difficult for the followers of Shevchenko as for the disciples of Marx.

The third reason for questioning the class/nationality dichotomy is that both formations are not only social but intellectual constructs that have been produced and reproduced in remarkably similar ways. Much recent historical and sociological writing on class, as on nationality, has specifically rejected any essentialist argument that these formations arise 'objectively' as the result of disembodied social forces or that they are the manifestation in time of eternal, irreducible essences. Rather than always and permanently inhabiting history, classes and nationalities have been conceived as relatively modern, historically created, and often ephemeral formations. Class can 'happen' or not happen, can be made and unmade, and the same is true for nationality. Similarly the particular conjunctures that create mobilised classes or nationalities, class consciousness or political nationalism, are often fleeting (one remembers Lenin's desperate plea to his comrades when they failed to appreciate the fragility of the workers' and soldiers' militancy in October 1917 and take action: 'History will not forgive us').

During the first year of the revolution hopes for a constitutional solution to the problem of multinationality moderated the demands of the nationalists, and social concerns were far more widely articulated than ethnic ones. But after the October Revolution, the domestic armed opposition to Bolshevism and the intervention of foreign armies abruptly launched a more vociferous nationalism among many non-Russian peoples. In part this was due to the spread of the revolution outside urban centers into the countryside where the non-Russian majorities lived. Lines of conflict were drawn up that emphasised ethnicity (Russian workers against Ukrainian peasants, Armenian bourgeois against Georgian workers and peasants). In part it was the product of the hostility felt by nationalist intellectuals to the ostensibly internationalist, but evidently Russocentric Bolsheviks; and in part it was a phenomenon encouraged and financed by the interventionists. In any case the rise of nationalism in the Russian Civil War was no more the natural outcome of an inevitable historical process, the inherent and organic working out of the 'natural' aspirations of the minorities, than was the rise of class consciousness during the first year of revolution the inevitable maturing of inarticulate proletarians. Both the development of class consciousness in the cities in 1917 and the subsequent spread of nationalism beyond the intelligentsia were products of both long-term social, cultural, and intellectual processes that began in the past century, and of more immediate experiences of the revolutionary years. In this understanding, 'class interests' or 'national interests' are seen not as objective or existing outside the discursive practices and experience of the participants themselves but as arising in particular historical experiences, short- or long-term.

Seeing class and nationality as social constructions produced by specific historic conjunctures and intellectual and popular discourses parallels the way many feminist historians and theorists have been discussing gender. Most notably, Joan Wallach Scott has called for a deconstructive approach toward the given wisdom of the natural differentness of men and women and offers 'gender' as an alternative to the term 'sex'. Gender, she writes, is

> used to designate social relations between the sexes. Its use explicitly rejects biological explanations, such as those that find a common denominator for diverse forms of female subordination in the facts that women have the capacity to give birth and men have greater muscular strength. Instead, gender becomes a way of denoting 'cultural constructions' – the entirely social creation of ideas about appropriate roles for women and men. It is a way of referring to the exclusively social origins of the subjective identities of men and women. Gender is, in this definition, a social category imposed on a sexed body.[4]

But for Scott gender is not only 'a constitutive element of social relationships based on perceived differences between the sexes', but also 'a primary way of signifying relationships of power'. Following the French anthropologist and social theorist Pierre Bourdieu, she argues that 'concepts of gender structure perception and the concrete and symbolic organization of all social life'.[5] Gender indeed is ubiquitous in the languages of social analysis and politics and reflecting on it becomes the means to decode meaning. 'Hierarchical structures rely on generalized understandings of the so-called natural relationship between male and female. The concept of class in the nineteenth century relied on gender for its articulation.'[6] While Scott does not claim that gender is the only field through which power is articulated, she does believe that it has had an extraordinary run in Judaeo-Christian and Islamic civilizations. And her critique of the common-sense understanding of sexual differences assists a deeper questioning of given social understandings.

Similarly, it has been argued in much of the historical and theoretical literature on nationality and class that these social categories are neither natural, eternal, nor fixed categories inherent in social relations or certain periods of history. Rather, to paraphrase E. P. Thompson on class, they happen when people 'as a result of common experiences (inherited and shared), feel and articulate the identity of their interests as between themselves, and as against other[s] . . . whose interests are different from (and usually opposed to) theirs'.[7] As part of that common experience people find themselves in historically-created productive relations or enter them voluntarily, and those relations make up the context and much of the content of their social experience that may create a sense of class loyalty. Thompson again: 'Class-consciousness is the way in which these experiences are handled in cultural terms: embodied in traditions, value-systems, ideas, and institutional forms. If the experience appears as determined, class consciousness does not'.[8]

Thompson's 'ethnographic' and cultural notion of class fits neatly into a discussion of nationality. Like a Thompsonian class, a nationality has been seen to be the product of 'common experiences', and the articulation of common, shared understandings of interests, on the one hand, and opposition to others who do not share them. Theorists and historians of class, like Thompson, Eric J. Hobsbawm, Ira Katznelson, William H. Sewell, Jr., Gareth Stedman-Jones, and others, as well as those of nationality (Benedict Anderson, Ernest Gellner, Geoff Eley, and Hobsbawm again), have stressed that these social and cultural processes cannot be conceived simply as objective forces existing outside the given class or nationality but rather are mediated and shaped by the social and cultural (even linguistic) experience of individuals and groups within the social group. Class and nationality make themselves as much as they are made; individuals, parties, newspapers, and activist intellectuals were the keys to the creation of social and national consciousness in the nineteenth and twentieth centuries. Class and national traditions are invented and reinvented, discarded and revived; their rhetoric, symbols, and rituals are borrowed, refined, and passed down by intellectuals and activists. Thus, not only nationalism but the formation of nationality has a history, one that can be empirically elaborated and placed in time. Like other social and cultural relationships, nationality has a reality in the social world and is not merely the liberation of an *a priori Volksgeist*, the realisation of a timeless essence.[9]

The actual emergence, then, of class or nationality becomes an historical problem capable of theorisation and empirical demonstration. It is here that the work of the Czech historian Miroslav Hroch on emerging nationalism is particularly revealing. Hroch argues that the nationalist movements he has studied, largely those of smaller east European peoples, grew through three stages: Phase A: when a small number of scholars first demonstrated 'a passionate concern . . . for the study of the language, the culture, the history of the oppressed nationality'; Phase B: 'the fermentation-process of national consciousness', during which a larger number of patriotic agitators diffused national ideas; and finally Phase C: the full national revival when the broad masses have been swept up into the nationalist movement.[10] Hroch, like those who have worked on the 'invention of tradition' in the process of nation-building, underscores the active intellectual and political intervention of educated strata in the process of national formation.[11] One might add here that modern nationality was rooted in pre-existing cultural milieus, and that the work of the intellectuals took hold in those places where some kind of ethnic community (or 'ethnie' in Anthony Smith's work) provided a receptive environment for the new formulations of the patriots.

The social historical study of nationalist movements is in its infancy, and the bulk of the research on such movements in the Russian Empire has remained almost exclusively concentrated on the intellectual and political leaders and institutions of the non-Russian peoples. As a result there is little sense of the different stages of development of different national movements and a regrettable tendency to compress the experience of the whole nationality into that of the patriotic intelligentsia, as if the two were identical. Like the ambitions and actions of workers, which have often been collapsed into those of trade unionists and socialists, so the actions of ethnic masses have been equated or confused with the activities of their leaders, the writings of their intellectuals, or the votes of bodies that claim to represent them. Not only must the actual sociology of nationalism be more carefully examined, but in order to understand the varieties of national movements and the varying stages of development, the very concept nationality (and class) must be decomposed into its various meanings.

In a thoughtful and lucid introduction to a collection of essays on working-class formation, political scientist Ira Katznelson has argued that 'as a term "class" has been used too often in a congested way, encompassing meanings and questions that badly need to be distinguished from each other', and he suggests 'that class in capitalist societies be thought of as a concept with four connected layers of theory and history: those of structure, ways of life, dispositions, and collective action'.[12] This useful decomposition of the term 'class' is equally valuable for the discussion of nationality. In examining class structure Katznelson is careful to note that along with general characteristics of capitalism, specific national histories of capitalism must be considered, each with distinct 'family patterns, demography, cultural traditions, inherited practices, state organization and policies, geopolitics, and other factors [that] help determine the specific empirical contours of macroscopic economic development at this first level of class'.[13] Ways of life and dispositions are, of course, culturally specific, and are central to the analysis of both class and nationality. And finally for some nationalities at some times, though not necessarily for all, a specific conjuncture of circumstances and attitudes will lead to collective action, to the mobilisation of part or all of the nationality in the nationalist movement.

All of this is not meant to suggest that class and nationality (or gender for that matter) are in all aspects the same kind of formation, only that in their generation and evolution there are striking similarities and useful comparative points. Class, at least in the Marxist tradition, is both the product of and an integral part of productive relations; nationality, it is usually argued, arises on the basis of common culture, language, geography, and historical experience; gender starts with the biological differences of men and women. The weight given to these various inputs – production, culture, and biology – will probably differ in the histories of these categories. When one recognises that there are correspondences between the

boundaries of certain ethnicities and social classes, as in eastern
Europe and Russia, then productive relations also play a part in the
making of nationality and nationalism. If one believes that class is
made historically in a cultural process, then common or different
languages, ethnic ties or divisions, and social geography will have
profound effects on class cohesion or fragmentation, consciousness,
and the ability (or inability) to act collectively. 'Ethnicity,' writes
Anthony Smith,

> is largely 'mythic' and 'symbolic' in character, and because myths,
> symbols, memories and values are 'carried' in and by forms and
> genres or artefacts and activities that change only very slowly, so
> *ethnie*, once formed, tend to be exceptionally durable under 'nor-
> mal' vicissitudes and to persist over many generations, even cen-
> turies, forming 'moulds' within which all kinds of social and
> cultural processes can unfold and upon which all kinds of circum-
> stances and pressures can exert an impact.[14]

Once the naturalness of these categories is rejected, the analysis
turns toward the intellectual and social construction of differentness
and the social and intellectual processes of generation. In nationality,
class, and gender the representation of the category of the female or
male, the class, or the ethnicity includes the distance and differentness from 'the other'. This making of the other is part of the
construction of the category. For Karl W. Deutsch, one of the most
influential theorists of nationality, the 'making' of nationality is an
historical process of political integration that increases communication among the members of an ethnic group or a 'people'. A
people, 'a group of persons linked . . . by complementary habits and
facilities of communication', has the ability 'to communicate more
effectively, and over a wider range of subjects, with members of one
large group than with outsiders'.[15] Deutsch links the increase of social
communication that is basic to the formation of nationality to other
processes of social change – urbanisation, development of markets,
railroads and other forms of communication. A progression is made
from a 'people' to a 'nationality' ('a people pressing to acquire a
measure of effective control over the behavior of its members . . . .,
striving to equip itself with power') and eventually (though not
necessarily) to a 'nation-state'. Deutsch's notion of social communication and the greater ability to 'communicate' with the insider than
with 'the other' is very suggestive as a way of looking at the formation

of social classes and gendered groups. Certainly there is a subjective sense among members of particular class, ethnic, or gender groups that they share a special kind of understanding that is unique to them, and that grants them an ease of communication that includes a sense of trust and security.

Two possible scenarios now might be envisioned for the emergence of fully-conscious classes or nationalities. The first separates analytically the pre-conscious class or nationality from its more mature stage. A class in itself (or an *ethnie* in Smith's sense or a 'people' in Deutsch's sense) exists as a collection of persons with shared characteristics, a similar position in the production process or shared linguistic and cultural practices. With the development of the modern world, capitalism, markets, industry and urban life, these classes and peoples coalesce into more coherent and conscious formations ready in time to take action in their own 'interests'. In this reading the position of workers or ethnics, the social context in which they find themselves, leads to certain understandable responses. In the Marxist understanding the full realisation of working-class interests is a product (somewhat mysteriously) of capitalist development and ultimately requires revolution and the overthrow of capitalism. In the nationalist understanding the nationality's position in an unequal relationship with an imperial power pushes it to react to realise its full interests, which include the achievement of nationhood, perhaps ultimately state sovereignty.

A second scenario is more suspicious of the teleology, determinism, and failure to account for agency implicit in the first. Rather than positing a strict disctinction between classes or nationalities 'in themselves' and 'for themselves', this approach conceives of these formations at all stages of development as being constituted by myriad social and intellectual processes, by various forms of collective action, but with different self-images and senses of purpose. Classes and nationalities are at all stages the consequence of struggles, victories and defeats, that define and bind, differentiate and reject certain kinds of understanding.[16] Full modern nationalism is merely one phase, the latest or current one, of the movement of ethnicities but is neither the only stage in which self-realisation takes place nor the end of the evolution of national formations. Likewise, classes in the earlier stages of formation are far from inert demographic conglomerates waiting to achieve (or receive in the Leninist version) enlightenment, but in fact are active in their own constitution, vary in their makeup and self-representation, often borrowing and reshaping older traditions and languages to meet new situations. The working class, for example, which hardly fits, even in later stages, the model of full proletarianization envisioned by Marx, is never really fully 'made'. Socialist class consciousness in this scenario represents merely a moment only occasionally realised in social development and existing under very particular historical conditions (and usually only at the level of cities and regions, and not as a nation-wide phenomenon).

In other words, whatever the degree of cohesion and consciousness of classes and peoples before their mass mobilisation, they represent authentic points of development, and, rather than being conceived as premature, adolescent, or primitive, should be appreciated in their full constellation of influences, initiatives, and responses. An ethno-religious formation, such as the ancient Jews or the medieval Armenians, was not yet a modern nationality with its self-conscious sense of the value of its ethnic and cultural (in contrast to religious) traditions and with consequent claims to territory and autonomy or independence. But the earlier history of classes and nations cannot be read simply as the prehistory of their present state, but rather as a series of varied developments whose trajectories remain openended.

When the formation of class and nationality is understood to be a contingent and historically-determined occurrence rather than an essential working out of a natural or historical logic, one must discard the comfortable notion (for socialists) that a militant revolutionary class-conscious working class was the natural outcome of labour's history, as well as the equally dearly-held conviction (of nationalists and their supporters) that nationalism leading to the goal of an independent, sovereign (and fairly homogeneous) nation-state was the natural and inevitable outcome of the national struggle. Classes and ethnicities in one form or another exist in various historical periods, but their political claims are the specific product of historically-derived discourses of our own times.

A SINGLE CIVIL WAR

From the starkly contrasting perspectives of the Marxists and nationalists the revolution of 1917 and the subsequent civil war have been interpreted by some as a national war of Russians against minorities, the centre against the peripheries, and by others as a civil war of class against class, worker against peasant and bourgeois, city against country.[17] The perspective of a single, gigantic revolutionary process engulfing the whole of the now-defunct empire was proposed by many Bolsheviks and other Russian socialist and non-socialist parties during the revolution and civil war. On the other hand, nationalist parties viewed the experiences of the borderlands as unique events, in many ways fulfilling a particularly national historical evolution.

Their example has been followed by most of the monographic studies of individual nationalities. Most often in the West the history of the non-Russian peripheries is sharply distinguished from that of central Russia. While much of the new social history depicts the revolution in the central Russian cities as a struggle between increasingly polarised social classes, or at least an intense pulling-apart of the *verkhi* (top) and *nizy* (bottom) of society, historians of the revolution in the less developed borderlands have traditionally emphasised ethnic rather than social struggles.[18] Yet woven through the monographic literature on the non-Russian regions, both Soviet and Western, is a red thread of social conflict of very great intensity in the national borderlands, obscured at times by the ethnic coloration but in fact made all the more ferocious by cultural as well as class cleavages. Here the social and the ethnic are so closely intertwined that separation of the two can be artificial and misleading.

Rather than two kinds of revolution, one in the centre, the other in the peripheries, one gigantic social upheaval engulfed the whole of the Russian Empire in the third year of the First World War, bringing down the integrating imperial authority and launching a prolonged crisis of authority that continued well into the civil war years. For that whole period an ever-widening economic disintegration shredded the social fabric of the old order. Everyone everywhere was affected, and physical survival became the first requirement for millions of people. In this great turmoil various regions, some of them ethnically distinct, had their own particular experiences, but rather than dozens of separate national histories they were part of the general experience fatally linked to the whole history of Russia. The sundering of political and economic links opened the way for some parts of the empire, like Finland and Poland, to opt for a viable independence (though not without dissenters and, in the case of Finland, a bloody civil war); other parts were simply set adrift (like Azerbaijan and Armenia); and still others found neither the opportunity nor the will to break with revolutionary Russia (for example, Tataria).

The story of national formation and nationalism in the revolutionary years in seen here as part of the intricate mosaic of the Russian civil war with social and ethnic conflicts inextricably mixed. The civil war in the disintegrating Russian Empire was a civil war everywhere, right up to its pre-World War I borders, and though in the national peripheries it took on aspects of national wars, the social struggle between workers and peasants, *tsentsovoe obshchestvo* and *demokratiia*, city and countryside, remained determinant.

From the civil war perspective Soviet power or Bolshevism never simply meant Russia, and the extension of its power was not simply a Russian conquest of other peoples. Bolshevism, for better or worst, was the actual achievement of the revolution of the *demokratiia* of the central Russian cities as it stood after October 1917, and Russian and Russified Ukrainian workers in Kiev and Kharkov, Russian and Armenians in Baku, and Russians and Latvians in Riga supported local soviet power (and even Bolshevism) as the preferred alternative to a national independence promoted by a small nationalist elite in the name of a peasant majority. The difficult choice placed before both the Russians and the non-Russian peoples was whether to support the central Soviet government and the revolution as now defined by it, or accept a precarious existence in alliance with undependable allies from abroad with their own self-aggrandising agendas. In making that choice social structure, experience, and the options available were often much more determinate than ethnic considerations.

Almost everywhere the nationalist movements were either strengthened or fatally weakened by the nature of their class base. Because ethnic solidarity, activism, Russophilia or Russophobia were very often primed by social discontents, where nationalist leaderships were able to combine social reform with their program of self-definition, autonomy, or independence, their chances for success were increased. Where social, particularly agrarian reform, was delayed or neglected, ethnic political aspirations alone did not prove strong enough to sustain nationalist intellectuals in power. For those ethnic leaders facing a peasant majority indifferent to their claims to power, and rivalled by the Bolsheviks, an appeal to the Great Powers of central and western Europe became the last resort. And the intervention of foreigners, particularly the Germans, in the crucial first months after the October Revolution, radically distorted the development lines of the first revolutionary year. 'By interposing itself between the peoples of the Russian Empire and their practical rights of self-determination at a crucial moment of revolutionary political rupture', writes Geoff Eley,

– after the old order had collapsed, but while the new was still struggling to be born (to adapt a saying of Gramsci) – the German military administration suspended the process of democratic experimentation before it had hardly begun. The Germans' essentially destructive impact explains some of the difficulty experienced by the competing political leaderships in the western borderlands of Russia during 1918–20 in creating a lasting relationship to a large enough coalition of social support. The various political forces – Bolshevik, left-nationalist, autonomist, separatist, counter-revolutionary – operated more or less in a political vacuum in a fragile and indeterminate relationship to the local population, not just because the Belorussian and Ukrainian societies were so 'backward' (the explanation normally given), but because the cumulative effects of war, Imperial collapse, and German occupation had radically dislocated existing social organization, strengthening old antagonisms between groups and inaugurating new ones.[19]

Because fifty or sixty years later, after decades of Soviet or independent development, many of the incipient nations of 1917 forged national-cultural identities, established state structures, and manifested political nationalism, in retrospective histories the revolutionary years are viewed as if that future had already existed in 1917. The nationalist representation of an essential if concealed national consciousness, ever-present and emerging when opportunity knocked, seemed borne out by subsequent events and therefore was read back into an earlier age. Though this is not a subject for this paper, one could argue that much of the story of nationbuilding, and even nationality formation, for many peoples of the Russian empire belongs more appropriately in the Soviet period than in the years before the civil war.[20]

Though most scholars of Russia and the Soviet Union write exclusively about either ethnic Russia or one of the non-Russian peoples, sharply separating the history of the two, the approach adopted here attempts to reintegrate the history of the non-Russian peoples into the history of the whole empire. The modest hope of the author is that in the future more of his colleagues will adopt such a perspective and understand Russia and the Soviet Union in its multi-national dimensions, rather than as a series of discrete ethnic histories, or as ethnic Russia writ large.

NATIONAL MOVEMENTS IN THE RUSSIAN EMPIRE IN 1917

While most of the non-Russian peoples of the tsarist empire were overwhelmingly peasant, they differed radically one from another both in their internal class differentiation and in degree of national consciousness. In a longer version of this paper (and, hopefully, in a future monograph) I look at nine major nationalities in the Russian Empire at the time of the revolution – the four Baltic peoples, the three Transcaucasian peoples, and two Western Slavic peoples – to illustrate the variety of socially and ethnically generated responses to the new opportunities offered by the revolution. It is useful to divide them into five groups based on their identifications with class or nationality. The first group includes the Belorussians, Lithuanians, and Azerbaijanis, and is distinguished by their almost completely peasant composition and low level of national consciousness. The second group – the Ukrainians and Estonians – is marked by social and geographic divisions and a profound ambiguity in their national and class orientations. The third group – Georgians and Latvians – resolved the tension between nationality and class through a socialist-oriented national movement. The fourth – the Finns – divided radically into fiercely opposing camps, one socialist, the other nationalist, that resolved their conflict through bloody repression. And, finally, the fifth group – the Armenians – subordinated class divisions to a vertically-integrating nationalism. Space does not permit reviewing the experiences of all nine of these nationalities here. In order to illustrate the complexities of class and national identifications I shall use here the example of the Ukrainians.

In the Ukraine, scholars agree, 'to an unusual degree, nationality coincided with economic class. Ukrainians were, with the exception of a small intelligentsia, almost entirely peasants; the landowners and officials were Poles or Russians, while the commercial bourgeoisie was largely Jewish'.[21]

Class and ethnic cleavages were closely related . . . . Russians manned the oppressive bureaucracy and were heavily represented among the principal landowners. Poles dominated the *pomeshchiki* class in the right bank provinces of Kiev, Podolia, and Volhynia. Petty trade, commerce, and much of industry on the right bank were controlled by Jews who were therefore the peasantry's most visible creditors. As a consequence, the ethnic and socioeconomic grievances of the Ukrainian peasant proved mutually reinforcing and provided the foundation for a political movement which combined nationalism with a populist social program.[22]

The Ukraine had developed a distinct ethnic culture and language in the long period from the fall of Kiev to the Mongols (1240) through the Polish dominion (1569) to the union with Russia (1654). Early in the nineteenth century nationalist intellectuals articulated a notion of Ukrainian distinctiveness, and the Romantics Taras Shevchenko and Panko Kulish formed a Ukrainian literary language from the vernacular of the southeast.[23] The brief flourishing of Eastern Ukrainian intellectual culture in the first two-thirds of the nineteenth century, however, was curtailed after the Polish insurrection of 1863, and particularly in 1876 when the tsarist power prohibited public expression in Ukrainian. With the restrictions on 'Russian' Ukrainian culture, Galicia, the Western Ukrainian regions under Austrian rule, became the centre for literary expression and a popular nationalism.[24] Part of a vast territory divided between empires, with severe constraints on ethnic intellectual life, and with non-Ukrainians dominating urban centres, 'Russian' Ukraine developed neither a coherent mass-based national movement, nor even a widely-shared sense of a Ukrainian nation in the decades before the revolutions of the twentieth century.

Ukrainian peasants were very active in 1905–7, though the movement in the first revolution had only very superficially nationalistic characteristics. Largely a protest over land shortages, which were blamed on the large holdings by noble landlords (most of them Polish and Russian), social discontent led to violence, but with minimal ethnic expression. Even the supposedly traditional Ukrainian anti-Semitism was largely absent, and Jewish revolutionaries were welcomed as supporters of the peasant movement. Peasant grievances were sufficient to generate protests without consistent intervention from outsiders, though on the Right Bank *Spilka* (the Ukrainian Social Democratic Union) and on the Left Bank the SRs and the Peasants' Union were active.[25]

Historians differ in their evaluation of Ukrainian nationalism in 1917–18. Without question an articulate and active nationalist elite, made up of middle-class professionals, was prepared to confront both the Provisional Government and the Sovnarkom with its demand for autonomy and self-rule.[26] John Reshetar, the author of the first major scholarly monograph on the Ukrainian Revolution, writes:

Immediately after the March Revolution, leadership in the Ukrainian national movement was assumed by the democratically inclined petite bourgeoisie, the intelligentsia with nationalist sympathies, and the middle strata of the peasantry which supported the cooperative movement. The peasant masses, the soldiers, and the urban proletariat were not participants at this early period, and it cannot be said that the national movement permeated their ranks to any significant extent in the months that followed since it was competing with more urgent social and economic issues.[27]

The Rada was committed to a democratic solution to the political crisis, to remaining within a federated Russian state, and to a radical program of land reform. Its support in the cities was minimal – in the elections in July to the municipal *duma* in Kiev Ukrainian parties won only 20 per cent of the vote while Russian parties garnered 67 per cent (Russian socialists, 37 per cent; 'Russian voters', 15 per cent; Kadets, 9 per cent; Bolsheviks, 6 per cent) – but it was backed by Ukrainian soldiers, particularly interested in the formation of ethnic military units (see the resolutions of the First Ukrainian Military Congress in May 1917).[28]

Far more problematic, however, is the estimate of the level of national cohesion among Ukrainians and the degree of support for the national program among the peasants. For Reshetar nationalism is a middle-class movement and the peasant 'was enslaved by his locale and regarded the inhabitants of the neighboring villages as a species of foreigner'. The absence of a Ukrainian bourgeoisie of any weight and

the essentially agrarian character of late nineteenth-century Ukrainian society, with its emphasis on the locale, tended to retard the development of that sentiment of group cohesiveness which transcends localism and is termed national consciousness. The peasant, because of his conservatism, was able to retain his language, peculiarities of dress, and local customs despite foreign rule, but initially he resisted the notion that all Ukrainians, whether living in Kharkiv province, in Volynia, or in Carpatho-Ukraine, belonged to the same nation.

Though this peasant parochialism was partially broken down by the spread of currency, the building of railroads, and the dissemination of newspapers and periodicals, the protracted process of nationality formation 'had not been consummated as late as 1917'. Reshetar points out that even in 1917 peasants in Ukraine referred to themselves not as a single collective but with regional terms: *Rusiny* (sons of Rus), Galicians, Bukovinians, Uhro-rusins, Lenki, and Hutsuli. Russophilia was still strong in many parts of the country, even among the peasantry, and much of the middle-class and working class was Russified.[29]

In his encyclopedic study of nationalism in the revolutionary years, a work sympathetic to the aspirations of the nationalists and repelled by the opportunism and centralism of the Bolsheviks, Richard Pipes repeatedly demonstrates that social environment – the isolation of the nationalists from urban society and the working class, and their dependency on and difficulties in mobilising the peasantry – confounded the plans of the Ukrainian ethnic parties.[30] Agreeing with Reshetar that 'the weakest feature of the Ukrainian national movement was its dependence on the politically disorganized, ineffective, and unreliable village', Pipes emphasises their 'political immaturity, which made them easily swayed by propaganda, and . . . their strong inclinations toward anarchism'. Nevertheless, nationalism was a reality in Ukraine, 'a political expression of genuine interests and loyalties', which had its roots in

> a specific Ukrainian culture, resting on peculiarities of language and folklore; a historic tradition dating from the seventeenth-century Cossack communities; an identity of interests among the members of the large and powerful group of well-to-do peasants of the Dnieper region; and a numerically small but active group of nationally conscious intellectuals, with a century-old heritage of cultural nationalism behind them.

But 'the fate of the Ukraine, as of the remainder of the Empire, was decided in the towns, where the population was almost entirely Russian in its culture, and hostile to Ukrainian nationalism'.[31] Contingent factors such as the inexperience of the national leaders and the shortage of administrative personnel are mentioned as part of the toxic mix that destroyed the Ukrainian experiment in independence.

While one might hesitate to accept Reshetar's firm requirement that a middle class must exist for a nationalist movement to succeed, or Pipes' assumption that there was a conscious community of interests between intelligentsia and peasantry in 1917, the argument that the movement would stand or fall on the backs of the peasantry seems compelling. In a most intriguing article Steven L. Guthier argues, in contrast to Reshetar, that the Ukrainian peasantry was nationally conscious in 1917, as demonstrated in their choices in the November elections to the Constituent Assembly when they overwhelmingly supported Ukrainian parties. In the eight Ukrainian provinces (Kiev, Poltava, Podolia, Volhynia, Ekaterinoslav, Chernigov, Kherson, and Kharkov) '55 per cent of all votes cast outside the Ukraine's ten largest cities went to lists dominated by the UPSR [Ukrainian Party of Socialist Revolutionaries] and *Selians'ka Spilka* [All-Ukrainian Peasants' Union]; another 16 per cent went to Left PSR/UPSR slates'.[32] The cities, on the other hand, went for Russian and Jewish parties, though heavy turnouts among Ukrainian soldiers gave substantial backing to Ukrainian parties.

Guthier concludes that 'Ukrainian nationalism as a substantial political force was a one-class movement', but one in which identification between peasant aspirations and the programmes of the national parties was quite close.[33] He assumes that peasants voting for the Ukrainian peasant parties were aware of and accepted the national planks in their programmes. 'The peasants were committed to the creation of a Ukraine which was both autonomous and socialist. They wanted land rights to be reserved for those who farmed the land with their own hands.'

A useful distinction, however, might be made between cultural or ethnic awareness and full-blown political nationalism, i.e., an active commitment to realising a national agenda. While the election results show that peasants in Ukraine preferred parties and leaders of their own ethnicity, people who could speak to them in their own language and promised to secure their local interests, they do not provide sufficient evidence either that the peasantry conceived of itself as a single nationality or that it could be effectively mobilised to defend ideals of national autonomy or independence. Though more work is needed to determine the mentality of the Ukrainian peasants of 1917, an impression is left that they had some ethnic awareness, preferring their own kind to strangers, but were not yet moved by a passion for the nation and certainly not willing to sacrifice their lives for anything beyond the village. For defeated nationalists, as well as 'class-conscious' Bolsheviks, the peasants of Ukraine were considered 'backward', 'unconscious', unable to be mobilised except for the most destructive, anarchistic ends. But more generously one might argue that rather than backward, Ukrainian peasants had their own localistic agenda in the chaos of the civil war, one that did not mesh neatly either with that of urban intellectuals, nationalist or Bolshevik, or with workers, many of whom despised those living in the villages.

Guthier may be closer to the mark when he sees the momentary coincidence of peasant voters and Ukrainian populists as the specific conjuncture when 'national autonomy was seen as the best guarantee that the socioeconomic reconstruction of the Ukraine would reflect local, not all-Russian conditions'.[34] Here once again both the contingent and evolving character of nationalism (and class, for that matter) and the closeness of ethnic and social factors become clear. At least in 1917–18 the Ukrainian peasants were most concerned about the agrarian question and their own suffering in the years of war and scarcity.[35] They thought of themselves as peasants, which for them was the same as being 'Ukrainian' (or whatever they might have called themselves locally). Their principal hope was for agrarian reform and the end of the oppression identified with the state and the city. Russians, Jews, and Poles were the sources of that oppression, and it is conceivable that for many peasants the promise of autonomy was seen as the means to achieving the end to their condescension and arbitrary power. But ethnic claims had no priority over social ones in these early years of revolution, and alliances with nationalists (or more frequently, ethnic populists) could easily be replaced by marriages of convenience with more radical elements.[36]

When the nationalist Rada was unable to resist effectively the Bolshevik advance in January 1918, it turned as a last resort to the Germans, who requisitioned grain and terrorised the peasants. When the nationalists failed to back up their own agrarian reform, support for the first generation of revolutionary nationalists rapidly evaporated among many peasants. As a consequence of the German occupation, the nationalist forces in Ukraine splintered into competing groups; the nationalist cause was identified by many as linked to foreign intervention; and to anti-nationalist elements, particularly in towns, the only viable alternative to social chaos, foreign dependence, and Ukrainian chauvinism appeared to be the Bolsheviks. A German report of March 1918 gives a sense of the fragmentation in Ukraine at the time, the uncertainty of nationalist influence, and the relative strength of the Bolsheviks:

It is not true that the Bolsheviks are supported only by the Russian soldiers who remained in the Ukraine . . . . They have a large following in the country. All the industrial workers are with them, as is also a considerable part of the demobilized soldiers. The attitude of the peasants, however is very difficult to ascertain. The villages that have once been visited by Bolshevik gangs . . . are, as a rule, anti-Bolshevik. In other places Bolshevik propaganda seems to be successful among the peasants.

The peasants are concerned chiefly with the dividing up of the land; they will follow the Rada if it allows them to take the estates of the landlords . . . as proclaimed in the Third and Fourth Universals . . . . Otherwise they will go with the Bolsheviks. Although the Bolsheviks lost out in many places because of their system of terror, their slogan 'Take everything, all is yours' is too attractive and tempting to the masses.

The Ukrainian separatist movement, on which the Rada is relying, has no true roots in the country and is supported only by a small group of political dreamers. The people as a whole show complete indifference to national self-determination.[37]

Sadly for the nationalists and happily for the Bolsheviks, the peasantry proved to be an unsteady social base for a political movement. A British observer in May 1918 confirmed to the Foreign Office the lack of national consciousness among the Ukrainian peasants.

The peasants speak the Little Russian dialect; a small group of nationalist *intelligentsia* now professes an Ukrainian nationality distinct from that of the Great Russians. Whether such a nationality exists is usually discussed in terms in which the question can receive no answer. Were one to ask the average peasant in the Ukraine his nationality he would answer that he is Greek Orthodox; if pressed to say whether he is a Great Russian, a Pole, or an Ukrainian, he would probably reply that he is a peasant; and if one insisted on knowing what language he spoke, he would say that he talked 'the local tongue'. One might perhaps get him to call himself by a proper national name and say that he is 'russki', but this declaration would hardly yet prejudge the question of an Ukrainian relationship; he simply does not think of nationality in the terms familiar to the *intelligentsia*. Again, if one tried to find out to what State he desires to belong – whether he wants to be ruled by an All-Russian or a separate Ukrainian Government – one would find that in his opinion all Governments alike are a nuisance, and that it would be best if the 'Christian peasant-folk' were left to themselves.[38]

When the Directory, which came to power in November 1918 and tried to place itself at the head of the peasant risings against the Hetmanate,

> faltered in its implementation of new programs, turning cautious and conservative in order to preserve its very life, the forces of the Jacquerie swept past it to embrace another, more radical political group, which seemed to promise a program that *would* suit peasant tastes. Specifically, even before the year 1918 had run its course, many of the Directory's peasant-Cossack supporters were already going over to the Bolsheviks . . . . For a few months in early 1919 there was an illusion that the two forces had joined for a common cause.[39]

But the Bolsheviks effectively disenfranchised the middle and wealthier peasantry and instituted a new round of requisitioning. Formerly sympathetic villagers turned against the Soviets, and the final Bolshevik victory depended on support from the workers, Russian and Russified, of the cities, and Donbass and the Red Army. Here the Bolsheviks were stronger than any of their contenders.

Though in much of the Russocentric writing on the revolution the varied experiences of the non-Russian peoples have often been homogenised into a single nationalist impulse toward national independence, closer examination exposes very different patterns. Like Ukrainians, Estonians vacillated between nationalism and other social movements, but Latvians and Georgians combined their ethnic and social grievances in a single, dominant socialist national movement. While Belorussia, Estonia, and Latvia had never been historically independent states, and the Ukraine had existed more as an idea of a nation than a unified ethno-political unit, Georgia, like its neighbour Armenia, had existed as a state (actually a number of states) long before the first Russian state had been formed. The sense of a continuous existence was fundamental to the national self-conceptions of the Armenian and Georgian intelligentsias of the late eighteenth and early nineteenth centuries as they revived the study of national history and literature. Their struggles for national emancipation began as liberal and democratic movements of writers, journalists, and teachers, but by the last decade of the nineteenth century the first generations of nationalist intellectuals had been shunted aside by younger, more radical, socialists.[40] For these peoples, as for other small nations in Hroch's analysis, the struggle for national

emancipation was also a struggle against the non-national or dena-
tionalised bourgeoisie.

The parallels between Latvia and Georgia are particularly striking.
In both countries the older generation of national patriots (in Latvia
'Young Latvia'; in Georgia the *pirveli dasi* and the *meore dasi*) were
supplanted by Marxists (the Latvian 'New Current' and the Georgian
mesame dasi). The brunt of national hostility was directed, not
against the Russians, but against the locally dominant nationality (in
Latvia, the Germans; in Georgia, the Armenians). Independence
resulted from unpropitious political circumstances, rather than the
plans or intentions of the dominant political movement. In both
countries class and ethnic identities overlapped and reinforced one
another, but the form of expression was socialist rather than predominantly nationalist.

The experience of Finland is closer to that of Georgia and Latvia
than to that of its other neighbors, Estonia, Lithuania, or Belorussia.
'Although ultimate control was exercised in St. Petersburg', writes
Risto Alapuro,

> domination within the country – political, economic, and cultural –
> was in the hands not of the Russians but of the Swedish-speaking
> upper class. Thus, although linguistic, social, and educational
> barriers coincided within Finland, the local elite was not an exten-
> sion of the metropolitan elite.[41]

The position of the Swedish-speakers – nobles, bureaucrats, and
middle class elements – was similar to that of the German nobles in
the Baltic and Polish landlords in Lithuania, though the Swedish-
speakers had never enjoyed feudal privileges, did not have control
over land, and exercised their hegemony through the bureaucracy
and literary culture. While the status of Finns as a subordinate people
within a region in which they composed the majority echoes the
social position of most non-Russian peoples in the nineteenth century, the unique juridical status of Finland provided a radically
different political environment for the development of Finnish
nationality. In Finland, then, one finds yet another variant of the
class/nationality relationship: by late 1917 all social groups favoured
independence, but the common national programme did not overcome class and regional cleavages. The result was a bloody civil war,
the defeat of the Social Democrats who had led the struggle for
democracy and independence, and the coming to power of a conservative, pro-German elite.

Finally, the experience of the Armenians as a geographically divided and endangered people led to the rapid decline of class allegiances and a commitment to a vertically-integrating nationalism. Though the absolute number of Armenians continued to grow in the nineteenth and early twentieth centuries, and they continued to dominate the largest cities of the Caucasus economically and politically, Armenians found themselves in a vulnerable demographic position. The relative position of Armenians in the Armenian plateau of eastern Anatolia worsened. The in-migration of Balkan Muslims, Circassians, and the rapid growth of the Kurdish population combined with the out-migration of Armenians, particularly after the massacres of 1894–6, made the Armenians even more of a minority in a heavily Turkish and Kurdish population.

Impressed by the urgency of a political solution, the nationalist intelligentsia disavowed joint solutions with other parties of the Russian Empire. The Armenian revolutionary parties took the battle to Turkey, and by means of 'propaganda of the deed' and examples of militant sacrifice, attempted to mobilise a rather passive and demoralised peasantry. The war, however, and the subsequent genocide of Armenians in eastern Anatolia created an entirely new situation. For Armenians the principal source of danger came from their ethnic and religious enemies, the Ottoman Turks and the Azerbaijanis, and the very acuity of that danger completed what two decades of revolutionary propaganda had been working to accomplish – the effective mobilisation of the Caucasian Armenian population to vote for and fight for the national future as defined by the Dashnaktsutiun. The central political issue became self-defence, and in the context of Russian retreat and Turkish-German advance it quickly took on an ethnic dimension. The ostensibly socialist ideology of the Dashnaktsutiun was largely neglected, and the party became the representative of all classes of Caucasian Armenians as they faced together the common threat from Ottoman and post-Ottoman Turks. Class divisions had become irrelevant as a reluctantly-independent Armenia, a tiny enclave of migrants, refugees, and local people, attempted to provide a last refuge for Armenians.

SOME PRELIMINARY CONCLUSIONS

Nationalism, like class consciousness, was a disturbingly ephemeral phenomenon among most non-Russians in these turbulent years, especially once the revolution outgrew the cities. Whatever their cultural and ethnographic preferences, non-Russian peasants did not automatically opt for the national programme of their urban ethnic leaders. Neither nationality nor class, in the Russian case or in general, is objective in the sense of existing outside the constitutive practices of its members and its opponents. Nor are these identities completely subjective in the sense that they exist only when they are perceived to exist by their members or opponents. Rather how class or nationality exists is determined by the social and intellectual activities that unify and make uniform internal differences among groups, the real and perceived interconnections between members of the group and the distance from the 'other'. These constitutive activities, contesting other forms of integration or imposition, are part of a process of social and cultural construction, the making of new socio-cultural identities, that are shaped both by existing and shifting structures and by political and cultural practices. Class or ethnic identity of many individuals is often ambiguous until solidified, however briefly, in political confrontations when less ambiguous choices must be made.

The relative strength or weakness of class and nationality in various areas of the empire were both determined by the nature of the political struggles and also crucial in determining the lines of battle and the commitment of actors. In the great sweep of the Russian Revolution and civil war nationalism was for most nationalities still largely a phenomenon centered in the ethnic intelligentsia, among students and the lower middle classes of the towns, with at best a fleeting following among broader strata. Among Belorussians, Lithuanians, and Azerbaijanis, rather than a sense of nationality, the paramount identification was with people nearby with whom one shared social and religious communality. For these peoples neither nationalism nor socialism was able to mobilise large numbers into the political struggles that would decide their future.

For several other nationalities, among them the Latvians and Georgians, class-based socialist movements were far more potent than political nationalism. Socialism as presented by the dominant intellectual elite answered the grievances of both social and ethnic inferiority and promised a socio-political solution to the dual oppression determined by class and nationality. For still other nationalities, like the Ukrainians and the Estonians, nationality competed with a sense of class for the primary loyalty of the workers and peasants, with neither winning a dominant position. In Finland a deadly polarisation between social groups led to a civil war between parts of a population relatively united on the question of national independence and commitment to Finnish culture. For the Armenians, a rather unique case of a people divided between two empires, without a secure area of concentration, and faced by the imminent danger of extermination, a non-class, vertically integrating nationalism overwhelmed all competitors.

The reasons for the relative weakness of nationalism and the strength of local and social identities in 1917-18, and even further into the civil war, require further attention by scholars, but tentatively one might suggest that the social distance between villagers and townspeople, between peasants and intellectuals, was great enough to make the supraclass appeal of nationalism difficult to buy. The most successful appeals were populist or even socialist, especially when they were enhanced by ethnic arguments. Furthermore, long-established trade patterns and complex economic relations tied most of the non-Russian peoples of the old empire to the centre (Finns and Poles are perhaps an exception here). The way the empire had developed economically was a powerful force for integration with the rest of Russia rather than for separate nations. Separation from Russia was almost always a political decision based on need for support by an outside power, at first Germany and Turkey, later the Entente powers, and had far less intrinsic appeal to the mass of the population than has been customarily accepted.

The ebb and flow of socialism or nationalism was tied to the ebb and flow of the war and revolution, to the relative fates of the Great Powers and their ability to act within Russia. In the twentieth century intervention has become an unwelcome but ubiquitous guest at the revolutionary table. When Bolsheviks were relatively weak and Germans strong, separatism and the fortunes of the nationalists rose; when the Germans were defeated and the Entente withdrew, the appeals of the Bolsheviks in favour of social revolution, land to the peasants, and even a kind of greater 'all-Russia nationalism' found supporters. Neither nationalism nor a sense of class were ends in themselves for ordinary people, as they often were for intellectuals. They resonated within the *demokratiia* in so far as they were believed to be a means of solving the aggravated social dislocation that had only got worse with war and revolution.

Lenin's estimation that national separatism would be reduced by central Russian tolerance and a willingness to allow national self-determination to the point of independence has appeared, understandably, to be either a utopian fantasy or an example of political dissembling. But if in fact nationalism was far weaker than most nationalists have allowed; if in Russia it was almost invariably connected with real social and political discontents caused by years of discrimination and hardship under tsarism; and if, indeed, significant groups within the non-Russian peoples responded well to the socialist programme of social transformation and national self-determination, then perhaps Lenin's views on the near future of the nationalities was less a fantasy than another example of his political style, an uneasy combination of hard-nosed realism and the willingness to take extraordinary risks.

NOTES

1. This paper is a much-revised version of a presentation made at a conference to mark the seventieth anniversary of the Russian Revolution, held at the Hebrew University of Jerusalem in January 1988. An earlier version of the paper will be published in the conference volume, *From February to October: A Reassessment of the Russian Revolution of 1917*. The author would like to thank Geoff Eley, Frank Sisyn, and Roman Szporluk for their critical reading and comments on earlier drafts. This paper is very much conceived as a work-in-progress, hopefully the embryo of a future monograph.

2. 'Nationalism and Social Class in the Russian Revolution: The Cases of Baku and Tiflis', in Ronald Grigor Suny (ed.), *Transcaucasia, Nationalism and Social Change: Essays in the History of Armenia, Azerbaijan, and Georgia* (Ann Arbor: Michigan Slavic Publications, 1983), pp. 239–58; 'Tiflis, Crucible of Ethnic Politics, 1860–1905', in Michael F. Hamm (ed.), *The City in Late Imperial Russia* (Bloomington: Indiana University Press, 1986), pp. 249–81; *The Making of the Georgian Nation* (Bloomington and Stanford: Indiana University Press and Hoover Institution Press, 1989); *The Baku Commune, 1917–1918: Class and Nationality in the Russian Revolution* (Princeton: Princeton University Press, 1972).

3. Suny, *The Baku Commune*, p. 14.

4. Joan W. Scott, 'Gender: A Useful Category of Historical Analysis', *American Historical Review*, 91, 5 (December 1986), p. 1056.

5. Ibid., p. 1067; Pierre Bourdieu, *Le sens practique* (Paris, 1980).

6. Scott, 'Gender', p. 1073).

7. E. P. Thompson, *The Making of the English Working Class* (London: Victor Gollancz, 1963), pp. 9–10.

8. Ibid.

works by Ernest Gellner, *Thought and Change* (Chicago: The University of Chicago Press, 1964); *Nations and Nationalism* (Oxford: Basil Blackwell, 1983); by Benedict Anderson, *Imagined Communities: Reflections on the Origin and Spread of Nationalism* (London: Verso, 1983); Maxime Rodinson, *Cult, Ghetto, and State: The Persistence of the Jewish Question* (London: Al Saqi Books, 1983); Eric Hobsbawn, 'Some Reflections on the "Break-up of Britain"', *New Left Review*, 105 (September-October 1977), pp. 3–23; Geoff Eley, 'Nationalism and Social History', *Social History*, 6 (1981), pp. 83–107; and the prolific output of Anthony D. Smith, for example, *The Ethnic Origins of Nations* (Oxford: Basil Blackwell, 1986).

10. Miroslav Hroch, *Social Preconditions of National Revival in Europe: A Comparative Analysis of the Social Composition of Patriotic Groups among the Smaller European Nations* (Cambridge: Cambridge University Press, 1985), pp. 22–3. See also his earlier work, *Die Vorkampfer der nationalen Bewegung bei den kleinen Volkern Europas* (Prague, 1968). As Eley points out in an important essay, Hroch 'pioneers a social-historical approach to the study of nationalist movements and their uneven penetration. In some ways it amounts to a much-needed specification of Deutsch's theory of social communication through the kind of concrete historical investigation that Deutsch himself never really engaged in'. (Eley, 'Nationalism and Social History', p. 101.)

11. E. Hobsbawm and T. Ranger (eds), *The Invention of Tradition* (Cambridge: Cambridge University Press, 1983).

12. Ira Katznelson and Aristide R. Zolberg (eds), *Working-Class Formation: Nineteenth-Century Patterns in Western Europe and the United States* (Princeton: Princeton University Press, 1986), pp. 13–14.

13. Ibid., p. 15.

14. Smith, *The Ethnic Origins of Nations*, p. 16.

15. Karl W. Deutsch, *Nationalism and Social Communication. An Inquiry into the Foundations of Nationality* (New York-Cambridge, Mass.: MIT, 1953), p. 70–71.

16. This critique of the two-stage model follows the review essay of the Katznelson/Zolberg volume by Margaret Ramsay Somers, 'Workers of the World, Compare', *Contemporary Sociology*, XVIII, 3 (May 1989), pp. 325–9. As Somers points out, it is an error to attribute 'to class structure a conceptual independence from the formative role of collective action, retaining an a priori directionality from structure to action in the conceptual definition'. Action should not be reduced to response. Furthermore, structure should not be reduced to economics. The intervention and contribution to class (and nationality formation) from culture, politics, gender, religion, law, demography should not be eliminated in favour of a notion of a separate, causally dominant economic sphere.

17. The classic text for the interpretation of the civil war as a national war of Russia against the borderlands, as a series of 'conquests' of the peripheries by the centre, is Richard Pipes, *The Formation of the Soviet Union:*

9. Particularly suggestive for this approach to nationality and ethnicity are

Communism and Nationalism, 1917–1918 (Cambridge, Mass.: Harvard University Press, 1957).

18. For a review of Western writing on 1917 in Russia proper that emphasises the importance of deep social polarisation as an explanation for Bolshevik victory, see Ronald Grigor Suny, 'Toward a Social History of the October Revolution', *American Historical Review*, 88, 1 (February 1983), pp. 31–52.

19. Geoff Eley, 'Remapping the Nation: War, Revolutionary Upheaval, and State Formation in Eastern Europe, 1914–1923', paper presented to the McMaster Conference on Jewish-Ukrainian Relations in Historical Perspective, 19 October 1983, p. 4.

20. This, indeed, is the argument of much of my work on the republics of Transcaucasia. See, for example, Ronald Grigor Suny, *Armenia in the Twentieth Century* (Chico, CA: Scholars Press, 1983); *The Making of the Georgian Nation* (Bloomington and Stanford: Indiana University Press and Hoover Institution Press, 1985); 'Nationalist and Ethnic Unrest in Soviet Union', *World Policy Journal*, 6, 3 (Summer 1989), pp. 503–28.

21. John Armstrong, *Ukrainian Nationalism* (New York and London: Columbia University Press, 1963), p. 10.

22. Steven L. Guthier, 'The Popular Base of Ukrainian Nationalism in 1917', *Slavic Review*, 38, 1 (March 1979), p. 32. In 1897 Ukrainians made up only 35 per cent of the population in the 113 towns in Ukraine; the larger the town the smaller the Ukrainian proportion. In Kiev Ukrainians made up 22 per cent, Russians 54 per cent, Jews 12 per cent, and Poles 7 per cent; in Kharkiv Ukrainians were 26 per cent, Russians 53 per cent, Jews 6 per cent, and Poles 0.3 per cent (Steven L. Guthier, 'Ukrainian Cities during the Revolution and the Interwar Era', in Ivan L. Rudnytsky (ed.), *Rethinking Ukrainian History* (Edmonton: Canadian Institute of Ukrainian Studies, University of Alberta, 1981), p. 157; Patricia Herlihy, 'Ukrainian Cities in the Nineteenth Century', ibid., p. 151).

23. On the formation of the Ukrainian literary language, see, George Y. Shevelov, 'Ukrainian', in Alexander M. Schenker and Edward Stankiewicz (eds), *The Slavic Literary Languages: Formation and Development* (New Haven: Yale Concilium on International and Area Studies, 1980), pp. 143–60.

24. John-Paul Himka, *Socialism in Galicia: The Emergence of Polish Social Democracy and Ukrainian Radicalism (1860–1890)* (Cambridge, Mass.: Harvard Ukrainian Research Institute, 1983); *Galician Villagers and the Ukrainian National Movement in the Nineteenth Century* (New York: St Martin's Press, 1988); Andrei S. Markovits and Frank E. Sysyn (eds), *Nationbuilding and the Politics of Nationalism: Essays on Austrian Galicia* (Cambridge, MA: Harvard Ukrainian Research Institute, 1982).

25. For a recent treatment of the peasant movement in Right Bank Ukraine (Kiev, Podolia, and Volhynia provinces), see Robert Edelman, *Proletarian Peasants: The Revolution of 1905 in Russia's Southwest* (Ithaca: Cornell University Press, 1987).

26. Most of the men who undertook the propagation of the national idea in Ukraine were intellectuals with a middle-class background although

many of them were of peasant stock. Hrushevsky was the son of an official in the Russian ministry of public instruction, and Dmitro Doroshenko was the son of a military veterinarian. Colonel Eugene Konovalets and Volodimir Naumenko were the sons of teachers. Nicholas Mikhnovsky, Volodimir Chekhovsky, Valentine Sadovsky, Serhi Efremov, and Colonel Peter Bolbochan were the sons of priests (John Reshetar, *The Ukrainian Revolution, 1917–1920: A Study in Nationalism* (Princeton: Princeton University Press, 1952), pp. 320–321).

27. Ibid., p. 48.
28. Pipes, *The Formation of the Soviet Union*, p. 63; Reshetar, *The Ukrainian Revolution*, pp. 50–1, 102n–103n.
29. Reshetar, *The Ukrainian Revolution*, pp. 319–23.
30. See particularly the conclusion in Richard Pipes, *The Formation of the Soviet Union*, pp. 283–6.
31. Pipes, *The Formation of the Soviet Union*, p. 149.
32. Guthier, 'The Popular Base of Ukrainian Nationalism in 1917', p. 40.
33. Ibid., p. 46.
34. Ibid., p. 41.
35. The Central Rada and the Directory failed to solve the agricultural problem; the hetman government did worse. It was constantly a step behind the revolutionary spirit of the peasants. Its policy was to carry out the land reform legally for approval by a future Constituent Assembly. For this reason it was not able to compete with the Bolsheviks, who were promising the land to the peasants immediately, or even with Makhno, who was giving the land to the peasants as soon as it was captured. For the peasants, the land was a primary question and those forces that would not interfere in the division of land would get their support (Michael Palij, *The Anarchism of Nestor Makhno, 1918–1920: An Aspect of the Ukrainian Revolution* (Seattle: University of Washington Press, 1976), pp. 54–55).
36. For another point of view on Ukrainian nationalism and the peasantry, see Andrew P. Lamis, 'Some Observations on the Ukrainian National Movement and the Ukrainian Revolution, 1917–1921', *Harvard Ukrainian Studies*, II, 4 (December 1978), pp. 525–31. Lamis argues that Ukrainian nationalism from Taras Shevchenko on had a dual nature: glorification of the homeland and a demand for social reform. Often these two components 'remained separate and in a state of dialectical tension' (p. 528). He takes issue with Arthur Adams, who claimed that Ukrainian peasants revolted during the German occupation primarily because of the grain requisitions and fear for their land. Lamis contends that the jacquerie was nationalist, aimed at one and the same time toward national and social freedom, even though the peasants and the intelligentsia did not act in concert (p. 530). For the Adams argument, see his essay, 'The Great Ukrainian Jacquerie', in Taras Hunczak (ed.), *The Ukraine 1917–1921: A Study in Revolution* (Cambridge, Mass.: Harvard Ukrainian Research Institute, 1977), pp. 247–70.
37. The report authored by the German writer Collin Ross was first published in *Arkhiv russkoi revoliutsii*, I, pp. 288–292, and translated and

reprinted in James Bunyan, *Intervention, Civil War, and Communism in Russia, April–December 1918: Documents and Materials* (Baltimore: The Johns Hopkins Press, 1936), pp. 4–5.

38. [Colonel Jones], 'The Position in the Ukraine', Public Records Office, London, Cab 24/52, ff. 117–18. I would like to thank Professor George Liber for a copy of this document, which was – to my knowledge – first referred to by Professor David Saunders in his paper 'What Makes a Nation a Nation? Ukrainians Since 1600', presented at the Conference on Premodern and Modern National Identity, University of London, 30 March–3 April 1989.

39. Adams, 'The Great Ukrainian Jacquerie', pp. 259–60. See also his *Bolsheviks in the Ukraine: The Second Campaign, 1918–1919* (New Haven: Yale University Press, 1963).

40. On the formation of the Armenian national intelligentsia, see the articles by George A. Bournoutian, Ronald G. Suny, Sarkis Shmavonian, Vahe Oshagan, and Gerard J. Libaridian in *Armenian Review*, 36, 3–143 (Autumn 1983); Suny, 'Populism, Nationalism, and Marxism: The Origins of Revolutionary Parties Among the Armenians of the Caucasus', ibid, 32, 2–126 (June 1979), pp. 134–151; and 'Marxism, Nationalism, and the Armenian Labor Movement in Transcaucasia, 1890–1903', ibid, 33, 1–129 (March 1980), pp. 30–47. On the Georgians, see Suny, 'The Emergence of Political Society in Georgia', in R. G. Suny (ed.), *Transcaucasia, Nationalism and Social Change* (Ann Arbor: Michigan Slavic Publications, 1983), pp. 109–40.

41. Risto Alapuro, *State and Revolution in Finland* (Berkeley and Los Angeles: University of California Press, 1988), p. 90.

11 The Background to *Perestroika*: 'Political Undercurrents' Reconsidered in the Light of Recent Events
Peter Kneen

In his speech to the Central Committee plenum in June 1987 Gorbachev announced that commodity-money relations or, in other words, the market, were becoming an organic part of the socialist system.[1] The Law on the State Enterprise, accepted by that meeting, anticipated that during 1988–9 all enterprises would become subject to the disciplines of full cost-accounting and self-financing.[2] Aganbegyan, one of Gorbachev's principal economic advisers, subsequently made it clear that enterprises which persistently failed to support themselves would, in effect, be considered bankrupt and closed.[3] At the June plenum Gorbachev left no doubt that, in his estimation, the causes of the present difficulties, which he identified as a pre-crisis situation, fundamentally arose from adhering to the command-administrative methods developed under Stalin, alternatives to which had been spurned by Brezhnev.[4] During the course of 1988, Bukharin, the leading proponent of market socialism in the 1920s, was rehabilitated as increasing public attention was directed to scrutinising the impact and legacy of Stalinism.[5] It appeared as if Soviet economic policy had come full circle, a circumnavigation that had taken sixty arduous years.

The plans to restructure economic relations coincided with a programme of radical changes to political institutions which was announced in January 1987.[6] During the course of 1988 and 1989 these changes assumed a higher profile and achieved greater momentum than those directed towards the economy. The pace of political developments rapidly quickened during the fractious process of selecting delegates for the special Nineteenth Party Conference, the first of its kind since 1941, which, when convened in late June 1988, witnessed frank public debate within the framework of a national party forum.[7] The Conference nevertheless lent general support to the programme of *perestroika*, including proposals to introduce far-reaching changes in the political system. These resulted in fundamental decisions allowing for the creation of the Congress of People's Deputies, the election of a permanent parliament in the shape of a reduced and reformed Supreme Soviet, together with the creation of a new executive presidency.[8] The enhanced powers of the soviets were complemented by a reduction in the scope of the Party which saw in the autumn of 1988 the transfer of the executive powers of the Central Committee Secretariat to six newly-created Central Committee commissions corresponding to the main areas of policy. At the same time the apparatus serving the Secretariat was drastically reorganised, resulting in the abolition of virtually all those departments which had previously supervised the various branches of the economy.[9]

The Party apparatus duly resisted this diminution of the powers which it had for so long wielded in the Soviet political system. In spite of Gorbachev's success in securing the retirement of over 100 members of the Central Committee and the Central Auditing Commission in April 1989, it remained to be seen whether the Supreme Soviet would imbue him with adequate sources of independent authority to cope with continuing conservative pressure from Party officials and to sustain the momentum of the reforms as well as maintaining his own security.[10]

The belief that political and economic reforms were interdependent has characterised Gorbachev's policy from the outset, although the ambitiousness of his programme has only become apparent with the passage of time. This interdependency was implied by the criticism of command-administrative methods of management which became established under Stalin, survived under Khrushchev and were sustained and refurbished by Brezhnev. Whereas Khrushchev had drastically reduced, even perhaps abolished, the capacity of the state to terrorise the population, he had, nonetheless, refrained from publicly criticising the circumstances in which the Stalinist system was formed as the means of collectivising peasant agriculture and rapidly industrialising the country.[11] In contrast, Gorbachev's attempts to revitalise the Soviet economy have been predicated on the withdrawal of the state and the release of suppressed initiative. They have been pursued against a background of the close public scrutiny of the past in general and Stalinism in particular, which has called into question the official claim that socialism was established by the mid-1930s in consequence of Stalin's policies.[12]

The socialist credentials of the current reforms have therefore been sought in the pre-Stalinist period of the NEP, 'the first revolutionary *perestroika*', according to one description.[13] This was the period of mixed economy which was sharply curtailed by the adoption of the strategy of crash industrialisation and forcible collectivisation, signalling the end of the debates about the appropriate pace and methods of state-guided economic development. Thus Gorbachev's policies and the public discussions which have so volubly accompanied them relate to socialist political traditions which predate the Stalinist system, and which provided alternative strategies for socialist development to that which was subsequently imposed. In order to understand the links between the perceived alternatives of the 1920s and the problems and possibilities of today there are few better places to begin than with Moshe Lewin's *Political Undercurrents in Soviet Economic Debates*, written in the early 1970s, and his more recent, and complementary, book entitled *The Gorbachev Phenomenon*.[14]

In the first of these books Lewin pursues four main themes. Firstly, that the social and economic transformation of the Soviet Union from 1929 was carried out by a centralised state which expanded the scope of its activities to establish a unique degree of control over the Soviet economy and society. In so doing it created a kind of total system in which it became hard to disaggregate the economic from the political system. Secondly, that this 'Leviathan state' was anticipated and fought against most consciously by Bukharin. Thirdly, that this centralised, total system eventually began to curtail economic growth and constrict the social processes which it had initially precipitated with such vigour. Fourthly, that the diagnosis of economic problems of the 1950s and 1960s, in particular economic slowdown and inefficiency, automatically touched on proscribed social and political themes and resuscitated the ideas of earlier opponents of this system, especially Bukharin. In the process of elaborating these themes the question is posed as to whether the Soviet system can escape from the two models of War Communism, which prevailed in the civil war and strongly influenced the system developed by Stalin from 1929, and the NEP which intervened in the years between, by finally abandoning monolithic Party dominance and developing a political system which would be more responsive and capable of sustained compromise than that briefly experienced during the 1920s.

As Lewin shows, Bukharin's sensitivity to the potential power that could accrue to the state as a result of its involvement in managing the economy was substantially derived from his studies of modern capitalism.[15] This allowed him to disassociate himself from the automatic identification of the expansion of economic control by the socialist state with the advance of socialism, an idea which gained credence during the civil war emergency to the point where it became fundamental to popular conceptions of socialism. From Bukharin's perspective, the incorporation of the market into a strategy of socialist economic development provided the essential means of protecting socialism from the growth of the state and the threat this entailed to the integral values of freedom and democracy.

Views such as these became heretical as the mixed economy of the NEP was abruptly curtailed by the radical policy of attempting to replace the market with the plan. The notion of an evolutionary path to socialism based on co-operative principles within the framework of the NEP was superseded by the language of the civil war, a campaign against the kulaks and the assertion that class conflict would sharpen as socialism was approached. But unlike the civil war, which witnessed the destruction of much industry and a flight from the cities, the collectivisation and industrialisation drives massively increased the rate of capital accumulation and the expansion of the urban population.

The industrialisation policy recommended by the Fifteenth Party Congress of December 1927, described by Lewin as 'very balanced and considered',[16] was soon replaced by progressively more ambitious plans, which eventually broke the linkage between available means and anticipated ends. Economic constraints therefore became irrelevant and the public discussion of them politically unacceptable. This not only made the idea of planning synonymous with the imposition of arbitrarily-chosen political priorities, but, once these priorities had been imposed as the unquestioned means of achieving the breakthrough to socialism, any semblance of political life, as conventionally understood, was replaced by a coercive system of economic and social mobilisation. In consequence, it was not only 'planning' that was lost in the five year plan but also 'politics'.

The attempt to replace markets immediately increased the state's involvement in almost all areas of society. In the first place the process of imposing a radical change on virtually all economic activity called forth a massive effort by the Party. Nowhere was this more graphically illustrated, along with the discrepancy between the level of preparedness of the Party cadres and the tasks they were required to perform, than in the collectivisation drive.[17] Once the majority of agriculture had been collectivised and industrialisation begun, the state incurred the job of administering an expanding area of economic activity without recourse to the independent criteria of market forces which, for the most part, had been driven underground.

In so far as the plan could not, whatever its claims to comprehensiveness, incorporate all the facets of economic behaviour, human initiative was not effectively channelled or controlled in its entirety. Unrealistically ambitious targets unrelated to available resources immediately produced incoherence in the system, expressed in numerous forms of uncoordinated activity. This was exacerbated by the pressure not only to fulfil, but to overfulfil plans, leaving managers with ill-defined and often moving targets which, in turn, sharpened the competition for the scarce resources needed to achieve them. Managers thus concentrated on the most important indicators of plan fulfilment, essentially quantitative physical output, at the expense of quality and cost. The reliability of the 'umbilical cord' of the economy, the centralised material-technical supply system, through which resources designated in the plan were channelled to enterprises, became uncertain. This arose because of several related factors. In the first place the economic activity incorporated by the plan was too complicated for it to be controlled coherently. The consequences of this were experienced by the enterprises in the form of a poor fit between the demands made upon them and the resources they received to meet them. In the second place the ambitiousness of the national plan meant that there were not enough resources to go around. Finally, the scramble to meet targets sometimes reduced the quality of production to the point where it could not be used by the receiving enterprise. Faced by a combination of intense pressure to overfulfil targets, an unreliable supply system and an inexperienced and unstable work force, managers endeavoured to protect themselves by hoarding resources and disguising capacity. The discrepancies between the real economy and the planned economy resulted in constant intervention by commissariats, the Party and the secret police, to adjust, check, exhort and threaten. In this way the foundations of the Stalinist state were rapidly established in the early 1930s and, as Lewin observes, they became fixed and highly resistant to change.[18]

The centralised economy inaugurated under Stalin's leadership had been operating for nearly three decades before Soviet economists were permitted to subject it to public scrutiny. From 1929 empirically-based assessments of Soviet economic potential were usually interpreted as evidence of ideological deviation and effectively suppressed. In his last published work Stalin had ruled out the analysis of policy as a legitimate area of concern for economists, a situation which had long been appreciated by all but the most courageous.[19] Only under Khrushchev's influence, when hitherto impressive rates of economic growth began to slow, was the expertise of economists tapped. The scrutiny of the assumptions which had underpinned Stalinist economic policy, and thus acquired the status of socialist axioms, such as the superiority of Sector A producers' goods over Sector B consumers' goods, together with the use of the language of economic analysis, immediately precipitated conflict with Stalinist 'economists' who were unwilling and, perhaps, incapable of breaking free from the essentially propagandist role which they had been taught or obliged to play.[20] Similarly the rapidly identified irrationalities of the planning system which resulted in sharp differences between what was good for the plan and what was good for the economy, unavoidably raised sensitive political questions about the constraining relationship between the state and industrial enterprises. Indeed, the economists were probing a huge system of official self-deception, the scale of which has only become fully apparent in the Soviet Union with the advent of *glasnost'*.[21]

In the face of a state planning system which was seriously defective in that it was failing to guarantee sustained growth, insensitive to cost, deficient in the provision of incentives and profligate in the use of resources, the economists' recommendations amounted to a reform of the planning system to make it sensitive to market disciplines and capable of extending greater independence to enterprises. Given the integration, even fusion, of the economic and political systems which had followed from the decisions of 1928 and 1929, the economists' conclusions were unavoidably fraught with political connotations. By asking why the productivity of Soviet labour was in decline, they immediately confronted the Marxist-Leninist axiom that the state represented the interests of everyone, for, if it was true that the workers owned the means of production and were therefore working for themselves, as officially claimed, then why was it that they worked so ineffectively? If it was contended that they were not working for themselves then for whom were they working, and if they did not own means of production who did and who benefited? Clearly all this posed fundamental questions about the nature of the Soviet state. Furthermore, the idea that the plan was not adequately meeting the basic requirements of the population or reliably supplying enterprises, introduced the novel concepts of the consumer, and of reciprocal relations between the individual and the state institutions that ran the economy. As Lewin notes, the notion of the 'consumer' led on to the introduction of the concepts of social needs and interests, which were not assumed to be necessarily compatible with the official values of the state.[22]

The essential general point being made by the economists of the 1950s and 1960s was that the state was acting as a brake on Soviet economic progress and that the solution lay in the direction of loosening its grip on the economy, in a word, decentralisation. Protected by the technical language of their discipline and the primary focus of their analyses, economists were able to address, with varying degrees of directness, issues of fundamental political importance. Ideas which are now central to the attempt to reconstruct the Soviet economy such as the integral role of the market, the need to transfer to full cost accounting and self-financing, together with the abolition of the material technical supply system and its replacement with a market in the 'means of production', were all initially floated in the 1960s. The link between then and now was explicitly acknowledged by Gorbachev in June 1987 when he cited the seminal criticisms made of the command-administrative system by Nemchinov, perhaps the most influential of all the reform-minded Soviet economists of that time.[23] With the rehabilitation of Bukharin, together with other leading Bolsheviks of the 1920s, it may be surmised that Gorbachev is sensitive to the idea that a new set of heroes are needed to re-establish the socialist credentials of current policies. With the thoroughgoing scrutiny and vigorous condemnation of so many aspects of Stalin's system, the longstanding official claim that socialism was established under his leadership has been substantially discredited as journalists, playwrights, film directors and, more latterly historians, have openly explored the origins of the system, the economic shortcomings of which were so thoroughly examined more than twenty years ago.

The limited, if effectively exploited, opportunities extended to the economists, were not made available to other social scientists who remained more securely incorporated by official disciplines such as Historical Materialism and Scientific Communism. The perception that the state planning system was acting as a brake on the development of the economy coexisted with the official version which claimed directly the opposite, emphasising the dynamism of Party leadership and the harmonious relationship it enjoyed with the Soviet people. It was within the constraints of this model that the other social scientists had to operate much more explicitly than their economist colleagues. Sociologists thus faced almost insurmountable barriers when designing empirical research projects of attempting to interpret findings which complemented the more heretical implications of the economists' conclusions. Locked in by an official model of social structure, dating back to the mid-1930s, which stipulated that Soviet society consisted of two non-antagonistic social classes, the working-class and the peasantry, together with a social stratum supposedly identifying those engaged in mental as opposed to physical labour, social scientists had to exercise considerable ingenuity even to obliquely discuss the major lines of conflict or the dynamics of Soviet society. When these barriers were challenged too boldly remedial action was decisively taken, as when leading sociologists were attacked in the early 1970s and the USSR Academy of Sciences' social research institute was reorganised.[24] In consequence of this rigidity the massive social changes which occurred in the wake of industrialisation could not be adequately investigated or credibly interpreted. Similarly the political system did not remain immune from all significant change, but in this sphere explicit public comment continued to be monopolised by ideologists.

The informed and provocative discussions of the dynamics of the Soviet economy were not, therefore, matched by the same kind of social and political analysis. This did not, of course, mean that developments in these areas were any less significant, nor that symptoms were lacking for those willing to notice them. Lewin's responses to these symptoms are mostly to be found in his more recent book, *The Gorbachev Phenomenon*, in which he develops the themes of social and political change initially broached in his earlier work.[25] The main point which Lewin makes about the Gorbachev phenomenon is that, in spite of the obvious importance of individual leaders in the Soviet Union, Gorbachev is responding to a new Soviet reality which has been forming for several decades. The key social and economic changes have already taken place: Gorbachev and what he represents are symptoms rather than causes of the emergence of a civil society to which the political system is only now being consciously adapted. Only by appreciating what this means can the current potential for political change in the USSR be adequately understood in the sense of whether it can develop beyond the two models of War Communism and the NEP which have, in Lewin's estimation, demarcated to a great extent the parameters of change in the past.[26]

In elaborating on the circumstances in which a Soviet civil society has grown up, Lewin begins by focussing on some of the key processes which he has explored elsewhere in his detailed studies of Soviet interwar history.[27] It is, for example, pointed out how the new Soviet state, committed to modernisation, confronted this task in the absence of a nascent capitalist class equipped with the necessary industrialising skills. The ambitions of the Soviet leadership thus contrasted with the human resources available in a society which had recently undergone the experiences of revolution and civil war, which had dispersed and exiled capitalists, emptied the cities and generally disrupted the inherited economy. To use Lewin's term, this resulted in the 'archaization' of Soviet society.[28] When Stalin dispensed with the more cautious approach to economic development which prevailed during the NEP, his industrialising ambitions extended not only well beyond the available physical resources, but also beyond the human and cultural resources. The initial dramatic process of urbanisation which took place in the 1930s reflected the fragility of the modern elements of society by swamping the cities with displaced peasants. As a result, the cities were 'ruralised'. Thus Lewin argues that a modernising state, unrestrained by independent and established urban classes, mobilised a traditional agrarian society which, as it responded to the sharp impulses of rapid industrialisation, further diluted the culture and influence of the pre-existing urban sector. The Soviet dictatorship which developed during the 1930s was thus sustained by what Lewin refers to as the 'rural nexus'.[29]

A particularly important aspect of this process arose from the attempt to replace the inherited 'bourgeois' intelligentsia with a new Soviet stratum of specialists. The frenetic effort to mobilise recruits from worker and peasant backgrounds for enrolment in a rapidly expanded system of higher technical schools coincided with the harassment and frequent arrest of those equipped with the technical knowledge and skills these new recruits were meant to be acquiring. The new Soviet stratum of technical experts was thus hurriedly and inadequately trained. It was from the ranks of these upwardly mobile workers and peasants that Soviet hierarchies were rapidly stocked and restocked in the face of industrial expansion and purge. It was to the most favoured section of this stratum that Stalin referred in 1939 when he reported that half a million young Bolsheviks had been promoted to managerial positions in the state and the Party in the period between the Seventeenth and Eighteenth Party Congresses.[30]

In spite of the inauspicious initial conditions, the expanded Soviet educational system began to produce the elements of a recognisable scientific and technical intelligentsia, which together with continuing urbanisation began to overcome the disruption of Soviet society. These processes continued in the more stable and less threatening environment of the 1950s and 1960s to the point where the Soviet Union became predominantly an urban society with a large proportion of the population concentrated in the larger cities. Of particular importance to Lewin has been the impressive growth of scientific and technical skills, because the deployment of knowledge and technique cannot be effectively exploited unless professional autonomy is to some degree recognised and respected.[31] With the increasing reliance of the Soviet economy on science and technology, illustrated by the high profile given to the slogan of the 'Scientific Technical Revolution' in recent decades, Soviet society has developed sources of autonomy, both cultural and social, which the state has not been able to identify clearly or respond to sympathetically but which are, nevertheless, largely a consequence of its own modernising policies. It is in this way that some of the key building blocks of a civil society were laid down in the Soviet Union.

By rigidly adhering to traditional ideological precepts and its authoritarian organisational structure, the Party deprived itself of the means of perceiving and coming to terms with these changes. In consequence it became overloaded by the tasks involved in attempting to render the unpredictable predictable, and coped in a largely piecemeal way with the results of failure to do this. Just as economic development exposed the inherent weaknesses of Stalinist economic planning, so uncharted social change exposed the myth of the vanguard Party. In both cases, as Lewin demonstrated in the early 1970s, the signs of dissonance between the Soviet political system and the economy and society it claimed to be leading were clearly apparent.[32] More recently he has persuasively interpreted the economic debates of the 1960s and the abortive economic reform which they gave rise to in 1965, as the precursors of the changes which have taken place under Gorbachev in the 1980s, changes which can be usefully seen as responses to the long-term strengthening of the elements of a 'civil society' in the Soviet Union.[33]

Does all this mean that the Soviet Union is now equipped with the means to progress beyond the limits of the War Communism/NEP model which has dominated its past? A positive answer to this question is clearly implied by Lewin, although when writing *The Gorbachev Phenomenon* he was, of course, not in a position to take account of the subsequent broadening of *glasnost'* and the dramatic unfolding of the democratisation process. The 'liberal dictatorship' of the NEP was a political system that existed in a society with a small educated urban sector. Restraining social groups associated with bourgeois democracy had been weakened, dispersed, or depleted by exile. The possibilities of compromise within the political system were limited by the measures taken to hold the Communist Party together at the end of the civil war, and by the general commitment throughout the leadership to identifying the one true line. These factors combined to undermine the legitimacy of sustained debate and the value of compromise. Notwithstanding the rehabilitation of Bukharin, Soviet historians have neither closed their eyes to these features nor mistakenly represented the NEP as some kind of golden age of Soviet democracy. Some of them have specifically focussed on the instability of institutions and the fragility of tolerance during this period, for which all contemporary leaders, including Bukharin and Rykov, have been held responsible.[34] Whereas the politics of the NEP can be interpreted, in Lewin's terms, as reflecting the 'archaization' of Soviet society, the political development of recent decades can be seen as representing the obverse of the situation in the twenties, with the state remaining in its archaic Stalinist mould in the face of an increasingly, if by no means uniformly, modernised society.

The symptoms of the essentially conflictual relationship between the state and society are not hard to find, nor insignificant when attempting to understand the current changes, not least their scale, pace and potential. It might be argued, for example, that the ideology of Marxism-Leninism has been fundamentally threatened by the development of *glasnost'*, indeed this anxiety has been regularly voiced by the more conservative leaders, surfacing, for example, with some vigour at the July 1989 meeting of the Central Committee.[35] However, sustaining the basic ideological beliefs, in particular the notion that there is somehow a true line which has been consistently followed by the Party and which brought about socialism and will, one day, deliver Communism, has depended upon an official account of the past so selective in its choice of events and personalities that it became seriously deficient in terms of empirical content. Whilst the inadequacy of official histories has been graphically demonstrated by the criticism of textbooks used in educational institutions and the cancellation of history examinations in 1988,[36] the effect of subjecting generations of increasingly sophisticated young people to ideological education of this type has probably contributed at least as much to the 'de-ideologising' of Soviet society as the fresh air of *glasnost'*. This possibility was even belatedly recognised by the Brezhnev leadership which, in 1979, issued a resolution which recognised the deficiencies of the propaganda effort in surprisingly frank terms and declared that the Party was losing the struggle for the hearts and minds of the Soviet people.[37] In an analogous fashion, the reliance on authoritarian methods of social control unsympathetic to social change during the eighteen years of Brezhnev's leadership perhaps contributed as much to undermining the pre-*perestroika* system as the current programme of democratisation, which is seen as so threatening by sections of the apparatus.

The erosion of the Party's ideological credibility and organisational integrity has been apparent at the grass-roots level for many years. Charged with supervising the administration of the establishments in which they were located, primary Party organisations could often only replicate the functions of the institutional managements they were meant to be overseeing. This left those whom the Party was supervising, supervising themselves, only wearing their 'Party hats' to signify the change of role. This was especially prevalent in establishments employing highly trained specialists such as research institutes and high technology plants. Here, Party organisations merely incorporated most of those filling the more important managerial posts and, in spite of the claims made on behalf of the rituals of socialist competition and ideological education, they could not contribute to enhancing the effectiveness of work in any convincing way. This presented the Party with an insuperable problem. Where people of genuine professional competence were recruited, the Party had to cope with those who either would not unquestioningly accept its authoritarian practices or, perhaps more usually, would go through the motions of Party membership in order to minimise the Party's influence in their own working environments. If, on the other hand, the Party organisation sought to place reliability above competence then its authority suffered accordingly. Faced with the problem of controlling not only those outside the Party but also those within it, primary Party organisations and the lower apparatus were repeatedly called upon by the Central Committee to take energetic steps to ensure greater discipline and reliability which were invariably regarded as the prerequisites of efficient working practices.[38] Thus the information explosion, from which the USSR could not remain immune, brought forth more censorship. The proliferation of technical specialisms was met with an extension of the Party's supervisory activities to incorporate research establishments as well as factories, whilst persistent signs of intellectual independence led to the more vigorous pursuit of dissidents.[39] In consequence the Party became, in Lewin's terms, overloaded and overcommitted, concentrating on the containment rather than the exploitation of social change, and adopting a reactive posture to the society its propaganda claimed it was leading and guiding.[40]

The consequences of the Party's methods of control have not been entirely negative or fully anticipated. In the attempt to substantiate its claim to represent the society it ruled, the Party has carefully recruited from all segments of society whilst placing particular emphasis on those occupying positions of responsibility. As Lewin has argued, the entire spectrum of Soviet society is mirrored by the Party membership.[41] Along with the disciplined and reliable there are the careerists and the corrupt. Similarly, along with the nostalgic Stalinists and those wedded to the recently disturbed *status quo* are the advocates of democracy and openness. These political tendencies were observed within the Party some twenty years ago by Roy Medvedev[42] and suggested by the analyses of Western political scientists who, like Jerry Hough, emphasised the sources of variety and conflict within the Party apparatus.[43] Although it remained committed to a self-image stressing absolute unity, the composition of the CPSU has not been insulated from the changes taking place in its social environment. Whilst it retained a monolithic facade buttressed by the public rituals of unanimity, the emergence of the current leadership, along with the now visible conflicts that occur in Party forums, lend fresh credence to the view that along the way the Party has acquired at least some of the means to engage in conventional as opposed to bureaucratic politics. Whether these will prove to be sufficient to sustain its credibility as a participant in constitutional politics remains a crucial, but as yet unanswered, question.

The strategy of reform adopted by Gorbachev can in part be understood as an attempt to unpick the mesh which has bound the economic and political systems together so tightly since the first five year plan. In order to achieve this he has tried to reduce the powers of the central ministries to interfere in the routine management of enterprises, and, as mentioned earlier, the Central Committee apparatus has lost most of its supervisory functions over the economy. In consequence, the Party has been deprived of one of its most important traditional roles, leaving it to concentrate on the strategic questions of national leadership, the supervision of ideology, and the control of the Party professional functionaries, together with the management of the rank-and-file membership, and the many responsible posts throughout society which require the Party's approval before they can be filled.

In conditions of open political discussion, the Party is having to try to rebuild its ideological role on new foundations. Faced with a new set of publicly acceptable values, stressing performance and accountability, its methods of personnel control through the *nomenklatura* system are also under threat. With the turn towards market socialism with its potentially economically independent factories and farms, the Party professionals may have to contemplate redundancy unless they can reformulate their activities to cope with the demands of an environment which they have been resisting for so long.

During this transitional period much depends on the resilience of Soviet citizens and the form this takes. Clearly the expansion of *glasnost'* and democratisation has been met by a variety of popular responses, some of which have been contained by the recently institutionalised opportunities for more genuine political participation and some, as in Azerbaidzhan and Armenia, which have not, and which have boiled over into violent conflict. In the economic sphere it is by no means clear how much time will need to elapse before a full transfer to market disciplines and the independence that goes with them can be achieved. It is apparent that the skills, instincts and inclinations required by managers to survive in a competitive market environment either need time to be cultivated, or else are being suppressed by the reluctance of those running the industrial ministries to give up their administrative powers. In the agricultural sector formidable obstacles continue to face those attempting to respond to the newly developing opportunities for independent farming. In almost all areas of economic activity, including the private co-operative sector, local Party organisations are proving reluctant to give up their controls.

It cannot, therefore, be assumed that because the political system has lagged behind economic and social change, that once its activities are curtailed the vacuum will automatically be filled by an appropriate level of hitherto suppressed initiative on the part of the population. There are bound to be areas of discontinuity which will take time to be straightened out. It is these discontinuities that help to fuel the arguments of those most anxious about the direction of the current changes and hopeful of preserving traditional centralised methods of rule. But whilst the momentum of the reforms may flag, or go into reverse, the changes which have so far occurred are likely to leave many indelible traces, for the political undercurrents in the Soviet economic debates of the 1960s, exposed so thoroughly by Lewin, have now surfaced with considerable vigour and much turbulence.

NOTES

1. *Pravda*, 26 June 1987, p. 3.
2. *Pravda*, 27 June 1987, p. 3.
3. Abel Aganbegyan interviewed, *Guardian*, 30 November 1987, p. 21; see also Abel Aganbegyan, *The Challenge: Economics of Perestroika* (London: Hutchinson, 1988) p. 187.
4. *Pravda*, 26 June 1987, p. 3.
5. *Pravda*, 6 February 1988, p. 1. See also the article entitled 'Vozvrashchenie k pravde', *Pravda*, 9 October 1988, p. 3. and the introduction of Moshe Lewin's *Political Undercurrents in Soviet Economic Debates* (London: Pluto Press, 1975) p. xiii.
6. *Pravda*, 28 January 1987, pp.1–5. For a useful summary and analysis of the democratisation process, see Stephen White, 'Democratising the Soviet State', *Politics*, No. 9 (1989) pp. 3–7.
7. For an interpretation of the significance of the Nineteenth Party Conference and the events leading up to it, see Michel Tatu, '19th Party Conference', *Problems of Communism*, 37, No. 3/4 (May/August 1988) pp. 1–15; see also Stephen White, ibid.
8. *Pravda*, 22 October 1988, pp. 1–2, *Pravda*, 3 December 1988, pp. 1–2 and *Pravda*, 4 December 1988, pp. 1–3.
9. *Pravda*, 1 October 1988, p. 1 and *Pravda*, 29 November 1988, pp. 1–2. See also Alexander Rahr, 'Who is in charge of the Party Apparatus?', *Report on the USSR*, 1, No. 15 (April 14, 1989) pp. 19–24.
10. On 25 April the resignations of 110 members of the Central Committee and the Central Auditing Commission were announced. See *Pravda*, 26 April 1989, p. 1 and Dawn Mann, Alexander Rahr and Elizabeth Teague, 'Gorbachev Cleans Out Central Committee', *Report On The USSR*, 1, No. 18 (May 5, 1989) pp. 8–10.
11. Stephen F. Cohen, *Rethinking the Soviet Experience* (Oxford and New York, 1984) pp. 106–7.
12. See, for example, Yu. Afanas'ev, *Pravda*, 26 July 1988, p. 3.
13. *Moscow News*, No. 6 (3358), 5 February 1989, p. 10.
14. Moshe Lewin, *Political Undercurrents*, op. cit., and *The Gorbachev Phenomenon* (Chatham: Hutchinson, 1989).

15. Moshe Lewin, *Political Undercurrents*, pp. 5–9, and 82–3.
16. Moshe Lewin, *Political Undercurrents*, p. 50.
17. See, for example, Daniel R. Brower, 'Collectivised Agriculture in Smolensk: the party, the peasantry and the crisis of 1932', *Russian Review*, 36, No. 2 (April 1977).
18. Moshe Lewin, *The Gorbachev Phenomenon*, p. 24 and *The Making of the Soviet System* (London: Methuen, 1985) p. 209.
19. J. V. Stalin, 'Economic Problems of Socialism', in Bruce Franklin (ed.), *The Essential Stalin* (Garden City, N.J.: Anchor Books, 1972) pp. 445–81. For a useful commentary, see Werner G. Hahn, *Postwar Soviet Politics: The Fall of Zhdanov and the Defeat of Moderation* (Ithaca and London: Cornell University Press, 1982) pp. 149–53.
20. R. Judy, 'The Economists', in H. Gordon Skilling and Franklyn Griffith (eds), *Interest Groups in Soviet Politics* (Princeton N.J.: Princeton University Press, 1971).
21. Vasilii Selyunin and Grigorii Khanin, 'Lukavaya tsifra', *Novyi Mir*, No. 2 (February 1987) pp. 181–201, and B. P. Orlov, 'Illyuzii i Real'-nost'', *EKO*, No. 8 (1988) pp. 3–20.
22. Moshe Lewin, *Political Undercurrents*, pp. 179–183, and *The Gorbachev Phenomenon*, pp. 96–7.
23. *Pravda*, 26 June 1987, p. 3.
24. Criticism mainly focussed on Yu. A. Levada's 'Lektsii po sotsiologii' published by the Institute of Concrete Social Researches of the USSR Academy of Sciences. See Rolf H. W. Theen, 'Political Science in the USSR', *Problems of Communism* 22, No. 3 (May-June 1972) pp. 64–70.
25. Moshe Lewin, *Political Undercurrents*, especially chs 10 and 11.
26. These themes run through the book but for specific commentary, see *The Gorbachev Phenomenon*, Preface, p. x and pp. 80–2, 152–3.
27. Moshe Lewin, *The Making of The Soviet System*.
28. Moshe Lewin, *The Gorbachev Phenomenon*, p. 18 and *The Making of the Soviet System*, pp. 209–240.
29. See Moshe Lewin, *The Gorbachev Phenomenon*, especially p. 24 and *The Making of the Soviet System*, pp. 209–40. An interesting comparison can be made between Lewin's analysis of social and political change in the USSR, and Barrington Moore's ideas on the politics of modernisation. At one point Moore comments 'we may simply register strong agreement with the Marxist thesis that a vigorous and independent class of town dwellers has been an indispensable element in the growth of parliamentary democracy. No bourgeois, no democracy' (*Social Origins of Dictatorship and Democracy* (London: Allen Lane, 1967) p. 148; see also p. 481 and Part 3).
30. See Stalin's report to the Eighteenth Party Congress in Bruce Franklin *op.cit.* p. 376. For detailed studies of the creation of the new Soviet scientific and technical intelligentsia see Sheila Fitzpatrick, *Education and Social Mobility in the Soviet Union 1921–34* (Cambridge: Cambridge University Press, 1979) and 'Stalin and the Making of a New Elite 1928–1939', *Slavic Review*, 38, No. 3 (September 1979) pp. 377–402; Nicholas Lampert, *The Technical Intelligentsia and the Soviet State* (London: Macmillan, 1979) and Kendall E. Bailes, *Technology and Society*

under Lenin and Stalin, (Princeton N.J.: Princeton University Press, 1978).

31. Moshe Lewin, *The Gorbachev Phenomenon*, p. 73.
32. Moshe Lewin, *Political Undercurrents*, particularly chs. 10 and 11.
33. Moshe Lewin, *The Gorbachev Phenomenon*, pp. viii, 1–2 and 61–2.
34. See the two-part article entitled 'Vremya Trudnykh Voprosov', *Pravda*, 30 September 1988 p. 3 and 3 October 1988 p. 3. In the first part it is claimed, for example, that Bukharin and Rykov did not shrink from the use of exceptional measures.
35. On this occasion the most explicit concern with the 'de-ideologising' of Soviet society was expressed, perhaps surprisingly, by N. I. Ryzhkov, see *Pravda*, 21 June 1989, p. 3.
36. In January 1989 it was announced that history examinations would be held again in 1989. See Vera Tolz, *Report On The USSR*, 1 No. 6 (10 February, 1989) p. 33 and 'New History Textbook for Secondary Schools', *Report On The USSR*, 1, No. 35 (1 September 1989) pp. 5–7.
37. The relevant decree can be found in *Spravochnik partiinogo rabotnika*, vyp. 20 (Moscow: Politizdat, 1980) pp. 319–31.
38. Moshe Lewin, *Political Undercurrents*, ch. 11; for studies of the role of the party in science and technology see Stephen Fortescue, *The Communist Party and Soviet Science* (London: Macmillan, 1986) especially pp. 124–59, and Peter Kneen, *Soviet Scientists and the State* (London: Macmillan, 1984) pp. 82–105.
39. See Roy A. Medvedev, *On Socialist Democracy* (London: Macmillan, 1972) pp. 164–74 and Stephen Fortescue, 'Research Institute Party Organisations and the Right of Control', *Soviet Studies* 35, No. 2 (April 1983) pp. 175–95.
40. Moshe Lewin, *Political Undercurrents* p. 292.
41. Moshe Lewin, *Political Undercurrents*, pp. 262–3 and 283–4.
42. Roy A. Medvedev, *On Socialist Democracy*, pp. 50–9.
43. Jerry F. Hough, 'The Party Apparatchiki', in H. Gordon Skilling and Franklyn Griffiths, *Interest Groups in Soviet Politics*.

12 Legality in Soviet Political Culture: A Perspective on Gorbachev's Reforms
Peter H. Solomon, Jr.

At the Nineteenth Party Conference in July 1988 the Gorbachev leadership made a commitment to far-reaching judicial reform and the extension of the role of law in public administration. In response to a public movement for legal reform the leaders went so far as to adopt as a goal the creation of a socialist state based on law (*Rechtsstaat*). The actual shape of the reforms remained to be determined, but it was clear that they would deal with such issues as the independence of judges, the right to defence, and the role of courts in both supervising criminal investigations and protecting citizen rights.[1]

The adoption and implementation of reforms of this kind was bound to encounter difficulties, if only because of the traditional Soviet condescension toward law. Soviet officials and politicians were not used to subordinating their interests to law. Many of them treated the law as an instrument to be embraced when useful and ignored when expedient. In short, their actions reflected the syndrome known as 'legal nihilism'.[2]

In a recent essay of remarkable breadth and insight veteran legal reporter Yuri Feofanov provided striking examples of legal nihilism. A classic was the infamous case of Ian Rokotov.[3] In 1958 police in Moscow apprehended this leader of a gang of hard currency speculators with a briefcase containing millions of rubles and a large quantity of jewels. At the time, speculation in hard currency brought a maximum punishment of eight years in prison, but just as the trial began an edict extended the maximum term to fifteen. How did this happen? The investigatory agencies had held a public exhibition of the goods seized, and the exhibition received a visit from a 'high, very high person, who was beside himself with rage'. On the very next day the edict appeared. Accordingly, the Moscow city court followed suit and sentenced Rokotov to fifteen years, but this did not assuage the wrath of the very high person. Within weeks the law changed again, this time to allow capital punishment in cases of hard currency operations in large amounts, again retroactively. On appeal the RSFSR Supreme Court sentenced Rokotov and one of his young companions to death.

In the case of Rokotov a leader (if not the leader) placed himself above the law and openly violated the legal prohibition against retroactivity. But this was not all. While most Moscow jurists of Feofanov's acquaintance were shocked, the public at large in the USSR actually approved Rokotov's fate! The mailbag to the newspapers featured comments like 'This is how you deal with scoundrels' and 'with speculators, beatniks (*stiliagi*) and persons who sell out their country, there is no reason to be tender'. In these emotional outbursts against the villains, Soviet citizens – like their masters – lost sight of legal principles.[4]

In the 1980s Soviet leaders and officials continued to violate the spirit of legality (*pravo*). For example, upon request from the Procuracy the Supreme Soviet issued special edicts authorising the extension of pretrial detention of individual suspects beyond the legal limit of six months.[5] Also commonplace was the distortion of laws, as when economic agencies issued instructions and regulations that twisted their meaning, even contradicting legislative intent. Bureaucratic creativity applied also to the criminal law, where instructions from agencies stipulated punishments for particular sorts of violations.[6] In short, the continuation of 'legal nihilism' was likely to prove an obstacle to the achievement of judicial and legal reform. The question was, how great an obstacle?

Negative attitudes to law have had a long history in the USSR. Some observers have blamed the most fervent Marxist legal theorists of the 1920s for promoting the idea of the withering-away of law. Others have found signs of a cavalier and condescending attitude toward law among the Bolshevik leaders, such as those attending the Fifteenth Party Congress in 1927.[7] It is also possible to blame historical events. The conduct of collectivisation, or the war against the peasantry, depreciated the value of law, which appeared more as an obstacle to the accomplishment of political goals than as a facilitator. Then too, the system of economic administration established in the early 1930s made regulations issued by central agencies, including party bodies, more important than laws.[8]

Still, the deep roots and long history of legal nihilism in the USSR should not prejudice the question of the strength of this tradition in the 1980s and 1990s. The challenge is to recognise when attitudes and habits of different social groups begin to change. Even the Brezhnev era, written off by Soviet publicists as a time of stagnation, may have witnessed developments that influenced how Soviet publics and officials viewed law. As Moshe Lewin has argued, social change does not observe the boundaries set by political periods. During the decades after World War II, and especially during the Brezhnev years, Soviet society became increasingly urbanised, educated, and exposed to Western values, including legality. At the same time, the views of Soviet publics became increasingly important to politicians. 'The Soviet Union,' Lewin wrote, 'has developed into a complex social body, with classes and publics, cultures and countercultures' to which politicians are responding more than ever before.[9]

The maturation of Soviet society and the new prominence of law in Gorbachev's reform programme suggest questions. What was the nature of public attitudes toward law and legality in the mid and late 1980s? How attached were Soviet jurists to legality and legal principles? How had the attitudes of the public and jurists in the USSR alike changed over the previous decades? In singling out jurists, I am paying special attention to the group most likely to serve as the bearers and promoters of legal culture. In a pathbreaking study of the origins of the Legal Reform of 1864, Richard Wortman showed how a legal consciousness took hold among jurists working within the tsarist bureaucracy and how this group made spreading legality a mission.[10] Were there signs of a similar movement in the USSR of the late 1980s?

My answers in this essay will be tentative, because the sources are far from ideal. For one thing, surveys of popular legal consciousness in the USSR began only in the late 1960s, and most of those in the 1970s did not ask the right questions or were not well reported. Moreover, I lack sufficient access to the best sources of the historian, such as memoirs of the actors involved or a large sample of letters from the public. For this essay I rely on Soviet analyses of surveys, reports on the content of the mailbags of central newspapers, letters, speeches and articles by officials, and the writings of jurists and journalists.

I shall start by considering how the general public in the USSR regarded legality in the late 1980s; than analyse the changing postures of jurists toward legal values and legal reform; and finally illustrate how the views of public and professional jurists interacted.

THE PUBLIC AND LEGALITY

Using the opportunity provided by *glasnost'*, journalists and legal reformers aroused within the Soviet public in 1986–8 a new concern with legality and legal procedures. The question was whether this concern ran deep enough to withstand competition from other values, such as giving corrupt leaders their just deserts or restoring law and order.

In the USSR as in other countries public opinion does not develop in a vacuum. Public attitudes and moods are products of information and messages directed at the public through the media. While these attitudes reflect underlying values and dispositions, they are subject to moulding by the media and social forces communicating through them.

Public concern with legality in the USSR was awakened by a band of muckraking journalists. Starting in the spring of 1986, with Yuri Feofanov of *Izvestiia* and Arkady Vaksberg of *Literaturnaia gazeta* in the lead, journalists relentlessly exposed the full gamut of abuses in the administration of justice. They wrote about cases of blatant injustice, in which innocent persons had been convicted, even executed, in which confessions had been extracted by force, and in which party and other authorities had intervened in the work of procuracy and courts. In the fall of 1986, legal scholars and judicial officials joined the discussion, tracing the roots of these practices and calling for a judicial reform. A number of writers and other intellectuals joined the crusade, and finally the political leadership made its commitment to judicial reform.[11]

To the press coverage of abuses in the administration of justice, the public responded. Each article elicited a volley of letters (counts provided by the newspapers and journals give figures in the hundreds as the norm).[12] For example, in response to an interview in *Literaturnaia gazeta* with legal scholar A. M. Iakovlev on infringements of judicial independence, the paper received hundreds of letters in which ordinary people related their own stories of injustice, supported positions taken by Iakovlev, offered remedies, and opposed some reform proposals. By late 1987 public outcry had become so loud that legal themes came second only to housing as the leading subject in letters received by newspapers.[13]

Another example of the arousal of public concern about abuses in the administration of justice is provided by a recent poll. Using a telephone survey and written questionnaires, sociologists questioned readers of *Izvestiia* in twenty-eight different cities (of varying sizes and significance). The researchers elicited reactions of readers to both a particular article by Yuri Feofanov and criticism of abuses of legality in general. The large majority of those polled approved of the newspaper's criticisms of law enforcement agencies and agreed that criticism made those bodies more accountable (69 per cent); a minority of 7 per cent opined that the muckraking 'undermined the authority of the administration of justice'. When asked to explain why the accused in Feofanov's article had sat in prison for two years before the trial that eventually acquitted him, readers cited 'pressure on the part of interested parties'. Most readers (74 per cent) supported Feofanov's call for a new law subjecting to criminal prosecution authorities who interfered in the administration of justice. Finally, more than three quarters (77 per cent) of readers polled indicated support for providing suspects with access to defence counsel from the initial moment of detention by the police (and not merely from the beginning of the preliminary investigation). This position represented the most radical version of the reformers' dreams for expanding the right to counsel, and the one supported by the writer Feofanov himself.[14]

The findings of this poll from late 1987 illustrate how easy it was for journalists and jurists writing in the newspapers to develop public concern with legality and sympathy for legal reform. The poll does not show how difficult it would be to entrench those values, refine them, and make them strong enough to withstand competition. There were signs that public attachment to legal principles did not run deep. For one thing, other surveys indicated that while the public might support law in the abstract, it had a limited understanding of what law meant. Nor did most Soviet citizens think of law as a guide for sorting out difficult life situations. Respondents in another survey gave more weight to the opinion of their peers than to guidance supplied by laws.[15]

Even more telling, scrutiny of letters from ordinary citizens to the newspapers suggests that what moved the Soviet public to react and support legal reform was not violations of legality *per se* as much as infringements of the administration of justice on fairness.[16] Admittedly, it can be hard to separate the two. But it appears that more often than not the Soviet public supported legal procedures and principles only as a means of achieving results that they considered correct. In fact, most members of the public seemed to have reserved for themselves the right to judge what was right or wrong, and they made their judgment on *moral* rather than legal grounds. The priority given by the Soviet public to its own appreciation of what was morally just gave its attachment to legal procedures a shallow quality, and rendered it vulnerable when legality came into conflict with the moral judgments of the public.

It is hardly suprising to discover that the Soviet public did not treat legality as an end in itself. The training in civics received by most members of the Soviet public and the legal propaganda directed at the adult population during the Brezhnev period did not emphasise legality. Since the late 1960s all high schools in the USSR offered a thirty-hour course on the Fundamentals of Soviet Law. In practice, this course emphasised respect for the criminal law (to encourage obedience) and information about family and labour law (to enable young people to function in society).[17] Likewise, adult legal propaganda – for example the popular journal *Man and the Law* ('Cheloveki zakon') and the television show of the same name – stressed knowledge of substantive law, and respect for law and order.[18] The television programme devoted more attention to police investigations than trials and showed movies relating to juvenile crime, alcoholism, and the apprehension of offenders. When *Man and the Law* aired a programme in September 1989 about the sad case of a former police captain who had been falsely charged and illegally arrested, but escaped and remained on the run, viewers greeted the programme as a novelty. One of the hosts of 'Man and the Law', the legal scholar A. M. Iakovlev, told an interviewer that he favoured the introduction of the theme 'Reports from the Courtroom' (to raise public respect for adjudication) and of broad coverage of the 'legal dimensions of the most significant events and changes in our society'.[19]

Along with the development in the 1970s and 1980s of adult legal propaganda came research on legal consciousness and socialisation. However, the researchers did not emphasise the public's sensitivity to principles, protections, or rights. In the published reports, researchers described findings about knowledge of the law, respect for its particular prohibitions and the prestige and attractiveness of legal careers.[20]

One additional source of concern with legality (that might encourage the public to support legal reform) was the avalanche of revelations in the late 1980s about breaches of legality under Stalin. The movement to secure the rehabilitation of the victims of the Great Purge trials not yet rehabilitated (especially Bukharin) and the rolling-back of denunciation and rehabilitation to virtually all victims of Stalin

should have increased public sensitivity about legal procedures.[21]
Still, it is not clear how much the general public made firm connec-
tions between past and present.

A telling indicator of the depth of a public's concern with legality
and legal procedures is how it reacts when this value comes into
conflict with other values. The investigation and trial of Yuri Churbanov provides a fine example. This case forced the public to face a
direct conflict between principles of legality – fair investigation and
trial – and the public's sense of what was morally just. The trial was
the product of a five-year investigation by a special team of 200
investigators from the All-Union Procuracy in Moscow of corruption
in Uzbekistan and beyond. The investigators uncovered bribes and
payoffs involving enormous sums. Their suspects ranged from the
leading politicians of the republic all the way to high officials of the
Ministry of Internal Affairs in Moscow and included one of its deputy
ministers, Yuri Churbanov, the son-in-law of Brezhnev himself. The
investigation, which stemmed from the crusade against corruption
initiated by Andropov, started quietly, but under the conditions of
glasnost' the public learned some horrifying truths. Not only did the
bribes extend high into the establishment, but the source of the
bribes was often organised crime. In the late Brezhnev years gang-
sters had started to act as predators on and protectors of illegal
private business, and in this capacity had infiltrated the centres of
power.[22]

The chief investigators in the case, Telman Gdlian and Nikolai
Ivanov, enjoyed muckraking and occupying the public eye. During
the investigation they appeared repeatedly in the press and on radio
and television, referring at all times to the suspects as 'criminals'.
Gdlian and Ivanov frightened the public with references to the Soviet
mafia and gave the producers of the news programme *Vremia* the
chance to photograph jewels and banknotes allegedly seized from the
defendants. Close to a hundred million people saw the physical
evidence and reached their own conclusions about the guilt of the
defendants.[23]

By the trial (in autumn 1988) – itself given close coverage by journalists – the public was primed, ready to wreak vengeance on evil representatives of the elite. Nonetheless, the presiding judge, M. Marov of the
USSR Supreme Court's Military Collegium, subjected the evidence
collected during the preliminary investigation to careful review. It
emerged during the trial that many of the charges found no support in
the evidence and in some instances rested only upon forced con-

fessions! As a result, the court dropped a number of the charges against the defendants. The principal accused, Churbanov, was convicted of taking bribes totalling 90,000 rubles (instead of the many hundreds of thousands cited in the indictment, and over 2 million mentioned in the press earlier on) and received a sentence of twelve years' imprisonment (the maximum possible was fifteen). Churbanov's accomplices received terms of six to nine years, and one codefendant, a police official from Uzbekistan, gained an acquittal, reportedly the first given by the USSR Supreme Court in ten years.[24]

A few day after the verdict two legal reporters greeted the outcome as a victory for legality. In *Izvestia* Yuri Feofanov described the trial as 'a sensation'. The court had not fallen for the 'myths' created about the size of the sums involved but had checked everything. (Judge Marov explained, 'As a judge I was obliged to doubt every conclusion of the investigation and check them again and again'.) Wrote Feofanov: 'The court acted in a courageous and principled way, answering to the law rather than to any suppositions about the danger of the actions'. Almost simultaneously a correspondent for *Literaturnaia gazeta*, Aleksandr Borin, praised the hearing as the first non-political trial of politicians in Soviet history. The trial's value, he claimed, lay in the fact that it was juridicial. Yet another commentator, Oleg Temushkin from the staff of the USSR Supreme Court, went even further and criticised the investigatory methods of Gdlian and Ivanov.[25]

In contrast to the reaction of the journalists (and with them reform-minded jurists), the public at large was puzzled, dismayed, and angered. Letters began pouring into the newspapers and political bodies alike, in the main questioning the result of the trial. Already in mid-January correspondents of *Pravda* decided to air the issue. Its readers, *Pravda* explained, had long ago concluded that the defendants represented corruption and mafia activity in high places. Consequently, the public expected the harshest outcome from the trial; anything less suggested a political deal! The public reportedly paid no attention to the first reports of the extraction of forced confessions by the Gdlian team, a prime example of which was described already by Feofanov on 2 January (and repeated in the *Pravda* article). Defending the court's decision, the *Pravda* correspondents explained that the court had departed from the usual 'accusatory deviation', but 'public legal consciousness, and one must say this openly, was not ready for this step'. To some, the acquittal was a sure sign of a 'weak investigation' and must have spelled big trouble for the investigators.

'We have received many phone calls,' reported *Pravda*, 'asking what had happened to Gdlian. Had he already been fired from the procuracy?'[26]

The intensity of public reaction to the outcome of the Churbanov trial becomes even clearer from an article written by Borin in March in answer to letters sent to his newspaper *Literaturnaia gazeta*. The paper had been hit by a 'tornado of angry letters from its readers'. 'In all my years of journalism', Borin reported, 'I never encountered such an explosion of indignation directed at me and my newspaper.' 'Where is your conscience?' wrote one irate reader. 'You are an experienced journalist? Can you be content with the outcome simply as a person? The sentence and your articles (yours and Feofanov's) evoked indignation, and not only from me.' Said another, 'I have doubts about your objectivity', and a third, 'you tried to demonstrate what is a just and independent court . . . . Were you given this assignment?' And a fourth mused, 'How hard it must be for our General Secretary . . . that he must act alone, when there are such persons as your journalist A. Borin fighting against *perestroika*, consciously and professionally!'

The readers displayed not only emotion but also open rejection of the need to observe legality in cases of officials accused of corruption. One wrote, 'These are government people . . . They belong to the ruling circles of the party. The material loss is nothing to compensate with the political one. The trial should have been political'. 'It is necessary', wrote another, 'to judge Churbanov for participation in an anti-Soviet organisation.' For obviously corrupt officials, there was no need for a proper defence. 'How could one defend Churbanov as a person [as one of the counsel claimed was necessary]? We live on 100-200 rubles per month and someone gets 500 and presents worth 130,000. You are going to defend him as a person, while we remain as we were?' Many readers showed disdain for the idea of presumption of innocence. A scientist from Tiumen wrote 'they were not judging simply "people" but "criminals"'. Even legal officials joined in the chorus. According to a representative of the central procuracy that supervised the investigation 'the sentence may have been legal, but it was not just'.

Topping it off was nostalgia for the way scapegoats were served up in the past. 'How can one not recall the father of the people, who believed no one, and would not have believed the fairy tales of Churbanov.'[27] This reader was referring to Joseph Stalin.

The reaction of the readers of *Literaturnia gazeta* is all the more telling when one takes into account the nature of its readership. These were not average workers, or a particularly conservative part of the population. A sociological study of *LG's* readers, conducted just a few months after the letters discussed, revealed that 90 per cent had higher education, 40 per cent were under thirty years of age and 65 per cent subscribers to *Ogonek*, a sign of interest in revelations if not also reform. Anti-corruption sentiment and anti-establishment feeling seemed to permeate the clientele of *perestroika*, as much as the more conservative layers of the population.[28]

The trial not only created a sensation, but also produced an intricate trail of political conflict over the methods of investigation used by the fight against corruption. The conflict itself revealed much about the place of 'legality' in the public's hierarchy of values. Accustomed to using the media for their purposes, Gdlian and Ivanov started a campaign to discredit the trial and the judges involved with it. Appearing on Leningrad television and Moscow radio, in a series of lesser journals and newspapers (*Moskovskii komsomolets, Vodnyi transport, Sovetskaia Tatariia*), and on stage, at public discussions organised at the film club (*Dom kino*), the actors' club (*Dom aktera*), factory clubs, and conference halls of institutes, they described the sentences as 'criminal' and accused judges of having been paid off or having conflicts of interest.[29] The two investigators gained such a strong following that they decided to embark on campaigns for election as deputies to the new Congress of Deputies.

Supreme Court Judge Marov answered the charges against him at public meetings in the capital, but Chairman Terebilov decided that stronger actions were needed to stem the crusade against his Court. Terebilov called for a review of another case from the past in which, he believed, an investigation by the Gdlian/Ivanov team had used illegal methods. To protect the investigators and the reputation of the procuracy Procurator General Sukharev refused to support a review of the Khint case (he may have had instructions from higher up), but Terebilov himself issued the protest and the review commenced. This action prompted Gdlian to attack Terebilov and in a private meeting with the Deputy Chairman of the Supreme Soviet Lukianov to provide sufficiently embarrassing material about Terebilov's past to compel Lukianov to fire the Chief Justice![30]

Shortly before this round of political hardball, the public began to hear criticism about the improper investigatory methods of Gdlian and Ivanov. After a blackout of discussion of their activities, Yuri Feofanov succeeded in publishing in *Izvestia* on 1 April an article denouncing the investigators for reviving the methods of Vyshinskii, that is forced confessions. Later in April, probably in revenge for the firing of Terebilov, the USSR Supreme Court met in plenary session to reexamine the Khint case. By unanimous vote the full court overruled the Khint decision and roundly criticised its investigators.[31] At the same time, the USSR Supreme Court issued a scathing supplementary judgment criticising Gdlian and Ivanov for their conduct of the investigation of Churbanov. The ruling on the Khint case was published immediately, but the supplementary judgment on the Churbanov investigation was held back until the conclusion of a meeting in May between the investigators and none other than M. S. Gorbachev himself. Far from exonerating themselves, Gdlian and Ivanov took the opportunity to accuse Secretary Ligachev of involvement in corruption! Within a few days, after Gorbachev had checked the findings of an inhouse Central Committee commission examining the affair, he authorised publication of the Supreme Court's damning supplementary judgment. Within two weeks, on 20 May, a report by a commission of legal officials and experts attached to the Praesidium of the Supreme Soviet also publicised its finding, while Gdlian and Ivanov extended their attacks to more high politicians.[32]

This saga of political intrigue continued through the summer and autumn of 1989; its details and denouement have yet to emerge. What matters here is how the public reacted to the first authoritative reports on the illegalities committed by the investigatory team. Some members of the public did display concern with legality. Both the Central Committee of the CPSU and the Praesidium of the Supreme Soviet received letters protesting the investigatory methods of the Gdlian team and in some cases offering further examples.[33] But for most of the Soviet population the anti-corruption fighters remained heroes, and the methods used by Gdlian and Ivanov irrelevant, as long as they were used to ensure that corrupt officials received their just deserts.

The evidence was unmistakeable. In Leningrad on 14 May the electorate of that city gave Ivanov 61 per cent of the votes cast for deputy to the Congress of Deputies in a contest that involved twenty-seven other candidates! (Gdlian had already been elected in Moscow two months earlier.) On 23 May, days after the publication of the report from the Commission of the Praesidium of the Supreme Soviet condemning the pair, workers in Zelinograd declared a political strike in support of their heroes. Newspapers, including *Izvestiia* and *Sovietskaia Rossia*, were bombarded with letters, accusing them of one-sidedness and defending the investigators. In the early autumn of 1989, long after the peccadilloes of the investigators had received an airing at the Congress of Deputies and made the subject of yet another commission, a political demonstration in Moscow placed Gdlian and Ivanov on the same plane as Boris Yeltsin! Finally, in the spring of 1990, when the USSR Procuracy announced its intention to prosecute the two investigators for their illegal acts, the Supreme Soviet itself came to their rescue. In response to public sentiment the delegates voted against removing parliamentary immunity from Gdlian and Ivanov, thereby blocking the prosecution.[34] The public did not want its heroes made into scapegoats for what most believed to be the usual illegal methods of the Procuracy. Nor did the public believe that observing legal norms mattered in the fight against corruption in the establishment. Fighting corruption in the establishment was an end more important than the observation of legal means.

This should not come as a surprise. The juxtaposition of legal principles with strongly-held moral judgments makes a hard test for citizens anywhere. A series of polls in the USA in the 1950s showed that among the American public support for civil liberties was 'as shallow as it is broad'. While most Americans supported principles like free speech in the abstract they did not tolerate the realisation of these principles by Communists. US survey analysis also showed that public application of principles could change. In the 1970s, when fear of communism had abated, Americans were prepared to extend these rights to members of the American Communist Party.[35]

The fact remains, however, that in the USSR of the late 1980s the nascent attachment of the public to legal principles and procedures was especially shallow. For most of the Soviet public ends like justice in the moral sense of the word justified illegal means of criminal investigation.

JURISTS AND JUDICIAL REFORM

If the attachment of the general public to legal values was shallow, then the attitudes of professional jurists toward legality assumes special significance. Yet, it was unlikely that Soviet jurists as a group would stand as defenders of legal principle. To begin, even legal education of quality would not eliminate the influence of the society in which young jurists were reared. Moreover, after completing studies, Soviet jurists did not join a legal profession, with its own organisation and corporate ethos, but rather embarked upon one of the series of legal careers. Each legal career produced its own norms and expectations, and some of them were reinforced by bureaucratic structures. Investigators who wanted praise and promotion had to fulfil expectations of superiors, expectations that included meeting indices of performance (percentage of cases sent to court; percentage of convictions, etc.) The pressures impinging upon investigators in the procuracy would not encourage them to support extension of the rights of the accused to counsel, or judicial supervision of the legality of investigations. (Remember that Gdlian and Ivanov were both jurists.)

It was our starting assumption that attachment to legal principles varied across the spectrum of legal careers in the USSR. A small group of legal scholars and advocates had taken the lead in judicial reform, and it appeared that those groups as a whole were starting to promote legal values. On the other hand, members of such state legal professions as judge, procurators and investigator, were more likely to display conservative tendencies. One reason was institutional. The routines of these officials and to some extent the power of their agencies as well required the continuation of the old rules of the criminal process. Another reason was sociological. Many of the jurists who worked as legal officials in the 1980s came from social and educational backgrounds that encouraged a more conservative approach. A substantial proportion came from non-intelligentsia urban backgrounds, had pursued legal studies at night or by correspondence (while working full-time), and used their legal careers to achieve social advancement. In contrast, the majority of advocates and legal scholars came from intelligentsia backgrounds, experienced the richer form of legal education offered at day divisions of legal faculties and institutes, and pursued careers in law partly out of commitment.[36]

The best published data on the attachment of Soviet jurists to legal principles appeared in a survey that examined the attitudes of legal officials toward proposals to improve legal protection for suspects and accused persons. Conducted in Moscow in spring-summer 1988, the survey questioned 212 judges, sixty-four procurators, and sixty-eight investigators.[37] These officials hailed from all parts of the USSR and had come to Moscow to attend sessions of the All-Union Institute for Improvement of Justice Workers. Most of those questioned, therefore, were in their thirties or early forties, a fact that enhanced the representativeness of the sample. Soviet legal education had expanded sufficiently in the 1970s so that of Soviet jurists working in 1989 nearly three-quarters had graduated from law faculties and started their careers after 1970. To be sure, selection to attend these courses may have indicated that the individuals had been marked for promotion in the particular 'hierarchy'. But this classification may have rewarded conformity and trustworthiness as much as special talent.

The survey revealed, first of all, that judges were strongly in favour of key reforms. 52.4 per cent supported judicial review of pretrial detention; 75.5 per cent approved of judicial supervision of investigations; and 63.7 per cent favoured the admission of defence counsel at the moment when a suspect was detained. Some of these reforms would increase judicial power, and the earlier admission of defence promised to make trials into contests. Yet, the habits of decades of conformity to the norms of the judicial bureaucracy might have dampened reformist tendencies among judges more than it did.

Also striking were the findings about the attitudes of investigators and procurators. Naturally, there was considerable opposition to reforms among these groups, but at the same time a substantial minority of these officials claimed to support radical positions on judicial reform (in contrast to some of their superiors in Moscow). Thus, 26.5 per cent of investigators supported judicial review of pretrial detention; and 41.2 per cent of investigators supported the admission of defence counsel at the moment of detention (37.5 per cent of the procurators questioned). Almost all of the remaining investigators and procurators supported the admission of defence at the beginning of the preliminary investigation, itself an advance on current practice. Moreover, 40.6 per cent of procurators and 20.6 per cent of investigators agreed that the criminal process in the USSR had a bias in favour of the prosecution.

The Soviet researchers were prepared neither for the strength of support for judicial reform among judges, nor the strong minority support among investigators and procurators, for these findings suggested major changes in the dispositions of the state legal professions. First, in the late 1950s, when some of the same judicial reforms were under consideration, legal officials provided little if any support. According to studies by John Gorgone and Morris McCain, legal officials serving on the commission drafting new fundamental Principles of Criminal Procedure in 1958 opposed judicial review of pretrial detention and admission of defence counsel at the start of the preliminary investigation. In addition, most judges and all procurators who took part in the public debate over these proposals expressed marked opposition to the reforms. In 1958 the reform positions drew support only from a narrow swathe of jurists – advocates, some academics, and a few high-level judges. Secondly, more recent studies conducted by the Procuracy Institute's sector on the psychology of the fight against crime showed that many procuracy workers still had a low attachment to the principle of legality. Thus, in 1985–7 one-third to one-half of investigators and assistant procurators were ready to ignore procedural norms when expedient, and most of those surveyed supported reforms to simplify criminal procedure. To the researchers from the Procuracy Institute such data signified the continuation of legal nihilism within the Procuracy.[38]

How to explain, then, the 1988 survey that found considerable support for judicial reform among many judges and a minority of investigators of procurators? One possibility was that the support reflected the natural inclination of conformists to shift with the times. At least some Soviet legal officials may have read the signals from the leadership (some commitment to legal reform was apparent by late 1987) and made the appropriate changes. No doubt, some feared appearing backward or uncultured and adopted an exterior of liberal attitudes. Perceptive Soviet observers found this shift in posture too swift and sudden to represent deep-seated attitudes and warned that jurists' support for legal reform might have shallow roots.[39]

Another possibility was that the views expressed reflected attitudes of somewhat longer standing that their possessors had developed during the Brezhnev era and only brought into the open under *glasnost*. Most Soviet jurists of the late 1980s were young persons who had started their careers in the 1970s and 1980s. They had grown up in cities and absorbed an urban culture, which, as Moshe Lewin has suggested, laid stress on individualism and gave concepts of rights new meaning. According to the SIP survey, exposure to higher education of any kind made these same urbanites more likely to value protection of the individual over the collective.[40] Not only was the new generation of Soviet lawyers more urban and more educated than previous generations, it also came of age at a particular moment in history. Growing dissatisfaction with conditions under Brezhnev led some young people into a world of countercultures and networks of informal groups. While most of these upwardly mobile young jurists may not have taken part directly, they were aware of the concerns of these groups. Nor could they have been shielded from the concern with legal values promoted in the literature of *samizdat* and the activities of the dissidents. Even within the mainstream jurists were searching for ways to develop legality. In the 1970s and early 1980s legal scholars paid special attention to legal reforms initiated in the countries of eastern Europe. Moreover, most of the jurist who emigrated from the USSR during the 1970s (especially between 1979–81) were sharply critical of the administration of justice in their homeland and ready to support major reforms. These persons included persons who had once worked as investigators, procurators or judges.[41]

Finally, there were probably many jurists who experienced these influences in the years before Gorbachev but also crystallised their positions on legality under the impact of *glasnost'*. However much judges and investigators knew about abuses in investigations, judicial control and early admission of advocates were only abstract possibilities in the Brezhnev years. Legal officials knew that political pressures had made acquittals rare and judges responsive to influence 'from the side and from above', but these practices were simply the rules of the game until 1986. The opening of the press to discussions of abuses in the administration of justice, their graphic illustrations, and the exploration of their origins gave officials the chance to generalise beyond their personal experiences, come to terms with their consciences, and adopt positions supportive of reform. In this way, *glasnost'* encouraged the growth of a culture of legal reform.

It is important not to exaggerate the support of Soviet jurists for judicial reform. Among no group of jurists did reform attitudes prevail fully. Among advocates, who generally favoured reforms, there was an unwillingness to support admission to cases at early stages until a payment for the extra work was provided. Concern ran so deeply that the head of the Moscow Bar refused to enter into an experiment with the procuracy of that city (in summer 1989) in which Moscow lawyers would meet clients from the time of arrest.[42] Among judges, who, as we have seen generally supported reform, there remained a sizeable minority who did not. Consistent with this was the finding in another survey from mid-1987. One third of judges questioned disagreed that 'the conviction of the innocent caused greater harm than acquittal of the guilty'.[43] Furthermore, for every reform-minded investigator or procurator (and their numbers included some higher level officials), there were two others who clung to traditional practices, and the leadership of the procuracy did its best to frustrate formal proposals that threatened that agency's power and interest. Yet, to have reached a point where if not a majority at least a substantial proportion of jurists supported reforms promoting legality, in words if not yet in deeds, represented a major step forward.

Moreover, the prospects for further spread of a culture of legal reform were good. As the number of new lawyers reared in the USSR expanded in the 1990s, so the share of those trained at day divisions was scheduled to rise, ensuring a higher degree of idealism and professional commitment.[44] And, with the continuation of *glasnost'*, a new generation of young lawyers would be reared with full exposure to questions of legal and moral values.

In the meantime, though, the world of jurists in the USSR remained divided about the appropriateness of legal reforms and the prominence they were willing to give to protection of rights. While some jurists provided the engine for change, others supplied opposition. A critical question for the early 1990s was how much conservative law enforcement forces would arouse a public concerned with corruption, and whether as a result they would succeed in checking the momentum of legal reform.

CONSERVATIVE JURISTS AND PUBLIC OPINION: THE CRIME SCARE OF 1989

We have seen that the Soviet public's newfound attachment to legal values was shallow and vulnerable to competition from others (like fighting corruption). At the same time, jurists themselves divided into supporters and opponents of reforms that promoted legality. From this snapshot as of 1988 and early 1989 there could develop a number of different scenarios. One possibility was that the legal reformers would find new ways of delivering their message and mobilising support from the public at large. Equally plausible, though, was the possibility that the more conservative jurists would find an issue through which they could turn public opinion against the expansion of legal protection and rights. In 1989 fear of crime emerged as just such an issue, ready for exploitation by conservative, especially legal officials, and journalists.

The crime scare of 1989 originated in a real rise in crimes of violence. The rates of murder, rape, and assault went up dramatically in the USSR during 1988, partly because of the renewed availability of alcoholic beverages and partly because of the self-confidence of organised criminal groups. The rise represented the resumption of a trend that started in the late 1970s (only during the height of the anti-alcohol campaign did violent crime fall off), but this did not make violence less real.[45] On the contrary, with the help of *glasnost'*, the public became far more aware of violent crime in 1988 than it had been in 1985 when its frequency was even higher. Journalists exacerbated the situation by reporting the most egregious examples in sensational ways and putting the spotlight on a previously hidden dimension of Soviet crime, organised criminal groups. A whole series of articles in 1988 told the public about the mafia that reigned in particular regions of the USSR, kept officialdom at bay through payoffs, and extracted protection money from the new cooperative business. The rise of organised crime dated from the Brezhnev era, but only with *perestroika* did the public become aware of its scope.[46] As if this were not enough, the Ministry of Internal Affairs (MVD) began releasing hard data on crime and in February 1989 published figures showing the dramatic rise in crimes of violence between 1987 and 1988. The Ministry went on to supplement this data with periodic reports on trends (monthly, quarterly) often accompanying the data with 'briefings' by top officials. Press releases and briefing reports appeared in newspapers throughout the USSR.[47]

Almost as soon as the figures were released, law enforcement officials started connecting the crime rise with legal reforms. Their objects of attack included reform proposals designed to protect the rights of defendants and make the criminal process subject to legal control; the 'humanisation' of the criminal law, as embodied in the draft Fundamental Principles of Criminal Legislation published in December that reduced penalties for most crimes and restricted the use of the death penalty; and even democratisation and *perestroika* in general.[48] Thus, the police chief of Moscow, P. Bogdanov, equated concern about the presumption of innocence with softness on crime and described the implementation of this principle as 'the presumption of all-forgiveness'. (Within two months Bogdanov was promoted to Deputy Minister of Internal Affairs.) Investigator Ivanov (from the Churbanov case) speculated in the Moscow youth newspaper that the authors of the new criminal legislation must have been paid off by criminals to have introduced such leniency into Soviet law. In an election speech in Moldavia Chebrikov, the Politburo member supervising legal matters, complained about the discouragement and passivity of law enforcement officials, who, he claimed, were afraid to stop crimes in progress, lest they be accused of violating the democratic rights of citizens.[49]

All these arguments came together in a sensational article in *Pravda* on 23 March, 'I'm Buying a Pistol' The author, Georgii Ovcharenko, started with the story of a cooperative manager who had given up with the police and decided to protect himself from 'racketeers'. A friend on the police assured Ovcharenko that this was not unusual. 'The population is arming itself. People are making pistols and bombs right at their workplaces . . . for self-defence.' The author went on to blame this situation and the rise in crime that produced it on democratisation and *glasnost'* in general, and judicial and criminal reform specifically. 'Somehow it often happens, and not without help from the press, that humanising the administration of justice turns into protecting the lawbreaker's rights rather than the victim's.' The result of the new concern with 'fair' investigation and trial was that 'the law enforcement agencies have lost their bearings. Afraid of going too far, they aren't going far enough'. And, according to a leading conservative spokesman in the Procuracy, the investigator E. Myslovskii, his colleagues had lost heart when they read the draft Fundamental Principles of Criminal Law. Ovcharenko agreed that the law paid too much attention to helping the 'criminals' and did nothing for the victims of crimes.[50]

Within days this emotional article was followed by similar flailings against judicial and criminal law reform by police officials in Leningrad and Uzbekistan, and by a speech from Moscow police chief Bogdanov at the *gorsovet*.[51] And investigator Myslovskii himself gave an interview in the best-selling newspaper *Argumenty i fakty*, claiming that the new judicial policy 'practically paralysed the work of investigators'. Asked what he meant by the new judicial policy, the senior investigator replied, 'Put in a nutshell, it is humanisation taken to the point of absurdity, that is insisting upon taking as evidence only testimony given at trial'.[52] For its part, the public responded quickly to these charges, swamping the Central Committee and newspapers alike with letters confirming its concern with crime and readiness to connect its rise with democratisation and humanisation.[53]

Promoters of legal reform recognised the gathering storm clouds. As early as February Yuri Feofanov responded with an interview with a high Procuracy official. (While the latter joined Feofanov in defending legality and judicial reform, he conceded that investigators had become afraid of pressing cases which they might lose and for which they would be held responsible!) In early April, the chairman of the USSR Supreme Court V. I. Terebi-lov denounced the current passions about crime 'as artificially created by interested persons'.[54] Finally, in May a chorus of voices defended legal reforms, voices that included scholars, judicial and law enforcement officials. They explained to readers that the recent rise in crime had resulted from the resumed availability of alcohol and other social factors that had nothing to do with law enforcement. They reminded readers of the importance of legality, noting how easy it would be to slip back in to Stalinist practices. And they urged the public to be mature. The public should not fall for the emotional appeals of the fear-mongerers, but instead let common sense prevail. It was up to the public to recognise the 'tendency to use the real growth in crime to attack the administration of justice, discredit the democratic principles of judicial reform, and undermine the democratic basis of the law-based state'.[55] Even the top police official Vadim Bakatin tried to reassure the public that the new concern with fair trials had not generated extra crime. Bakatin also introduced a cause of his own, the underfunding of police. Confronting crime, he warned, called for more policemen, better paid, and better equipped (the police budget per capita in the USSR stood officially at 10 per cent of that in the USA).[56]

Despite all these reassurances the Soviet public's fear of crime did not vanish. A poll taken in May of residents of Moscow found that they were nearly as afraid as New Yorkers of going out alone at night, despite having a much lower crime rate, and more afraid that Bostonians, though Boston had much more crime than Moscow.[57]

To prevent fear of crime mushrooming into a social panic called for action by the regime. The leaders' response began with a special meeting on 17 May 1989 of the Central Committee's commission on Legal Policy devoted to the struggle against crime. The commission members agreed on the need not only to give law enforcement more money, but also to make the struggle against crime a priority once again for party activists and the mass media. Newspapers and television programmes that had sought to strengthen law and order received special praise. Moreover, the commission agreed that a 'general governmental programme for the fight against crime should be established and specific measures elaborated'. A long account of this session of the commission was published in most Soviet newspapers, in some instances on the front page.[58]

At the Congress of Peoples Deputies and the first session of the new Supreme Soviet the issue of crime received much prominence, reminding the huge television audience of its concern with the issue. In the confirmation hearings on Anatolyi Lukianov's appointment as Deputy Chairman of the Supreme Soviet, Gdlian himself (now a deputy) challenged the former secretary of the Central Committee in charge of the legal portfolio to explain why there had been such a dramatic rise in crime, why organised crime was flourishing, and why law enforcement agencies were demoralised.[59] Likewise at a July session of the Supreme Soviet Vadim Bakatin, the new Minister of Internal Affairs, had to defend his agency's record in fighting crime.[60] In response Lukianov and Bakatin stressed that the objective causes of crime had nothing to do with democratisation, but related to the renewed availability of alcoholic beverages and underlying social problems.

Finally, the Soviet leadership decided that to allay public fears about crime called for more than words. Accordingly, in early August it established a Temporary Commission for the Struggle against Crime at the all-union level and provided for similar commissions in the republics and provinces. The organisation of these commissions to coordinate a campaign against violent crime made sense even to some reform-minded jurists, who hoped that the commissions would counter the potentially destructive effects of the panic over crime. But what shocked the reformers was the inclusion of judges among the members of the commissions, a provision that seemed to counter-act the policy of strengthening judicial independence. As members of the commissions, judges would learn about the priorities in the fight against crime and be expected to adjust their sentencing practices accordingly. In fact, the text of the edict establishing the commissions made this explicit. The edict told judges 'to treat with maximal severity allowed by law cases of robbery, theft, rape, trade in narcotics. . .'.[61] Political direction of sentencing policy for Soviet judges was not new. In most cities and provinces judges had joined colleagues in law enforcement for regular meetings at Party head-quarters to discuss policy for the coming months.[62] However, the treatment of judges as administrators ready to implement the pro-gramme of fighting crime, rather than neutral arbiters of criminal responsibility, contradicted the efforts to strengthen legality.

It was not clear to what degree involvement with the temporary commissions would curb the willingness of judges to review cases independently (even acquit) or compromise their autonomy in sentencing. In the spring of 1990 the All-Union Commission was eliminated in favour of a Standing Committee of the Supreme Soviet on the Struggle against Crime. The fate of commissions at lower levels, though, remained to be seen, and might depend upon the choices of lower levels of government. In any event, their impact on judicial behaviour might prove small, especially if the Constitutional Amendments of December 1988 and the new law on the status of judges (August 1989) succeeded in reducing judges' dependence on local politicians.[63] Still, the manifestation of the traditional Soviet view of judges as crime-fighters illustrated the fragility of the public's and politician's commitment to promoting legality. When the chips were down and the reality and fear of crime emerged as political issues, nourished by conservative forces, the leaders made concessions that contradicted the spirit of judicial reform.

This did not mean that the judicial reform would not move ahead. An encouraging sign was the promulgation in November 1989 of legislation admitting defence counsel to criminal cases at the initial moment of detention.[64] But the tension between the concerns of reformers and law enforcement officials ready to play upon the fears of the public was likely to continue. How it would influence the implementation of this new law, not to speak of the passage of further measures, such as the draft Fundamental Principles of Criminal Legislation, known for their humanisation of the criminal law, remained to be seen.

CONCLUSION

As of 1990 legal values still did not have a strong hold over the Soviet public. To be sure, many citizens appreciated how the law could protect personal rights and stand in the way of injustices perpetrated by public officials. But few Soviets were willing to place abstract principles of legality ahead of satisfaction of their own views of what was morally correct. For most Soviet citizens the law remained an instrument, if not for their masters, then one that could serve their own views of morality and justice. This popular conception of the instrumentality of law remained as the legacy of a decades-long expedient approach to law on the part of state officials, what Feofanov and other Soviet observers described as 'legal nihilism'.

In contrast to the general public, some Soviet jurists had developed a strong attachment to legal principle. According to survey research, the support extended beyond the normally progressive groups like legal scholars and advocates and permeated the state legal professions, especially judges. Overall, support for legal reform and legal values among jurists was much greater than it had been thirty years before.

There remained a substantial bloc of conservative opinion among legal officials, especially within the Procuracy. This syndrome derived from not only institutional interests but also social and educational background. As a result, there were prospects for a greater appreciation of legal values among legal officials as their profile changed. In the meantime, conservative legal officials proved a powerful political force that could mobilise public opinion. These officials succeeded in 1989 in playing upon public fears of crime to make judicial and criminal law reforms more difficult to pursue.

The place of law in Soviet political culture was starting to change, but slowly. The development of the kind of legal culture that would support a greater dependence upon legal regulation in public life was unlikely to emerge on its own. It would come only as political and economic reforms led to an increased use of law to resolve conflicts, and jurists, public, and politicians alike came to appreciate the benefits of a principled and unconditional attachment to legality.

NOTES

1. 'O pravovoi reforme', 'Rezoliutsiia 19 partiinoi konferentsii', *Kommunist*, 1988, No. 10, pp. 85–7; Peter H. Solomon, Jr., 'Judicial Reform under Gorbachev and Russian History', in Albert J. Schmidt (ed.) *The Impact of Pereistroika on Soviet Law* (Alphen aan der Rijn: Kluwer, 1989), and Peter H. Solomon, Jr., 'The Role of Defense Counsel in the USSR: The Politics of Judicial Reform under Gorbachev', *Criminal Law Quarterly*, 31; 1 (December 1988), pp. 76–93.
2. Peter H. Solomon, Jr., 'Soviet Criminal Justice under Stalin', unpublished manuscript, ch. 1; A. Vaksberg, 'Tsarina dokazatelstv', *Literaturnaia gazeta*, 27 January, 1988, p. 13. Eugene Huskey reserves the term 'legal nihilism' for attempts to eliminate or avoid using laws altogether. See his 'A framework for the analysis of Soviet law', *Russian Review*, 50 (January 1991) pp. 53–70.
3. Iurii Feofanov, 'Vozvrashchenie k istokam', *Znania*, 1989, No. 2, pp. 138–57. On the Rokotov case, see also Yuri Luryi, 'The Use of Criminal Law by the CPSU in the Struggle for the Reinforcement of its Power and in the Inner-Party Struggle', in D. A. Loeber et al. (eds), *Ruling Communist Parties and their Status under Law* (Dordrecht: Martinus Nijhoff, 1986), pp. 95–7.

4. Feofanov, 'Vozvrashchenie', 140.
5. Ibid., Arkady Vaksberg, lecture at Harriman Institute, Columbia University, 25 April 1989.
6. A. M. Iakovlev, 'Vedomstvennoe ugolovnoe pravo: Razmyshlenii o psikhologii zapretov', *Izvestiia*, 8 February 1988, p. 2; 'Opiat ob instruktsiiakh', *Izvestiia*, 23 September 1987, p. 3; Eugene Huskey, 'Government Rule-Making as a Brake on Perestroika', *Law and Social Inquiry*, 15 (1990) pp. 419–32.
7. Harold Berman, *Justice in the USSR* (New York, 1963), ch. 1; M. Vyshinskii, 'K chemu vedet pravovoi nigilizm', *Nedelia*, 1989, No. 14. p. 12.
8. Solomon, 'Soviet Criminal Justice under Stalin', chs 3 and 4; Eugene Huskey, 'A framework'.
9. Moshe Lewin, *The Gorbachev Phenomenon: A Historical Interpretation* (Berkeley, 1988) pp. 81–2.
10. Richard Wortman, *The Development of a Russian Legal Consciousness* (Chicago and London, 1976).
11. Solomon, 'Judicial Reform under Gorbachev'.
12. 'Chitateli o problemakh pravosudiia i ukreplenii zakonnosti: V polzu spravedlivosti', *Literaturnaia gazeta*, 19 November 1986, p. 13; 'Otkliki, mneniia, vozvrashchaias k napechatannomu "Podnozhka prokuroru"', *Pravda*, 24 August 1987, p. 4; 'Sensatsii ne poluchilos', *Literaturnaia gazeta*, 16 September 1987, p. 13; 'Demokratizatsiia i zakonnost', *Pravda*, 27 April 1988, p. 3; 'Demokratiia i zakon: Khod perestroiki pravovoi sistemy volnuet chitatelei', *Pravda*, 12 May 1988, p. 1; 'Zhitie polkovnika militsii', *Druzhba narodov*, 1988, No. 5.
13. 'Chitateli o problemakh pravosudiia'; Conversation with Louise Shelley, 12 November 1987.
14. 'Poslednii list odnogo ugolovnogo dela', *Izvestiia*, 12 December 1987, p. 3.
15. *Organizatsiia i effektivnost pravovogo vospitaniia* (Moscow, 1983), ch. 3; E. L. Bonk, 'Ob odnoi probleme sotsiologicheskikh issledovanii obschchestvennogo mneniia o prave', *Sovetskoe gosudarstvo i pravo*, 1986, No. 8, pp. 120–123.
16. See especially 'Zhitie polkovnika militsii'. A similar point was made by N. Radutnaia in her review of N. Ia. Sokolov, *Professionalnoe soznanie iuristov*, *Sovetskaia iustitsiia*, 1989, No. 8, p. 31.
17. For recent critique of popular legal education, see E. Lukianova, 'Nuzhen iuridicheskii vseobuch', *Izvestiia*, 9 August 1988, p. 3; and A. Nikitin and Ia. Sokolov, 'Femida u shkolnoi doski', *Pravda*, 8 December 1988, p. 2.
18. *Chelovek i zakon*, 1980s, passim.
19. 'TV: v efire peredacha "Chelovek i zakon"', *Sovetskaia iustitsia*, 1987, No. 16, pp. 20–3; S. Mostovshchikov, 'Beglii inspektor prosit zashchity', *Izvestiia*, 22 September 1989, p. 7.
20. Two fine representative examples are *Lichnost i uvazhenie k zakonu. Sotsiologicheskii aspekt* (Moscow, 1979) and Alex Targonsky, 'A Research Project on Legal Consciousness Carried Out by the All-Union

Institute for Study of the Causes of Crime', Hebrew University, Soviet and E. E. Research Centre, Soviet Institutions Series, Paper No. 9 (August, 1977). For an overview of such studies, see Peter H. Solomon, Jr., 'Sociology of Law', in F. Feldbrugge (ed.), *Encyclopedia of Soviet Law* (Dordrecht: Martinus Nijhoff, 1983).

21. See R. W. Davies, *Soviet History in the Gorbachev Revolution* (Bloomington, Indiana, 1989).

22. For background see Julia Wishnevsky, 'The Gdlyan-Ivanov Commission Starts Its Work', *Report on the USSR*, 1, No. 26 (1989), pp. 1–7. On organised crime see Iurii Shchekochikhin and Alexsandr Gurov, 'Lev prygnul!' *Literaturnaia gazeta*, 20 June 1988, p. 13; 'Pryzhok l'va na glazakh izumlennoi publiki', ibid., 28 September 1988, p. 13; and T. Gdlian and N. Ivanov, 'Protivostoianie', *Ogonek*, 1988, No. 26, pp. 26–9.

23. Ibid.; Wishnevsky, 'The Gdlyan-Ivanov Commission'; Iu. Feofanov, 'Unter v lampasakh: Sesantsii i zakonomernosti tolko chto zakonchiv-shegosia protsessa', *Izvestiia*, 2 January 1989, p. 4; Oleg Temushkin, 'Verdict Announced, Problems Remain', *Moscow News*, 1989, No. 2, p. 5; Olga Chaikovskaia, 'Mif', *Literaturnaia gazeta*, 24 May 1989, p. 13; Iu. Feofanov, 'Toska po Tsaritse', *Izvestiia*, 1 April 1989, p. 4.

24. 'Prigovor', *Pravda*, 31 December 1988, p. 3. Coverage of the trial appeared in *Pravda*, *inter alia*, on 10 September, 2 November, 3 December, 14 December, and 22 December 1988.

25. Feofanov, 'Unter v lampasakh'; Aleksandr Borin, 'Churbanovskii prot-sess', *Literaturnaia gazeta*, 4 January 1989, p. 2; Temushkin, 'Verdict Announced'.

26. V. Itkin, et al., 'Posle suda: Razmyshleniia o nashumevshem protsesse', *Pravda*, 21 January 1989, p. 3.

27. Aleksandr Borin, 'Eshche raz o 'Churbanovskom protsesse' – otvet moim opponentam', *Literaturnaia gazeta*, 8 March 1989, p. 13.

28. F. Sheregi and B. Nikiforov, 'Chitateli o "Literaturnoi gazete"', ibid., 27 September 1989, p. 14.

29. Feofanov, 'Toska po Tsaritse'; Chaikovskaia; 'Mif'; Wishnevsky, 'The Gdlyan-Ivanov Commission'; T. Gdlian and N. Ivanov, 'Sledstvie o prigovore', *Novoe vremia*, 1989, No. 6.

30. Ibid.; V. I. Terebilov, 'Kto osudit sudiu?' *Ogonok*, 1989, No. 14, 26–9; 'S'ezd narodnykh deputatov SSSR – stenograficheskii otchet; piataia sessiia', *Izvestiia*, 30 May 1989.

31. Feofanov, 'Toska po Tsaritse'; 'V Verkhovnom sude SSSR', *Pravda*, 28 April 1989, p. 2.

32. Wishnevsky, 'The Gdlyan-Ivanov Commission'; 'V Verkhovnom sude SSSR: Chastnoe postnovlenie plenuma ot 25 aprelia 1989', *Pravda*, 7 May 1989, p. 2; 'V Prezidiume Verkhovnogo Soveta SSSR', *Izvestiia*, 20 May 1989, p. 4.

33. 'Pismo s kommentariem: Tolko po zakonu', *Pravda*, 30 April 1989, p. 2.

34. 'Kto kak ponimaet glasnost', *Izvestiia*, 23 May 1989, p. 6; 'The Gdlyan-Ivanov Commission'; 'Takovy fakty – Svidetelstva sledsvennykh rabotni-kov ne pozhelavshikh miritsia s protivopravnymi metodami T. Kh. Gdliana i N. V. Ivanova', *Sovetskaia Rossiia*, 25 May 1989, p. 6;

'Komissia dlia proverki materialov, sviazannykh s deiatelnostiu sledstvennoi gruppy Prokuratury SSSR vozglavliaemoi T. Kh. Gdlianom', *Izvestiia*, 2 June 1989, p. 2; V. Dolganov, 'Poisk istiny', ibid., 17 April 1990, pp. 1 and 3; V. Doganov and A. Stepovoi, 'Reshenie davalos nelegko', ibid., 19 April 1990, pp. 1–2; 'O vyvodakh komissii dlia proverki materialov, sviazannykh s deiatelnostiu sledstvennoi gruppy Prokuratury Soiuza SSR, vozglavliaemoi T. Kh. Gdlianom', Postanovlenie Verkhovnogo Soveta SSSR, ot 18 aprelia 1990, *Pravda*, 20 April 1990, p. 2.

35. Samuel A. Stouffer, *Communism, Conformity, and Civil Liberties* (Garden City, 1955); David G. Lawrence, 'Procedural Norms and Tolerance: A Reassessment', *American Political Science Review*, 70:1 (March 1976), pp. 80–100; Austin Sarat, 'Studying American Legal Culture: An Assessment of Survey Evidence', *Law and Society Review*, 11 (Winter 1977), pp. 427–88.

36. Vyshinskii, 'K chemu vedet pravovoi nigilism'; N. Ia. Sokolov, *Professionalnoe soznaie iuristov* (Moscow, 1988), p. 16; Interview with Elena Makeeva, 5 November 1989; *Vestnik MGU: Seriya pravo*, 1989, No. 3, pp. 15–16. I have no information about the attitudes of jurisconsults, lawyers in the economy, who represented the largest group of Soviet lawyers.

37. V. Kogan, 'Sudebnaia reforma: kto za chto?' *Sovetskaia iustitsiia*, 1988, No. 19, pp. 21–22; 'Puti sovershenstvovaniia sistemy ugolovnoi iustitsii', *Sovetskoe gosudarstvo i pravo*, 1989, No. 4, pp. 87–8. Of those interviewed, 77.9 per cent of investigators had worked for ten years; 62.5 per cent of procurators; and 42.5 per cent of judges. Personal correspondence from V. M. Kogan, 12 December 1989.

38. John Gorgone, 'Soviet Jurists in the Legislative Arena: The Reform of Criminal Procedure, 1956–1958', *Soviet Union*, 3:1 (1976), pp. 1–36; Morris A. McCain, 'Soviet Lawyers in the Reform Debate: Cohesion and Efficacy', *Soviet Studies*, 34:1 (January 1982), pp. 3–22; A. R. Ratinov and S. V. Kudriavtsev, 'Professionalnoe obshchestvennoe mnenie rabotnikov prokuratury', unpublished report (Moscow, 1987); Interview with A. R. Ratinov, 23 April 1990.

39. Lecture by Arkady Vaksberg at the Centre for Russian and East European Studies, University of Toronto, 22 September 1989.

40. Lewin, *The Gorbachev Phenomenon*, chs 5, 6 and conclusion; Brian D. Silver, 'Political Beliefs of the Soviet Citizen: Sources of Support for Regime Norms', in James B. Millar (ed.), *Politics, Work and Daily Life in the USSR: A Survey of Former Soviet Citizens* (Cambridge, 1987), pp. 100–41.

41. See, for example, V. M. Savitskii, (ed.), *Pravo obviniaemogo na zashchitu v sotsialisticheskom ugolovnom protsesse* (Moscow, 1982). My interviews with some fifty former Soviet jurists in emigration were conducted during 1985. On the sample see Peter H. Solomon, Jr., 'The Case of the Vanishing Acquittal', *Soviet Studies*, 39:4 (October 1987), pp. 531–55.

42. Arkady Vaksberg, 'Terminy, kotorye reshaiut vse', *Literaturnaia gazeta*, 27 September 1989, p. 10.

43. L. Aimkin, 'Dorogo stoit deshevoe pravosudie', *Literaturnaia gazeta*, 28 August 1987, p. 3.
44. 'Perestroika obrazovaniia na iuridicheskom fakultet LGU: rezultaty i perspektivy', *Pravovedenie*, 1988, No. 4, p. 7.
45. A. Larin, 'Ugolovnaia statistika i realnost', *Izvestiia*, 24 March 1989, p. 3; A. Iakovlev, 'Prestupnost i pravosudie', *Pravda*, 10 May 1989, p. 3; S. Borodin and Iu. Kudriavtsev, 'Prestupnost: ne panikovat, a razobratsia', *Kommunist*, 1989, No. 14, pp. 50–60; 'Iazykom tsifr', *Argumenty i fakty*, 1989, No. 28, p. 7.
46. See, for example, Shchekochikhin and Gurov, 'Lev prygnul!'; Vladimir Sokolov, 'Bandokratiia', ibid., 17 August 1988, p. 13; Aleksandr Radov, 'Shaika, banda, sistema', *Ogonek*, 1988, No. 48, pp. 5–8, 25.
47. A. Illesh, 'Eta statistika otkryta vpervye', *Izvestiia*, 14 February 1989, p. 6; V. Zaikin, 'Mery protiv prestupnosti', ibid., 12 May 1989, p. 3; V. Itkin, 'Trevozhnaia statistika', *Sovietskaia Rossiia*, 14 June 1980, p. 6; A. Illesh, 'MVD: SSSR! Analyz prestupnosti za polgoda', *Izvestiia*, 11 July 1989, p. 8.
48. 'Osnovy ugolovnogo zakonodatelstva Soiuza SSR i soiuznykh respublik (Proekt)', *Sovetskoe gosudarstvo i pravo*, 1989, No. 1, pp. 3–29.
49. L. Kislinskaia, 'Petrovka, 38, bez sekretov', *Sovetskaia Rossiia*, 19 February 1989, p. 6; 'Zakon i zloba dnia', *Izvestiia*, 17 April 1989, p. 3; V. M. Chebrikov, 'Predvybornaia platforma partii – realnyi put uglubleniia perestroiki', *Pravda*, 11 February 1989.
50. Georgii Ovcharenko, 'Pokupaiu pistolet', *Pravda*, 23 March 1989, p. 6.
51. 'Zakon i zloba dnia'; Claire Rosenson, 'Justice under Gorbachev: The Reform of the Soviet Legal System', unpublished essay, July 1989, pp. 51–8.
52. Cited in 'Kto ostanovit presupnosti?', *Literaturnaia gazeta*, 7 June 1989, p. 14.
53. 'Pravovye rychagi obnovleniia', *Pravda*, 11 May 1989, p. 11.
54. 'Zakon i zloba dnia', V. Terebilov, 'Kto osudit sudiu?' *Ogonek*, 1989, No. 14, pp. 26–7.
55. V. A. Abolentsev, 'Avtoritet suda', *Sovetskaia Rossiia*, 13 May 1989, p. 1; A. Larin, 'Borba s prestupnostiu meshaet zakon? O nekotorykh konfliktakh mezhdu sudom i sledstviem', *Izvestiia*, 18 May 1989, p. 3; E. Parkhomovskii, 'Prestupnost trevoga obshchestva', ibid., 23 May 1989, p. 3; Borodin and Kudriatsev, 'Prestupnost: ne panikovat'.
56. 'Militsiia i obshchestvo', *Argumenty i fakty*, 1989, No. 38, p. 7; E. Gonzalez, et al., 'Ministr vnutrennikh del i ego programma', *Izvestiia*, 10 July 1989, p. 1.
57. 'I'm Afraid to Leave my House', *Soviet News and Views*, 1989, No. 13, p. 6.
58. 'Zasedanie Komissii TsK KPSS po voprosam pravovoi politiki', *Sovetskaia Rosiia*, 17 May 1989, pp. 1–2; *Izvestiia*, ibid., p. 3.
59. 'S'ezd narodnykh deputatov SSSR – stenograficheskii otchet, piataia sessiia', *Izvestiia*, 30 May 1989, pp. 1–5.
60. Gonzalez, 'Ministr vnutrennykh del'.
61. 'O reshitelnom usilenii borby s prestupnostiu', *Izvestiia*, 6 August 1989, p. 1.

62. Interviews with former Soviet judges during 1985. See Peter H. Solomon, Jr., 'Soviet Politicians and Criminal Justice: The Logic of Party Intervention', (revised version, September 1989), to appear in James Millar (ed.) *The Communist Party and Soviet Bureaucracy* (Armonk, NY, 1991).
63. Interview with S. G. Kelina, 18 April 1990; 'Zakon SSSR. O statuse sudei v SSSR'. *Izvestiia*, 21 August 1989, p. 1.
64. 'Osnovy zakonodatelstva SSSR i soiuznykh respublik o sudoustroistve', *Izvestiia*, 16 November 1989, p. 1.

Index